KU-607-366

CONTENTS

LIST OF TABLES

LIST OF FIGURES

LIST OF EXHIBITS

Arthur W. Page Society

DEDICATION

Arthur W. Page—the "father of corporate public relations"—would have been enthusiastic about this book. It pursues many of the ideas he followed and furthered in his life's work.

One of those ideas is that sound planning and research are essential to the success of a public relations endeavor. Page bore the brunt of many jokes inspired by his habit of devoting more time to preparation for a task than to direct action upon it. A casual observer once reported to Page's boss that the PR man paced his office one end to the other time after time and seldom did any work. The boss is reported to have replied, "Thank God—he's thinking."

Another Page concept is the overriding importance of public opinion to the success (or otherwise) of public ventures of all varieties. The

(Prepared by the Research Committee on behalf of the members of the Arthur W. Page Society)

quotation most often associated with Page is: "All business in a democratic society begins with public permission and exists by public approval." He added that "the purpose of public relations is to deserve and maintain public approval."

Page's first efforts at researching public opinion came in the years just before World War I. He regularly gathered and then analyzed examples of American opinion and reaction to events. He summarized his comments in letters to his father, the ambassador to Great Britain. Page continued this watchfulness throughout his life, often sharing his findings with public leaders.

During his tenure (1927–1947) as the vice president of public relations at the American Telephone and Telegraph Company, he was an early proponent of public relations research. He established in his department a "public relations laboratory" where PR successes and failures were gathered, studied and the lessons learned passed on to his colleagues. AT&T efforts to monitor public opinion on a continuing basis were furthered under his leadership, and feedback from these opinion samplings went regularly to management for use in conducting the affairs of the corporation.

It was Page who authored six standards of institutional behavior which he believed made up the essence of sound public relations. Today—six decades later—these standards still describe the goal of the public relations professional.

The standards are:

TELL THE TRUTH. Page said, "... no more in business than in politics can you fool all the people all the time, and if you expect to stay in business long, an attempt to fool even some of the people some of the time will end in disaster."

PROVE IT WITH ACTION. "Publicity," Page once told a group of corporate executives, "is an important part of public relations, but in business as in most human affairs, what you do is more important than what you say."

LISTEN TO THE CUSTOMER. "The only safeguard for those of us in a large business, he advised, "... is to keep a pretty careful watch on the way people's minds are running, figure out the coming public attitudes, what the public decisions are likely to be—and then be ready for them."

MANAGE FOR TOMORROW. Page was always "future-minded," believing that today's actions are a prelude to tomorrow's performance.

CONDUCT PUBLIC RELATIONS AS IF THE WHOLE COMPANY DEPENDS ON IT. In Page's view, public relations is not only a necessary function but also a very broad one, involving service as the eyes, ears and conscience of the corporation as well as being its communicator.

AND (through it all!) REMAIN CALM, PATIENT AND GOOD-NATURED.

Page's total philosophy of institutional public relations is a synthesis of these and other basic ideas. This book, too, is a synthesis of the experiences of many practitioners and scholars who have contributed to the maturing of public relations.

Very shortly after its founding in 1983, the Arthur W. Page Society identified the support of research bearing on the successful practice of public relations as one of its principal reasons for existence. In this book the Society found its first support project. We believe the book furthers the search for knowledge about how public relations works—and can work better—so we are proud to dedicate this effort to the memory of Arthur W. Page and to the perpetuation of those high standards of public relations practice he personified.

PREFACE

Let's be up front about something: using research in public relations is better than not using research in public relations. We aren't suggesting that research will substitute for experience, judgment and power. Nor is avoiding research somehow "bad." We simply want to start by clearly stating that, in most situations, using research improves the management and practice of public relations.

With that assumption as prologue, we can get on with the business of introducing you to our goals for this book, the content of the chapters, and the purposes of the appendices.

We wrote this as a "reader friendly" research book. Many students and practitioners express a "fear of numbers," self-diagnose "math anxiety," or say they have little aptitude for research. Our challenges, then, are to explain research concepts and to present examples relevant to your interest in public

relations. That is what we mean by reader friendly. By discussing research in its public relations context, we hope to make this book both more relevant and more understandable.

Our first strategy was to interview highly qualified public relations professionals. As often as we can, we use their words. We picked these leading practitioners because they understand and use research. They also share our enthusiasm for the role of research in public relations practice. We want you to learn as much as we did when we interviewed these practitioners. You won't find many research books with as many direct quotes as in the pages that follow.

After you study the 14 chapters, you should understand how research fits into public relations management, how to plan and conduct research, and how to use the findings to improve both the public relations program and the organization's performance. In addition to knowing about each of these areas, you should acquire the technical research skills needed to gather research information, to analyze research information, and to interpret and report research results.

PART I provides the context for using research in public relations. *Chapter 1* sets the stage by defining research, reviewing important notions about the nature of public relations, and describing the functions of research in managing public relations. *Chapter 2* develops the uses of research to understand the problem situation and plan the program. In particular, we show how to use research findings to define the problem, identify publics, and set program goals and objectives. We make the point that the adequacy of the research done in the planning stage affects everything that follows. *Chapter 3* outlines the uses of research in monitoring program implementation and tracking progress on a day-to-day basis. Research results at the implementation stage are used to fine tune program tactics and adjust strategies. *Chapter 4* concludes PART I by outlining the uses of research in assessing program impact. This is the evaluation stage in which research findings help determine the worth or effectiveness of the program.

The next two parts explain research methods—gathering and analyzing information. In PART II, *Chapter 5* describes the research process, defines theory, discusses cause and effect, outlines different research designs, and shows how designs isolate program effects from other fac-

tors. *Chapter 6* explains the principles and techniques for selecting representative samples. Here we also talk about using findings from samples to estimate characteristics of publics and other populations of interest. *Chapter 7* outlines the many techniques available for gathering data. Ranging from unobtrusive measures and depth interviews to structured questionnaires, this chapter discusses strengths and weaknesses of observation techniques, as well as their uses in public relations program research. *Chapter 8* addresses measurement—the essence of research methods. The chapter explains different levels of measurement, concepts of measurement reliability and validity, and types of indices and scales most frequently used in public relations research.

PART III deals with analyzing information. It discusses subjects that scare more people than they should—data, statistics and computers. These topics immobilize even some of the heartiest among us. *Chapter 9* makes compiling and organizing data understandable and doable tasks. We outline the issues you must understand and decisions you have to make *before* analyzing the data. *Chapter 10* introduces concepts and techniques used to describe the findings. Much of this chapter explains the descriptive statistics used in research reports. *Chapter 11* takes the next step by showing how to measure relationships between sets of measures. We identify and explain the most commonly used inferential statistics and tests of relationships. *Chapter 12* provides examples and techniques used to isolate program impact. Here we address the cause-and-effect argument in the program evaluation context. Once you know the rules, you can move on to PART IV—using research results.

Chapter 13 describes how to interpret research results and report findings. The chapter shows how to interpret the analyses and relate those interpretations to the public relations program. Included here are suggestions for organizing, writing and illustrating research presentations. *Chapter 14* concludes our exploration with the most difficult task of all—making sure the research results are used in managing the public relations program and improving the performance of the organization. We outline obstacles to research utilization, strategies for increasing research utilization, and impacts of research utilization in the public relations function.

The book ends with two important supplements. First, we summarize major points and references from the book in a series of "how-to" guides addressing the most commonly asked questions about using research in public relations. Second, we present a glossary of the major terms used in public relations research. It helps if you speak the language!

To end this beginning, we must admit to having violated a principle of effective communication and defend our behavior. Throughout the book, we wrote to two of you at the same time, fully aware that addressing only one of you would be a more effective approach. One of you is an advanced student studying public relations in a formal course. One of you is a practitioner doing professional

development or using this book as a reference at work. We struggled with the decision of which one of you to address in our book, finally concluding that you have similar information needs. So we had you in mind all along. We hope you don't mind that the other is looking over our shoulders as we explore *Using Research in Public Relations*.

ACKNOWLEDGMENTS

We want to thank many people for their contributions and support. Heading that list are the members of THE ARTHUR W. PAGE SOCIETY whose development grant made possible the travel and research necessary to write this book. In particular, we appreciate the counsel and support of *Stanley J. Boulier,* Vice President-Public Relations and Public Affairs, MOUNTAIN BELL, Denver (retired). Stan also serves as chairman of the PAGE SOCIETY's research committee and as our liaison on the development grant. He and the other members of the PAGE SOCIETY demonstrated extraordinary patience and support during the seemingly endless process of researching and writing *Using Research in Public Relations*. We are proud to have received the PAGE SOCIETY's first research grant and pleased that our book is dedicated to Arthur W. Page in recognition of his high standards of public relations practice.

Our senior colleague, *Allen H. Center* (Distinguished Resident Lecturer in Public Relations, SAN DIEGO STATE UNIVERSITY), introduced us to the PAGE SOCIETY, supported our project proposal, and gently prodded us to completion. We—like most others in public relations—find inspiration and direction in Allen's words and deeds. We are just luckier than most of you, as we have the privilege of frequent luncheon conversations with Allen in which we solve the world's problems.

Stan and Allen played key roles in getting this book off the drawing table, but the people that follow made the important contributions you will read in the pages that follow. We interviewed them about how they use research. These professionals' generous sharing of experience, insights, and materials made this book come to life in public relations. Some changed employment while we worked on the manuscript, so we indicate in parentheses their affiliations at the time of our interviews. We extend thanks to:

Paul H. Alvarez, APR, Chairman and Chief Executive Officer, KETCHUM PUBLIC RELATIONS, New York

Don Bates, APR, President, THE BATES COMPANY, INC., New York

Ann H. Barkelew, APR, Vice President-Corporate Public Relations, DAYTON-HUDSON CORPORATION, Minneapolis

Gary F. Barton, APR, Science Communications Director, MONSANTO COMPANY, St. Louis

Walter L. Beiter, Division Staff Manager-External Communication, SOUTHWESTERN BELL TELEPHONE, St. Louis

Hilda M. Besand, News Relations Specialist, SOUTHWESTERN BELL TELEPHONE, St. Louis

Edward M. Block, Senior Vice President, AT&T, New York (retired)

David E. Clavier, Ph.D., APR, Executive Director, HUSK JENNINGS OVERMAN PUBLIC RELATIONS, Jacksonville, FL (formerly with AMERICAN TRANSTECH, Jacksonville)

Jerry W. Cooper, APR, Manager-Public and Government Affairs Operations, AMOCO CORPORATION, Chicago

Scott J. Farrell, Vice President-Client Services Manager, BURSON-MARSTELLER, Chicago

Mary Ann Ferguson, Ph.D., Associate Professor and Director-Communication Research Center, College of Journalism and Communications, UNIVERSITY OF FLORIDA, Gainesville

Sandra Fuhrman, Public Policy Specialist, SOUTHWESTERN BELL CORPORATION, St. Louis

Larissa Grunig, Ph.D., Assistant Professor, College of Journalism, UNIVERSITY OF MARYLAND, College Park

Blair C. Jackson, Senior Vice President, ROGERS & COWAN, INC., New York (formerly with FLEISHMAN-HILLARD, INC.)

Larry Johnson, District Manager-Public Relations, PACIFIC BELL, San Francisco

Gray Kerrick, Vice President-Corporation Communication, SOUTHWESTERN BELL CORPORATION, St. Louis

Lloyd Kirban, Ph.D., Executive Vice President and Director of Research, BURSON-MARSTELLER, New York

Duncan M. Knowles, APR, Vice President and Director-Leadership Communications, BANK OF AMERICA NT & SA, San Francisco

Jack A. Koten, APR, Senior Vice President, AMERITECH, Chicago

Harold F. Leiendecker, Opinion and Communication Research, Public Affairs Department, EXXON CORPORATION, New York (retired)

Walter K. Lindenmann, Phd, APR, Vice President & Director of Research, KETCHUM PUBLIC RELATIONS, New York

John V. Pavlik, Ph.D., Associate Director for Research and Technology Studies, GANNETT CENTER FOR MEDIA STUDIES (COLUMBIA UNIVERSITY), New York (formerly with School of Communications, PENNSYLVANIA STATE UNIVERSITY, University Park)

Paul M. Sanchez, APR, National Practice Director for Employee Communications Consulting, THE WYATT COMPANY, San Diego

Gary L. Schmermund, Senior Vice President LOUIS HARRIS & ASSOCIATES, INC., New York

Roger Sennott, Ph.D., General Manager, MARKET DEVELOPMENT, INC., San Diego (formerly with BURSON-MARSTELLER, Chicago)

Jennifer Strohl, Staff Manager-Issues Development, SOUTHWESTERN BELL TELEPHONE, St. Louis

Charlotte M. Vogel, President, THE RESEARCH GROUP, New York

Franklin J. Walton, Ph.D., President-Public Affairs Communication, RESEARCH & FORECASTS, INC., New York

Three colleagues provided comments and suggestions on an early draft of the manuscript. Prof. *John V. Pavlik* (mentioned above), Prof. *Mark Larson,* Ph.D., Chair, Department of Journalism, HUMBOLDT STATE UNIVERSITY, Arcata, California, and Prof. *Nick Trujillo,* Ph.D., Center for Communication Arts, SOUTHERN METHODIST UNIVERSITY, Dallas, Texas. We thank them for taking time to study our work and give useful feedback.

Four San Diego associates and their organizations provided extended examples of using research in public relations to illustrate concepts in several chapters. We thank *James O. Boylan,* Vice President, CHILDREN'S HOSPITAL AND HEALTH CENTER, *Mary Ann Burnett,* Director of Corporation Communications, HARTSON MEDICAL SERVICE; *Marsha L. Gear,* Publications Editor, SAN DIEGO STATE UNIVERSITY, and *James F. McBride,* Public Affairs Director, KAISER-PERMANENTE MEDICAL CARE PROGRAM.

Books often have unheralded sponsors. We don't want to leave out our patient and supportive editor at PRENTICE-HALL, *Alison Reeves,* Senior Managing Editor, Management & Industrial Relations. She did not snicker when we gave her yet another unrealistic estimate for completing the manuscript. She was understanding during times of need. And finally, she believed in our project and provided support to see it to completion. Other authors should be so lucky as to have Alison as their editor.

Naturally we want to thank our significant others—*Betty Broom* and *Lorri Anne Green.* We recognize that this book could not have happened without their support and understanding. Dozier thanks daughters *Sara* and *Lara Dozier* for their tolerance of days missed on the beach and their willingness to do their household chores so Dad could keep on task. Dozier also thanks *Patricia Jean Head,* closest friend during his illness in the early days of writing this book.

Finally, we want to thank our parents—*Ralph* and *Audrey Broom,* and *Jack* and *Elena Dozier.* As we collaborated on this manuscript and struggled with words and deadlines for more than two years, we often wondered what it was about our upbringing that drove us to such extremes. We conclude that whatever success we have with this and other projects surely can be traced back to the early influence of our parents. For that we are grateful. At the same time, we absolve them and the others mentioned here of any responsibility for the errors and misstatements included in this book. For those we have each other to blame.

Glen M. Broom, Ph.D.   *David M. Dozier, Ph.D.*

Department of Journalism

SAN DIEGO STATE UNIVERSITY

CHAPTER 1

THE ROLE OF RESEARCH IN PUBLIC RELATIONS

Jerry W. Cooper, APR, Manager–Public and Government Affairs Operations, AMOCO CORPORATION, Chicago.

We have a three-part charge in this department: First, look out there and report what is happening to management. Second, look at what is happening in the company and report it. And finally, analyze and try to make sense out of all of that. Research is the basis for all three aspects of our mission.

Gary L. Schmermund, Senior Vice President, LOUIS HARRIS & ASSOCIATES, INC., New York.

The role of public relations—and therefore the role of public relations research—has changed dramatically over the last few years. It has become much more of a policy-impacting function. For instance, when I directed public relations research at AT&T, we still did the traditional communication tracking research. In fact, most of our money, most of our interest, and certainly most of our interesting findings were in the areas of tracking social values, tracking what is on the minds of social leadership, and tracking how individual issues are evolving. We did this to help us under-

stand when to make decisions, create policy, modify policy, or when to make no change at all. This continues today, I believe.

Ann H. Barkelew, APR, Vice President–Corporate Public Relations, DAYTON-HUDSON CORPORATION, Minneapolis.

Research saves me time. If I don't know the opinion climate or environment for a project or program, then I don't know—first— if I am on target, and—second—if I am starting some place different than where the audience is. So I find that the research step saves me time and almost guarantees—as close as anything can guarantee—that the program we put together is going to end up with the results that we want. I think it helps us manage the public relations function.

Lloyd Kirban, PhD, Executive Vice President, BURSON-MARSTELLER, New York.

Practitioners need research for precisely the same reasons that any business activity would benefit from the use of a knowledge base. Public relations people make decisions. They make decisions on the kind of program that would be suitable for a particular client. They make decisions about the best combination of elements in that program to maximize the impact of the program. Practitioners need some way of diagnosing and then demonstrating that programs have achieved some kind of an intended effect.

Blair C. Jackson, Senior Vice President, ROGERS & COWAN, INC., New York.

*The most compelling reason for using research is to make sure that your program is the best it can be—that what you are doing is as "right on" as it can be. You will be confident that you are addressing the right audiences, that you are using the right messages, and that you are focusing on the right perceptions or attitudes. Evaluation research will tell you whether or not it works. The second reason is **program justification**. What if the research shows that "the needle did not move," or did not move as much as the client thinks it should have? Then it means that you don't do the program again next year, the budget does not get increased, or the program gets stopped in the middle without rolling out in the remaining nine markets. On the other hand, research is the way to prove that you are doing the job, to make sure the program is continued, or to get the budget increase.*

Gary F. Barton, APR, Science Communication Director,
MONSANTO COMPANY, St. Louis.

*You sit in a number of meetings in the company in which the
need for surveys and survey results are discussed. In modern business, you need some background in research and statistics in order to understand what people are presenting—concepts like confidence intervals, how items get coded, and how to pull things out
of the computer. From my perspective, you will most likely be a
consumer or evaluator of research who works with an expert. But
when people start talking about the various elements of research—what can and cannot be done, how many people you have
to interview to have a certain confidence in the results, and the
way you construct questions—you need some background.*

This book is about research and how to use research in public relations.
It does not contain everything you need to know about research, but it gives you
the basic understanding and skills for using research in practice.

We do not contend that research solves all problems or replaces experience, judgment, or even less likely, power in decision making. The assumption
underlying the pages that follow, however, is that research makes the practice of
public relations more responsive, effective, useful, and professional.

For example, assume that you are assigned the task of developing a public relations program to increase various publics' understanding of biotechnology
and willingness to have field tests conducted near their communities. How could
you do that without first finding out what people in the target publics already
know—or don't know—about biotechnology, their perceptions and fears of biotechnology, and the extent to which they have confidence in your company and
the governmental agencies charged with protecting public safety?

Once the program is underway, what if your client or boss asks you how
effective your program has been in getting messages to those target publics? Or,
how would you know if changes in the strategy were required in order to reach
community "thought leaders" on this topic?

And what if at the next budget meeting, you are asked to show results to
justify continuing the program? Or, as program manager, how do you know the
extent to which the program is achieving the objectives?

Welcome to *using research in public relations!* In the pages that follow, you
will learn how to employ research to help you plan, monitor, and evaluate public
relations programs.

THE MEANING OF RESEARCH

You could try to answer the preceding questions—as have generations of public
relations practitioners—by citing expert judgments or by calling on your own
experiences. In fact, when we have questions or face problems, all of us turn to

authorities and make personal observations. Experts are in their positions because of their previous experiences and records of success. Individual observations are filtered through each of our past experiences and unique perspectives.

Our answers often reflect yet another powerful determinant—our past behavior in similar situations. Responses are programmed as a result of history. Repeating past practices often is simply easier, less time-consuming, and cheaper than developing new programs and specifically targeted responses. Routine behavior removes the need to engage in decision making.

Authority, personal observation, and history do not provide satisfactory answers to many of the questions asked in managing public relations. Enter the need for research. Simply defined, *research is the controlled, objective, and systematic gathering of information for the purposes of describing and understanding.* In other words, it is the *scientific* approach to answering questions, providing more reliable answers in most situations than authority, personal experience, and historical precedent. People who do research want to know something, to understand what is happening. They want to learn in such a way, however, that they themselves have confidence in the answers and that others will accept the answers as valid and reliable.

One of the key motivations for using scientific research is to reduce the influence the researcher or observer has on the findings. Done correctly, the scientific approach produces findings that result more from the phenomena under study than from the researcher's views, interests, or expectations. As a result, the researcher has confidence that the findings accurately reflect reality, not just the researcher's perceptions of reality. Furthermore, by knowing and following the "rules" of scientific inquiry, researchers produce results that are verifiable by and credible to others who also understand research.

You should study research to learn how to *systematically* and *objectively* gather information for increasing your own knowledge of situations and to learn how to communicate this knowledge in a form persuasive to others. How can you plan public relations program strategies without such understanding? How do you counsel clients or management without being able to present evidence persuasively?

Research is but one of many sources of information in the mixed and frequently confusing assortment of inputs. Without depreciating the value and roles of other methods of knowing, this book deals with the orientation, concepts, and methods of scientific research in the public relations context. Our thesis is that scientific research is fundamental to effective public relations practice and management.

THE CONCEPT OF PUBLIC RELATIONS

Historically, practitioners typically moved from positions in journalism into public relations, then operated akin to "journalists in residence." Probably because of their backgrounds in news media, "putting out our story" (to both internal

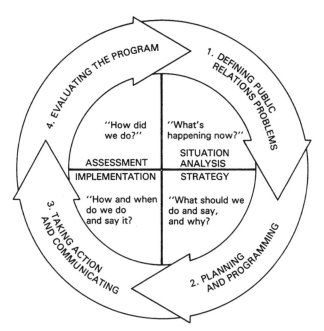

Figure 1-1 Four-step public relations process. Source: Reprinted with permission from Prentice-Hall, Inc.

and external publics) and serving as the media contact occupied the majority of their work days. Viewing public relations as something requiring scientific research departs from the dominant paradigm in practice—public relations as the communication "art" of informing and persuading.

Cutlip, Center, and Broom define public relations with the focus on the relationships between an organization and its publics:

> *Public relations is the management function that identifies, establishes and maintains mutually beneficial relationships between an organization and the various publics on whom its success or failure depends.*[1]

To effect and maintain these relationships, these authors see research as the "foundation of effective public relations."[2] They detail a four-step public relations process that casts research as central to defining public relations problems, monitoring public relations programs, and assessing program impact.[3]

Grunig and Hunt define public relations as the "management of communication between an organization and its publics."[4] They argue that in the ab-

---

[1]Scott M. Cutlip, Allen H. Center, and Glen M. Broom, *Effective Public Relations*, 6th ed. (Englewood Cliffs, N.J.: Prentice-Hall, Inc., 1985), p. 4.

[2]Ibid., p. 202.

[3]Ibid., pp. 199–310.

[4]James E. Grunig and Todd Hunt, *Managing Public Relations* (New York: Holt, Rinehart and Winston, 1984), p. 6.

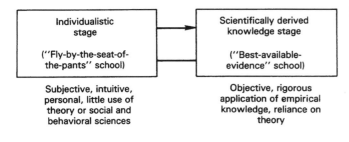

Figure 1–2 Robinson's problem-solving continuum. Source: Edward J. Robinson, *Communication and Public Relations* (Columbus, Ohio: Charles E. Merrill Publishing Company, 1966), p. 48.

sence of research, *managers* "would have to rely on intuition rather than informational inputs...."[5] Marston defines public relations as "planned, persuasive communication designed to influence significant publics," then goes on to outline a four-step process that begins with research and ends with evaluation.[6]

These and other textbooks, professional publications, and professional societies have long defined public relations as a management function and outlined the public relations problem-solving process as beginning and ending with research. Many practitioners, however, serve as communication technicians and do not use scientific research. As a result, public relations practice tends to focus on the *means* or strategies, paying little attention to the specific *ends* to be achieved. Few programs have measurable objectives specifying measurable outcomes, and even fewer use systematic research to determine the nature of problem situations, progress toward achieving objectives, or program success or failure. It is apparently the case that practitioners take on faith—and ask their clients and managers to accept assertions—that certain strategies should be used and that programs using those strategies are working.

In this style, public relations is practiced more as a creative art than as an applied social and behavioral science. Robinson refers to this as the "individualistic" or "fly-by-the-seat-of-the-pants" approach to problem solving, in contrast to the "scientific" or "best-available-evidence" approach at the other end of his problem-solving continuum.[7]

In his preface to *Public Relations and Survey Research* (1969), Robinson inaccurately observes, "The old 'flying by the seat of the pants' approach to solving public relations problems is over." He goes on to say that the public relations practitioner functioning as an applied social and behavioral scientist will rely upon "the proper use of research to help in the problem solving process" and that research is "the most powerful tool available."

[5]Ibid., p. 108.

[6]John E. Marston, *Modern Public Relations* (New York: McGraw-Hill Book Company, 1979), pp. 3 and 185–203.

[7]See either Edward J. Robinson, *Communication and Public Relations* (Columbus, Ohio: Charles E. Merrill Books, Inc., 1966), p. 48, or Robinson's *Public Relations and Survey Research: Achieving Organizational Goals in a Communication Context* (New York: Appleton-Century Crofts, 1969), p. 12.

David Clavier, executive director at Husk Jennings Overman Public Relations, Jacksonville, Florida, contends that this concept of public relations presents problems:

I see two basic problems with bringing research into daily practice. First, we don't have a large supply of practitioners who are trained and are skilled in research techniques, methodologies, and interpretations. Secondly, the fact is that research and evaluation are not part of the status quo. Research is beyond contemporary practice, it's the next step and it's a little bit harder to take that next step in business application. My sense is that practitioners want to move in that direction, and that organizations are almost demanding it. I see the profession as growing and moving constantly in the direction of research and evaluation.

In summary, the *concept* of public relations—if not always the current practice—as a management function calls for systematic research in the formulation, conduct, and evaluation of programs. Also central to this concept of public relations is the imagery of organizations as open systems using inputs to adjust to their constantly changing environments.

THE OPEN SYSTEMS MODEL

Unlike relatively closed systems, open systems engage in *exchanges* of information, energy, and matter with their environments. These exchanges make possible the adjustments and adaptations required for systems accommodating to changes in their environments. Close off the input of information, energy, and matter, and the relatively closed system that results will be insensitive to environmental change pressures. Without inputs, most such systems become dysfunctional and eventually cease to output. They become inert or disintegrate.[8]

The model of open systems exchange processes leading to structural and activity change and adaptation depicts the function of public relations in organizations. In systems theory terms, public relations most closely fits as part of the *adaptive* subsystem. It supports the *production, supportive/disposal, maintenance,* and *managerial* subsystems.[9] When an organization functions consistent with the open

---

[8]For more complete descriptions of systems theory and its application to public relations, see "Adjustment and Adaptation: A Theoretical Model for Public Relations" (Chapter 8), in Cutlip, Center, and Broom, *Effective Public Relations,* 6th ed., pp. 183-98, and Grunig and Hunt, *Managing Public Relations,* pp. 8-9 and 92-104.

[9]Explications of these concepts applied to organizations appear in Chris Argyris, *Integrating the Individual and the Organization* (New York: John Wiley & Sons, Inc., 1964); and Daniel Katz and Robert L. Kahn, *The Social Psychology of Organizations,* 2nd ed. (New York: John Wiley & Sons, Inc., 1978).

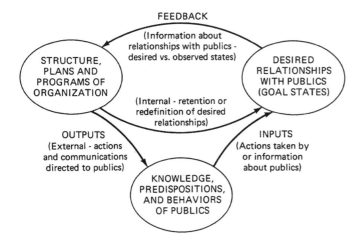

FEEDBACK
(Information about relationships with publics - desired vs. observed states)

STRUCTURE, PLANS AND PROGRAMS OF ORGANIZATION

DESIRED RELATIONSHIPS WITH PUBLICS (GOAL STATES)

(Internal - retention or redefinition of desired relationships)

OUTPUTS (External - actions and communications directed to publics)

INPUTS (Actions taken by or information about publics)

KNOWLEDGE, PREDISPOSITIONS, AND BEHAVIORS OF PUBLICS

Figure 1-3 Open systems model of public relations. Source: Scott M. Cutlip, Allen H. Center, and Glen M. Broom, *Effective Public Relations*, 6th ed. (Englewood Cliffs, N.J.: Prentice-Hall, Inc., 1985), p. 194.

systems model, the public relations adaptive subsystem emphasizes input and "may be viewed as not only influencing the environment but also as influencing the organization relative to environmental conditions."[10]

In their important article outlining the "functionary" versus the "functional" modes of public relations, Bell and Bell describe what they see as an expansion of the concept of public relations in organizations. They contend that there is a "growing schism" between those who see public relations as "selling" a favorable image of the organization and those who include surveillance, interpretation, and advising management in an expanded role. As they note, however, "Technical rather than scientific proficiency has traditionally been the dynamic of public relations."[11]

The Bells draw a parallel with the development of the marketing function in organizations:

> *Marketing was born in the disposal subsystem and there it remained until changes in the environment dictated changes in function. . . .*
>
> *Marketing management, on the other hand, has expanded the dimensions of its gatekeeping activities to bring information about the environment into the organization. It has great impact on decisions concerning goods and services offered by the organization and it provides a body of knowledge on which the activities of marketing (disposal subsystem) are based. The management of marketing has become a part of the adaptive subsystem by virtue of its ability to keep the company's outputs in harmony with its environment.[12]*

[10]Sue H. Bell and Eugene C. Bell, "Public Relations: Functional or Functionary?" *Public Relations Review*, Vol. 2, No. 2 (Summer 1976), p. 51.

[11]Ibid.

[12]Ibid., p. 54.

EXHIBIT 1-1
Role of Research
in Public Relations

In public relations, the most important role we play is in policy formulation. The basis for our participation is our understanding of what the public is thinking or feeling. That is our *primary* function. That we do press releases and such derives from the need for somebody to do it, and who better than us? But our principle role in the governance of our organizations is to act as listening posts in which research is a major tool. That ability and that information are our major contributions to policy formulation.

In a perfect world, as a public relations manager, I would want to use research to understand what the problem is in the first place. Too many times, public relations departments and firms spend their time conceiving of a solution when they don't know enough about the problem to know what the indicated solution should be. You must understand the problem, and research is your best tool for developing the understanding. And obviously you want a benchmark— a starting point.

Having an understanding of the problem, you create a public relations program to deal with it. Assuming that communication will be a large part of it, with target audiences, you want to pretest your creative to see if in fact it communicates what you had intended to communicate. Then you would launch the effort and set milestones, at which you would go back and test to see if your program is making a difference. You would also use these tests to fine-tune the program, to see where it needs to be "tweaked."

And finally, at some point you use research to see if you have solved the problem or have been overwhelmed by a new problem—which is probably the case.

So in a perfect world, research has a crucial role to play in every step in the understanding of problem, creation of the program, and monitoring of the outcomes of that program. Now, obviously, there are some programs that we do that are simply not important enough to invest that kind of money in. There are other times when the problem is consuming you *today* and you have got to use your judgment—you don't have time for this neat and orderly model using research. But that model should be the basic tool in any public relations operation.

Edward M. Block, Senior Vice President (retired), AT&T, New York.

Without the research orientation and skills necessary to make public relations truly part of the adaptive subsystem, it cannot function as part of the management decision-making process. Our own research demonstrates the link between research activities and participation in management decision making.[13] Several studies show that environmental scanning activities appear to put public relations practitioners on the management team.[14] It's as though you don't get invited to the table where decisions are being made unless you have systematically gathered information—research—to contribute to the process.

Walter Beiter, a public relations manager with Southwestern Bell Telephone in St. Louis, captures the essence of this relationship:

> *An important part of what we do is to help ensure that external considerations are applied to operational decisions that are made with regard to deploying new services and avoiding difficulties. So it goes way beyond just determining what we do in public relations.*

Our data also show that becoming part of the management team does not happen simply as a result of years of experience or tenure in position. Rather, how much research practitioners do to manage their programs has more to do with the increases in decision-making participation we observed in a six-year follow-up study of practitioners.[15] Most surveys show, however, that only a minority of practitioners do systematic research.

RESEARCH AND PUBLIC RELATIONS MANAGEMENT

Not only does research play a minor part in public relations practice, it often is greeted with skepticism or hostility. Of course, some of these reactions reflect previous experiences with research projects that "over promised and under delivered." Skeptics also find research an easy target for assertions that the "sample was too small," "they asked the wrong questions," or "the findings are out of date." Then there is always the fallback position that public relations deals with

[13]Glen M. Broom and David M. Dozier, "Advancement for Public Relations Role Models," *Public Relations Review,* Vol. 12, No. 1 (Spring 1986), pp. 37–56, and David M. Dozier, "Program Evaluation and the Roles of Practitioners," *Public Relations Review,* Vol. 10, No. 2 (Summer 1984), pp. 13–21.

[14]David M. Dozier, "The Environmental Scanning Function of Public Relations Practitioners and Participation in Management Decision Making," paper presented to the Public Relations Division, Association for Education in Journalism and Mass Communication, Norman, Oklahoma, August 1986, and Sharon Bradley Kraemer, "Public Relations Practitioner Involvement in Environmental Monitoring Research as a Predictor of Involvement in Corporate Planning" (MS thesis, San Diego State University, 1981).

[15]Glen M. Broom and David M. Dozier, "Determinants and Consequences of Public Relations Roles," paper presented to the Public Relations Division, Association for Education in Journalism and Mass Communication, Memphis, Tennessee, August 1985, p. 34.

"intangibles not amenable to research and measurement." Try that in a group of operations managers! Remember that some of them have MBAs and would probably agree with Lord Kelvin's pronouncement, "When you cannot measure it, when you cannot express it in numbers, your knowledge is of a meager and unsatisfactory kind."

Also, historically, many managers and clients did not require research-based programs, or were not willing to pay for the research needed to manage public relations. But times are changing. According to Blair Jackson, senior vice president at Rogers and Cowan:

> *In general, public relations people are being asked more and more by either their management or their clients to justify the expenditures for a project or the program. For example, after spending $200,000 or whatever for a program, they ask, "Did that change people's minds? Do they think differently now? Are they more aware of the company?" In other words, did it accomplish the objectives you said you were going to accomplish? That is the evaluative use of research at the end of the program. Without research, it is much harder to show results.*

Exxon's opinion and communications research specialist Harold Leiendecker (now retired)—an engineer by training—told us that the public affairs department there is "quantitatively oriented" because of the corporate culture. "Chemical engineers are the ones who manage the company. These are people who like to quantify things generally in helping make decisions." Gary Barton at Monsanto summarized his similar perceptions of Monsanto managers this way:

> *I think senior managers are receptive to programs with numbers. They feel more comfortable when they have numbers and results, than when they don't have polls and other research. It is sort of, "Show that you've moved the needle." Everybody throughout senior management now says they want public relations to demonstrate that it can "move the needle."*

If not based on research, Professor William Ehling says public relations is "incomplete and flawed" and technician behavior replaces management-level functioning.[16] He outlines public relations management as:

> *. . . a decision-making, problem-solving activity, essentially concerned with selecting and specifying end-states (goals, objectives) to be attained by an organization or group and with developing,*

---

[16]William P. Ehling, "Application of Decision Theory in the Construction of a Theory of Public Relations Management. II," *Public Relations Research & Education*, Vol. 2, No. 1 (Summer 1985), pp. 4–22.

programming, and implementing efficient and effective means (courses of action, strategies) for attaining or accomplishing the desired end-states.[17]

Using Ehling's outline, the role of public relations management includes the following:

1. *Conceptualizing specific tasks and responsibilities such as budgeting, goal-setting, strategic planning, staffing, organizing, administering, and evaluating.*
2. *Monitoring the organization's environment to analyze and evaluate opportunities and threats as that arise out of the interaction and relationships with other organizations and social groupings.*
3. *Planning public relations programs to deal with the opportunities and threats found in the environment.*
4. *Organizing and coordinating required resources inside and outside the organization to implement programs.*
5. *Activating and administering programs of communication.*
6. *Reviewing and evaluating program performance against stated objectives.[18]*

This clearly positions public relations as a purposive, goal-directed, and problem-solving management function. It uses both corrective action and communication to build and maintain what Ehling refers to as "cooperation over conflict," or what we noted earlier as "mutually-beneficial relationships between an organization and the various publics on whom its success or failure depends." The program itself calls for many technical implementation skills, but management of the function calls for well-developed decision-making and counseling skills. Research gives you the valid and reliable information you need for making decisions and for counseling clients and managers.

In short, research is essential to the rational management of the organizational adjustments, adaptations, and responses to changing environments. Without a basis in research, public relations is little more than a low-level technical activity in support of management decisions in which the practitioner did not participate.

RESEARCH AND PUBLIC RELATIONS MANAGEMENT BY OBJECTIVES

If you don't know where you want to end up, then you need not fret about which direction you go! That is the dilemma you face in programs with goals and objectives stated in such a way that intended outcomes cannot be measured, or pro-

[17]Ibid., p. 18.
[18]Ibid., pp. 19–20.

gram theories and strategies tested. Yet this fairly characterizes the majority of public relations programs. In these programs, implementing the program activities tends to be viewed as achieving the objectives. When implementation tasks are substituted for genuine impact objectives, practitioners engage in *pseudoplanning*. Because the intended outcomes and program impact have not been spelled out specifically, the mere effort expended and program activities produced become the observable consequences of the public relations effort.

To move away from this focus on the activities, research provides the detailed information you need to precisely define the existing situation—internal and external aspects of your organization's environment. Armed with this information, you and other managers can make judgments about what needs to be maintained and what must be changed. You can write specific statements describing what you want the situation to be at the completion of the program—*goals*. And given the detailed understanding of the publics involved, you can write specific statements describing the intended outcomes you hope the program achieves with each public—*objectives*. John Koten, senior vice president of corporate communications at Ameritech, Chicago, put it this way:

All goals and objectives ought to be rooted in something that can be described as research. I think this is important because we're driving more and more toward accountability. In setting objectives, we ask, "If we do this, what are the results going to be?" Later on we ask if we actually achieved those results. That's accountability and fixing responsibility. To determine whether you made your objective, you need to do some pre- and post-research.

Many people rebel to accountability and management by objectives. Most who are trained as public relations people view public relations as some kind of art form. Anything that's structured is viewed as a natural enemy. They don't like to have to deal with structure.

If we didn't insist on using management by objectives, the process would probably ebb away. As it ebbed away, so would—in my judgment—the influence of our entire corporate communications department. The discipline that management by objectives provides gives us credibility with management that couldn't be obtained by any other means.

In their book, *Public Relations Management by Objectives*, Nager and Allen define MBO as "a *total management system that focuses on results* rather than activities *for performance evaluation*" (their emphasis).[19] No doubt, you see the parallel be-

---

[19]Norman R. Nager and T. Harrell Allen, *Public Relations Management by Objectives* (New York: Longman Inc., 1984), p. 10.

tween MBO and the concept of public relations as a purposive, goal-directed function designed to produce *consequences* in both the external environment and organization itself. You probably also appreciate the tension among practitioners primarily trained as communication (usually journalistic in nature) artists who find themselves operating in the numbers-oriented MBO environment.

The tension associated with an increased emphasis on accountability— the shift from the activities that make up public relations to the results of those activities—motivates this book. As Professor Ehling observes, an *effects* orientation is central to public relations management, and " . . . much of what passes for public relations practice falls far short of this, usually manifesting itself instead, as nothing more than low-level, non-managerial preparation and presentations of journalist messages."[20]

SCIENTIFIC PUBLIC RELATIONS MANAGEMENT

Robinson's continuum (Figure 1–2) highlights differences in approaches to decision making and problem solving—the essence of management. Based on the role of research in public relations practice, we see five major approaches to program management.

No-Research Approach

Public relations technicians operate on the basis of their intuition and artistic judgment, and what Simon calls "programmed decisions."[21] They do not use research to plan, monitor, or evaluate their programs or specific activities. Job descriptions indicate prescribed activities to be carried out and call for a minimum of management-level decision making. The "goal" under this approach is to generate a steady flow of public relations output, usually in the form of communications from management to internal and external publics.

In the no-research approach—unlike open systems public relations—the boundary between the organization and the environment is relatively impermeable to inputs. Public relations structure and process increasingly reflect routine, institutionalized strategies and activities. Explanations of public relations under this "closed systems" approach call to mind the imagery of perpetual motion machines. The original motivations for activities or programs are lost in history and current strategies cannot be linked to specific conditions in the environment.

[20]Ehling, "Application of Decision Theory," pp. 21–22.
[21]Herbert A. Simon, *The New Science of Management Decision* (New York: Harper & Row, 1960), pp. 5–6.

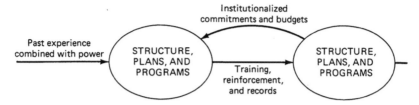

Figure 1–4   Historicist causal model of public relations. Source: Glen
M. Broom, "Public Relations Roles and Systems Theory:
Functional and Historicist Causal Models." Paper
presented to the International Communication
Association, Chicago, Illinois, May 1986.

Figure 1–4 depicts the historicist causal model that leads to public relations as the product of institutionalized power and "sunk costs." Checking the
files to see what was done in previous years and relying on existing routine activities preclude the need for research. From a budgetary perspective, it is easier
and less costly in the short term to maintain current program activities than to
invest in research and program adjustments. It also is easier to budget using past
program records rather than a yet-to-be-implemented program designed to respond to a changing environment.

Changing management goals and dynamic environments all but doom
this approach to a low-status, technical support function that must be *managed* by
others. Practitioners operating under this approach often complain that they are
told about decisions after the fact and are then in the uneasy position of trying
to explain management decisions and actions on which their counsel was not
solicited.

Informal Approach

You can do some things without regard to rules and rigor. Research is
not one of those things. It is not that so-called informal research methods serve
no purpose; rather, it is that they are often asked to serve inappropriately. For
example, it is obviously useful to interview people you perceive to be well-
informed on some topic—just as we did for the insights and quotations we gathered for this book. It would not be useful to suggest, however, that these few
people are representative of some larger population of interest. Yet this is the
type of error made in much of what passes as public relations research.

When viewed as explorations or pretests providing tentative answers,
then informal "pre-scientific" probing serves valuable purposes. But when the
results of such exploratory methods are used to manage a program, they are
misused. Walter Lindenmann, vice-president and director of research at Ketchum Public Relations, New York, pulls no punches on this problem:

Say you did one focus group of consumers in one particular community. On the basis of that focus group you reached the conclusion that people really loved this particular company and that they wanted to get their message one particular way. Then you built a public relations program based on that, not recognizing that people were just responding to a friendly moderator or to the particular topics that were on the agenda for that particular focus group. Maybe people really hate the company or maybe they don't know the company at all. You're making all sorts of assumptions about that public that simply aren't supported by adequate data. You might then build a campaign on that wrong set of data.

I've discovered that there is an awful lot of ignorance, an awful lot of naivete, on issues relating to research that really rests within the public relations function. It's sad to say, but that's not the problem in other parts of the organization. . . . Public relations people are very often their own worst enemy because they are so unsophisticated in this area.

Media-Event Approach

Practitioners know that media people and their audiences are interested in research results, particularly polls on topics or persons currently in the news. As part of program strategy, then, research is done to generate newsworthy or attention-getting information. Frank Walton at Research and Forecasts, Inc., calls this use "public issues studies":

These are done to attract public attention to the client, much in the way that a client will sponsor an art exhibit or sponsor something on public television. They support a research project and get their name associated with the project. Then as the media pick up on the facts and figures, the source of the information is always mentioned.

We did one for the American Association of Critical Care Nurses—four questions about attitudes toward organ transplants. They got an enormous amount of publicity—a clipping book this thick! It was an issue that people are talking about and want to think about—it's in the news. So here—coming from a responsible source, using a research methodology above reproach, with a 1,000-sample weighted to match census data—we come out with some statistics that say, "Here is the way Americans really think about this."

Four questions. The whole thing cost a few thousand dollars and they have a product that gets them a lot of publicity. It's research done for the sake of publicity geared to a specific audience that you want to reach with a message about the client.

EXHIBIT 1–2
Publicity based on American
Association of Critical Care
Nurses Survey

Courtesy of Research & Forecasts, Inc., New York.

Paul Alvarez at Ketchum Public Relations calls this "pop research." He defines it as "good, strong validated research that has news value in and of itself."

Evaluation-Only Approach

The push for accountability and demonstrated results produces what we choose to call the "evaluation-only" use of research. Research is not seen as essential for planning the program so much as it is for tracking the implementation and assessing the impact. It may be this notion of the use of research that causes practitioners to view research in the threatening performance control and program adjustment roles. As we were told:

> *You might just find that you didn't change the numbers. What if that happens? Why cause trouble? The client may be perfectly happy with what we did. Now if you go in there and do research*

and find that those three or four articles did not do anything,
that's not so good. I mean this is the cold, hard reality of it.

The evaluation-only role of research limits its contributions to the lower levels of feedback depicted in Figure 1–5. For research to make its fullest contribution to organizational adaptation to changing environments, the open systems approach calls for research to play the central and major role in managing public relations.

Scientific Management Approach

Science attempts to provide more reliable answers than those provided by other generally used ways of knowing. To the extent that you can use the scientific method for decision making in public relations management, then you elevate the function from the intuitive enterprise of the artist and make it part of an organization's management system. In this approach, research is at the core of how the function is managed.

First, research is done to define the problem situation for the purpose of developing a public relations program. In other words, research is the basis for planning. The conception, purpose, and design of the program are consequences of what you learn from this intelligence-gathering step. You design the intervention—so to speak—based on the diagnosis. Research findings are one of your key inputs for program planning. This is our topic for Chapter 2.

Second, research is done to monitor program implementation for performance accountability and for strategic adjustments. Clients and managers alike demand specific evidence that the program is being implemented as planned, on schedule, and within budget. Such systematic monitoring also provides practitioners objective evidence upon which to make program changes. You need not worry about program impact unless the program is being implemented in ways to reach target publics with the planned strategies. Research provides you the feedback necessary to keep the program on course. We expand on this use in Chapter 3.

Third, research is done to measure program impact or effectiveness with respect to goals and objectives. Unless you can measure your program's impact, you will have a difficult time assessing its success or failure. You will also have difficulty assessing the relative worth of your efforts with respect to program costs. But even more importantly, without impact measures, you will not detect the changes your efforts caused that now dictate adjustments in the program that follows. Research gives you feedback about program impact on the organization's environment. This use of research guides our discussion in Chapter 4.

Research adds a layer of complexity to the practice of public relations and elevates the function from its relatively safe haven as an artistic endeavor. Knowing how to do research is essential, according to Ann Barkelew at Dayton-Hudson Corporation:

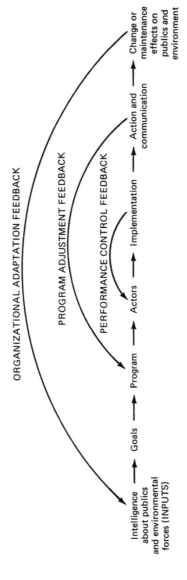

Figure 1-5 Public relations feedback model. Source: Glen M. Broom, "Public Relations Roles and Systems Theory; Functional and Historicist Causal Models." Paper presented to the International Communication Association, Chicago, Illinois, May 1986. Model adapted from Jerald Hage, *Communication and Organizational Control: Cybernetics in Health and Welfare Settings* (New York: John Wiley & Sons, 1974), p. 239.

It is as important as knowing how to write a news release. I would say it is basic, because you can't do public relations today without that element. You can't practice public relations today— successfully or effectively—without research. Saying you don't know how to do research is like asking, "Is it OK that I don't type? No. "Is it OK that I don't do research?" No!

As Ed Block at AT&T told us, "One thing students and early career public relations people need to know is that research is not just the domain of the researcher. It is a crucial part in the combination of skills of a public relations generalist." Gary Schmermund at Louis Harris & Associates added, "If you are going to come out with a degree in public relations, then it is wrong if you can miss taking research. 'Appreciation of Research 101' ought to be part of the training of a public relations person."

That is our mission. It's not that we think research is the total answer, or that it will solve all your management problems. We just can't find a better approach to public relations management.

CHAPTER 2

USING RESEARCH TO PLAN PROGRAMS

Lloyd Kirban, PhD, Executive Vice President and Director of Research, BURSON-MARSTELLER, New York.

When our people go into a brainstorming session or a business pitch, it's valuable for them to have a background or situation analysis. They use everything we can put together about the problem or the target audiences to be reached. We use whatever we can find from secondary research, even what I call "quick and dirty" primary research, to arm our people. That way, they can give informed creativity rather than uninformed creativity.

Blair C. Jackson, Senior Vice President, ROGERS & COWAN, INC., New York.

First of all, we use research to pin down demographics of who you should be communicating with. Secondly, to identify the most important issues that you should focus on. Also, to identify existing attitudes that might need to be changed. In other words, you might feel there is a problem, but you don't know what it is— exactly. If it is an attitude problem, which attitudes—in particular? And what are the "hot buttons" in the problem areas? Once we know these things, we can develop a campaign, conduct the campaign, and then test again to see what kind of difference it made.

Scott J. Farrell, Vice President, Group Manager, BURSON-MARSTELLER, Chicago.

We do more research than we used to. Our approach to our clients on the need for research is that we don't think that we can develop a sound strategy until we know what the starting point is.

Don Bates, APR, President, THE BATES COMPANY, INC., New York.

Before you launch any program that asks people to do something, you've got to do research not only to find ways to succeed, but more importantly, to avoid problems. And how do you validate a proposed public relations program without some sense of the reality you are working in? The only way you can get that in a quantitative and qualitative sense is through research.

Gray Kerrick, Vice President–Corporate Communications, SOUTHWESTERN BELL CORPORATION, St. Louis.

We perform research to provide strategic direction for the vast majority of our corporate communication activities. Strong, scientific research helps guide both internal and external initiatives—including advertising, cultural and community activities, media relations, and employee communications.

Roger Sennott, PhD, General Manager, MARKET DEVELOPMENT INC., San Diego.

Ideally, research is set up so it becomes a piece of strategic research to tell you what kinds of messages to come up with, the first step in a pre-post study to tell you if you produced change, and a data base for the client. You can analyze the data by region, by age, by level of education, or any number of ways to help them understand their publics.

An accurate description of the setting for most public relations work is that few situations are simple and the only constant is change. The more complex and dynamic your organization's environment becomes, the more important it is to use research for planning public relations programs. New publics form around new issues. Coalitions of publics tip the balance of power on old issues. Old publics split as interests change. About the time you think you understand what is happening, things change. In short, public relations operates in an unsettled and untidy setting.

As Charles F. Browne, nineteenth century humorist and lecturer, wrote under the pen name, Artemus Ward: "It ain't so much the things we don't know that get us in trouble. It's the things we know that ain't so." More than a hundred years later, an Ohio banker suggested that 3 percent of each year's profit be budgeted for research. When one of the directors challenged the proposal and asked why the bank needed research, the banker replied, "I don't know. That's what I want to find out."

This chapter outlines the use of research in helping you check out assumptions about situations and learn what you need to know in order to plan public relations programs. In this context, research begins the public relations planning process.

STRATEGIC PLANNING

Strategic planning is deciding where you want to be in the future (the goal) and how to get there (the strategies). It sets the organization's direction proactively, avoiding "drift" and routine repetition of activities. Not surprisingly, the reason people do research when planning is to make the information used by decision makers more comprehensive, accurate, and relevant. The intent is to improve strategic decisions so the program effectively responds to the problem situation and achieves the goal. The same thinking applies to your work in public relations.

The professional literature portrays public relations strategic planning as four basic steps in a cyclical process. For example, Cutlip, Center, and Broom list the steps as:

1. *Defining the problem.* This involves probing and monitoring awareness, knowledge, opinions, attitudes, and behaviors of those concerned with and affected by the acts and policies of an organization—research and fact-finding. In essence, an organization gathers intelligence it requires to determine "*What's happening now?*"

2. *Planning and programming.* This involves bringing the intelligence to bear on the policies and programs of the organization. It results in decisions affecting program publics, objectives, procedures, and strategies in the interests of all concerned. This step in the process answers "*What should we do and why?*"

3. *Taking action and communicating.* This involves implementing the plans and program through both action and communication designed to achieve specific objectives related to the program goal. With respect to each of the publics, the question is *"How do we do it and say it?"*

4. *Evaluating the program.* This involves determining the results of the program as well as assessing the effectiveness of program preparation and implementation. Adjustments can be made in the continuing program, or the program can be stopped after learning *"How did we do?"*[1]

Practitioners often cite Professor John Marston's R-A-C-E planning formula as the basis of their planning process: *Research, Action, Communication,* and *Evaluation.*[2] In building a case for using research in planning, Marston says, "The things that you don't know, or the things that you think you know that aren't so, usually have the capacity to hurt you most."[3]

The process begins when somebody senses a problem. At first this is a judgment call, but you must do research to really define the problem and understand the situation you hope to change.

RESEARCHING THE PUBLIC RELATIONS PROBLEM

The meaning of "problem" here is a condition in which someone thinks there is a gap between what is perceived and what is desired. Strategic planning uses research to define and redefine the perceived problem. Research of all kinds is used to gather information to help you understand the problem more completely and accurately. Without research, you are left with your own and others' unsystematic observations, views, and assertions, and a collection of intuitions and "gut feelings" about what is happening. Without ongoing research, you cannot update your understanding of the problem as conditions change—sometimes as a result of your own program!

The definition often begins, however, as the result of informal, even unsystematic monitoring of the environment. "Scanning for planning" applies here. *Environmental scanning is the detection, exploration, and description of public relations problems through informal and formal research. Detection* of something perceived to be a discrepancy between observed and desired states—without regard to frequency or intensity—escalates the surveillance to a higher level of rigor. *Exploration* of the potential problem includes probing the environment to confirm the presence of a problem and to expand your understanding of the situation. *Description* of the problem situation calls for systematic, objective information gathering to accurately and precisely define the nature and scope of the problem. As you employ increasingly rigorous surveillance methods, you increase the probability that your findings represent reality (see Figure 2–1).

[1]Scott M. Cutlip, Allen H. Center, and Glen M. Broom, *Effective Public Relations,* 6th ed. (Englewood Cliffs, N.J.: Prentice-Hall, Inc., 1985), p. 200.
[2]John E. Marston, *Modern Public Relations* (New York: McGraw-Hill Book Company, 1979), pp. 185–95.
[3]Ibid., p. 188.

EXHIBIT 2–1
Public Relations Strategic
Planning Process

Four-step process for public relations	Strategic planning process steps and outline for program plan
1. *Defining public relations problems*[1]	1. *The problem*
	2. *Situation analysis*—background information, data, evidence
(Research)[2]	A. Internal factors/forces
[The issue or opportunity][3]	B. External factors/forces
2. *Planning and programming*	3. *Program goal*
(Planning)	4. *Publics*
[Goals and objectives]	A. Who is involved/affected?
	B. How are they involved/affected?
	5. *Program objectives*—for each public
3. *Taking action and communicating*	6. *Action program*—for each public
	7. *Communication program*—for each public
(Execution)	A. Message strategies
[Implementation]	B. Media strategies
	8. *Program implementation plans*
	A. Assignment of responsibilities
	B. Schedules
	C. Budget
4. *Evaluating the program*	9. *Evaluation plans*
(Evaluation)	10. *Feedback and program adjustment*
[Evaluation and results]	

[1]Chapters 9–12 in Scott M. Cutlip, Allen H. Center, and Glen M. Broom, *Effective Public Relations*, 6th ed. (Englewood Cliffs, N.J.: Prentice-Hall, Inc., 1985), pp. 199–310.

[2]Categories of judging criteria for Public Relations Society of America "Silver Anvil Awards" in parentheses.

[3]Categories of judging criteria for International Association of Business Communicators "Gold Quill Awards" in brackets.

Whereas informal and opportunistic scanning of the environment may alert you to a potential problem, you use more formal and systematic observations to explore, confirm, and describe the problem. At a later stage in the problem definition process, you can recycle to a less formal method to scan the environment from a new perspective or to pursue more in-depth understanding. Harold Leiendecker, opinion and communications research specialist at Exxon Corporation, New York, describes the process:

The latest trend is to go beyond the traditional qualitative-to-quantitative. Now the trend is to do additional qualitative research to follow up on quantitative research. When they get the quantitative results, people often say, "Geeze, what did they mean by that? Why that?" They go back to qualitative research to find out.

The process might go like this: Somebody tells you that employees are concerned about a rumored reduction in staff, which you determine is not the case by checking with management. You follow up on the report by talking with some supervisors in the cafeteria. They confirm that there is such a rumor and that "a lot of our people are worried." You decide to see how widespread the concern is by polling a systematic sample of employees working all three shifts—100 on each shift. Based on the results of that survey, you call in three people from each shift to talk about why employees think a layoff is imminent and to explore how such a rumor got started.

Southwestern Bell's public policy development specialist, Hilda M. Besand, describes an example of using methods at the informal level to explore something identified at the formal level:

When we do an employee survey, it is usually a printed, mailed questionnaire. We generally sample about ten percent of the employees—every employee in some small departments—so we can get department-specific results.... Then sometimes we use focus groups to probe some of the reasons behind the findings.

To define public relations problems, you use a variety of informal and formal research methods for environmental scanning and surveillance. Figure 2–1 shows how some of the methods we discuss in Part II can be ordered according to their function in defining problems and the confidence you can place on how accurately the results represent reality. Chapters 6 through 8 outline both the techniques and characteristics of each of the methods used to gather information for defining and redefining the problem. The results of this phase of information gathering take two forms—the *problem statement* and the *situation analysis*.

WRITING THE PROBLEM STATEMENT

Generally, nothing has more influence on the strategic planning process than the form and content of the problem statement. If it points to a particular cause, other causes are ignored or given less weight in developing the strategies. If it suggests a particular course of action, then other courses are ignored or given less opportunity for selection. If it blames a particular person or group, then

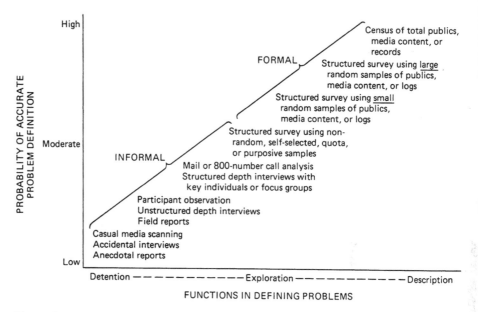

Figure 2-1   Accuracy of environmental surveillance techniques.

others are ignored or given less attention in program planning. In short, the problem statement determines the focus and direction of strategic planning.

The problem statement should describe *"What's happening now?"* in specific and measurable terms. It summarizes what your research tells you about *what* the source of concern is, *where* it is of concern, *when* it is a concern, *who* it involves or affects, *how* it involves or affects them, and *why* it concerns your organization and its publics. No easy task! Remember that the problem statement not only sets the course for strategic planning, but also must serve as the benchmark for later measures of progress and program success.

To help illustrate how research is used in the problem definition process, consider the case of a regional blood bank with the problem, "We simply need more donors." First of all, the problem statement does not describe a specific situation in measurable terms. Secondly, it directs attention to the external donor publics. And thirdly, it suggests something about the future—a vague goal of expanding the pool of donors. In other words, it does not describe the current situation, nor does it describe in detail the attributes listed in the preceding paragraph. The problem definition process might go as follows:

Questioning the Initial Problem Statement

Interviews with the director and key staff members reveal that they do not have specific data on the frequency and size of the blood shortage that prompts them to see a need for more donors. The director continues to insist,

"The problem is we always need more donors, pure and simple!" Others, how-ever, describe what could be a frequent, but not continuous, problem of demand outstripping supplies. "Usually we have plenty of blood, but it is a serious prob-lem around here when we run short," one says. Responses also include details about how the problem causes some hospitals to postpone elective surgeries and creates crisis conditions as blood is moved among hospitals to meet needs. One staff member shares copies of letters from hospitals describing the consequences of the demand-supply problem and copies of internal memos detailing staff reas-signments during the crisis situations. Certainly, the interviews and anecdotal reports indicate a blood supply and demand problem has been detected.

Refining and Sharpening the Problem Statement

A census of records and shipment logs covering the past two years con-firms the existence of a blood supply-demand problem, but only in June, July, August, and December. After recording the data from these files in a two-column table, it is obvious that the shortfall is about 100 units each of those four months. A less systematic scan of previous years shows a similar pattern, though the short-ages have been increasing each year. These data begin to fill in details missing in the initial problem statement.

Expanding Your Understanding of the Problem Situation

Additional reviews of orders and shipment records indicate that not only does demand go up during the four months, but the number of units collected drops. Analysis of shipment logs shows that demand increases during the same four months at hospitals along the major interstate highway and during the sum-mer months at hospitals near large lake resort areas. Detailed study of the collec-tion records uncovers the finding that the blood mobile does not operate on the university and college campuses in the region during summer months. The staff member who does scheduling explains that, because students leave campuses during the summer, there is little reason to schedule campus blood drives then.

Identifying the Forces For and Against Solving the Problem

The internal analysis begins with a study of staffing, policies, and proce-dures of the blood bank. Highlights of the findings include the staff schedules for the previous twelve months that show vacation time is taken during the summer months. Extra blood drives are not scheduled in place of campus drives. Findings also show that complete files on donors are maintained and that special recogni-tions go to individuals and groups reaching donation goals. Externally, increased traffic during summer vacation and Christmas periods correlates with increased numbers of highway accidents and hospital emergency room admissions, as well as increased blood demand from the blood bank. Calls to the university and college registrars' offices turn up surprisingly large numbers of summer school enrollments. Thousands of summer school students reside on campuses in the region. Published results of a survey conducted by a Red Cross blood program in another state suggest a possible explanation for why fewer people donate blood during the critical shortage months. Even regular donors indicated that they sometimes forget about donating blood during the summer and Christmas holidays because of busy schedules and children home from school. However, the majority of those who say they often forget about donating checked that they "would like to be reminded" to the next survey question. These and other findings about the internal and external conditions, groups, and forces begin to build a rather complete and detailed mosaic of the problem situation. (Recognize that this summary does not include all the detailed findings.) When organized and interpreted, this part of the planning process constitutes the *situation analysis.*

Restating the Problem Definition

Armed with a more detailed understanding of the problem situation, we can rephrase the problem statement as follows:

> *During the months of June, July, August, and December, demand for blood exceeds blood bank supplies by approximately 100 units each month. The blood bank's inability to fulfill its supply mission causes critical blood shortages for emergencies at hospitals in the region, postponements of elective surgeries, increased costs of transferring blood among hospitals, and diversion of blood bank staff effort away from donor recruitment and blood collection activities.*

Notice that this version details a) *what*—demand for blood exceeds supply by an average of 100 units; b) *where*—the region served by the blood bank; c) *when*—June, July, August, and December; d) *who*—emergency and surgery patients at the region's hospitals, the hospital and blood bank staffs; e) *how*—increases risks to hospital patients, decreases hospitals' ability to meet patient needs, increases costs, and takes blood bank staff away from other activities; and f) *why*—concern about blood bank's ability to fulfill its mission of providing for the region's blood needs. Of course, given the actual data from the various research efforts used in the definition process, we could make these elements of the problem statement even more specific.

This example illustrates the use of research in developing a specific and measurable problem statement, starting with a vague assertion motivated by the perception of a discrepancy between demand and supply. It also illustrates the uses of research for detection, exploration, and description in developing the problem statement and understanding of the situation. The sharpened problem statement focuses attention on current conditions and motivates the program of corrective action and communication.

EXHIBIT 2–2
An Example of Research for Identifying the Problem

I can give you an example—getting the special session of the legislature called in order to pass the amendment to Minnesota's anti-takeover law. It strengthened the law and prevents a raider from coming in, busting up a company, and then using the assets of the company to pay back the money it had to borrow to buy the company in the first place. We thought that was wrong and we had only a few days to act. There was an urgency about the situation.

The legislators were squeamish about the idea of a special session. It was therefore important to us to find a way to help them over this hurdle. We used our customer research firm to survey a statistically representative sample of the people of Minnesota to determine if the public would support legislators taking part in a special session. The results showed overwhelming support for the special session. We never had to reveal the results publicly, but we used them to let the legislature know what the public opinion climate was . . . and it let us know if we were asking for something within reason.

Ann H. Barkelew, APR, Vice President-Corporate Public Relations, DAYTON-HUDSON CORPORATION, Minneapolis.

Organizing the Situation Analysis

The situation analysis represents the unabridged edition of the problem definition, as it contains all the information and data collected about the internal and external environments. Whereas the problem statement directs the planning effort to a particular set of conditions, the situation analysis provides details about the internal and external contexts. The presentation format varies to suit the needs of each situation, but the following outline serves as a guide:

I. INTERNAL FACTORS

    A. Statements of organization's mission, charter, bylaws, history, and structure

B. Lists, biographical sketches and photos of key individuals—officers, board members, and program managers

C. Detailed descriptions of programs, products, services, etc.

D. Statistics about resources, budget, staffing, and programs

E. Summaries of interviews with key personnel about the problem situation

F. Copies of policy statements and procedures related to the problem

G. Complete descriptions of how the organization currently handles the problem

H. Lists and descriptions of the organization's controlled communication media

II. EXTERNAL FACTORS

A. Clippings from newspapers, magazines, trade publications, and newsletters tracing print media coverage of organization and problem situation

B. Reports of radio, television, and cable placements

C. Content analyses of media coverage

D. Lists of media, journalists, columnists, and free-lance writers who report news about your organization and related issues

E. Lists and descriptions of individuals and groups that share organization's concerns, interests, and views (including their controlled print and broadcast media)

F. Lists and descriptions of individuals and groups that oppose organization's positions on issues (including their controlled print and broadcast media)

G. Survey results of publics' awareness, knowledge, opinions, and behaviors related to the organization and problem situation

H. Schedules of special events, observances, and other important dates related to the organization and problem

I. Lists of government agencies, legislators, and officials with regulatory or legislative power affecting your organization and the problem situation

J. Copies of relevant government regulations, legislation, bills pending, referenda, publications, and hearing reports

K. Copies of published research on topics related to problem situation

L. Lists of important reference books, records, and directories, as well as their locations in the organization

No such outline can include all the information you will need to understand a problem situation. It should be obvious, however, that a great deal of research goes into developing the information base for program planning. Some of the research will have to be specifically designed for the particular problem situation—surveys of publics, analyses of media content, and depth interviews with key individuals. Other information gathering is ongoing—clipping print media, monitoring broadcast reports, and tracking relevant legislation and regulation. The research includes both informal and formal, qualitative and quantitative. All of it represents your attempt to develop a more complete understanding of the problem situation, including the publics.

IDENTIFYING THE PUBLICS

Researching the problem situation includes the discovery or confirmation of who is involved and who is affected, in the context of their relationship with the organization. From those identified as somehow contributing to or touched by the problem, *you* select and assign priorities to the target publics of the program. This is as much a part of strategic decision making as any other step. Too often, however, publics are selected from static "laundry lists" without taking into account the specific problem situation. You've seen the lists of so-called "publics": employees, stockholders, customers/consumers, analysts, community groups, government officials, etc. As seductive as these lists may be—because they reduce the need for research and decision making—such cross-situational typologies may or may not apply in a particular problem situation.

Publics, then, are defined on the basis of their connection to the organization in a particular situation. Whereas this linkage is useful for conceptually defining publics, it does not provide the observable attributes needed to identify publics. For that purpose, we need operational measures that help us determine who is "in" and who is "out" of a particular public. The following approaches provide useful referents you can use to define and describe publics:

Geographics

Geographic boundaries provide a gross indication of where to find those involved or affected, but give little useful insight about important differences among those residing within boundaries. Geographic segmentation may be most useful for determining media strategies and allocating program resources according to population density. Geographic boundaries are also useful for selecting samples for scanning organizational environments and measuring program impact. For example, Southwestern Bell Telephone Company "Customer Attitude Survey" samples are large enough in each of the five states to permit state-by-state analyses. These results are then weighted according to the distribution of customers served by the company.

Demographics

Used alone, this most popular approach to describing publics often provides little understanding of why or how people are involved or affected. Sex, age, income, education, marital status, religion, etc., help make the first "cut," but typically you need additional information about how people with particular cross-situational characteristics intersect specific situations. Often, demographic attributes interact with aspects of the situation, thereby usefully identifying publics. For example, not all eighteen- to twenty-four-year-old males are targets of a campaign to reduce highway fatalities associated with alcohol abuse. Rather, accident records indicate that one priority public can be identified as eighteen- to twenty-four-year-old males who try to drive home from bars at closing time on two-lane highways on the outskirts of the city.

Psychographics

Psychographics are psychological and life-style characteristics of individuals. They are used widely under the tradename VALS™ (an acronym for SRI International's values and lifestyles psychographic research program). Ketchum Public Relation's Paul Alvarez says, "We recognized much useful information in VALS™ about government and about people's attitudes, about who votes and who doesn't vote. VALS™ helps show where the issues emerge from. We are using VALS™ very, very heavily." Specifically, the proprietary VALS™ program segments the adult population into nine lifestyle types based on their "psychological maturity."[4]

Marketers and others have used psychographics—sometimes referred to as "people research" or "lifestyle analysis"—to segment populations since about 1970. However, the cross-situational categories are useful only when combined with other attributes tied to the particular situation of interest. For example, one advertising executive says that psychographics is "one of many inputs" and that his agency uses "a little bit of everything." Another points out that it is "just a *different* and *additional* way" to describe people relevant to your problem situation.[5]

Covert Power

This approach to describing publics is similar to what Floyd Hunter found in his influential study of "Regional City" (probably Atlanta).[6] People at the top of a power pyramid (often covert and economic) operate across situations. They exert power over others on a wide range of issues, but not in ways easily observed. Discovering who these people are requires a combination of careful observation over a long period, depth interviews with overt leaders, and analyses of official records documenting major public policy actions.

---

[4]See Arnold Mitchell, *The Nine American Lifestyles* (New York: Macmillan Publishing Company, 1983).

[5]James Atlas, "Beyond Demographics: How Madison Avenue Knows Who You Are and What You Want," *The Atlantic Monthly,* October 1984, pp. 49–58.

[6]Floyd Hunter, *Community Power Structure: A Study of Decision Makers* (Chapel Hill: University of North Carolina Press, 1953).

Position

The position-occupant approach uses positions held by individuals, not attributues of the individuals themselves. Analysts, farm advisers, doctors, teachers, and business reporters are descriptions of publics selected because these categories of individuals hold positions of influence. It is not that these individuals are either male or female, old or young, white or black. Rather, their positions make them important to an organization in a particular situation. For example, to determine science and technology policy leaders' attitudes toward biotechnology, Northern Illinois University's Public Opinion Laboratory surveyed full-time science journalists at national print and broadcast media as one important public.[7]

Reputation

This approach helps identify "knowledgeables" or "influentials" based on others' perceptions of these individuals. After starting with a purposive sample of people in relevant positions or those you perceive to be knowledgeable, "snowball sampling" (see Chapter 6 for description of this technique) identifies those seen by others as having influence in the social network on a specific issue (overt power). Of course, you could include items in any survey asking respondents to identify "opinion leaders" on the issues or concerns motivating the research. In community development programs, for example, positional leaders are asked to name persons other than elected officials whom they consider to be most influential in the community. Those receiving the most nominations are designated as a key public for community development efforts.[8]

Membership

This approach uses organizational membership—based on rather loose definitions of what constitutes an "organization" and "membership." The simple act of joining, affiliating, belonging, or aligning qualifies one to be included in a public. For example, membership in a professional association or community group is the qualifying attribute. These publics typically appear on mailing lists and receive controlled media from the organizations with which they affiliate. Whereas not every member is necessarily involved or affected in a particular situation, membership often is a useful indicator of potential publics.

For example, in the NIU survey of attitudes toward biotechnology, another public sampled included members of the National Academy of Sciences, National Academy of Engineering, and the Institute of Medical Sciences. Belong-

---

[7]Jon D. Miller, *The Attitudes of Religious, Environmental, and Science Policy Leaders Toward Biotechnology* (DeKalb, Illinois: Northern Illinois University Public Opinion Laboratory, 1985), p. 11.

[8]Larry R. Meiller and Glen M. Broom, "Communication Experiments in Building Community Consensus," *Journal of the Community Development Society,* Vol. 10, No. 2 (Fall 1979), p. 67.

ing to one of these scientific societies is a useful—though hardly foolproof—way to describe and identify the science policy leaders public.

Role in Decision Process

To identify individuals using this approach, you typically have to observe the decision-making process, interview participants to determine who plays what role(s), or later check records of who actively influenced a decision. It may even call for detailed analysis of minutes of meetings, logs, reports, and other records pertaining to decisions made or actions taken. In other cases, as a public relations practitioner, you may have to employ unobtrusive field observation techniques to discern who plays key roles in situations important to your organization. (See Chapter 7 for more on unobtrusive observation.) These typically small but influential publics often call for specially targeted program efforts, but would be overlooked except for careful observation. The same NIU survey defined yet another science policy leader public as persons who testified before a congressional committee or served on an executive branch advisory panel on science or technology issues during the previous two years. These people exert greater or lesser influence on the public policy decision-making process regarding science and technology. Participation in public policy forums is a pragmatic indicator of an individual's role in the policy-making process.

Communication Behavior

Professor James Grunig provides an overlay to all of the other strategies for describing publics. He uses measures of *problem recognition, constraint recognition,* and *level of involvement* to categorize publics and predict their communication behaviors. Of interest to Grunig and public relations program planners is the extent to which people passively process information versus actively seek information. Publics who do not recognize a particular problem, he calls *latent* publics. These people may passively process information about the problem situation. If and when they recognize the problem as relevant to their interests, Grunig calls them *aware* publics. If they begin to seek information or take other actions related to the problem, he says they become *active* publics. Grunig's research on publics shows a pattern of four types: a) publics that are active on all of the issues, b) publics that are apathetic on all issues, c) publics that are active only on issues that involve nearly everyone in the populations, and d) single-issue publics.[9] Furthermore, the communication behavior approach identifies publics that "cannot be identified by demographic indicators and personal activities or attitudes . . . ."[10]

The nine approaches to describing publics are generic techniques for

[9]James E. Grunig and Todd Hunt, *Managing Public Relations* (New York: Holt, Rinehart and Winston, 1984), pp. 144–60.

[10]James E. Grunig, "Communication Behaviors and Attitudes of Environmental Publics: Two Studies," *Journalism Monographs,* No. 81 (March 1983), p. 41.

refining your understanding and definitions of publics. The techniques supplement the conceptual statements about how publics are linked to your organization in a particular situation. You may find one approach more useful than the others in a particular situation, but most likely you will use combinations to pinpoint target publics for planning and evaluating purposes.

The objective is to end up with what Harvey Rosen, vice-president of Simmons Market Research Bureau, calls "actionable" definitions of publics—descriptions of publics that help you make program decisions. For example, *geodemographics* combines the geographics with demographics—the nation is divided into neighborhoods with similar characteristics. Contrasting this approach with VALS[tm], Rosen says geodemographics gives you information you can use: "VALS helps you understand who does what and why. But geodemographics lets you buy lists [for direct mail and other such purposes]."[11]

One thing is clear, however. Publics do not exist as static and monolithic entities. Rather, they vary from situation to situation, and from one time to the next. In short, they are dynamic—as are their relationships with your organization.

Researching each of the internal and external publics must include measures of their *knowledge, predispositions,* and *behaviors.* You need this information to write program objectives. The objectives guide the development of program strategies and establish the benchmarks for program evaluation. "When you are trying to get across a particular message," says Claritas president Bruce Caroll, "it's useful to know what the people are like, that they do these particular things."[12] The research effort must also determine each of the publics' *media sources* and *communication networks* concerning your organization and issues relevant to the problem situation. You need these insights to select the communication channels and media for each public. In other words, you use research to increase your understanding of the publics—a vital part of the situation analysis.

ANALYZING PUBLIC-ORGANIZATIONAL RELATIONSHIPS

The relationship between an organization and one of its publics results in part from what the individuals in that public *know* about the organization and related issues. Similarly, organizational intelligence about the public and related issues affects the public-organizational relationship. Likewise, how people in the public and organization *feel* about each other and issues in common has impact on the public-organizational relationship. And finally, what people in the public and organization *do* to each other and things in common determines the nature of their relationship. Public reactions to the organization and organizational reac-

---

[11]Michael Winkleman, "Their Aim Is True," *Public Relations Journal,* Vol. 43, No. 8 (August 1987), p. 22.
[12]Ibid.

tions to the public result from their respective knowledge, predispositions, and behaviors regarding each other and issues in common.

The most frequently used "audit" for researching the public-organizational relationship involves: a) doing interviews or document reviews to establish the organization's position on an issue, b) surveying members of the target public to determine the prevalent view of the same issue, and c) calculating the distance between the two sides on the issue. What typically follows, of course, is a public relations effort designed to move one side—usually the public—closer to the other side.[13] Such audits use what social scientists call the *individual agreement* approach to studying the relationship. There is an alternative, however, that takes into account a more complete diagnosis of the relationship—the *coorientational* approach.[14]

Consider this possibility: A public relations audit shows that an organization and one of its publics hold similar knowledge and opinions of an issue important to both. For example, management of a paper products company and members of a wildlife conservation group share concern that certain logging practices endanger bald eagle habitats and think that precautions should be taken to protect habitats. In other words, there is no distance between the two sides to calculate. Yet, angry representatives of the public force their way into the office of the director of public relations protesting the company's actions. Going beyond the typical audit, the director interviews protestors, discovering that they think the company's position on protecting bald eagle habitats differs from the group's views. Group members inaccurately *perceive disagreement,* which motivates their protest. The possibility of such inaccurate perceptions of the other side's views makes the coorientational approach a useful model for framing the research effort.

A public relations audit using such cross perceptions requires data answering four questions:

1. What are the organization's views on the issue?
2. What is the dominant view within the organization of the public's views?
3. What are the public's actual views on the issue?
4. What is the dominant view within the public of the organization's views?[15]

Answers to these questions make it possible to calculate the three coorientational variables illustrated in Figure 2–2—agreement, accuracy, and perceived agreement.[16] *Agreement* represents the extent to which the organization and public hold

[13]Joyce F. Jones, "Audit: A New Tool for Public Relations," *Public Relations Journal,* Vol. 31, No. 7 (July 1975), pp. 6–8.

[14]Thomas J. Scheff, "Toward a Sociological Model of Consensus," *American Sociological Review,* Vol. 32, No. 1 (February 1967), pp. 32–46.

[15]Glen M. Broom, "Coorientational Measurement of Public Issues," *Public Relations Review,* Vol. 3, No. 4 (Winter 1977), pp. 110–19.

[16]For a more complete explanation of the coorientational model, see Jack M. MeLeod and Steven H. Chaffee, "Interpersonal Approaches to Communication Research," in *Interpersonal Perception and Communication,* ed. by Steven H. Chaffee and Jack M. McLeod, special edition of *American Behavioral Scientist,* Vol. 16, No. 4 (March/April 1973), pp. 483–88.

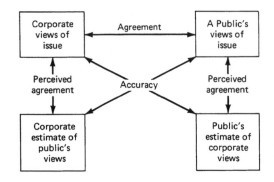

Figure 2-2 Coorientational model of relationships.

similar views on the issue (including both their definitions and evaluations of the issue). *Accuracy* indicates the extent to which one side's estimate of the other's views is similar to the other's actual views. *Perceived agreement* represents the extent to which one side's views are similar to their estimate of the other's views. Unlike agreement and accuracy, however, perceived agreement does not describe the relationship between the organization and the public. Rather, it describes how one side views the relationship and no doubt affects how it deals with the other side in the relationship. Recall, for example, that it was the wildlife members' perceptions of disagreement over the need to protect bald eagle habitats that motivated their protest in the paper company offices.

This approach expands the description of the relationship beyond simply calculating the distance between the organization and its public on the issue—agreement. The problem situation may be one best portrayed as an inaccurate perception of the public's views held within the organization—the accuracy variable. To the extent that perceptions of high agreement, for example, dictate strategy directed to a public that actually holds differing views, then the organization's behavior toward that public will be inappropriate. Likewise, there can be a problem in the relationship if an active public is inaccurate in its perceptions of the organization's views on issues of mutual interest.

If the two sides hold accurate views of each other's positions on an issue, two types of relationships are possible. *True consensus* occurs when both the organization and the public actually agree and accurately perceive that agreement. For example, if the wildlife group members and paper company management hold similar views regarding the protection of bald eagle habitats—and know that they agree—then the relationship can be described as one of true consensus. *Dissensus* occurs when there is actual disagreement that is accurately perceived. If, for example, management of the paper company and wildlife group members disagree on the importance and nature of protecting bald eagle habitats—and know that they disagree—then dissensus exists.

If one or both of the sides in the relationship hold inaccurate views of the other's positions on the issue, two false states are possible. *False consensus* occurs when there is actual disagreement that is inaccurately perceived as agreement. If the paper company only created "cosmetic" programs demonstrating concern for endangered bald eagles and was able to convince members of the wildlife group, then the relationship is based on a state of false consensus. Typically, a critical event produces undeniable evidence that the perceived agreement is not accurate. The relationship then suffers when one side realizes it has been misled. *False conflict* occurs when there is actual agreement that is inaccurately perceived as disagreement. In our example, members of the wildlife group *thought* that paper company management attached no importance to protecting habitat, but as it turned out they were wrong. Management shared the group's concern and had established a record—albeit not publicized—of research and practices to reduce their operations' impact on bald eagle habitats. Inaccurate perception of disagreement produced a state of false conflict in the relationship.[17]

In true consensus and dissensus, the two sides relate on the basis of accurately held perceptions of the other's views. In the case of dissensus, one or both could develop strategies for changing their own or the other's positions on the issue to improve the relationship. In the cases of false consensus and false conflict, however, strategies developed on the basis of inaccurate perceptions of the other's views will not be appropriate responses to the situation.

Research evidence that shows relationships are based on inaccurate perceptions calls for public relations objectives that use coorientational variables as outcome criteria. For example, the paper company public relations director's finding of false conflict would lead to an information program strategy designed to improve the *accuracy* of wildlife group members' perceptions. If the research produced evidence of low agreement, then the program strategy could be designed to change views held by *both* sides in the relationship. It is even possible that the appropriate strategy could be to develop a persuasive effort to change management's positions to make them closer to those held by important publics.

As these hypotheticals illustrate, you can develop internal and external strategies to improve the accuracy of each side's views of the other's perceptions, as well as to increase levels of agreement. The program goal is to improve the relationships between an organization and its publics by not only changing what people know and how they feel about an issue and each other, but by increasing the accuracy of their perceptions of each other's views. The objectives spell out what needs to be changed in order to achieve the improved relationships.

WRITING PROGRAM GOALS AND OBJECTIVES

In practice, writing program objectives for each public appears to be one of the most difficult and befuddling tasks you will face. As Burson-Marsteller's Lloyd Kirban observes:

> *By and large, the current objectives in public relations are not measurable. But we're asked to measure them. When this happens, you can see the change in how those objectives are stated.*

---

[17]Adapted from Scheff's typology of consensus in "Toward a Sociological Model of Consensus," p. 39.

The change is toward statements that spell out specific results to be achieved. *Public relations objectives specify change in or maintenance of measurable levels of knowledge, predisposition, and behavior.* (Coorientational agreement, perceived agreement, and accuracy are subsumed by the knowledge and predisposition outcomes.) To write such objectives, you need the detailed measures and understanding of the situation that only research provides.

Goals Versus Objectives

Writers sometimes use the terms "goals" and "objectives" interchangeably, but the usual meanings make goals the more global statement of program results. *Goals* indicate the more general and ultimate outcome the total program is designed to achieve. *Objectives* describe the specific results to be achieved by a specified date for each of the well-defined target publics. Goals specify what will be accomplished if the objectives for each of the publics are achieved. Both goals and objectives, however, specify measurable results.

Goals give the program direction. Objectives spell out the sequence of operational-level program consequences—sometimes referred to as *key results*—for each public. Objectives:

1. *give focus and direction to developing program activities,*
2. *provide guidance and motivation to those working in the program,* and
3. *spell out the criteria for assessing program impact.*

You cannot just pick these elements out of the air. You have to have a detailed understanding of the publics and their knowledge, predispositions, and behaviors. The baseline established by your research provides the information needed to cast meaningful objectives. For example, the most frequently asked question in our classes and workshops is, "How do you know how much change to call for in an objective?" The simple reponse is, "By researching the situation to learn what is possible." As is usually the case, the real answer is not nearly so simple.

The research part is true. Because most objectives require specific descriptions of the starting points, you must have that intelligence in the situation analysis. For example, the Dairy Council of California learned that 41 percent of adult women surveyed said they consume some form of calcium supplement. One of the objectives for the public information campaign that followed was: "To decrease the use of calcium supplements by 20 percent among adult women by January 31 [one year after the survey]." That translates into a decrease roughly from two out of five, to one of three—20 percent of 41 is about 8, so 41 percent less 8 is 33 percent. Program planners *judged* this to be a realistic expectation for their program. They had additional evidence that adult women recognize that they need more calcium in their diets but are unsure about the best source. If the survey results had shown that women were strongly convinced that they are using the best calcium supplement, then a less ambitious objective would have been proposed—given no other data to suggest a supportive "climate" for changed behavior. By the way, the follow-up survey after the year-long program indicated that the percentage of women taking calcium supplements dropped from 41 to 30 percent—a 27 percent decrease. Naturally, the results pleased the cooperating nutrition, dietetic, medical, and other health groups concerned about the long-term effects of widespread use of vitamin and mineral supplements. No doubt, the program sponsor—the dairy industry—also appreciated the results, in light of the threat these supplements pose to achieving their goal of maintaining or increasing dairy food consumption.[18]

The objective in this example takes the form of a *relative* objective, as it states the desired outcome as a proportionate change in the observed problem situation—to reduce the percentage by 20 percent. An even clearer form of the objective would be: "To reduce the percentage of adult women using calcium supplements from 41 percent to at least 33 percent by January 31." Notice that the program planners did not propose the unrealistic objective of eliminating all use of calcium supplements. If they had, the statement would be an *absolute* objective. Absolute objectives call for the total elimination of some condition or the creation of something that did not exist before the program.[19] For example, opposing sides on a piece of legislation might have objectives about how individual senators vote on the bill. Another example would be the objective of getting targeted authors to include—for the first time—information about an issue in new and revised textbooks.

The key to setting realistic and useful objectives is the adequacy and completeness of the research done in diagnosing the problem situation. Objectives established on the basis of individual values and assumptions may have to be modified based on research evidence and program experience. In fact, you may have to rewrite absolute objectives as relative objectives as a result of new information.

> *For example, the planners of an antismoking program may start out with the absolute objective of eliminating all cigarette smoking. But the planners may soon find that the stubborn persistence of smoking habits necessitates reducing their aspirations to the relative objective of reducing the number of smokers by some specified percentage.[20]*

And of course, once the program is underway, objectives cannot be viewed as fixed targets. In the open systems approach to public relations management, structures and activities change in response to environmental changes—including changes brought about by the program itself. If the research effort to

---

[18]Example adapted from Chapter 1 in Kerry Tucker and Doris Derelian, *Public Relations Writing: A Planned Approach for Creating Results* (Englewood Cliffs, N.J.: Prentice-Hall, Inc., 1989).

[19]This typology of objectives suggested in Peter H. Rossi and Howard E. Freeman, *Evaluation: A Systematic Approach*, 3rd ed. (Beverly Hills: Sage Publications, Inc., 1985), p. 65.

[20]Ibid., p. 67.

monitor the environment and track the program detects changes in the problem situation, then you may have to make changes in the objectives. More on this follows in Chapter 3. The point here is that objectives should be treated as dynamic reflections of the changing environment. However, make changes on the basis of a consensus among key line managers and program staff, as program implementation and evaluation are guided by the criteria spelled out in the objectives.

Elements of Objectives

"Mushy" objectives give vague guidance for those charged with implementing the program. Mushy objectives prevent meaningful evaluation by not spelling out the standards for measuring progress. Use detailed research findings to make objectives specific. The elements and stylistic requirements for writing useful objectives follow.

1. *Begin with "to," followed by a verb that describes what you want to happen with respect to the criterion outcome.* The most frequent problem with this element is the confusion of *process* versus *outcome* in the verbs chosen. For example, "to educate" describes the process, not the outcome. What is the outcome you hope to achieve with education? "To inform" describes the process. What is the outcome of informing someone? "To encourage" describes what *you* plan to do. What outcome do you hope to achieve by encouraging the target public? This is not just a matter of semantics. These examples show how such verbs direct attention to the program, away from the intended results. The list of verbs is actually rather limited—increase, decrease, and maintain are the most frequently used.

2. *Specify the criterion outcome to be achieved.* The outcomes specified by program objectives derive from the functional definition of public relations—to identify, establish, and maintain relationships between an organization and its publics. The nature of such relationships is determined by a) what both sides know about each other—including how accurate both are in estimating the other's views—and things common to both, b) how both sides feel about each other and things common to both, and c) what both sides do to each other and to things common to both. Recognize that these also determine the outcome criteria for public relations objectives: *knowledge, predispositions,* and *behavior.*

Survey results show what people know or do not know, what they are aware of or not aware of, and what they understand or do not understand. Using this evidence, you can formulate knowledge outcome objectives. Survey results also indicate how people feel—opinions and attitudes.[21] These data serve as the

---

[21]Here and throughout the book, we use "opinion" to mean the predisposition expressed in a particular situation. "Attitude" refers to the predisposition carried from one situation to another. In other words, attitudes are cross-situational predispositions, whereas opinions are what get expressed when an attitude interacts with a set of circumstances in a particular situation. This distinction represents the mainstream of social psychology and serves as a useful way to differentiate the two types of predispositional outcomes sought in public relations.

baseline information for setting predispositional outcome objectives. Surveys and other observations document what people do or do not do. Measures of behaviors in the target publics establish the levels that must be changed or maintained as behavioral objectives. However, *each objective should specify a single criterion outcome.*

The reasons we suggest only one criterion outcome in each objective are that a) more than one outcome may require more than one program strategy, and b) more than one outcome confounds the evaluation step by creating multiple criteria.

3. *State exactly and in measurable terms how much change is to occur or what outcome level is to be maintained.* To be useful and verifiable, objectives must indicate the magnitude of the outcome expected. "To increase" or "to decrease" leaves open the level desired or needed for program success and raises the possibility of conflict over how much is enough. The key is to make objectives as quantifiable as possible, even if at the level of an absolute objective. The more you specify, the better. For example, it is better to say "to increase from 40 to 60 the number of senators," rather than to say "to increase by 50 percent the number of senators." The first version is a richer description of the intended change than is the version using percentage of change. The more concrete, specific, measurable, and observable you make objectives, then the more useful they are for guiding program planning and evaluation.

How much change is enough? That decision calls for both judgment and knowledge. Clients and employers may impose minimum levels of change. Experience in previous program cycles or similar programs may suggest realistic levels. Research evidence from different situations may indicate what is *possible* under certain conditions—suggesting what can be *expected* if the program produces those conditions. In short, however, there is no easy answer to questions about what levels of change should be set in program objectives and goals. "It depends," may have more meaning than usual when trying to answer, "How much is enough?"

Our recommendation is to gather all the evidence you can and call on the experiences of others, then factor in your own judgment about what is possible given the resources available and the nature of problem situation. As you begin to use research to manage and evaluate programs, your ability to set realistic and useful levels will increase.

4. *Say when the outcome is to be achieved.* Set the target date and put it in the objective. When the deadline for the desired change (or maintenance) is clearly displayed, it guides those charged with carrying out the program and with assessing program impact.

Notice that the objective in Figure 2–3 does not indicate how the objective will be achieved, only what will be achieved by when. Deciding which strategies to use for achieving the objective follows the management decisions of what will be accomplished by when. As several strategies may be used, and even changed during the program, they should not be included in the statement of the intended outcome. If written properly and based on an accurate assessment

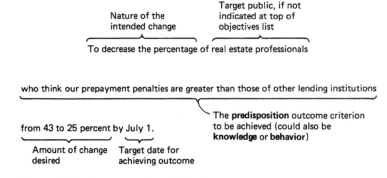

Nature of the
intended change

Target public, if not
indicated at top of
objectives list

To decrease the percentage of real estate professionals

who think our prepayment penalties are greater than those of other lending institutions

from 43 to 25 percent by July 1.

The **predisposition** outcome criterion
to be achieved (could also be
knowledge or **behavior**)

Amount of change
desired

Target date for
achieving outcome

Figure 2-3   Anatomy of an objective.

of the problem situation, public relations objectives make you a *results-oriented manager.* To do so, however, two points deserve special attention: First, the *objectives must be in writing,* with copies kept and periodically referred to by those implementing the program. Second, the *objectives must be discussed* often in regularly scheduled program review meetings, serving as the basis for monitoring and evaluating the program.

DEVELOPING AND PRETESTING STRATEGY

Research points the way for developing and pretesting the means for achieving objectives. However, some view selecting program strategies as essentially a creative process calling on both intuition and experience. Research evidence provides the foundation for educated judgment. Harold Leiendecker, of Exxon Corporation, describes using research to determine message strategies:

We participate heavily early in the planning process. What we've done in recent years is to first have focus-group exploration of "political-social actives" (a population segment identified by the Roper Organization and Exxon in the 1940s). That's about 11 percent of the population who respond positively to questions like: "Are you registered to vote? Have you made a political speech? Did you vote in the last election? Have you contributed to a political campaign in the last year?" We typically do two groups in each of four communities. We explore their interest in communications from oil companies on an open-ended basis and then on a more structured basis. "What about this? What about that?" Then we use relatively low-cost quantitative exploration to check out those same issues. We do that through add-on questions in omnibus surveys. We have people select from a card listing topics that they would most like to hear about from oil companies.

Pretests provide reliable estimates of how program strategies will work. In fact, pretesting gives you the opportunity to compare alternative strategies before putting together the final program. Amoco Corporation's Jerry Cooper outlines how message pretesting with treatment and control groups helped planners evaluate their choice of cartoon characters for a corporate film:

You can set up research in a scientific way so that you can measure differences. For example, we put together a cartoon economic education film some years ago. It used Fred Flintstone type characters. We were most concerned that we might have some adverse reactions to the stereotyped characters in the film. After all, these were cartoon characters. So we tested it—first, right here in the company. The first group of employees saw the "gels" from the film and another group did not. Afterwards, both groups were given a very simple questionnaire that included questions about knowledge of economic concepts, opinions of the company, and views toward the media. We compared the answers and in fact found that the group that saw the film did learn economic concepts, did feel better about the company, and did not have adverse reactions to the film characters. From there we went to the Museum of Science and Industry and did the same kind of experiment with school kids—an experimental group and a control group. We found similar differences. We went ahead and did the film. It has been seen by about 75 million viewers in the past ten years and I can't recall a half dozen letters that protested the characters. In fact, it has been so successful that we are about to do a sequel that talks about world trade. That is an example of the kind of research that shows whether or not what you are doing makes a difference.

In Chapter 4, we discuss using research to measure program impact. In Chapters 5 through 8, we outline research designs and methods for planning and conducting the actual research procedures. As these issues also apply to using research for pretesting program strategies, we will not summarize the information from those chapters here.

In this chapter, we argue that research is essential for planning a public relations program. Research provides the information necessary for defining the problem, identifying the publics, writing the goals and objectives, and selecting the program strategies. Without a solid foundation of research, program decisions are made on the basis of individual intuition and experience. Even the collective intuition and experience of the management team is no substitute for research findings that describe the specific conditions affecting the relationship between an organization and its publics. As Harry W. O'Neill, president of Opinion Research Corporation, says:

> *Public relations or corporate communications research has as its purpose providing the practitioner with intelligence on how business, industry, and one's company stand in the eyes of those important publics—and how those perceptions are changing. This is needed to manage a corporate reputation. It should be gathered systematically, on a continuous basis—not, as too often occurs, a little bit here and a little bit there, or when a problem already has reached serious proportions. Properly conducted, such research also prevents practitioners and managers from falling victim to preconceived notions about **what** to communicate to **whom**.*[22]

In conclusion, there simply is no substitute for good organizational intelligence when it comes to planning a public relations program. Creative and artistic decisions employing all the intuition and experience you can muster are then made in the context of a strategic plan based on research.

[22]Harry W. O'Neill, "How Opinion Surveys Can Help Public Relations Strategy," *Public Relations Review,* Vol. 10, No. 2 (Summer 1984), pp. 11–12.

EXHIBIT 2–3
An Example of Research for
Program Planning

An example of using research to plan a program occurred right before divestiture. We used research to plan our announcement. As it happened, the assistant attorney general had granted an interview to an obscure trade publication many months before the settlement. Nobody had paid any attention to it, even though in the interview he precisely laid out his terms for the settlement. So at the time we agreed to his deal, I had that interview upon which to base our public opinion research. We went into the field and got a reading on how the public would react—what they thought was good and what they thought was not.

That research became my touchstone for planning the announcement. That was my star to steer by in planning what we had to stress in the press conference, and in the information given to employees and the public. Then after the press announcement, we went back to the field to see if we had succeeded. In the main we did, but in the days and weeks following the announcement we were able to use advertising to correct some of the impressions that had not come out straight.

The point is that we had only one public relations objective and that was to make sure the deal stuck. The worst thing that could happen to us was to have made the deal with the government and then have Congress, shareholders, or whomever reverse the deal. That public relations effort *had* to succeed, and research was absolutely the key to planning what we did and quickly getting back to the field in order to make course corrections—in real time.

Edward M. Block, Senior Vice President (retired), AT&T,
New York.

CHAPTER 3

USING RESEARCH TO MONITOR PROGRAMS

Roger Sennott, PhD, General Manager, MARKET DEVELOP-
MENT INC., San Diego.

*We have two criteria for judging our creative work. First, does it
say what is necessary to influence the target audience? Second, to
what extent are those things said in ways that the media people
will use the messages? So our research on the creative side of
message strategy has to deal with both the ability to influence an
audience and the ability to get picked up by the media. And those
can be very different. For example, I've heard it said that, "I know
this is not the best way to say it to our target public, but it is the
kind of thing that media people like."*

*What I see as the biggest challenge is finding a way to ap-
proach the traditional measures of the process in a more scientific
fashion. We need to get back to the idea of tracking what we call
output, which is the initial result of what we do, in order to learn
what is going to work in getting mentions or placements. This is
something we should know to better serve our clients. The emphasis is on measuring impact, but there is a great deal we need to
learn about what happens to what we produce.*

*Other than that, we do research for the same reasons they do
it in marketing. Beforehand, we want to know what we have to
say. Afterwards, we want to know whether enough people got the
message enough times and were influenced the way we wanted
them to be. It is the research on the process of obtaining media
coverage that makes public relations research different.*

Edward M. Block, Senior Vice President (retired), AT&T, New York.

In the case of our media measurement research, it changed the way we do things. Here we are in New York reading the New York Times, Wall Street Journal, *and* Washington Post. *So the bylined beat reporters who cover us for those newspapers condition our notions of what the publics are getting about us from the press. Of course, most of our publics don't read those newspapers, and the media study showed us that most of the news reaching them is wire service copy. So we put more resources against servicing the wire services, as opposed to putting all our attention on that one guy at the* New York Times. *So that study changed our approach to day-to-day media relations.*

Blair C. Jackson, Senior Vice President, ROGERS & COWAN, INC., New York.

Another example of where ongoing measurement is needed is publicity campaigns. Typically, that involves looking at how many clips you get. To take that further—as more and more public relations people are doing—it's not just counting the clips, but evaluating the clips in terms of how many of our copy points got across—quantifying the publicity coverage in some way for the client.

Paul H. Alvarez, APR, Chairman and Chief Executive Officer, KETCHUM PUBLIC RELATIONS, New York.

Should you admit errors and make mid-course corrections? That depends. By and large, we're dealing with MBAs. MBAs know that if the world were a perfect, foolproof place, there wouldn't be any reason to have an MBA degree. If you go to somebody and admit that something didn't work, the world doesn't end. It happens all the time in the rest of the business world. Of course, PR people think they've got to be nearly perfect. I think that we do have an obligation to make reasonable judgments and estimates about what is likely to happen. That doesn't mean you can't be wrong.

We spent a lot of time and money to come up with a public affairs issues tracking model. Our current tracking model really measures target audience and the delivery of copy. It doesn't say anything about whether anything is getting through. It is designed to answer, "Was the promised program delivered?" And if not, "Why wasn't it delivered?"

After using research to plan the program, but before using research to measure program impact, you use research to document and monitor the program. Certainly, your need to document the program for *accountability* motivates the research, but your primary purpose is to track program implementation in order to make needed program *adjustments*. Documentation produces an accurate record of what was done, where it was done, when it was done, and to whom it was done, so that you can later describe exactly what the program included. Documentation also systematically calls your attention to how the program is being implemented and how closely it conforms to the strategic plan. Monitoring, along with measures of who the program is reaching with what effects, provides the basis for modifying the plan.

In Figure 1–5 (page 19), we refer to performance control and program adjustment feedback loops in public relations. These are analogous to the two uses of research for monitoring program implementation. First, the performance of program staff is documented for later evaluation along with program impact or effectiveness. Second, the program activities themselves are monitored for the purpose of detecting implementation problems that call for program adjustment.

Evaluation researchers distinguish between these two purposes for research done to monitor the program based on how the results are to be used.[1] Documentation for accountability is *summative* research in that the program record is intended to help decision makers assess the overall effectiveness of the program or its parts. As Morris and Fitz-Gibbon put it, "You cannot evaluate something without describing what that something is."[2] We will hold our discussion of the summative use until later in this chapter, as it complements the summative research done to measure program impact outlined in Chapter 4. Research done to monitor program activities with an eye for implementation problems and program adjustments is *formative* research. That is because such research is done for the purpose of changing the program as a result of what is learned from the research. In effect, the program is "reformed" on the basis of new evidence about the problem situation or feedback on how the strategies are working.

Some refer to the formal methods used to collect and report information about program progress as the *management information system,* or MIS. Another title for using research to monitor a program is *decision analysis,* which focuses on using information to make program decisions. Decision analysis attempts to make explicit "every assumption made in deriving a solution."[3] This use of re-

---

[1] Lynn Lyons Morris and Carol Taylor Fitz-Gibbon, *How to Measure Program Implementation* (Beverly Hills: Sage Publications, Inc., 1978), pp. 13–14.

[2] Ibid., p. 7.

[3] Gordon F. Pitz and Jack McKillip, *Decision Analysis for Program Evaluators* (Beverly Hills: Sage Publications, Inc., 1984), p. 35.

search reflects four features commonly associated with public relations situations:

1. *High stakes riding on the outcome.*
2. *Complicated information structure*—numerous issues involved and no obvious appropriate method for dealing with these issues.
3. *No identifiable authority to provide correct answer*—no single authoritative expert to turn to for answers.
4. *Need to justify the decision*—rationale for decision demanded by clients and employers.[4]

In short, research is used to monitor public relations programs in order to make adjustments and to document what was implemented.

We first look at the formative uses of research, because they logically follow the program planning uses outlined in Chapter 2. You will notice, however, that research done at this stage often serves both documentation and adjustment purposes.

FORMATIVE RESEARCH
FOR PROGRAM ADJUSTMENT

Why wait until the program is completed to do research? If you do, isn't it often too late to make changes if it is not working? If you use research to monitor the program in progress, then you avoid the risk of wasting resources that do little to change the problem situation. You would think that the possibility of these outcomes would drive even the most reluctant employer or client to use research. Blair Jackson at Rogers & Cowan makes the point, however, that in the real world not all clients are so enlightened or motivated:

> *In an ideal world, if the research shows the program is not working, then you go to the client and say, "Look, this program is just not hitting the mark the way we thought it would. Stop right now. Save your money. Let's use the remainder of the budget to try a different approach." Some clients would say, "Gee, that's great. Thanks for being right on top of this." But most clients would say, "Sorry you couldn't handle it. I'm going across the street and get another agency that can." It is such a competitive field. Getting accounts and keeping accounts—that's what gives us ulcers and keeps us up nights. In the agency business, that is the motivation. On a more personal level, it is often your job at*

[4]Ibid. Adapted from list on pp. 34–35.

stake. If your client leaves, then it sometimes means that you leave. That is why research that shows how the program is working can be scary.

"How the program is working" apparently can be a confusing notion for some, however. So, before delving further into the uses of research to monitor the program, we must inject an important reminder about the difference between *means* and *ends*.

Substituting Efforts for Results

Keep this distinction in mind as you study the next two chapters. Confusing means with ends has a long history in public relations. The problem persists. We can illustrate this problem with just one of many examples of this confusion found among Public Relations Society of America (PRSA) Silver Anvil Award-winning programs. The American Association of Yellow Pages Publishers' program's short-term "objective" focuses attention on program *efforts,* not *results,* as outcome criteria:

> *In the short term, to encourage and facilitate Yellow Page coverage in the **classroom** immediately and as a continuing part of the curriculum by meeting educators' needs for usable information and supporting tools.[5]*

When *Public Relations Journal* described this award-winning program, it added to the confusion by reporting, "Short term public relations objectives included providing educators with teaching materials and information that could be used in the classroom, by September 1986."[6] Notice that the program planners emphasized *what they plan to do* ("encourage," "facilitate," "meeting ... needs," and "providing"), not what they hope will happen as a *result* of these efforts. It is probably safe to assume, however, that they hope to achieve some yet-to-be-specified level of classroom use. The point is that measuring the activity described in the "objective" fits under this chapter on monitoring the program effort, not in Chapter 4—"Using Research to Assess Impact."

Here are two more "objectives" from actual programs that illustrate how program activities get substituted for program impact:

> *To promote an understanding of the work and contributions of associations with specially selected target publics.*

This first statement describes the general nature of the strategy to be implemented—a promotional campaign. It provides a vague indication of the

---

[5]"1987 Silver Anvil Winners: Index and Summaries." Published by the Public Relations Society of America, New York, p. 71.

[6]Gail Bernstein, "Not-So-Mellow-Yellow," in "Briefings," ed. by Celia Kuperszmid Lehrman, *Public Relations Journal,* Vol. 43, No. 7 (July 1987), pp. 8–9.

message strategy—something will be said about what associations do and accomplish. It says that the program will be directed to "specially selected target publics." As readers, we are left with the task of guessing what specific and measurable increases in understanding are to be achieved and the extent to which and by when these changes are to occur. As stated, the "objective" directs the research effort to monitoring the nature of the promotional effort, the content of the messages and activities used in the program, and the recipients of the messages (and, by necessity, the media used to carry those messages to the target publics). This statement describes more about the program than about the results to be achieved. But it could be worse! How about this?

> *To tell the story of Nipper's rejuvenation to the widest possible audience via the news media.*

What specific and measurable *result* is this program designed to achieve? You cannot tell from this "objective." Again, the statement directs research attention to measuring the extent to which the Nipper story is told, the success of placing the story in the news media, and the reach or penetration achieved by the publicity effort. Whereas these are entirely appropriate aspects of program *effort*, they do not represent outcome criteria. They fail to state the intended *impact* of such effort. (If you do not understand the distinction between these so-called "objectives" and the type outlined in Chapter 2, review pages 39-44.)

More examples would be redundant. Suffice to say that this chapter deals with those attributes of the program itself that so often are confused with program impact. Despite this confusion, measuring program effort is an essential research enterprise. You simply cannot substitute the implementation level measures for those needed at the impact level. For example, measures of employee readership of the monthly corporate magazine provide feedback on how effectively the program attracts employee attention to the messages. They do not, however, substitute for measures of program impact. These measures don't tell you what message content those same employees know, how they feel about the topics discussed, or what they do as a result of reading the magazine. Readership measures one aspect of message attention; not the knowledge, predispositions, and behaviors of those attending to the messages. Readership does not equal impact.

That may seem obvious to you, but we see many publication evaluations using readership as the only or major criterion for judging success in achieving publication objectives and goals. Is it simply easier to measure readership than the intended results? Probably. This may explain why so many countable and measurable aspects of the communication *process* get substituted for measures of intended *outcomes*.

Monitoring Content

Like readability, content cannot substitute for measures of program effects on target publics. To explain or understand what did or did not work to produce effects, however, research designed to track and document program content is essential. Again, like readability, content often is a necessary but not sufficient condition for program effects. Rather, you need evidence of publication, broadcast, or appearance of program content in order to later link *what* was said or done to *whom* such messages were communicated with *what effect*.

Probably the most frequently used definition of content analysis appears in Berelson's 1952 book on the topic: "Content analysis is a research technique for the objective, systematic, and quantitative description of the manifest content of communication."[7] Kerlinger offers a similar but more recent definition:

> **Content analysis** *is a method of studying and analyzing communications—documents of all kinds, including existing documents and documents deliberately produced for research purposes, books, letters, and so on—in systematic, objective, and quantitative ways to measure variables or to accomplish other research purposes.*[8]

Notice the key words from both definitions—*objective, systematic,* and *quantitative*. Objectivity has to be a primary concern to ensure that the results reflect the procedures used, not the persons making the observations. In other words, if different people used your system to determine the topics covered in your employee newsletter during the past year, they would get results very similar to your own. Being systematic means that your coding categories and procedures are complete and applied the same way for all content. It also means that what actually appears is coded, not what coders *think* is intended or suggested. And finally, the content of communication is reduced to some quantity—number—that can later be used in mathematical analyses.

Given a system that meets these conditions, you can usefully measure and track the content of stockholders' letters, press releases and other materials sent to media, media coverage of your organization, minutes of meetings, annual reports, brochures, flyers, films, video tapes, recordings or transcriptions from focus groups, speeches, and almost any other medium. Using content analysis, you can systematically monitor the extent to which communications match the outcome criteria spelled out in the objectives. In Chapter 7, we go into more detail on how to do the actual observations for content analyses.

Comparing Content with Outcomes

Analyzing the content of program materials helps detect three types of problems: a) content does not address issues related to intended outcomes, b) not enough content relates to outcome criteria, and c) content is unsystematic or varies across target publics. In other words, you can use content analysis results

---

[7]Bernard Berelson, *Content Analysis in Communication Research* (New York: The Free Press, 1952), p. 18.

[8]Fred N. Kerlinger, *Behavioral Research: A Conceptual Approach* (New York: Holt, Rinehart and Winston, 1979), pp. 256–57.

to determine the extent to which program efforts address the intended outcomes. If they do not, you can make changes in the program during implementation.

Content analysis specialists Krippendorff and Eleey describe a hypothetical scenario to illustrate this use:

> **1.   *Surveillance information from public opinion measures*** *at* T₁ *shows the prevailing belief about a public utility company to be that there is a trade-off between the quality of consumer home service provided and development of high-technology services for commercial clients. The public feels (albeit wrongly) that an improvement in one is at the expense of the other, and that the company is currently ignoring consumer home service in favor of commercial clients.*
>
> **2.   *Surveillance information from media content measures*** *also taken at* T₁ *indicates that recent news items have dealt with high-technology commercial service twice as frequently as with consumer home service. To counter this potentially adverse opinion trend, it is felt that the ratio of attention to the two types of services should be reversed. . . .*
>
> **3.   *In order to achieve this desired effect, the decision is taken to increase the company's press releases on home service themes. It is expected that a change in the public relations "mix" will stimulate a corresponding change in media coverage.***
>
> **4.   *Joint measurement of media content and public relations activity at time T₁ and later repeated at time T₂ provides control*** *information on what has actually been achieved. . . .* [9]

You can imagine other scenarios by substituting other findings: Program content would be redirected if the findings show that for the past six months rate structures and the upcoming rate hearings dominated both press coverage and your own public relations output. Likewise, program content would be focused on the high priority given to consumer services if the content analysis findings show little consistency in program messages now directed to various publics. There is also the case of a program objective not being achieved simply because the intended outcome is not being addressed in the program content. By comparing program content with the outcome criteria spelled out in the objectives, you can detect mismatches between effort and intended impact while there is still time to modify the program.

Estimating Readability

When talking about estimating readability of program materials, the emphasis is on the word "estimating." This narrowly focused approach to content

---

[9]Klaus Krippendorff and Michael F. Eleey, "Monitoring A Group's Symbolic Environment," *Public Relations Review,* Vol. 12, No. 1 (Spring 1986), pp. 30–31.

EXHIBIT 3–1
Examples of Using Research to
Monitor and Adjust Programs

In short, we do research on everything we do: We do regular reader research on every publication. We do a survey and include an open-ended question. Then we do follow-up interviews with some of the people who respond. This helps us justify the existence of a publication when we are determining budget priorities for programs. Some may think that this or that publication is a frivolous thing to do, but the research shows us that the customers, the media, management, employees, or whomever, feel that it is really important.

Our audience research has helped us improve our publications. For example, we dropped monthly sales figures from our management newsletter, because in one of our surveys managers told us we were covering too much that doesn't seem to be "news" to them. So we made some mid-course corrections and the next survey showed much higher ratings on that newsletter.

When we do a quarterly financial news release, we do an analysis of the coverage generated to determine how many of the key message points are picked up. We also do analyses of *Wall Street Journal* coverage to find out how many times our CEO is mentioned high up in articles, compared to other retail company CEOs. We do follow-up interviews after analyst meetings to find out if our presentation hit the target and got our message across.

For instance, if I see that the Associated Press picked up only 30 percent of our messages, then I have a problem. That has resulted in me going to New York and meeting with those people to find out why they aren't picking up the messages we send. At one time, AP was incorrectly identifying us as the sixth largest retailer and not correctly reporting a couple of other things about our operating companies. My visit resulted in the next AP story correctly giving our size and correctly identifying our companies. But, if we had not been looking at what AP reports about us, how Reuters covers us, how the Dow Jones wire covers Dayton-

Hudson; then it could have been a year before we scratched our heads and said, "Oh, we really missed the boat on that!"

Ann H. Barkelew, APR, Vice-President–Corporate Public Relations, DAYTON-HUDSON CORPORATION, Minneapolis.

analysis takes into account some—but certainly not all—aspects of how effectively content is presented. It results in reading ease or difficulty scores. Most readability measures use syllable and word counts to compute scores indicating the level of education required to comprehend printed messages. Commonly used measures of readability, however, do not take into account the topic or its relative interest value to potential readers. So while readability measures can usefully detect potential stylistic problems in messages, they may not consistently predict reader comprehension across various target publics.

As it turns out, the major approaches to measuring readability or comprehensability of communication correlate highly. This means that even though they use slightly different inputs plugged into slightly different formulas, the resulting indices give similar *relative* measures of readability.

Figure 3–1 shows how to use Edward Fry's readability grade level chart. Two other commonly used techniques are Rudolph Flesch's Readability Score (sometimes referred to as Reading Ease score) and Robert Gunning's Fog Index. To estimate readability using the Flesch Readability Score, randomly select at least two 100-word samples from the manuscript.[10] For press releases or other short copy, you could use the entire manuscript rather than introduce sampling error. Here are the steps:

1. Count the number of sentences, the number of words, and the number of syllables. (Count numbers, abbreviations, symbols, and hyphenated words as single words.)

2. Compute *average sentence length* by dividing the number of words by the number of sentences.

[10]Rudolf Flesch, *How to Write Plain English: A Book for Lawyers & Consumers* (New York: Harper & Row, Publishers, 1979), pp. 23–26.

3. Compute *average word length* by dividing the number of syllables by the number of words.

4. Use these averages in the Readability Score calculation formula.

$$Readability\ Score = 206.835 - [(\text{average sentence length} \times 1.015) \\ + (\text{average word length} \times 84.6)]$$

In other words, first multiply average sentence length by 1.015. Next, multiply average word length by 84.6. Subtract the sum of these two numbers from the baseline value of 206.835.

5. Estimate the relative difficulty by using the Readability Score. Flesch says that Plain English should score at least 60. Conversational English should score at least 80. Table 3–1 shows the ranges and approximate school grades for interpreting readability scores.

In a study of twenty-four annual reports, for example, readability scores ranged from 12 ("very difficult") to 51 ("fairly difficult"). Using the Fry readability chart shown in Figure 3–1, the most difficult annual report required seventeen or more years of education (4.2 sentences per 100 words and 203 syllables per 100 words). The easiest to read annual report came in at eleven years of education on the Fry chart (4.6 sentences per 100 words and 159 syllables per 100 words). It was also the only one written at a level comprehensible by someone with less than a college education, according to the Fry chart. The other twenty-three annual reports rated seventeen or more years of education required![11]

The Gunning Fog Index formula uses sentence length and percentage of words with three or more syllables to estimate reading difficulty.[12] Select at least two samples of 100 words and count the number of whole sentences.

Table 3–1 Interpretations of Flesch Readability Scores

SCORE	READABILITY	GRADE LEVEL
90–100	Very Easy	5th
80–90	Easy	6th
70–80	Fairly Easy	7th
60–70	*Plain English*	*8th and 9th*
50–60	Fairly Difficult	10th to 12th
30–50	Difficult	college
0–30	Very Difficult	college graduate

SOURCE: Adapted from Rudolph Flesch, *How to Write Plain English: A Book for Lawyers & Consumers* (New York: Harper & Row, Publishers, 1979), pp. 25–26.

[11]Robert L. Hoskins, "Annual Reports I: Difficult Reading and Getting More So," *Public Relations Review,* Vol. 10, No. 2 (Summer 1984), pp. 49–55.

[12]Robert Gunning, *The Technique of Clear Writing,* rev. ed. (New York: McGraw-Hill Book Company, 1968), pp. 38–40.

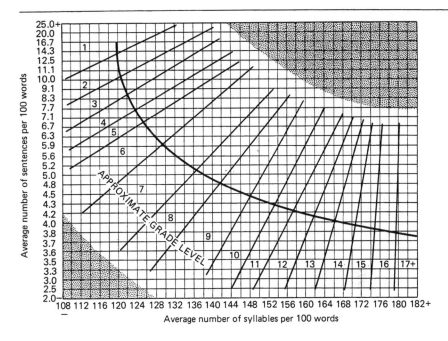

Average number of sentences per 100 words

Average number of syllables per 100 words

DIRECTIONS FOR WORKING READABILITY GRAPH

1. Randomly select three sample passages and count out exactly 100 words each, beginning with the beginning of a sentence. Do count proper nouns, initializations, and numerals.

2. Count the number of sentences in the hundred words, estimating length of the fraction of the last sentence to the nearest one-tenth.

3. Count the total number of syllables in the 100-word passage.

4. Enter graph with *average* sentence length and *average* number of syllables; plot dot where the two lines intersect. Area where dot is plotted will give you the approximate grade level.

5. If a great deal of variability is found in syllable count or sentence count, putting more samples into the average is desirable.

6. A word is defined as a group of symbols with a space on either side; thus "Joe," "IRA," "1945," and "&" are each one word.

7. A syllable is defined as a phonetic syllable. Generally, there are as many syllables as vowel sounds. For example, "stopped" is one syllable and "wanted" is two syllables. When counting syllables for numerals and initializations, count one syllable for each symbol. For example, "1945" is four syllables, "IRA" is three syllables, and "&" is one syllable.

Figure 3–1 Fry's Extended Graph for Estimating Readability.
SOURCE: Edward Fry, "Fry's Readability Graph: Clarifications, Validity, and Extension to Level 17," *Journal of Reading*, Vol. 21, No. 3 (December 1977), p. 249. Used with permission.

Simply divide the total number of words in the sentences by the number of whole sentences and insert the answer in the following formula. Next count the number of long words (three or more syllables, but not counting capitalized words; those ending in *es, er,* or *ed;* and those that combine simple words, such as "heretofore.") Enter that figure in the formula.

$$\text{Fog Index} = 0.4 \times (\text{Average number of words per sentence} \\ + \text{number of long words per 100 words})$$

The Fog Index for the 100 words preceding the formula is 12.8, indicating that you need almost thirteen years of education to find this passage readable.

Another study of corporate annual reports uses the Gunning Fog Index to compare report readability with that of the business publications usually read by investors. Annual reports average almost 15 on the index, whereas business publications score only slightly more than 11. The researchers point out that nothing about financial reporting requires complex and difficult-to-read writing. They conclude that, given the costs involved, "the least that can be done is to create a readable report."[13]

Professor Irving Fang's Easy Listening Formula (ELF) creates a comparable measure for estimating broadcast "listenability."[14] His original study included thirty-six television network news scripts and thirty-six newspaper samples totaling more than 150,000 words. True to its label, the technique is easy to use. To

Table 3–2 Interpretation of the Gunning Fog Index

FOG INDEX	GRADE LEVEL	
17	College graduate	
16	College senior	
15	College junior	
14	College sophomore	
13	College freshman	"Danger line"
12	High school senior	
11	High school junior	
10	High school sophomore	
9	High school freshman	"Easy-
8	Eighth grade	reading
7	Seventh grade	range"
6	Sixth grade	

SOURCE: Adapted from Robert Gunning, *The Technique of Clear Writing,* rev. ed. (New York: McGraw-Hill Book Company, 1968), p. 40.

[13]Robert L. Heath and Greg Phelps, "Annual Reports II: Readability of Reports vs. Business Press," *Public Relations Review,* Vol. 10, No. 2 (Summer 1984), pp. 56–62.

[14]Irving E. Fang, "The 'Easy Listening Formula,'" *Journal of Broadcasting,* Vol. 11, No. 1 (Winter 1966-67), pp. 63–68.

determine the ELF score for a sentence, simply count each syllable above one per word. The average of ELF scores for sentences in a passage is the estimate of listenability. Fang reports that his ELF scores correlate highly (r=0.96) with Flesch scores of readability computed for the same copy. On the basis of his study of network broadcast news, he concludes that:

> ... *the most highly rated television news writers use a style that averages an Easy Listening Formula score below 12 [emphasis his]. This does not mean that every sentence scores below 12. The key word is: averages. A sentence that scores 20, or higher, may be perfectly clear, and may be the best way to deliver a fact.*[15]

Certainly, readability (or listenability) measures quantify only a very limited aspect of writing quality in program materials. For example, jargon and technical terms may interfere with comprehensibility even when the Fog Index and Readability Score indicate otherwise. But, among the people you know, how many prefer reading long, complex sentences heavily sprinkled with polysyllabic words? (No snide comments about our writing, please.) Estimates of readability serve as useful reminders that brevity and simplicity add to clarity in communications and demonstrate sensitivity for the reader. More meaningful in the long run, of course, are measures of the extent to which messages achieve the objectives set for that part of the program. During program implementation, however, readability measures provide a quantitative and objective way to monitor an important stylistic quality of program content.

Tracking Output

Press and wire service clippings, broadcast placement, and counts of how many communications have been distributed are much maligned because the results are so often misused. Either the clippings themselves, or measures developed from media placements, are used to represent program impact. Used correctly, however, methods for tracking program output are essential to monitoring program implementation.

Tracking output begins with good records and copies of all program materials. This includes both controlled and uncontrolled media. For example, close counts of how many copies of the employee newsletter are actually picked up by employees versus how many are printed (or returned) may tip you off to a problem in the distribution method for this controlled employee medium. On the other hand, analysis of clippings indicates that some important business sections and publications are not using your announcements of appointments and promotions as frequently as in the past. A check of the mailing list used for such releases turns up names of several reporters no longer working at those newspa-

---

[15]Ibid., p. 68.

pers and business publications. These are examples of how good program records and monitoring output provide evidence for program adjustments.

The first distinction important to tracking program output is *distribution* versus *placement*. Whereas documenting distribution is primarily an internal staff responsibility, documenting placement often involves the services of clipping and monitoring bureaus. Not all the news releases, public service announcements, video news clips, photographs, and features are used by the media. What gets sent may not be printed or broadcast. Program adjustments may be called for when you decide that not enough of what is sent is used by the media, or when you do content analysis and find that not enough of the right messages is being used. In both cases, following up on what happens to the information you give to media begins with monitoring media content. As Paul Alvarez at Ketchum observes, clients expect you to monitor media content in order to make program adjustments.

> *What corporations really want to know is significant change in the level of activity on an issue. Are new things being reported that add weight to the issue? Are their public relations people doing something useful in response? They're looking for a device that says, "Look, I countered this stuff and this issue didn't get any worse. The controversy, at least, stayed where it is and that's because I have proactive public relations. I am fighting the issues out there, countering their messages with our messages." That's what they want to know. Figuring out for a client the proactive message and getting it through is really the role of research. That's what content analysis helps you do.*

The costs of systematic observation of media placements can be spread over many organizations by contracting with a media monitoring firm. Although most major cities have one or more local companies providing such services, Burrelle's Press Clipping Bureau may be the oldest and largest national media monitoring firm. Burrelle's reports that its readers and "cutters" scan and clip more than 15,000 publications—every daily, weekly, and Sunday newspaper in the United States (plus many in Canada, Latin America, and Europe); most trade, professional, and consumer magazines and newsletters; as well as the major wire services. Carol Holden at Burrelle's reports that the most commonly requested variables in print media monitor reports are:

Date	Company identification
Publication/origin	Subject identification
Size of story (column inches)	Product identification
Advertising cost equivalence	Reader audience
Headline	Editorial slant
Byline	Feature or mention[16]

---

[16]Information about Burrelle's media monitoring services provided by Carol W. Holden, Manager-Analytical Services, Burrelle's Newsclip Analysis Service, 75 East Northfield Road, Livingston, N.J. 07039.

Monitoring broadcast media requires recording equipment and capabilities for transcribing the recordings to document what was said and when it was said. Burrelle's, for example, monitors almost 200 stations in forty-eight cities. Clients get typed transcripts or summaries, noting the station, program, date, and time of airing. In addition, audience data for television programs make it possible to calculate *potential exposure* for information placed in the media. Some broadcast monitoring services provide video and audio tapes of programs containing client information.

Some public relations staffs do their own media monitoring for local issues and local coverage, because they routinely (but usually unsystematically) monitor local media anyway. The danger is that other pressing duties may interfere with attempts to monitor media content and placement. As with any other research activity, *systematic* observation procedures produce the most accurate feedback on media placement efforts.

Roger Sennott at Market Development Inc. says the need to monitor media placements is the big difference between publicity and advertising:

> *The area of research that is peculiar to public relations is the relationship between what we do and what ends up out there— sometimes nothing happens. I just saw a press kit from which nobody wrote a story. Good kit. Looked good. Nothing happened. So in public relations we have an extra phase to look at. That leads to some interesting problems in trying to determine how what we do is linked to our success in getting placements.*

How you define and measure placement depends on your needs. As a minimum, however, record the date published or broadcast, as well as the publication or station. Most practitioners also assign value to the size of story placement—either column inches or minutes of air time. In practice, however, you may find it difficult to decide when to begin and end the count, as surrounding information may be relevant. Still others assign different values based on where the story appeared—front page versus an inside page, or lead story versus later in evening news program. The key is to decide how you will use the information to make program adjustments *before* you do the content analysis. That way, what you use as measures will match your needs.

This brings us to what not to use—advertising equivalence. What is "equivalent" between purchased time or space identified as sponsored advertising and information reported as news or public service? In fact, we can find no theoretical or logical justification for equating a column inch of copy imbedded in a news story with a column inch of advertising space, or a minute on local news with a minute of advertising time adjacent to the news report. The pragmatic reasons, of course, are a) it is an easy way to assign "value" to media placements, and b) you get impressive dollar totals when you multiply the amount of space or time devoted to program content times the published advertising rates. Never mind that the totals are misleading or even meaningless!

Describing Audiences and Their Attention

If you really want big numbers, here is the place to turn on the calculator! While measures of audience size and attention are useful for monitoring program implementation, they indicate only the extent to which the program is reaching the target publics. Unfortunately, practitioners often erroneously substitute these for measures of program impact. But clearly, measures of audience size and attention to messages do not represent the changes in knowledge, predisposition, or behavior spelled out in program objectives.

You need to make another important distinction as you use research to monitor program audiences—*total audience* versus *target public*. Advertisers sometimes make a similar distinction when they talk about delivered audience versus effective audience. When they make media buying decisions, advertisers want to know how many in the delivered audience are real prospects for the advertising appeals. In the public relations context, of course, the total number of people reached is not important if they are not people you have identified as publics for your program. Keep this distinction in mind any time you use audience data from syndicated studies, such as those provided by A.C. Nielsen Company, Arbitron Ratings Company, and Audit Bureau of Circulation. In fact, syndicated audience research services seldom are able to break out target publics for a specific public relations program, except those defined on the basis of geographic and demographic variables. As a consequence, you typically must do your own research or contract proprietary research to gather data about target publics and their attention to particular media or program efforts. For example, Paul Alvarez at Ketchum Public Relations acknowledges that his firm had to revise its well-known Publicity Tracking Model:

> We're looking at it now as a planning tool as well as an evaluation tool. The tracking model tells us some very, very interesting things about the target audience, since we can get very sophisticated about the target audience. In the old days, we used to write programs involving very sophisticated target audiences and report in rough circulation. People are still getting away with reporting rough circulation, but I don't imagine that it is going to last very long. It can't. Clients are particularly upset by such crude measures.

Audience size data for print media (those independent of public relations staff control) usually come from the Audit Bureau of Circulation (ABC), Verified Audit Circulation Company (VAC), and Business Publications Audit of Circulation, Inc. (BPA). The most used index of print media audience size is *circulation*, which includes only paid distribution in the case of ABC, or both paid and "controlled" free distribution for VAC and BPA. Circulation for public relations print media is the number of copies distributed to potential readers. Notice, however, that this measure of audience size does not tell you how many people actually attended to a publication. That is a different measure of audience size—readership.

Readership may be greater than circulation if copies of the publication are read by more than one person. It can be less than circulation if more copies are distributed than people who read them. As with all measures, you must first carefully define what you mean by readership, then select the observable indicators that match your definition. One commonly used approach for measuring readership is the aided recall method, in which you show respondents the printed material and ask them questions designed to determine how much they recall reading. In the case of magazine advertising, the Starch INRA Hooper, Inc. aided recall studies illustrate how readership can be defined according to different levels of attention. The Starch Readership Report distinguishes among three levels of readership: a) Noted—when shown the advertisement, the respondent remembers seeing it but recalls no content, b) Associated—the respondent not only remembers seeing the ad but recalls the name of the advertiser, and c) Read Most—the respondent says he or she read at least half of the ad and recalls enough content to justify the claim. Similar levels of readership could be used for monitoring readership of public relations publications. (See Exhibit 8-1 for examples of different levels of measurement used in readership surveys.) It is important to note again, however, that readership—like viewership and listenership for broadcast and film—measures an audience activity—attending to the communications. Circulation, on the other hand, represents a count of copies distributed, not the audience.

For broadcast media, audience size is expressed in terms of *ratings* and *shares*. Syndicated research firms use meters attached to television sets, diaries completed by selected households, and telephone surveys to gather broadcast audience data. The telephone survey technique often takes the form known as *telephone coincidental,* meaning that the calls are made at the time the program is running.

You can easily adopt this technique to measure audiences of public relations program efforts. For example, let's say you want to know how many in a target public watch a corporate film being shown on the local cable system. You select a random sample of households (from the target public, if possible) and call them while the film is running. By asking the right questions of a large representative sample, you could immediately estimate how many in your target public(s) viewed the film. Telephone coincidental surveys are relatively inexpensive ways to measure audiences for particular programs, and they have the obvious advantage of giving you immediate results.

In addition to the audience size estimate as an absolute number, you could calculate another commonly used index to describe the film's audience— *audience rating.* Audience rating uses either the number of people *or* the number of households to calculate the percentage of the total population attending to your particular medium or communication. For example, to calculate the employee audience rating for the corporate program shown on cable television, divide the number of employees viewing the program by the total number of employees:

$$\text{Rating} = \frac{\text{Number of employees viewing program}}{\text{Total number of employees}}$$

The rating tells you how many employees among the total watched the program but does not tell you how the program fared against competing programs. If the telephone coincidental survey data show how many employees were watching television—regardless of channel or program—then you can calculate *audience share*. Audience share represents the percentage of all employees watching television who chose to watch the corporate program.

$$\text{Share} = \frac{\text{Number of employees watching program}}{\text{Number of employees watching television}}$$

Notice that in the preceding examples, both audience rating and audience share indices describe only the target public audience, not the gross audience viewing the program.

If you want to estimate the relative *cost-efficiency* of the cable program, simply divide the cost of production and distribution (or placement) by the number of employees viewing the program.

$$\text{Cost-Efficiency} = \frac{\text{Total cost of cable program}}{\text{Number of employees who watched}}$$

In this case, cost-efficiency of the cable program represents how much was spent for each employee who watched the program. If you had similar figures for other employee communication media, you could compare them on their relative cost-efficiency. In mass media advertising, cost-efficiency is usually calculated using audience size in thousands. Advertisers and representatives from media refer to this index as the cost per thousand (CPM).

Other commonly used measures for monitoring how effectively the media strategy delivers the message are *reach* and *frequency*. *Reach*—sometimes referred to as cumulative audience—is the total number of people exposed to your message at least once during a fixed period of time. For example, assume you want to know what the reach is for the three media used to make policy and procedure announcements. Seventy-seven percent of employees typically read the weekly employee newsletter. Of those, only 32 percent read *only* the newsletter. Fifty-one percent usually read the bulletin boards, but only 6 percent *only* read the bulletin boards. And finally, 16 percent monitor the internal electronic mail on their desk terminals, but only 5 percent use *only* the electronic mail system. Remember when computing reach for a medium or combination of media, count a person only once—regardless of how many times that person sees the

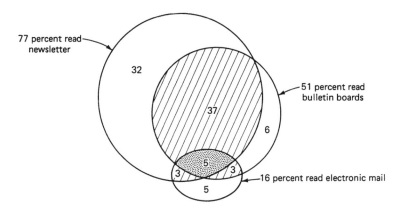

Figure 3-2 Calculating reach and frequency.

message. For our example, Figure 3-2 illustrates how reach is 91 percent for the media mix used for policy and procedure announcements to employees.

Frequency, on the other hand, is the average number of times a person is exposed to your message during a period of time. Compute frequency by totaling the number of times people are exposed to your message by all media during a period of time. Divide that total by the number of people reached at least once during the time period. Returning to our employee communication media for policy and procedure announcements, frequency is approximately 1.6 exposures per person reached. The calculations are as follows:

$$\text{Frequency} = \frac{\text{Total number of exposures}}{\text{Reach}}$$

$$\text{Frequency} = \frac{144 \text{ exposures}}{91}$$

$$\text{Frequency} = 1.58$$

Gross impressions is another measure used to summarize *potential exposures* for a public relations program. We urge caution here, however, because the large numbers produced tend to be grossly exaggerated with little connection with reality. Computing gross impressions usually involves multiplying the number of placements times the circulations and audiences for each of the placements. In media mixes of national, regional, and large local media, the gross impressions can easily add up to many millions—even billions—of potential readers, viewers, and listeners. Whereas such a figure indicates maximum program exposure, it is not a good substitute for the more useful estimates of actual audiences. In the final analysis, gross impressions is seldom the meaningful criterion for assessing the media mix. Rather, measures of the actual audience composition provide useful management information because these data can be compared with the profiles of your program target publics.

These are some of the major indices used for monitoring media placements and audiences for public relations programs. Media and audience research are specialized areas of research requiring large samples and sophisticated data gathering. In local and internal settings, however, you are often required to do your own media research in order to effectively monitor and manage the program. The key for managing public relations programs is to select in advance the criteria you will use for monitoring how effectively the program is being implemented, as well as for assessing audience size and composition. Only when you have adequate evidence of these criteria can you make rational decisions about how to adjust the program. Finally, using research to monitor the program provides the objective evidence of needed program changes. Research evidence then helps justify and support program recommendations to clients and employers who otherwise rely on their "gut feelings" and casual observations for assessing how the program is going.

SUMMATIVE RESEARCH FOR PROGRAM DOCUMENTATION

Research provides summary data for accountability and documentation. Clearly, such management information is useful for making program adjustments, but here we emphasize the need for using research in order to establish a record of time, expenditures, activities, and program efforts.

First, you need program records as evidence for *accountability*. Hill and Knowlton management information specialist Joel "Buff" Kizer emphasizes accountability as he outlines the benefits of systematic records in the agency setting:

- Accurate time records can help establish realistic project budget estimates for clients. Having good budget estimates is the first step in the process of collecting for an agency's work.
- An easy-to-use accounting system for client billing will result in more billable hours for an agency than a time accounting system that is difficult to use.
- One key to a successful project is the ability to match continuously actual charges against the budget and make adjustments as needed.
- Having complete and accurate service detail readily available when inquiries occur builds credibility with clients, resulting in bills being paid in their entirety.
- The activity reports of an agency, together with its time records, give management a quantitative feel for where the enterprise is expanding, where it is contracting, and where the real success stories are to be found.[17]

[17]Joel "Buff" Kizer, "Managing Client Service," in *New Technology and Public Relations*, ed. by Kalman B. Druck, Merton Fiur, and Don Bates. (New York: Foundation for Public Relations Research and Education, 1986), p. 151.

It is the systematic and objective imperatives of the scientific research process that shape the effort to monitor the program for purposes of accountability.

Second, you need complete program records to *document cause-and-effect.* Some time after the program, you will most likely want to know what program efforts "caused" the observed program "effects." In other words, another reason you keep counts and records of program efforts is to document what in Chapter 5 we call the "treatment." Without complete documentation of what you did in the program, you have no way of tracing what caused—or did not cause—the intended program results.

Stanford University professor Byron Reeves emphasizes the difficulty of scientifically demonstrating a program effect in his article, "Now You See Them, Now You Don't: Demonstrating Effects of Communication Programs."[18] His summary of what you must fully document in order to convincingly demonstrate a program effect suggests the types of information you should gather:

> . . . *(1) knowledge of the stimulus material; (2) control of its application; (3) assessment of impact; and (4) understanding of the mechanism or process underlying the effect. In question form: What's having an effect, who's affected, what changes, and when and how does it change?[19]*

In other words, research is used to monitor the program for the purpose of documenting what caused the changes measured later. It was, after all, your working theory of what would cause the desired changes that guided your selection of program strategies. Documenting what you did in the program provides the evidence you need to "test" your theories about public relations cause-and-effect relationships. It may just be the case that this is the missing link in a great deal of public relations programming—little effort is devoted to trying to causally link program efforts to program effects. Employers, clients, and—alas—practitioners are often so happy to see the desired effects that they do not make an effort to systematically determine what it was that contributed to their achievement. Missing that opportunity limits not only your own professional growth and development but also helps perpetuate the practice as a continuing series of discrete trial-and-error efforts. Building your own and the profession's knowledge base requires complete documentation and test of working theories using the criteria outlined in Figure 3–3.

In conclusion, you use research *during the program* to monitor program effort and activities. First, the evidence you gather provides the feedback during implementation on where and how the program needs to be adjusted. As Amoco's Jerry Cooper observes, "Research does not have to be elaborate to provide valuable information that will change how things are done." Second, systematic pro-

---

[18]Byron Reeves, "Now You See Them, Now You Don't: Demonstrating Effects of Communication Programs," *Public Relations Quarterly,* Vol. 28, No. 3 (Fall 1983), pp. 17–21, 27.
[19]Ibid., p. 17.

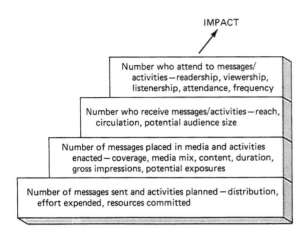

IMPACT

Figure 3-3 Levels of program implementation criteria.

gram records serve as the basis for accountability and tests of program strategies. David Clavier at Husk Jennings Overman Public Relations notes, "What you're looking at is stacking different techniques on top of each other over time, allowing you to make the best judgments you can for the corporation." Or, using terms from the Figure 1-5 public relations feedback loops, research to monitor the program provides two types of feedback—program adjustment and performance control. You use both types of feedback to increase program impact—the subject of our next chapter.

CHAPTER 4

USING RESEARCH
TO EVALUATE PROGRAMS

Duncan M. Knowles, APR, Vice President and Director of Leadership Communication, BANK OF AMERICA, San Francisco.

We conducted a survey to learn if senior management gives employees a clear picture of Bank of America's direction. From our own officers we learned that 49 percent felt that senior management did not. Of those same officers, 38 percent agreed that they had a sense of direction. A year later we had dropped the number that felt senior management did not give a clear picture from 49 down to 10 percent. We increased the number who felt they had a sense of direction from 38 up to 60 percent. And we were able to validate that through surveys.

John A. Koten, APR, Senior Vice President–Corporate Communications, AMERITECH, Chicago.

Accountability and objectives are part of the corporate world. If you work in a corporation, you can't be totally different to be successful. You should be willing to have your efforts measured the same way that other functions are measured. From my standpoint, there ought to be more accountability, because in the long run that's going to help us do our jobs better. If there aren't public relations managers trained in how to be accountable, it isn't going to happen. Our ultimate success is tied to our willingnesss to be accountable for our results.

Lloyd Kirban, PhD, Executive Vice President and Director of Research, BURSON-MARSTELLER, New York.

At the final point we need to learn how much did the client get for the money. This is traditionally a "bug-a-boo" to public relations. I don't understand why. That same question can be raised with advertising agencies, and they have as difficult a time demonstrating what the client got for $80 million. We're asked to demonstrate what the client got for $300,000. This is essentially the area of evaluation and measurement.

*The traditional approach has been to throw a book of clips on the desk and to talk about total impressions. Or, practitioners talk about number of minutes of air time and the like. Philosophically, we regard placements as a **necessary, but not sufficient,** condition. Obviously, you cannot communicate unless you fill the communication pipeline with your messages and get them out. But the mere fact that they got out is no guarantee that they have accomplished the objectives.*

If this were nirvana, the final arbiter would be some behavioral measure, but you can't do that in many cases. In some cases you can. Whenever that's possible, behavioral measures probably should be the criteria. On the other hand, if behavioral measures are not possible, then we believe that—at a minimum—the criteria should be communications driven. Sometimes that's not at all easy to accomplish. We are talking about dimensions like awareness, knowledge, interest, attitude, propensity to take action, or whatever.

I've come to the conclusion after being involved in measurement and evaluation that good public relations programs do good things and bad public relations programs don't do anything. It's no longer a question—in my mind—of the intrinsic worth of public relations activities. We're now past that. Most people who use us are past that. The real question is, "How do you make programs more effective?" Measurement and evaluation are not only good at demonstrating how successful you were; they also give you the opportunity to do diagnostics. The value of measurement is you can evaluate. Evaluation means you learn. If you learn, you do better the next time than you did the last time.

Two words come to mind as we begin this chapter—benchmarks and accountability. You don't have meaningful accountability without benchmarks. It's that simple. You plan, produce, and pay for a public relations program in order to achieve objectives and—finally—goals. In other words, your program is intended to cause observable *impact*—to change or maintain something about a situation. So, *after the program,* you use research to measure and document program effects.

Accountability is both the keystone of public relations management and a double-edged sword. If you use research to document program successes, you can leverage more resources for future public relations efforts. Even if the research shows only partial success, but helps explain why other parts failed, you strengthen your position for getting resources to change the program. On the other hand, research also provides evidence of program failure. Top management tends to reward success and replace those who repeatedly demonstrate ineffectiveness in achieving program objectives and goals. That's the other side of accountability. Little wonder so many cling to the rhetorical line that "public relations deals with intangibles!"

Public relations, however, "enjoys" a particularly vulnerable position during times of "downsizing"—the euphemism for personnel cuts during economic slumps, mergers, and restructurings. Could it be, as John Koten pointed out in the opening comments for this chapter, that until public relations becomes more accountable it will not share the status and security that other management functions have? In essence, this chapter addresses the issue of accountability by developing both a rationale and the guidelines for using research to assess program impact.

EVALUATION RESEARCH IN PUBLIC RELATIONS

PR Reporter newsletter says, "Evaluation is the profession's number 1 need."[1] "Evaluation" happens all the time and in all programs, however. What is really needed is *evaluation research* to add objective feedback on program impact to the subjective assessments and informal research now used to judge program effectiveness. *Evaluation* is determining the worth of something. Evaluation research uses scientific procedures to collect, analyze, and interpret information to *help* determine the worth of something.

The emphasis here is on "help" because research findings are only one of many factors that go into deciding the worth of public relations efforts. At the most general level, evaluation uses information from many sources—including research findings—and judgment. Judgment also includes a large number of factors—past experience, perceived constraints, values, and even estimates of what important others think about the program. So rather than mislead you by suggesting that research findings are omnipotent when it comes to program evaluation, we want to be candid about the complexity of both the evaluation context and task. But, if you don't have the power and authority to assert and make stick your individual assessment of program worth, then it's only rational to approach

---

[1] *PR Reporter,* Vol. 27, No. 25 (June 18, 1984), p. 4.

program evaluation as an applied research task. The research assignment is to find empirical evidence to replace or rebut assertions about what the program did or did not accomplish. That is the assumption underlying this chapter.

Focuses on Outcomes

Chapters 2 and 3 dealt primarily with the uses of formative research to plan and monitor programs. Research for these purposes includes measurement of the criteria spelled out in what some call *process objectives*—stated intentions regarding workflow, effort, timeliness, productivity, costs, and such. We would put those process criteria in the category of *program effort,* and refer you back to Chapter 3. Here we limit our discussion to measuring the criteria established in *impact objectives*—the statements describing *intended outcomes* related to what people know, feel, and do, as well as the nature of relationships between the organization and its publics. These are the same criteria established by the program objectives and referred to frequently while planning program strategies. At the point of measuring program impact, the general research question is, "How effective was the program in achieving what we intended?"

Provides Information for Decisions

Decisions about program effectiveness take on several meanings—depending on the criteria you select. Effectiveness may mean that the outcomes spelled out in the objectives were achieved, even though there is no way to *prove* that the program caused them to occur. Effectiveness may mean that you can show a cause-and-effect relationship between the program activities and some or all of the desired outcomes, usually by controlling for other factors that may have contributed. Effectiveness may mean that some outcomes have been achieved, providing evidence that more or others are possible in due time. Effectiveness may mean that the program was implemented within budget, indicating that management controls worked. Effectiveness may mean that costs for various levels of outcomes are acceptable—cost-effectiveness. Effectiveness may mean that there is a favorable relationship between program costs and the monetary value of the outcomes achieved—cost-benefit analysis. It is the latter that concerns those wanting to show how public relations "affects the bottom line," but it is only one of several ways to assess program effectiveness. In the sections that follow, we focus on measuring program *impact.*

PROGRAM EVALUATION AS A FIELD EXPERIMENT

The context for public relations program evaluation fits the model of a field experiment: You create an "experimental intervention" or "treatment"—the program. In effect, the program represents your working theory—your notions of why you think the program will "cause" the desired outcome (in some cases, to prevent an outcome). The target publics are the "subjects" in your experimental treatment. When possible, you also use "control groups" (the placebo condition) to help isolate program effects from those resulting from extraneous factors. You observe samples from both the treatment and control groups *before* the program starts, establishing that they are similar and therefore provide the basis for useful comparisons *after* the program. (You could also use the *after-only* approach, but more on these design issues follows in Chapter 5.) After the program, you again take measures on the criteria established in the objectives. After comparing changes in the treatment and control samples, you try to determine if there are real and meaningful differences that can be attributed to the program and projected to others. In the end, decision making also calls for experience and judgment, because public relations field experiments occur in dynamic settings. Under such conditions, it is often not possible to *scientifically prove* the program caused the observed differences. For the informed manager, however, research provides the best available evidence and strengthens claims of program effectiveness.

Limitations aside (and all research has limitations), systematic evaluations using scientific research methods increase credibility and provide the basis for improving the practice. As Fitz-Gibbon and Morris point out:

> *The very best summative evaluation has all the characteristics of the best research study. It uses highly reliable instruments, and it faithfully applies a powerful evaluation design. Evaluation of this caliber could be published and disseminated to both the lay and research community. Few evaluations of course will live up to such rigid standards or need to.* **The critical characteristic of any one evaluation study is that it provides the best possible information that could have been collected under the circumstances, and that this information meet the credibility requirements of its evaluation audience.**[2]

If you continually use research to plan, monitor, and evaluate programs, you add to your understanding of what works and what does not work under various conditions. In other words, through a series of field experiments, you test and revise your working theories. Impact measures also provide the information needed to help judge program effectiveness and efficiency. In the long term, what you learn from each field experiment adds to the body of knowledge guiding your practice and increases your professional competence. In the short term, you learn how well and why your program worked.

---

[2]Carol Taylor Fitz-Gibbon and Lynn Lyons Morris, *How to Design a Program Evaluation* (Beverly Hills: Sage Publications, Inc., 1978), pp. 13–14.

EVALUATION TIED TO OBJECTIVES AND GOALS

"Worked" usually refers to whether or not the program achieved the results you specified in the objectives. At some point, "worked" means the program accomplished the overall goal and solved the problem. To learn if your program worked, you must use the criteria established in the objectives and goals. If you have to define or refine the criteria in order to plan the evaluation, that means the objectives were not specific enough in the first place. It also means that because you had to change the after-program measures, the pre-program research probably will not provide the baseline data you need to demonstrate program effects. Figure 4–1 illustrates the before-after comparison basic to most public relations program evaluations.

The "Time$_1$" (T_1) stake describes the situation before the program—derived from the formative research done to define the problem and plan the program (Chapter 2). The small stakes—"Time$_{1a}$" and "Time$_{1b}$"—represent the formative research effects to monitor implementation and make adjustments during the program (Chapter 3). "Time$_2$" (T_2) stands for the summative research done to measure program impact, using the criteria established for T_1 and stated in the objectives and goals. Recall from Chapter 2 that each objective states an intended program effect—specifically *what* is to occur, *how much* of an effect is to be achieved, and *when* the effect is to be accomplished. The goal describes what will be accomplished—overall—if the objectives are achieved; that is, if the working theory is correct. The goal statement also conforms to the style of useful objective statements.

The most common problem we observe in public relations program evaluations is violation of the principle that the T_2 evaluation measures must be consistent with the T_1 criteria spelled out in the objectives. For example, a PRSA Silver Anvil Award-winning program was designed to (emphasis added): a) "Rally local residents' *pride* in the community." b) "Create regional *awareness* of Durham among civic and business leaders." c) "Generate national/international *interest* in Durham as a place to locate a business." The program summary, however, reports no measures of pride, awareness, or interest among the target publics. Instead, "the success of the campaign is being measured" by tracking media placements,

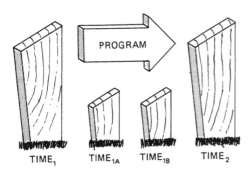

TIME$_1$ TIME$_{1A}$ TIME$_{1B}$ TIME$_2$

Figure 4–1 Impact assessment benchmarks model.

by counting participants at events, and by documenting new business inquiries.[3] As vague as the outcome statements are, it is easy to see that the evaluation measures are not consistent with the awareness and predispositional outcomes the program was designed to achieve. Either the desired outcomes are not correctly reported or the evaluation criteria don't match program intentions.

Criteria for Effects on Publics

In the Chapter 2 section on writing objectives, we outlined the usual range of program outcomes for specific public—change or maintenance of a public's knowledge (including awareness and understanding), predispositions (opinions and attitudes), and behavior. When specific knowledge, predispositions, and behaviors affect important organization-public relationships, then changes in or maintenance of these criteria are spelled out in the program objectives. In effect, they become the desired consequences of program strategies directed to internal and external publics. Once stated in the objectives, these same outcomes are the only appropriate criteria for assessing program impact.

1. *Knowledge.* When a national survey of science, environmental, and religious leaders showed that less than 20 percent considered themselves highly informed about genetic engineering, Monsanto Company saw potential problems in testing and marketing its new biotechnology products. Monsanto's surveys (conducted by Opinion Research Corporation) of community knowledge of genetic engineering included this two-question probe to measure *knowledge:*

> *What types of things do you associate with the term genetic engineering? When you read or hear the term genetic engineering, what comes to mind?[4]*

Interviewers coded answers into nineteen topical categories. "Other" (category 20) turned out to be an often-used option in the list, as did "Don't know/no response" (category 21). To illustrate this coding scheme, here are the first five categories:

1. Chemicals/chemical technology/biochemistry
2. Medicine/medical/medical equipment/medical developments
3. Cloning
4. Tampering with nature/dangerous/destructive/immoral
5. Improving agriculture/livestock

---

[3]*1987 Silver Anvil Winners: Index and Summaries* (New York: Public Relations Society of America, 1987), p. 7.

[4]Examples and statistics reported here and in following sections are reported in Monsanto summaries of Opinion Research Corporation survey findings and used with permission of Monsanto Company.

This open-ended probe and coding strategy produced a detailed profile of what people in the sample associate with genetic engineering. In other words, the survey item provided data on what people know and don't know about genetic engineering, their awareness or lack of awareness of its applications, and even their understanding or misunderstanding of its value. Based on insights gained from the first surveys, the Monsanto public relations staff designed a campaign a) to increase public awareness of genetic engineering and its potential benefits, and b) to increase public knowledge that Monsanto is a leader in biotechnology.

Follow-up surveys in two campaign test communities, as well as in control communities where there were no messages, produced clear evidence that people in the test communities learned message content. Before-campaign surveys indicate the levels of knowledge represented by the T_1 stake in Figure 4–1. Post-campaign measures indicate T_2 levels. The results show greater T_2-minus-T_1 knowledge gains in the campaign target communities—compared to the changes in the control communities. Also, awareness of Monsanto's involvement with biotechnology rose from 9 percent to 25 percent in one test community, and from 7 percent to 39 percent in the other. These significant changes are in contrast to the control communities, where no significant changes in knowledge occurred.

In this example, the criteria for assessing program impact are measures of the specific knowledge outcomes established in the program objectives. These are also the same criteria first used to describe the before-campaign state of knowledge. When the objectives call for specific changes in awareness, knowledge, and understanding, only measures of those particular cognitive outcomes provide appropriate evidence for assessing program impact.

2. *Predispositions.* Similar logic applies when the outcomes specified in the objectives have to do with changes in predispositions—*opinions and attitudes.* In the Monsanto example, community acceptance of field testing new products developed through genetic engineering is clearly an important concern, as is public opinion of Monsanto itself. The community surveys measured public opinions of field testing with this question:

> *Suppose that a company that is involved in biotechnology wanted to field-test an agricultural product that was produced through biotechnology. Would you favor or oppose letting them test such a product in your community?*
> *1. Favor   2. Oppose   3. No opinion/no response*

Among those who saw the Monsanto campaign messages, opposition dropped from 27 percent to 21 percent in one test community, and from 25 percent to 14 percent in the other. In contrast, essentially no changes occurred in the control communities during the same period.

This predispositional measure provides evidence of opinions related to field testing biotechnology products in their communities. Before-campaign surveys provide the benchmark evidence needed to write useful objectives specifying changes in public opinion. Subsequently, measures in the after-campaign surveys provide the data necessary for comparing T_2-minus-T_1 opinion changes in the test and control communities.

The campaign also influenced people's opinions about allowing Monsanto to field-test genetically engineered products. After the campaign, those in favor of field testing were asked:

> *Thinking of the six companies we have been talking about, which ones would you allow to field-test such a product in your community?*
>
> 1. *Dow Chemical*   5. *Johnson & Johnson*
> 2. *Du Pont*   6. *Monsanto*
> 3. *General Electric*   7. *None of these*
> 4. *IBM*   8. *No opinion/no response*

Among these who saw the campaign, 61 percent said they would allow Monsanto to conduct field testing. In contrast, only 40 percent of those who did not see the campaign supported field testing by Monsanto. This illustrates an "after-only" approach to measuring impact—comparing "treatment" and "control" groups after the program with no before-program measures. In essence, the control group serves the same purpose in the comparison as would a before-program measurement.

To help understand the makeup of public opinion of Monsanto, the survey asked a series of questions about how people view large industrial companies in general and Monsanto in particular. The items called for responses on four-point scales. The following examples of the general and specific versions measure respondents' perceptions of corporate concern about the environment:

> *In forming your opinion of a large industrial company, how important is it that they are concerned about the effect of their operations on the environment?*
>
> | Most Important | Least Important | No opinion/ No response |
> |---|---|---|
> | 4 – – – – 3 – – – – 2 – – – – 1 | | —— |

> *In your opinion, it is definitely true, probably true, probably not true, or definitely not true of Monsanto that they are concerned about the effect of their operations on the environment?*
>
> 1. *Definitely true*
> 2. *Probably true*
> 3. *Probably not true*
> 4. *Definitely not true*
> 5. *No opinion/no response*

The four survey questions in this section illustrate two approaches for measuring public predispositions. The first approach produces simple counts—frequencies. One question yields *counts* of how many favor or oppose field testing. Another shows how many pick each company as acceptable for conducting field tests. The second approach uses *scales* of varying values to indicate both the direction of opinion and its intensity or strength. Both approaches, however, measure how people feel about issues of concern to Monsanto and about Monsanto itself. (Chapter 8 discusses types of measures in more detail.)

In this section, we also illustrated two major research designs for showing program impact. In the first, before-after changes are demonstrated by comparing after program levels with those observed before the program $(T_2 - T_1)$. The second approach uses measures taken only after the program, contrasting levels among those exposed to the program with levels among those not exposed to the program (treatment-control). The same principle applies here that we stated for the knowledge impact measures: To assess program impact on public predispositions, you must use the very same criteria stated in the objectives.

3. *Behavior.* Our next statement should come as no surprise: When objectives call for *behavioral outcomes* (what people do or what actions they take), use only measures of those specific behaviors to indicate program impact.

As an example, assume that your before-after research shows that those opposed to field testing new biotechnology products are more likely to write letters to the editor than are those who favor field testing. You could write objectives and develop strategies to increase the number of people favoring field tests who write supportive letters to their newspaper editors. Writing supportive letters is the intended behavioral outcome—program *impact.* The following probe measured the behavior (self-reported) in the Monsanto surveys:

> *I am going to read a list of activities. As I read each one, please tell me whether you have done it in the past two or three years.*
>
> 1. *Presented your views to a public official or legislator*
> 2. *Written a letter to the editor*
> 3. *Urged someone outside your family to get out and vote*
> 4. *Urged someone to get in touch with a public official or legislator*
> 5. *Made a speech before an organized group*
> 6. *Been elected an officer of an organization*
> 7. *Run for public office*
> 8. *Taken an active part in a political campaign*
> 9. *Helped on fund-raising drives*
> 10. *Voted in the last two elections*
> 11. *None of the above*
> 12. *Refused/no answer*

Counting how many more in the target publics wrote such letters after the program compared to before the program is the only valid way to measure program impact on this behavior. (If you were to implement such a program, the follow-up survey would have to use exactly the same question as the foregoing one—in order to have measures comparable to the before-program measures.)

Whereas knowledge and predispositional outcomes typically require surveying samples selected from the target publics, often you can observe behavior without questioning the target public directly. In addition to the usual *obtrusive* techniques that make respondents aware that they are being observed—such as survey questionnaires and interviews—you may be able to use *unobtrusive* methods to observe behavior.

You could, for example, determine whom among the 300 respondents in each of the test and control communities had run for public office during the past three years, as this information should be a matter of official public record and media election coverage. Simply go to the city or county clerk's office and review the candidate filings and ballots from recent elections. Or, search local newspaper files to learn who ran for public office in each of the elections held during the past three years. The cost involved in gathering such information for each respondent, however, may not justify the increased reliability over other methods. Probably for that reason, Monsanto chose the less costly approach of adding "run for public office" to the list of self-reported behaviors.

Here is another example of an obtrusive measure that could have an unobtrusive counterpart: The United States Telephone Association (USTA) "National Customer Opinion Survey" (conducted by The Gallup Organization, Inc.) includes questions designed to determine what changes customers made in the telephone service during the preceding year. The survey asked:

> *Have you made any changes in your home phone service during the last year?* ___ *Yes* ___ *No*

> *(If Yes) In what ways did you change your phone service?*
> ___ *Bought new, additional phone(s)*
> ___ *Changed long-distance company(ies)*
> ___ *Moved to another residence*
> ___ *Added custom-calling features*
> ___ *Added another phone line*
> ___ *Changed phone number(s)*
> ___ *Added touch-tone service*
> ___ *Changed to unlisted or unpublished number(s)*
> ___ *Increased level of service*
> ___ *Decreased level of service*
> ___ *Discontinued service temporarily*
> ___ *Don't know, no answer*
> ___ *Other:* _____

Notice that the first question—sometimes called a screening question or base question—limits the number asked the second question to only those who answer "Yes" to the first. Whether or not the second question is asked becomes contingent on how the first is answered, making the second a contingency question—in the language of questionnaire construction, our topic in Chapter 8.

If one of the USTA member telephone companies wanted similar information about its customers' behaviors, it could simply study its own customer records—without ever asking customers directly. This unobtrusive approach, however, represents a different method of gathering the information and may yield different information. If the telephone company wants to compare its results with those from the national sample, then it would have to survey local customers using the same question used in the national survey. As the USTA report of findings states:

> *The primary objective of the survey was to establish national benchmarks ... against which future behavioral and attitudinal changes could be measured. ... In addition, it was felt that the national survey results could serve as a valuable comparison with studies of customers done by USTA member companies in their local operating areas.[5]*

Measuring program impact calls for credible evidence that withstands the scrutiny of skeptics—and even detractors. If you measure something not spelled out in an objective, then few skeptics will accept your data as evidence of having achieved that objective. If you have no comparison to establish a difference between those who received the program and those who did not (before and after measures at a minimum), then few skeptics will accept your "findings" of program effects. If you use different observation techniques to establish measures for comparisons, then few skeptics will accept your "differences" as representing anything more than artifacts of the research itself. So when it comes to designing and conducting research on program impact, use the test of how credible the findings will be in the eyes of skeptics. If you don't know any skeptics, then imagine some and keep them in mind as you read the chapters that follow.

The foregoing sections dealt with the most commonly used program impact criteria—changes in or maintenance of knowledge, predispositions, and behavior. Typically, these outcomes occur in a particular public—internal or external—but represent only one side of a relationship. The next section suggests criteria for measuring the relationship itself, using the coorientational variables introduced in Chapter 2.

Criteria for Effects on Relationships

Conceptually, public relations programs affect the *relationships* between organizations and their publics, but rarely is program impact on the relationships

---

[5]*USTA National Customer Opinion Survey* (United States Telephone Association, Public Relations Department, 1801 K Street, Washington, D.C. 20006).

themselves measured. In practice, impact measures are made on one or both sides of relationships and then inferences made—sometimes explicitly, usually implicitly—about how the relationships changed.

The coorientational model suggests two variables that describe the relationship—agreement and accuracy. The difference in this approach to measuring program impact, however, is that you must have measures from both sides of the relationship, not just from one side.

For example, recall from Chapter 2 that *agreement* measures similarity between organizational and public views. And, as noted in the sections describing impact measures on target publics, you can measure two aspects of those views— *what* people know about something and *how* they feel about something. That means you can determine two types of agreement: a) one type based on the extent to which the two sides in a relationship have similar definitions of a situation (knowledge held), and b) another type based on the extent to which two sides have similar evaluations of a situation (opinions and attitudes).

The other coorientational variable—*accuracy*—measures similarity between one side's perceptions of the other's views and the other's actual views. In other words, accuracy is a measure of how correct one side is at estimating the other's views. The estimates may be about one or both kinds of views—knowledge and predispositions.

For purposes of illustration here, assume that we want to use coorientational indices to determine program impact on Monsanto Company-public relationships in one of its campaign test communities. First, we determine corporate views of the meaning and uses of genetic engineering. This involves interviewing key scientists and top management, asking them to give importance ratings to each of the nineteen topical categories used for the community survey knowledge

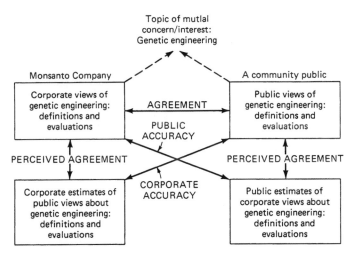

Figure 4-2 Coorientational relationships.

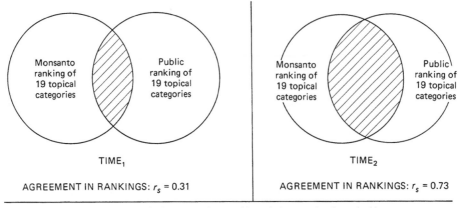

TIME₁   TIME₂

AGREEMENT IN RANKINGS: $r_s = 0.31$ AGREEMENT IN RANKINGS: $r_s = 0.73$

*This example is hypothetical, but uses the actual knowledge question from the Monsanto Company community surveys. Use similar calculations for determining T_1 - T_2 changes in perceived agreement and accuracy. As with other correlation coefficients, the range of possible values is + 1.0 to − 1.0. In this case, + 1.0 indicates perfect agreement between the two rank orders. The minimum value, − 1.0, means that the two rank orders are exactly the reverse of each other — total disagreement. A value of 0.0 indicates there is simply no pattern or relationship between the two sets of ordered items. Spearman's rho can take on any value in the range.

Figure 4–3   Rank-order correlation measures of organization-public relationships.

question (see page 77). Based on their answers, we rank order the set. Then we use the data from the public survey to rank order the same set of options based on how many people mentioned each—from most often mentioned to least often mentioned. We now have two sets of nineteen rank-ordered items.

The Spearman's *rho* (sometimes referred to by the symbol "r_s") would be an appropriate nonparametric index of the correlation between the two rank-ordered sets.[6] If the program has the effect of increasing agreement on the meaning of genetic engineering, then the rank-order correlation after the program should be greater than before the program, as Figure 4–3 illustrates.

[6]Calculation of r_s is actually quite simple. First, assign ranks to the two sets of items—with ties within a set given the arithmetic mean of the ranks they would have received if there had been no ties. For example, if two items would have occupied ranks 4 and 5, had they not tied, then each gets the rank of 4.5. Second, compute differences in ranks for each item by subtracting the ranking in one set from the ranking for the same item in the other set. You should have a difference score for each item in the ordered set. Third, square each of the differences. Fourth, total the squared differences. Plug those values into the following formula:

$$r_s = 1 - \frac{6 \times \text{Total of squared differences}}{\text{Number of items} \times (\text{Number items squared} - 1)}$$

For more information on how to calculate and use rank-order correlations, see Frederick Williams, *Reasoning with Statistics: How to Read Quantitative Research*, 3rd ed. (New York: Holt, Rinehart and Winston, 1986), pp. 138–40, or any other basic statistics book. Look in the index for "Spearman's *rho*," "Kendall's *tau*," or "rank-order correlation."

Instead of using rank orders, we could have both the public sample and corporate leadership group *rate* each of the items—say on a 1-to-10 scale in which 1 stands for "not at all important" and 10 stands for "very important." We could then compute mean scores for each item and then use an even more powerful correlation technique—Pearson product moment correlation. Chapter 11 explains correlations and their interpretation. Here we just need to point out that correlation coefficients are useful measures of association between two sets of measures. The point is that to calculate correlation coefficients for the coorientational measures of program impact on relationships, we need data from both sides of the relationship.

Another approach—often used in coorientational studies of communication relationships—is the *difference score* (sometimes referred to as a "*D*-score"). As in the case of the more powerful correlational method, you need rating scores—not ranks—for each item, from both sides of the relationship. The *D*-score is nothing more than the difference between the two sides' ratings for each item. The relative magnitudes of difference scores indicate the degree of agreement, perceived agreement, and accuracy. Relatively large *D*-scores indicate relatively little agreement, relatively low perceived agreement, or relatively low accuracy. Smaller *D*-scores indicate greater agreement, greater perceived agreement, and higher accuracy.

You could even calculate a mean difference score by simply averaging a set of *D*-scores, although by doing so you might lose important information about the specific sources of agreement/disagreement or accuracy/inaccuracy in the relationship. And finally, by subtracting the T_1 *D*-scores from the T_2 score, you have an indication of how much the program changed the organization-public relationship—in terms of agreement, perceived agreement, and accuracy on the set of items studied. For example, the hypothetical example in Figure 4–4 shows a $T_2 - T_1$ difference in *D*-scores of 2.1.

"In your opinion, how important is the contribution genetic engineering will make to improving agriculture and livestock?"

Not at all important									Very important
1	2	3	4	5	6	7	8	9	10

Figure 4–4   D-score measures of organization-public agreement.

TIME$_1$	TIME$_2$
Monsanto importance rating of "Improving agriculture/livestock" = 9.5*	Monsanto importance rating of "Improving agriculture/livestock" = 9.5
Public rating = 5.7	Public rating = 7.8
T_1 agreement D-score = 3.8	T_2 agreement D-score = 1.7
TIME$_2$ – TIME$_1$ = 2.1	

*Based on 10-point importance scale using hypothetical data.

As simple and as rough as they are, D-scores represent an easily understood way to show how far apart or how close two groups' ratings are. T_1-to-T_2 changes in D-scores provide useful indicators of program impact on agreement, perceived agreement, and accuracy. Analyses of the direction and amount of change in each group's ratings (back to the one-sided approach) provide insight as to which side changed most in the relationship. The combination of one-sided measures of program impact and coorientational measures provides the most complete picture of program impact on the organization-public relationship.

We conclude this discussion of coorientational measures of program impact by pointing out that this is a relatively new approach to program evaluation. Coorientational measures have been used more in scholarly communication research than in public relations program management. They are, however, consistent with the open systems and two-way symmetrical models of public relations—meaning that changes in knowledge, predispositions, and behaviors occur in both the organization and its publics.[7] And unlike the asymmetric models of public relations, in which programs are designed to affect target publics, two-way symmetrical public relations affects both components in the organization-public system. Coorientational measures describe characteristics of system relationships, but much work remains to refine this approach for measuring program impact.

LONG-TERM APPROACHES
TO IMPACT EVALUATION

To this point, we have outlined criteria, discussed some observation techniques, and given examples of a few measurement approaches used in assessing program impact. Figure 4–5 summarizes the levels of outcome criteria for a target public and extends the list to include *repeated behavior* and *social or cultural change.*

Maintaining desired behaviors and extinguishing undesirable behaviors over an extended time are outcomes sought by many public relations programs. Professional ethics and social responsibility call for sensitivity to the long-term impact of such public relations programs. For example, what are the consequences on public health, the health care system, the insurance industry, etc., of Tobacco Institute programs designed to contradict reported research findings of the effects of smoking? What are the long-term impacts of tobacco industry programs designed to affect public policies related to smoking in public settings?

Even if attempts to measure long-term effects are left to scholars in sociology and anthropology, the ultimate judgment of public relations programs will be based on their positive or negative impact on society and culture. Both individual practitioners and the profession as a whole must pass this test.

---

[7]See Scott M. Cutlip, Allen H. Center, and Glen M. Broom, *Effective Public Relations,* 6th ed. (Englewood Cliffs, N.J.: Prentice-Hall, Inc., 1985), pp. 192–97, and James E. Grunig and Farissa Schneider Grunig, "Toward a Theory of the Public Relations Behavior of Organizations: Review of a Program of Research," *Public Relations Research Annual,* Vol. L (1989), pp. 27–63

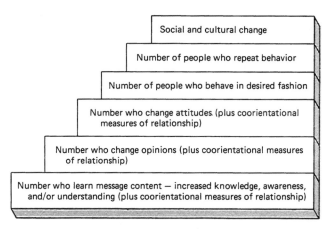

Figure 4–5 Levels of program impact criteria.

Social and cultural change

Number of people who repeat behavior

Number of people who behave in desired fashion

Number who change attitudes (plus coorientational measures of relationship)

Number who change opinions (plus coorientational measures of relationship)

Number who learn message content — increased knowledge, awareness, and/or understanding (plus coorientational measures of relationship)

Measuring program impact over an extended period requires measures repeated at regular intervals, producing data similar to the chart display of stock price fluctuations. Over time, the findings provide a series of benchmarks that can be viewed in relation to other factors that may or may not have been included in the original working theory that guided program strategies. Repeated measures help answer two important questions: a) How long does it take before the desired program effect shows up in the target public? b) How long does the effect last after the program activities cease? Hence, longitudinal studies give you not only data needed to monitor program impact, but also serve to generate new ideas and theories about programs and nonprogram forces.

IMPACT RESEARCH AS MANAGEMENT INFORMATION

Collecting repeated measures of public knowledge, predispositions, and behaviors, as well as indices of the organization-public relationships, provides the data base for the management information system (MIS). As Professor William Ehling puts it:

> Research, both factual and evaluative, plays an important role in the total process of public relations management. Without competent and thorough research of an organization's environment, there is no basis for assessing opportunities or threats facing the organization and, hence, no way of determining the existence or the possible emergence of a public relations setting or situation. Without an adequate review and evaluation of the program performance there is no basis for determining whether desired goal-

> *states have been attained or for determining what should be done*
> *if they are not attained.*[8]

MIS is the structure and procedures for gathering, storing, retrieving, and applying information to help managers make decisions. As part of the MIS, public relations program impact measures provide information about past program performance that managers can use to adjust current and future programs. In other words, feedback on program impact helps reduce uncertainty in decision making. The assumption underlying research to measure program impact is that the results will be used to improve future programs.[9]

T_2 program impact measures at the end of one program cycle are the T_1 benchmarks for the next planning cycle. The more extended the record, the more information you and other managers have on which to base judgments about resources, goals, and objectives. Impact measures can be used along with information about program inputs in the MIS to compute program efficiency and cost-effectiveness to aid in program management.

In the final analysis, impact measures are essential MIS ingredients for assessing program effectiveness and improving the next effort. The measures' usefulness, however, in part depends on the appropriateness of your research design, sampling procedures, observation techniques, and measurement tools. You will learn about these topics in Part II—Methods: Gathering Information.

[8]William P. Ehling, "Application of Decision Theory in the Construction of a Theory of Public Relations Management. II," *Public Relations Research and Education,* vol. 2, No. 1 (Summer 1985), p. 20.

[9]For detailed discussion of how information is used in decision making, see Arthur J. Kuhn, *Organizational Cybernetics and Business Policy: System Design for Performance Control* (University Park: The Pennsylvania State University Press, 1986).

CHAPTER 5

DESIGNING THE RESEARCH

Gary L. Schmermund, Senior Vice President, LOUIS HARRIS & ASSOCIATES, INC., New York.

Before doing research, I ask: Is the information already available someplace else? If it isn't, does the research have to be done? Finally, if the client can't answer how it's going to be used, then I'd be remiss if I didn't question whether the research should be done.

Roger Sennott, PhD, General Manager, MARKET DEVELOPMENT, INC., San Diego.

I have to be absolutely precise and sure about what the client needs to learn from the research. There is a hazy "getting started" part, but I never want there to be an ambiguity about what the research is about.

Scott J. Farrell, Vice President, Group Manager, BURSTON-MARSTELLER, Chicago.

The questions are "What do you want to learn?" and "What do you want to do with what you learn?" These have to be determined up front.

Walter K. Lindenmann, Vice President and Director of Research, KETCHUM PUBLIC RELATIONS, New York.

Nobody gives a damn about methodological tools or the validity of research. That's your problem to cope with as a researcher. As the practitioner, all I need is something that's going to prove that this program is working or not. When designing research, you've got to look at the real-world problem you're facing. In a sense, you almost always have to compromise from the ideal design to a certain degree.

David E. Clavier, PhD, APR, Executive Director, HUSK JENNINGS OVERMAN PUBLIC RELATIONS, Jacksonville, Florida.

*From a practical standpoint, there are three important issues. One, of course, is budget. One of the most difficult things to budget for in a corporate environment is research. It's not as tangible as budgeting for people on payroll or capital assets. Number two, how quickly do you need that information? How strong does the information have to be to sell to the management team? That is, how certain do you and the management team need to be about the conclusion? What kind of decision would the research play into? Number three is also critical. You must be able to clearly describe and explain the methodology—why you're asking the question and **how** you are doing the research—to other members of management. If you can't explain it to other managers in terms they understand, you run into resistance.*

Paul H. Alvarez, APR, Chairman and Chief Executive Officer, KETCHUM PUBLIC RELATIONS, New York.

Fear of cost is something we fight all the time when designing research. It's very easy to rationalize your way out of doing research in a PR agency. Research usually comes with the sharp edge of costly put in front of it. "Costly research" is like one word.

Lloyd Kirban, PhD, Executive Vice President, Director/ Research, BURSON-MARSTELLER, New York.

We would never advocate doing measurement if it cost more than 8 to 10 percent of program cost. That's our rule of thumb.

Research *design* is the organization of activities to answer research questions. In public relations, the scientific method can be applied to framing the research question, designing the study, collecting information, analyzing the data, and using the results.

After completing this chapter, you will be able to make decisions about research budgets, about timing and different design options, and you will be able to select designs that management will understand and accept. Before considering these practical issues, you must first understand the fundamentals of scientific research design.

THE CRITICAL ROLE OF THEORY

A *theory* is an explanation and a prediction of natural phenomena, including human behavior.[1] One might think that building theory would be the furthest thing from your mind when using research in public relations. After all, we're trying to answer practical, applied questions about programs and publics. We use research to help make decisions and measure program impact. What does theory have to do with the practice of public relations?

Theory helps us to organize what we learn from research. The bits and pieces of information that we gather from environmental scanning for planning (see Chapter 2), from monitoring programs (see Chapter 3), and from program evaluation (see Chapter 4) need to be organized. Some things we learn are specific. These research findings don't apply to other situations. Other things we learn in one research situation can be abstracted and generalized to a number of situations. This is how we build the theory of public relations, the foundation for all our actions.

Center and Jackson refer to this body of theories in public relations as the "emerging maxims" of the practice.[2] For example, they offer the following maxim about credibility:

[1]Fred N. Kerlinger, *Foundations of Behavioral Research,* 2nd. ed. (New York: Holt, Rinehart and Winston, 1973), pp. 5–6.

[2]Allen H. Center and Patrick Jackson, *Public Relations Practices: Managerial Case Studies and Problems,* 4th ed. (Englewood Cliffs, N.J.: Prentice Hall, 1990).

> *A source of information regarded as trustworthy, expert, or authoritative is most likely to be believed.*

In scientific terms, this maxim is a theoretical *proposition*. That is, the maxim is an abstract statement that shows how two or more concepts are related to each other. A *concept* is an abstraction formed by a generalization from particulars. The concept "trustworthy" is an abstraction, a generalization of that attribute of all those things in the real world that we trust. To varying degrees, we trust our parents, the braking system in our cars, and the system for grading student performance in public relations courses. Trustworthiness is generalized from these particular real-world manifestations of the concept of trust.

Testing Hypotheses

On the abstract level, we have a proposition that a source of information regarded as *expert* will be believed more than a source not regarded as expert. Is this proposition true? Does it really describe how credibility works in the real world? To find out, we might do an experiment. We might have one source regarded as expert provide one group of people information on a controversial topic like nuclear power. We have another group hear the same information from an information source they don't consider as expert. Then we ask members of both groups whether they believed the source. If Center and Jackson's maxim is true, we would expect the group exposed to the "expert" source to believe the information provided more than the group exposed to the "not expert" source.

When we apply a theoretical proposition to a real-world situation, we use hypotheses. An *hypothesis* is a statement of a relationship between real-world variables, deduced from a theoretical proposition. The process of taking concepts from propositions and deducing real-world indicators of those concepts for hypothesis testing is called *operationalization*. Operationalization is intricately interwoven with the process of measurement. Both topics are considered in detail in Chapter 8.

Modifying Theory and Elaboration

Theoretical propositions and the hypotheses they spawn are not cast in concrete. Rather, they are constantly evolving and changing as we rethink issues at the conceptual level and seek to apply theory to real-world research questions. Theory, then, is dynamic, growing, and changing as we use it.

One of the ways that theory is modified is when it is specified. *Specification* is stating limitations or conditions under which theory applies. For example, we may find that a source regarded as expert is not believed as readily if he or she is viewed as having a vested interest in our believing the information provided. Returning to our aforementioned experiment, we find that two nuclear physicists are rated by the two groups as "expert" on nuclear power. When we identify one physicist as working for a university, she is believed by one group when she provides information favorable to the nuclear power industry. However, the other group is told the physicist is an employee of a major nuclear power company. She is not believed as readily when she provides information favorable to the nuclear power industry. So expertness increases the believability of a source if and only if the expert has no vested interest in the outcome. Our original theory is true, but only under certain circumstances.

This process of testing and retesting the relationship under different conditions permits the *elaboration* of theory. That is, you move back and forth between theory and observation, thinking of different variables that may affect the original relationship. As these new relationships are tested, the theory grows and changes. The elaboration process is discussed in detail in Chapter 12. Research is a continuing process, wherein the results of one study become input for posing new research questions.

Grounded Theory

Research can start with theory and proceed to test hypotheses derived from theory. This hypothesis-testing approach to the research process is called the classical approach. However, hypothesis testing is not the only way in which research can be conducted. A second approach, called the grounded theory approach, reverses the process and favors alternative ways of collecting information.[3]

Center and Jackson's maxim about the credibility of information sources is based on a "bank of precedential cases and the experience of educators and practitioners."[4] That is, the theory rests on a body of prior research and experiences. But what if we had no prior theory to draw on? As is often the case in public relations, there are many aspects of the practice that do not rest on a strong theoretical foundation. How do you get started without theory?

Advocates of grounded theory argue that one starts with intensive observation. Using small samples of people (see Chapter 6) and qualitative techniques such as field observation (see Chapter 7), we might observe how people evaluate information sources and what characteristics of those sources are important in believing the information. Based on a small number of observations, we might conclude that people believe information sources that they previously regarded as being "expert" about that type of information. We find this to be true for many different information sources and many different information topics and many different audiences. This "conclusion" is called an *empirical generalization.* An empirical generalization is a statement of a relationship between two variables, based directly on the observation of that relationship in the real world.

---

[3]Grounded theory is explored in detail in Barney G. Glaser and Anselm L. Strauss, *The Discovery of Grounded Theory: Strategies for Qualitative Research* (Chicago: Aldine, 1967).
[4]Center and Jackson, *Public Relations Practices.*

Such empirical generalizations are the raw material for developing new theories that account for relations discovered in the real world.

The Spiral of Science

The process of scientific inquiry is illustrated in Figure 5–1. The spiral of science describes the cyclical process of moving from theory to observation and back again to theory. We deduce relationships from theoretical propositions and state them as operational hypotheses. These hypotheses are our predictions of how we expect two variables to relate to each other. We then test hypotheses by making observations. Our observations and hypothesis testing lead us back to theory. If our hypotheses are disconfirmed, then the theory needs to be rethought. Further, our observations may lead us to recognize patterns and relations that hypotheses had not predicted. These empirical generalizations also provide the basis for the discovery and reformulation of theory.

Working and Scientific Theories

Theories vary in their degree of specificity. For example, Lloyd Kirban of Burson-Marsteller had a "theory" that a spokesperson not directly affiliated with the company would have more credibility than an internal spokesperson. This is a more specific theory than the maxim provided by Center and Jackson about source credibility. Further, it applies to a specific real-world problem that Kirban was trying to solve for his client.

Our client was emphatic about using his own people as "spokespeople." We created a mock interview with two of their own people. The interview discussed a neutral issue—government guidelines on food and nutrition. We videotaped it and voiced over, changing the introduction to indicate who the guy worked for. In one version it was Dr. So-and-So, Director of Food and Nutrition for the company. In the second version, it was the Director of Food and Nutrition for the Harvard School of Medicine. In the third version, it was the Director from the Institute of Food and Technology. We showed it to three matched samples of 150 apiece and then asked them a series of questions. The credibility rating was 25 percent higher among the people who thought he was with Harvard, compared to those who thought he was with the company. In the middle was the Institute of Technology.

This is an example of a *working theory,* a relatively specific causal statement that links a public relations activity with an outcome. Kirban's theory may not apply to every situation in which a spokesperson speaks for the company.

The point is that all public relations practices are driven by some form of theory. When you write a press release or organize a special event, you do so

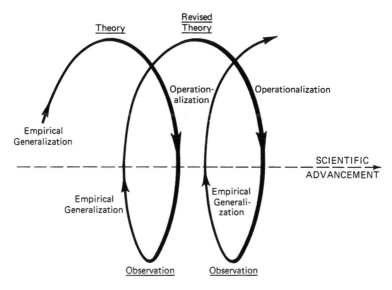

Figure 5–1   The spiral of science.

with the notion that these public relations activities will impact some public in some way. If not, why do it? Sometimes the linkage between a public relations activity and its intended outcome is not articulated. That is, nobody has specified exactly what to expect as the effect of a particular public relations activity. Nonetheless, the theories implicit in these activities are the bedrock assumptions that drive practitioner activities. When these assumptions are stated as relations between program activities and outcomes, a working theory emerges.

These situation-specific working theories can be contrasted with formal scientific theory. Formal *scientific theory* links relatively abstract concepts through propositions. *Propositions* are statements that describe the relationships between two concepts. Examples of concepts can be taken from another maxim reported by Center and Jackson:

> *In controversy, opposing views seeking major change of opinion tend to harden the positions held.*[5]

One concept is "messages seeking major opinion change"; a second concept is the "hardening of positions held." The maxim itself is a *proposition,* a statement that causally links the two concepts together. Theory in this example consists of a number of these propositions specifying the conditions under which the exchange of information and opinion change are related to each other.

The advantage of an abstract theory is that it applies to many different

[5]Ibid.

situations. One theory serves to guide decisions and actions in many different settings. The disadvantage of an abstract theory is connecting the abstract concepts to things that we can see, feel, and touch in the real world. The more situation-specific working theories are cumbersome. Many maxims are required to guide decisions and action in a myriad of situations. On the other hand, the connection between the ideas or concepts that make up a working theory and the things we see, feel, and touch in the real world is relatively direct.

THE PROCESS OF RESEARCH DESIGN

Making research design decisions is a logical process. The first step is to clearly and objectively define the information needs that are driving the research effort. Fundamental to that process is a clear understanding of the purposes for which the research findings will be used. As Gary Schmermund pointed out at the beginning of this chapter, if the client can't answer how research is to be used, you should question whether to do it at all.

Using principles of the Management By Objectives (MBO) philosophy, we can think of the initial curiosity driving a research activity as a "fuzzy."[6] A "fuzzy" is a preliminary statement of a research objective. "Fuzzies" are vague, imprecise statements that communicate a need for information but are generally too ill-defined to actually guide the implementation of a research project.

To convert a "fuzzy" into research objectives, the use of the information must first be defined. Is the research project concerned with answering questions about the current awareness, knowledge, opinions, or behavior of a public or publics? Will this information be used to plan programs? Or, is the research project measuring the impact of a new public relations program?

Once information needs have been specified, the next step is to precisely define the public or publics involved. The research objectives that emerge from this process specify the kind of information to be gathered, the publics from whom the information is gathered, and the purposes to which the information is to be put. (If media content—rather than publics—is studied, then the same principles apply.)

The research objectives of the research project suggest appropriate research design options. These design options are considered in detail later in this chapter. Once an appropriate research design (cross-sectional, longitudinal, experimental, quasi-experimental) is selected, you prepare a written research plan.

The Research Plan

As David Clavier said at the beginning of this chapter, you must consider budget, timing, and the ability of management to understand your research methods. You write down your budget, timing, and methods decisions in a research plan.

---

[6]Karl Albrecht, *Successful Management By Objectives: An Action Manual* (Englewood Cliffs, N.J.: Prentice Hall, 1978), pp. 73–82.

The *research plan* documents the information needs that drive the research project and explains how that information will be used. Part of your research plan is a data analysis plan. The *data analysis plan* provides step-by-step details on how the information (or data) will be collected and how that information will be analyzed. Research and data analysis plans are considered in more detail in Chapter 9. The research plan is the operations guide for conducting a research project. When doing research yourself, write a research plan to keep yourself on task, on time, and under budget. When contracting for research services (see Appendix B), the research plan is even more essential for keeping research consultants on task, on time, and under budget. Figure 5–2 is a flow chart of the research design and implementation process.

Selecting the Design Option

As indicated in Figure 5–2, you select an appropriate research design for your project based on your research objectives. Embedded in concrete design

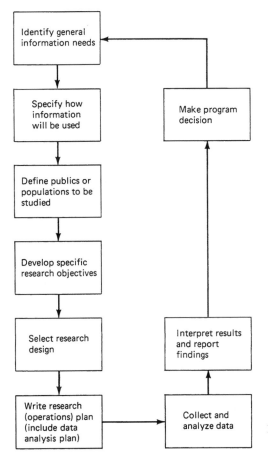

Figure 5-2 Flow chart for designing a research project.

issues of budget, timing, and methods are larger, more conceptual design issues. These design issues involve the strength or the amount of confidence you have in your research findings.

When you gather information for planning purposes, all you may need is an accurate "snapshot" or "freeze frame" of current knowledge, predispositions, or behavior of publics. A single survey—collecting data at one point in time—may suffice. Such designs are called *cross-sectional* designs.

Often, however, you want more than a "freeze frame" of the status quo among target publics. You want to know if a public relations program has achieved its goals and objectives. What worked and what did not work? To answer these questions, you must consider gathering data at several points in time, using *longitudinal* designs.

Panel Studies

One longitudinal design is the *panel* study, the systematic surveys of the same individuals on several occasions over an extended period of time. Panel studies are especially useful, because changes in a particular individual's knowledge, opinion, or behavior can be compared from survey to survey. You put panel studies together by identifying members of key publics and soliciting their agreement to participate in several surveys, perhaps one survey each six months for two years.

Panel studies are particularly vulnerable to *experimental mortality,* the dropping out of respondents during the period of study. This problem can be corrected by offering participants incentives for their continued participation. In addition, a large initial sample can be drawn, so that the final number of participants does not dwindle to a count too small for useful analysis. In addition, dropouts can be replenished with newly solicited participants during each wave of data collection. However, the new panel members must be analyzed separately from the regular, continuing members of the panel.

Commercial research firms conduct panel studies for multiple clients. In this way, the cost to each individual client is reduced. Called "caravan" studies, these panel studies provide a relatively inexpensive mechanism for tracking changes in publics over time.

Trend Studies

Another form of longitudinal study is the *trend* study, surveying different respondents in a series of surveys over time. Because the respondents are "new" in each survey, changes in knowledge, opinions, and behavior can only be compared between surveys in the aggregate. You may find, for example, that awareness of your organization's community relations program has increased from 20 percent to 30 percent over a six-month period. However, you will not be able to learn anything about those people (10 percent of the samples), who became aware of the program *during* that six-month period, who changed their level of awareness from the first to the second survey. Trend studies are generally easier to do than panel studies.

When collecting longitudinal data to measure program impact, data must be gathered according to an experimental design. In public relations, an experimental design is a strategy for exposing some people to a public relations program, then comparing them to people who were not exposed to the program. In a very literal sense, every public relations program is a field experiment in action and communication effects on publics and organizations.

EXPERIMENTAL DESIGN

Whenever a public relations program is evaluated, some kind of experimental design is used. Indeed, every research plan to evaluate program impact includes either an explicit or implicit experimental design. In an *experimental* design, a *treatment* (the public relations program or some part of it) is given to at least one group of subjects. Impact of that treatment is measured (change in awareness, knowledge, opinion, or behavior, for example) by comparing after-treatment levels with before-treatment levels.

When considering the appropriateness of any design, the issues of internal validity and external validity are key. *Internal validity* is the truth of conclusions reached from a study in terms of causes and effects. For example, in Kirban's experiment involving the organizational affiliation of spokespeople, he concluded that—under certain circumstances—spokespeople not directly affiliated with the company have greater credibility than do company spokespeople. Indeed, subjects in the experiment who saw the nonaffiliated spokesperson rated him as more credible than did other subjects who rated a spokesperson identified as an employee of the company. The conclusion is that the spokesperson's affiliation caused the difference in credibility. But what if the people who saw the nonaffiliated spokesperson, as a group, generally consider *anybody* more credible, when compared to the other group? That is, the difference in credibility ratings may not be due to differences in treatments (organizational affiliation) but to differences in subjects. As detailed in the following sections, you will see how Kirban controlled for these rival explanations that account for differences in credibility.

External validity is the generalizability of the study—the degree to which relationships identified in the study apply to other situations. You might think of external validity as how "exportable" your research findings are. If your study has low external validity, your findings are restricted to (only true for) the specific circumstances of your data collection setting. On the other hand, a study with high external validity has findings that apply to many different settings and situations.

For example, in Kirban's spokesperson experiment, subjects were placed in a room, exposed to a videotaped message about a neutral subject, and then asked to rate the credibility of the spokesperson. Clearly, this experimental setting differs from the way in which people are generally exposed to mediated messages in the real world. Does that difference between the research setting and the real world suggest that the effects would be different in the real world? This question is concerned with the external validity of the experiment.

Figure 5–3 illustrates the relevant internal and external validity questions for a study of the relationship between communication satisfaction and job satisfaction. The two concepts are posited to be positively related to each other. High levels of communication satisfaction lead to subsequent high levels of job satisfaction. A study is designed to examine this relationship in the real world. The internal validity questions seek to determine if a change in job satisfaction occurs when we manipulate communication satisfaction. Further, are there any other factors that might account for increased job satisfaction other than an increase in communication satisfaction? The external validity questions ask how generalizable or "exportable" our findings are. Suppose we conduct an experiment where we systematically increase the job satisfaction of one group of clerical workers in one large company. For another group of clerical workers in the same company, we systematically decrease communication satisfaction. We find that job satisfaction increases for the former group and decreases for the latter group. Would we find the same effect if we studied assembly line workers? Technical and professional employees? Workers at another company? These are all external validity questions.

Experimental Design Options

There are three types of experimental research designs: pre-experimental designs, true experimental designs, and quasi-experimental designs.[7] Pre-

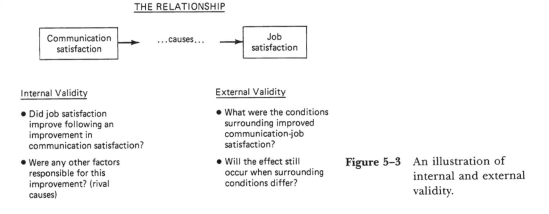

THE RELATIONSHIP

Communication satisfaction → ...causes... → Job satisfaction

Internal Validity

- Did job satisfaction improve following an improvement in communication satisfaction?
- Were any other factors responsible for this improvement? (rival causes)

External Validity

- What were the conditions surrounding improved communication-job satisfaction?
- Will the effect still occur when surrounding conditions differ?

Figure 5–3   An illustration of internal and external validity.

[7]For a comprehensive overview of experimental designs, see Donald T. Campbell and Julian C. Stanley, *Experimental and Quasi-Experimental Designs for Research* (Chicago: Rand McNally, 1963).

experimental designs are those which, due to characteristics of the design, do not permit causal inferences to be directly supported by the data. That is, the internal validity of such designs are weak.

True experimental designs, on the other hand, permit powerful causal inferences to be drawn, based on the information collected and analyzed. True experiments are able to do so through the random assignment of subjects to treatment and control groups. Treatment groups, for example, are people exposed to a prototype of a new public relations program, such as a persuasive TV advertisement about a public issue. Control groups, on the other hand, are exposed to a placebo. The *placebo* may be an advertisement about an unrelated public issue; people in the control group feel like they have received some kind of treatment but, in fact, have not. True experiments also often involve measurement of impact (change in opinion, for example) both before the treatment (pretest measures) and after the treatment (posttest measures).

Laboratory Experiments

While true experiments are strong on internal validity, the need to assign subjects to control and treatment groups often restricts such studies to a "lab" setting. People are exposed to treatments in "unnatural" settings. Thus, experiments are often weak on external validity, the ability to generalize the lab findings to similar situations in the real world. Therefore, it's often desirable to conduct experiments in a field setting.

Field Experiments

In a field study, subjects might be exposed to the same persuasive advertising message in their own homes under all the distractions of "natural" TV exposure. When doing field studies, it's often difficult to assign subjects to treatment and control groups. Due to this difficulty, designs have been developed that allow the researcher to use "naturally occurring" groups of people (employees in one plant versus employees at another plant) to serve as comparison groups. These are called quasi-experimental designs. Naturally occurring comparison groups replace the more rigorous randomly assigned treatment and control groups of experimental designs.

One-Shot Case Study Design

A baseline survey of publics, a single cross-sectional survey, uses a preexperimental design called a one-shot case study. Figure 5–4 displays this design.

Generally speaking, a cross-sectional survey of a public or publics does not occur in a vacuum. Often, the public under scrutiny has already been the focus of public relations activities. As illustrated in Figure 5–4, the public has been the focus of a public relations program. The single survey occurs after such program implementation. There are many things that can be learned from cross-

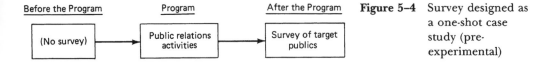

Before the Program   Program   After the Program   **Figure 5–4** Survey designed as
a one-shot case
study (pre-
experimental)

sectional surveys and one-shot case studies. We can quantify the awareness, knowledge, opinions, and behavior of key publics at the time of our survey. This is key to program planning (see Chapter 2).

Further, we can examine relationships between program activities and impact measures. For example, we may find in a readership survey that employees who regularly read our internal publications are generally more satisfied with their jobs than employees who do not read those publications. Can we conclude that reading employee publications caused the difference in job satisfaction? No! For one thing, high job satisfaction may lead those employees to seek out information about the organization through internal publications. That is, job satisfaction causes the employee to read the publications—not the other way around. Further, some third factor, unknown to us, may be the cause of both readership levels and job satisfaction.

Determining Cause and Effect

In experimental designs, we seek to determine the causes and effects involved in a relationship. (Causality is dealt with in greater detail in Chapter 12.) Does readership of internal publications cause an increase in job satisfaction? In a one-shot case study, we may find a *necessary* condition of causality. After all, if frequent readers of internal publications were no more satisfied with their jobs than infrequent or nonreaders, then there would be little reason to think that readership somehow causes job satisfaction. So the discovery of the relationship between readership and job satisfaction provides a partial answer to the question. But this answer is not *sufficient.* To establish causality—to show that readership is both necessary and sufficient for an increase in job satisfaction—we need a more rigorous experimental design.

TYPES OF EXPERIMENTAL DESIGNS

To measure the impact of a public relations program, one is attempting to learn if program activities cause a change in the awareness, knowledge, opinions, and behavior of publics. The most powerful tool for determining such cause and effect is the experiment. An experiment generally involves three basic concepts: random assignment of subjects to groups, pretest-posttest measures, and control-treatment groups. By assigning people to treatment or control groups at random, you can feel confident that the groups do not differ from each other at the beginning of the experiment. We can expose one or more groups (treatment groups) to the public relations program and expose other groups (control groups) to a placebo. By comparing the outcomes for the different groups, we can determine program impact—the causal relationship between the public relations programs and the awareness, knowledge, opinions, and behavior of publics.

Mary Ann Burnett is director of corporate communications for Hartson Medical Services. Hartson is a private contractor providing paramedic services to the city of San Diego. Part of Hartson's contract with the city specifies a community education program. Part of community education is to help school children understand the appropriate uses of the 911 emergency number. Abuses are common among children. (For example, a child may call 911 because a pet has been struck by a car.) Burnett has a number of awareness, knowledge, and behavioral objectives for her 911 in-school education program. Using a half-hour assembly at schools, she instructs children in how to access 911, and she tries to increase their understanding of paramedics and 911 emergencies. The overall program *goal* is to reduce abuses of 911.

The Hartson example permits illustration of several different types of experimental designs that allow Burnett to measure the impact of her 911 in-school program. The intervention in each case is a half-hour assembly in the school, using a number of presentation techniques designed to affect the awareness, knowledge, and behavioral predispositions of children toward 911. The impact of the program is measured through a brief questionnaire that measures the child's awareness of 911 and paramedics, their knowledge of the appropriate use of 911, and finally a hypothetical situation where the child indicates whether he or she would dial 911 under specified circumstances.

One Group Pretest-Posttest Design

In this design, Burnett provides a half-hour assembly for the entire student body at a particular middle school. The day prior to the assembly, all students fill out the questionnaire. Then, two months after the assembly, the students fill out the questionnaire again. The purpose is to determine if any lasting increase in awareness, knowledge, or behavioral predisposition has occurred as a result of the assembly. Figure 5–5 illustrates this design.

At the top of Figure 5–5, a description of the design is provided, describing the experiment in terms of evaluating a public relations program. In the middle of Figure 5–5, the same design is displayed using more generic language of experimental designs. At the bottom, a symbolic description is provided, where "X" represents the treatment (the program) and "O" represents observation of the dependent variable, the program impact. This design has several weaknesses, which are threats to its internal validity.

Returning to our example, Burnett sets several measurable objectives for her in-school program. One objective is to increase knowledge of appropriate use of 911 by 50 percent from pretest to posttest measure. That means that if 30 percent of the students are knowledgeable about 911 prior to the assembly, at

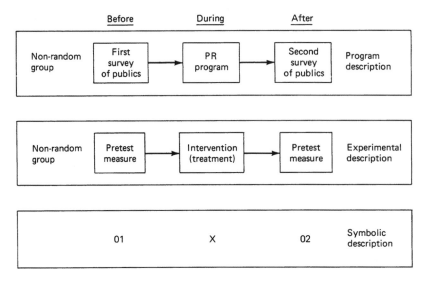

Figure 5-5 One-group pretest-posttest design (pre-experimental)

least 45 percent must be knowledgeable about 911 as indicated by the posttest measure (50 percent increase of 30 percent equals 45 percent).

Suppose 50 percent of the students are knowledgeable about 911 at the time of the posttest. Burnett apparently met her objective. However, due to weaknesses in design of this study, there are rival explanations for improvements in the children's knowledge of 911. Campbell and Stanley identify five threats to the internal validity of this design relevant to this research setting.[8]

One threat is *history*, events occurring between the pre- and posttest measures, besides the public relations program, that could account for the change. For example, a child at the school might have been involved in an abuse of 911 and receives extensive notoriety among classmates. A good deal of "incidental learning" about 911 occurs as the children discuss the incident among themselves. Part of the increase in knowledge about 911 occurs as a result of this historical incident; the public relations program (the assembly) can't take full credit for the increase in knowledge.

A second threat is *testing*. Children learn something about 911 just by answering the questions on the pretest questionnaire. Whenever awareness or knowledge change occurs as a result of the measurement activity itself, a testing effect has occurred. Part of the increase in knowledge, then, comes not from the public relations program itself but from the measurement activities of the pretest. In effect, the questionnaire communicates program content.

---

[8]These threats include history, maturation, testing, instrumentation, interaction of the pretest and the treatment, and regression to the mean. The regression threat is not considered here because it is not relevant to this research setting. For a detailed explanation, see Campbell and Stanley, pp. 6–16.

A third threat is caused by the sensitizing that occurs as a result of the pretest measure. This is the *interaction* threat to internal validity, the way that the pretest measure affects the impact of the treatment (program). The children at the assembly have already been sensitized to the importance of 911 because they were required to fill out a questionnaire about 911 prior to attending the assembly. Does filling out the questionnaire increase the attention that the children pay to the assembly? Is the public relations program (the assembly) as effective if the participants are not sensitized by the pretest measure? This design does not control for this effect. Therefore, we are unable to isolate the effect of the public relations program *by itself* from the interaction of the pretest measure with the treatment.

The *interaction* threat occurs whenever individuals are recruited for a research activity. Sandra Fuhrman of Southwestern Bell encountered this problem when customers were recruited to participate in a study of pricing information for phone services.

> *We called the customers in advance and told them that materials were going to be sent to them. So they had advance warning that they were going to receive the materials and that we were going to call. Otherwise, I think more customers would pitch the materials without reading them.*

This sensitizing effect causes the treatment (program) to appear to be more effective than it really is.

A fourth threat to internal validity is *maturation*. Students become more sophisticated about the world around them as they mature. Part of the improvement in knowledge scores from pretest to posttest measures may be due to maturation. This threat becomes more serious as the time between pretest and posttest measures is increased.

A fifth threat is *instrument decay*. Instrument decay is a breakdown in the reliability and accuracy of the measuring instrument. This problem is more pronounced when a human observer is measuring the dependent variable, the program impact. Observer fatigue or error, which can increase over time, can result in findings that the dependent variable has "changed" since the pretest measure. However, this change is the result of unreliable measures, not an actual change in the dependent variable. In this case, the students may not complete the questionnaire as completely or as carefully the second time. This results in measurement error that gives the appearance of "change" in the dependent variable that may not have actually occurred.

Pretest-Posttest Control Group Design

In her effort to isolate the effect of the assembly program on participant knowledge of 911, Burnett uses another design. Figure 5-6 illustrates this design, the pretest-posttest control group design.

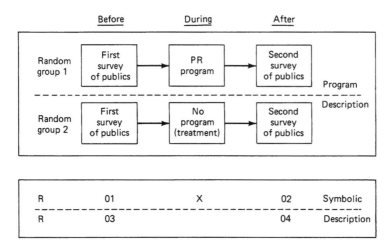

Figure 5–6 Pretest-posttest control group design (true experimental)

This design involves two groups, with assignment to each group made randomly. Burnett evenly divides the pretest questionnaires into two equal piles and staples a ticket numbered 1 to the top of each questionnaire in one pile. She staples a ticket numbered 2 to the top of the remaining questionnaires. She then mixes the questionnaires thoroughly so that each student has an equal chance of getting ticket 1 or ticket 2. Students in the school fill out the same pretest questionnaire, measuring their awareness, knowledge, and behavioral predispositions toward 911.

Students receiving ticket 1 (random group 1) attend the 911 assembly in Room 1. Students receiving the ticket 2 (random group 2) attend a different assembly in Room 2. The second assembly deals with drug and alcohol abuse prevention, another community education objective of Burnett and Hartson. Two months later, students from *both* assemblies fill out the same 911 posttest questionnaire.

Some 30 percent of the children attending the 911 assembly are deemed knowledgeable about 911 prior to the assembly. Some 32 percent of children attending the drug abuse assembly are deemed knowledgeable about 911 on their pretest questionnaires. It's not surprising that roughly equal numbers of students are knowledgeable about 911 during the pretest measure, since membership in groups is random. Following the two assemblies, Burnett expects the children attending the 911 assembly to post a larger increase in knowledge about 911 than students attending the drug abuse assembly.

The posttest scores show that students attending the 911 assembly increased their knowledge from 30 percent (pretest measure) to 60 percent, a 100 percent increase. However, the students attending the drug abuse assembly, where nothing is said about 911, also post a slight increase—from 32 percent to 37 percent. What factors could account for the increase in the control group (the drug abuse assembly group)? *Testing, maturation, instrument decay,* and *history* could account for the improvement in knowledge scores in the control group. Also, students at the 911 assembly could have talked to students at the drug abuse assembly about 911, causing secondary or two-step learning to occur from the 911 assembly.

Burnett reasons that the 5 percent knowledge increase in the control group can be attributed to the four threats to internal validity just noted. She further reasons that a like effect also occurred in the treatment group. That is, five percentage points of the thirty percentage-point improvement in the treatment group is due to *maturation, testing, instrument decay,* and *history* effects. The other 25 percent, she reasons, is due to the treatment itself. This logical process allows Burnett to *isolate* the treatment effects from all the other plausible threats to the internal validity of the design.

Posttest-Only Control Group Design

A remaining problem with the pretest-posttest control group design is that the treatment group received the pretest measure. As a consequence, the interaction of the pretest measure and the treatment remains uncontrolled. How much do children learn about 911 if they are not sensitized through a pretest measure? The pretest-posttest control group design does not allow Burnett to answer this question.

Burnett decides to repeat the experiment at another school. As before, she uses the two assemblies on 911 and drug abuse, assigning students to the two assemblies at random. This time, however, she eliminates the pretest measures for both groups. Her measures of awareness, knowledge, and behavioral predispositions toward 911 for both groups occur two months after the assemblies. Figure 5–7 illustrates this design, the posttest-only control group design.

Because of random assignment, the two groups should have roughly equal knowledge scores at the time of the assembly. Results show that, among students attending the 911 assembly, 50 percent are knowledgeable about 911 on the posttest measure. Among students attending the drug abuse assembly, only 30 percent are knowledgeable about 911. Burnett can make the assumption that, since the students attending the drug abuse assembly did not receive the treatment directly, their posttest scores approximate the pretest scores of the treatment group, had a pretest measure been made. Thus, Burnett concludes that the twenty percentage-point difference between the two groups is due to the treatment.

However, Burnett is not satisfied with this design. For one thing, she has no direct measure of change in knowledge levels in the treatment group. Further, the posttest knowledge scores for the control group include the effects of maturation and history over the two-month period since the assembly. Indeed, the control group's knowledge scores also include the two-step learning from students they talk to that did receive the treatment. The effects of the treatment may be underestimated by this design.

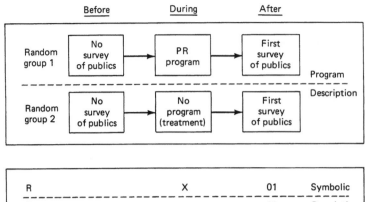

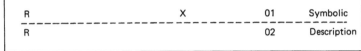

Figure 5–7 Posttest-only control group design (true experimental).

Solomon Four-Group Design

Burnett decides to use a more elaborate design at a new school that just happens to have facilities for four simultaneous assemblies. She combines both the pretest-posttest control group design and the posttest-only control group design. The resulting design is called the Solomon four-group design. Figure 5–8 illustrates this design.

This design requires four groups, randomly assigned from the same pool of subjects. Burnett accomplishes this through the random distribution of tickets to students in the school, numbered 1 through 4, which assigns them to one of four assemblies (random group 1 through random group 4). At two assemblies, students receive the drug abuse placebo. At the other two assemblies, students receive the 911 treatment. One group attending the 911 assembly completes the pretest questionnaire (random group 1); the other treatment group does not (random group 2). One group attending the drug abuse assembly completes the pretest questionnaire (random group 3); the other control group does not (random group 4). Two months later, all four groups complete a posttest questionnaire.

Burnett now is able to isolate the various "causes" that have led to increased knowledge levels among students receiving the 911 treatment. Turning to the symbolic description of this design in Figure 5–8, the first group provides a direct measure of change in knowledge scores for those receiving the treatment. But this group is sensitized to the treatment of the pretest measure. However, the third group—which also receives the treatment—is not sensitized. This group did not complete a pretest questionnaire. "O2" can be compared to "O5." If "O2" is greater than "O5," the difference can be attributed to the sensitizing effect of the pretest measure. In a similar manner, Burnett can isolate the effects of history, maturation, and testing by comparing the observations for the different groups in the design.

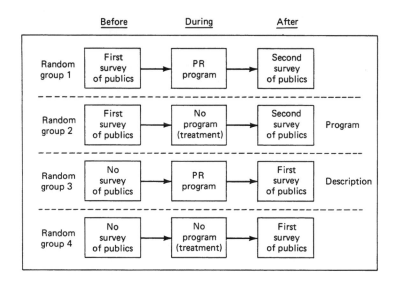

| Before | During | After |

Random group 1: First survey of publics → PR program → Second survey of publics

Random group 2: First survey of publics → No program (treatment) → Second survey of publics — Program

Random group 3: No survey of publics → PR program → First survey of publics — Description

Random group 4: No survey of publics → No program (treatment) → First survey of publics

R	01	X	02	
R	03		04	Symbolic
R		X	05	Description
R			06	

Figure 5–8   Solomon four-group design (true experimental).

Other Combinations

The preceding designs can be combined and modified in various ways to meet special research needs. One common variation is to examine not one treatment but several different versions of a treatment. This is common when prototypes of different message strategies are being scientifically compared as part of implementation evaluation. To do so, the pretest-posttest control group design can be modified by adding one or more additional treatment groups to the design.

Programs as Field Experiments

The 911 in-school community education program for Hartson's Medical Services is an example of a rigorous field experiment. The rigor is permitted because Burnett was able to randomly assign students to either treatment or control groups. Burnett's impact evaluation of her 911 school assemblies can be contrasted with Kirban's spokesperson experiment. Kirban's experiment is a laboratory experiment, in that the research setting (people assembled in a room to watch videotapes of spokespeople) differs from the real-world setting in which people watch television. This difference is a threat to the external validity of the design. Burnett, on the other hand, ran her experiment in the schools where she actually conducts her public relations program. Except for completion of questionnaires, the research setting is identical to the typical setting where the public relations program is actually conducted.

However, Burnett's field experiment is not without drawbacks. For one thing, students from the control and treatment groups are likely to interact during the two-month period from assemblies to posttest measures. This lack of control is typical of field experiments, making them somewhat weaker on internal validity than lab experiments. However, field experiments have stronger external validity.

Quasi-Experimental Designs

What about field experiments when random assignment to groups is not possible? Indeed, impact evaluations can be conducted using *comparison* groups, existing groups of people that can be used as substitutes for treatment and control groups. Figure 5–9 illustrates one such design, the nonequivalent control group design.

One application of this design was conducted by Susan Swanson, a public relations practitioner and paramedic coordinator for the city of San Diego. Working with the San Diego Fire Department, she sought to evaluate the impact of a community education program aimed at residential fire safety. The program used special events at shopping centers, door-to-door distribution of printed materials, and other techniques to communicate the basics of residential fire safety to citizens. Because the program was community based, people could not be as-

Figure 5–9 Nonequivalent control group design (quasi-experimental).

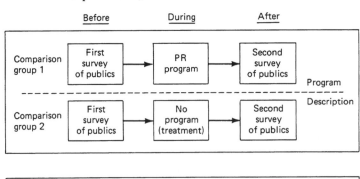

signed at random to treatment and control groups. However, it is possible to match two communities in terms of demographics, the age of most residential structures, and other characteristics. After comparing scores of communities within greater San Diego, the communities of Mira Mesa and Tierrasanta were selected because they closely matched each other for many important characteristics. A survey of several hundred people was conducted in both Mira Mesa and Tierrasanta prior to program implementation. The community-based fire prevention education program was implemented in Mira Mesa. No similar program was implemented in Tierrasanta. After one year, a second survey was conducted in both Mira Mesa and Tierrasanta. By comparing the changes in Mira Mesa to smaller or nonexistent changes in Tierrasanta, Swanson was able to identify community education components that worked and other components that did not achieve stated objectives.

Monsanto Corporation followed a similar strategy to evaluate community-based programs promoting biotechnology or genetic engineering. Genetic engineering involves the alteration of genetic materials of organisms, creating mutations. Some mutated microorganisms offer many benefits, such as economical production of insulin for diabetics. At the same time, some critics see danger in creating mutated organisms that might harm plants, animals, and humans. Monsanto, an emerging leader in biotechnology, sought to preempt critics through a broad-based community education program designed to build public support and appreciation of biotechnology and to position Monsanto as a leader in this field.

Prior to program implementation, large sample surveys (300 respondents) were conducted in two treatment communities, Columbus, Ohio, and Columbia, South Carolina. Surveys were also conducted in two comparison communities. Then extensive public relations campaigns were undertaken for three months in both treatment cities. Central to these programs were placements, media tours, direct mailings, and a science exhibit explaining biotechnology that operated at a museum in Columbus and at a shopping center in Columbia. In all, sixty-five media placements were credited to the campaign in the two cities.

Follow-up surveys were conducted in both treatment cities. Results indicated substantial increases in perception of Monsanto as a leader in biotechnology from pretest to posttest measures. More people perceived benefits of genetic engineering in both treatment cities after the programs, and more were willing after the programs to permit Monsanto to field test genetically altered bacteria.

The problem with this design and other quasi-experimental designs is that the groups—communities in this case—are not equivalent at the outset of the experiment. These differences may account for differences when posttest measures are compared. Controlling for plausible rival explanations is more problematic in quasi-experimental designs. Should such designs be discarded then? No! While they don't provide airtight control of rival explanations, and while their internal validity is not strong, such designs provide useful *estimates* of program impact. Very often, quasi-experimental designs provide the only viable evaluation strategies for many public relations programs.

BUDGET, TIMING, AND DESIGN

Ideally, research design decisions should seek to optimize the quality of information obtained to permit the best informed decisions about programs. When program impact is evaluated, true experimental designs in a field setting are ideal. Quasi-experimental designs are used when circumstances prohibit the use of true experimental designs. Often, however, other pragmatic factors affect design decisions. In an organizational setting, these other factors are very important elements of design decisions.

Research Budgets

As David Clavier of Husk Jennings Overman Public Relations puts it, "you don't want to spend more asking the question than the answer's worth." Budget constraints are a major factor in considering design options. Often the most rigorous and precise answer to a research question is provided by the most expensive design option. Therefore, your first step in making a design decision is to assess the value of the information sought. This is no easy task. Often, the information sought will help you and other managers make decisions. What is the dollar value of an informed decision? What are the consequences of making an uninformed decision?

Because these assessments of the value of informed decisions are difficult to make, some practitioners make the mistake of not conducting research. Clavier describes such decisions due to cost as "the first 'cop out' for not doing research at all." But Clavier cautions, "By not doing anything at all, we've saved the company maybe $2,000 in research costs but we've made an uninformed decision. Uninformed decisions can easily wipe out any such savings."

Are there any rules of thumb to guide research budget decisions? Lloyd Kirban of Burson-Marsteller points out that his firm holds research costs to less than 8 to 10 percent of total budget. This is a reasonable figure to use. First, the 9 to 1 ratio of program to research costs insures that the "tail doesn't wag the dog." Research costs are capped so that they never exceed a small fraction of overall cost. Second, because a top public relations firm uses that rule, it serves as expert endorsement of that figure. On the other hand, such a percentage is too low when a test market or pilot project is undertaken. When testing or piloting a new product, service, or program, research costs overshadow implementation costs because research is generally the sole reason for the test in the first place.

Over the long run, you need a strategy for building research costs into ongoing operating costs of the public relations department. Clavier notes that major research questions must be figured into the annual budget:

> *We know that during that projected time period other questions,*
> *maybe of more importance, are going to raise their heads. We've*
> *got to deal with them. You can plan out the big long-term research*

projects. But you have to have some kind of resources to deal with short-term, specific research questions as they come up.

The creation of "slack resources" for emerging, short-term research questions requires both a commitment to research within the public relations unit as well as the education of other managers as to the importance of public relations research. Key to that education of other managers is the successful use of research in the ongoing operations of the public relations unit and in counseling management on issues related to their operations.

Time Frame

As with research costs, timing limits research design choices. Just as the most rigorous and precise answer to a research question often costs the most, so too the superior research design may take the longest time to implement. But if the answer to a research question provides input to management decision making, a late answer may be of no value at all. Often decisions have to be made in a collapsed time frame. Knowing that time frame is key to decisions about design.

The first step is to determine when a decision must be made. If a decision is to be made within ten days, then such observation techniques as a large sample survey may be precluded. Limitations on observation techniques impact design decisions. Indeed, a focus group study or two may be the only observation techniques that can satisfy the time constraints. Limitation to this mode of observation also impacts design decisions.

The second step is to list all the design options that can be implemented within the time frame. The final step is to make trade-offs between design rigor, cost, and timing. It's key to realize that the least desirable option is to make a wholly uninformed decision. While the design chosen may not be optimum in terms of methodological rigor, it does provide some information that incrementally improves the quality of decisions by improving the quality of the information upon which decisions are based.

Understanding the Design

A third issue to consider is the ability of other members of the management team to understand the research design. A key question to ask yourself is: "How will I explain research findings to the management team?" Managers will have more confidence in your answer to a research question if they understand how the study was designed. As with budget and timing, the most rigorous design may be the one most difficult to explain. As a consequence, a trade-off should be made between design rigor, on the one hand, and design comprehension on the other. If a design option can't be explained to other managers in a manner that they can understand, then a simple design may be better for your organization.

CHAPTER 6

SAMPLING THE POPULATIONS

Frank Walton, PhD, President, RESEARCH AND FORECASTS,
INC., New York.

URPR: Outline how you approach sampling for your
surveys.

Walton: *If you want to do a survey that will be projectable to
some population, then there are strict methods, sample
sizes, and things to be concerned about. You can usually find local experts to help you with those things—
at a marketing research firm or at the local university.
The first question is: "Who should be in the sample?"
The second question is: "How many do you need?" You
have to focus on **who** you want to hear from or learn
about. For example, we got fairly far along in the design of a survey of physicians before we found out that
the client's product would not be used by maybe half
of the designated specialties. So here we were designing
a study in which half of our sample was going to be
worthless because we had planned to use the usual lists
of doctors to draw the sample. Once we learned that
only certain types of doctors would be involved, we
were able to cut out the other specialties. We also
learned that our client distributes the product in question only in the Northeast, North Mid-Central, and
West Coast regions of the country—with little distri-*

*bution in other regions. So in terms of the sample, it certainly was **not** all doctors. Rather, it was a few specialties in designated parts of the United States.*

URPR: Once you precisely define who you should include in the sample, what is your strategy for setting sample size?

Walton: *In social science methods literature, there are standard tables that indicate reliability of data. You can show your boss or client that if you interview 500, then you have a margin of error of five points—which means that we could find percentages of plus or minus five points if the survey were repeated tomorrow. You then ask, "Is that all right with you, or do you want it more reliable than that? Or can you stand plus or minus ten points of variation?" So whatever fits their **budget** and their concept of what is acceptable variability determine sample size. You have to find out what is **acceptable** and **affordable**. There is no "right answer" to the sample size question.*

URPR: How do you deal with the problem of people being enamored by large sample size, regardless of how the sample is selected?

Walton: *You can always use appeals to authority—in this case, the **industry standards**. You can easily cite for most publics the acceptable sample sizes in the industry. For example, for the Lou Harris **BusinessWeek** poll of CEOs, it's something like 75 to a 100, so that is the industry standard for CEOs. Let's face it, you can't get them on the phone. There are practical reasons why you don't even try to do more. For doctors, as another case, there are standards based on what the major research companies do and what the American Medical Association does when it polls its own members.*

URPR: Often your clients want to know about subsets of the population sampled. For example, the client may want to know employee opinions at each of ten widely scattered plant locations—in addition to the overall picture.

Walton: *If you are interested in knowing about a large number of subgroups in a heterogeneous population, then you may need a very large sample. In order to get enough people in each subsample, you may need 5,000 in the general sample.*

Many times you are unable to survey every member of a public or analyze all the media coverage of your organization. You must then select what you want to be a representative *sample* of the public or media reports. Based on the information gathered from the sample, you then make estimates about the entire public or media coverage.

Sampling requires careful attention to several methodological issues in order to avoid unrepresentative data and misleading pictures of reality. The objective of sampling is to select a representative subset of the population you want to know about.

Who should be included in the sample? How large should the sample be? To answer these questions, a basic understanding of sampling is needed. In this chapter, we first consider whether to sample at all. Sometimes, small publics permit the practitioner to conduct a census of the entire public. If time and cost prohibit a census, then different sampling strategies must be considered. All sampling techniques fall into one of two categories: nonprobability sampling and probability sampling. Although nonprobability samples have some useful applications, they do not permit precise knowledge claims about publics from which they are drawn. As detailed in a later section, inferential knowledge claims from samples to publics are extremely important. Such knowledge claims can only be made from probability samples. That's because probability samples—unlike their nonprobability counterparts—allow us to estimate the reliability or representativeness of the sample. For this reason, probability samples are sometimes called representative samples. Different types of probability and nonprobability samples are defined. Then sampling strategies are spelled out for applications in public relations research.

WHO TO INCLUDE IN THE STUDY

The first step in sampling is selecting precisely who to include and exclude. Useful concepts in making these selection decisions are the universe and the population of study. Although population and universe are often used interchangeably, a distinction can be drawn. The *universe* of study is relatively abstract. For example, the universe for a survey might be defined as "American adults." The *population* for that same study would be more precisely defined, in greater detail. The population might be defined as "native or naturalized citizens of the U.S. over seventeen years old and currently residing in the fifty states." These are the people who will actually be surveyed.

Further, in public relations, you are not solely interested in studying people. Sometimes you are interested in studying media content, such as newspaper articles that involve your organization. When newspaper clippings are under study, the *universe* of newspaper clippings is defined as *all* newspaper clippings that mention the organization. However, when defining the precise *population* of study, you may limit the study to newspaper clippings from general circulation daily and weekly newspapers within the metropolitan area where the organization is located.

One reason for carefully defining the population of study is to make sure that all people (or newspaper clippings) studied are relevant to the research questions and information needs that motivate the study. Walter K. Lindenmann, vice president of Ketchum Public Relations, underscores the importance of tightly defining the population of study.

We did a general public survey for a wine industry client with a thousand respondents, a tremendously decent sample size by anyone's ground rule. The sample is representative of the adult population of New York state. But actually, only one out of five people anywhere in the U.S. can be identified as wine drinkers. So out of my thousand respondents, I only had 200 wine drinkers. If my client wants to look at the really sophisticated wine drinker, then that 200 subsample becomes a bit shaky.

A clear specification of the information needs driving the research provides the basis for selecting who to include—and who to exclude. (See Chapter 5.) Once you have clearly defined the population you choose to study, then the issue of sampling must be considered.

CONDUCTING A CENSUS

Not every public is so large that sampling is necessary. For example, a small manufacturing company has 170 assembly line employees. To learn if these workers are reading the company's weekly employee newsletter, the internal communications practitioner decides to have all 170 workers complete a brief questionnaire. A *census* is the collection of information from all members of a population.

In order to conduct a census, you need to identify all of the people (or articles) that make up the population. The units making up a population are defined as *sampling elements*. A listing of all the sampling elements is defined as a *sampling frame.*

Sampling Frames

Generally, sampling frames are notoriously incomplete. For example, the internal communication specialist just mentioned wants to survey all current employees on the assembly line. Her sampling frame is a listing of current assembly line employees provided by the payroll department. However, the particular payroll listing of assembly workers is almost two weeks old. In that time, 6 of the 170 workers are on vacation and don't appear on the list. Further, 5 employees on the assembly line who receive the newsletter are part-time employees. Their names also do not appear on the list provided by payroll.

You should make an assessment of the completeness and currency of any sampling frame used to collect information about publics, media placements, and the like. Technically, the sampling frame defines the actual public studied. Is the public defined by the sampling frame really the one that you want to study? In the preceding example, the internal communication specialist will study full-time assembly line workers not on vacation during the time of the study. The difference between the ideal universe of study and the actual population defined by the sampling frame may not be important. That's a value judgment, based on the purposes of the research.

If the difference *is* important, seek to update and expand the sampling frame. The internal communication specialist, for example, could ask the payroll office for an additional listing of part-time workers on the assembly line, as well as a list of those on vacation. The sampling frame would then become the combination of all three lists. In other situations, updating and expanding the sampling frame to include all members of the universe of study may not be feasible or practical. When this is true, you may have to proceed with the research, keeping in mind that the population studied is *not* the one you originally selected as the focus of research. As we point out in Chapter 13, you should note this limitation in your report of the findings.

Advantages of the Census

The advantage of conducting a census of a target public (or of the organization's clip file) is simple. You gather exact information about the entire population, rather than having to make estimates about the population based on a sample. For example, the director of communications at a major university may study *all* of the newspaper articles that mention the university by name. She may find that the university is mentioned favorably in 63 percent of the articles, unfavorably in 22 percent, and in a neutral way by the remaining articles. Likewise, the internal communication specialist may find that fully 80 percent of the assembly line workers read the weekly newsletter at least twice a month. If the census is complete, if all newspaper articles and all employees in the population are studied, then these percentages are precise descriptions—not estimates.

Rarely, however, is a census 100 percent successful. The director of communications may have missed some newspaper articles that mention the university due to errors in the clipping process. More systematic problems occur when some newspapers are not tracked by the clipping service. The internal communication specialist may only get 142 complete and readable questionnaires from the 170 assembly line workers. This disadvantage of a census affects sampling-based research as well.

Sources of Bias

When a census collects information from less than 100 percent of the population or universe, the missing information is a form of possible *bias*. You cannot be sure that the missing elements are similar to the elements included in the census. When the missing elements are few, the potential bias is small. As the number of missing elements increases, the potential for bias also increases. Are the assembly line workers who do not fill out the questionnaire not interested in the newsletter? Does their nonparticipation make the research findings about the newsletter "look better" than the reality on the assembly line? These are the kinds of questions that you must consider when examining missing elements in a census or sample-based research.

The major disadvantages of census research are time and cost. As the population or universe size increases, the cost of collecting information increases proportionately. The research will also generally take longer to complete, and time is usually in short supply. Fortunately, as numbers of the target public or media placements increase, sampling provides an efficient substitute for census research. Properly drawn samples allow us to make estimates or knowledge claims about the entire population, based on information gleaned from a sample of that population.

Sampling and Knowledge Claims

You may decide not to collect information from every member of a target public, or to analyze every newspaper article in the clip file. This means you must decide how to study *some* members of the target public (or *some* newspaper articles in the clip file) in order to make knowledge claims about the total population.

A *knowledge claim* is a statement that describes the total population but is based on information gained only from a sample or subset of that population. The reliability of the knowledge claims about populations is very much dependent on the type of sampling strategy used. In the following sections, we consider two categories of sampling strategies. First, we discuss *nonprobability* sampling strategies. These sampling techniques permit only a limited and possibly biased understanding of populations from which they were drawn. However, they do have useful applications when the research is exploratory. Next, we consider *probability* sampling techniques. These techniques allow us to use probability theory to make precise knowledge claims about an entire population, based on a sample drawn from that population.

NONPROBABILITY SAMPLING

Nonprobability sampling techniques should be avoided when you are seeking to describe an entire public, wherein a truly *representative* sample is required. However, these techniques are of considerable value in the early exploratory research that practitioners do before launching a major study.

An internal communication specialist may drop by the cafeteria near the assembly line during coffee break some afternoon. She may ask a few of the workers there if they ever read the weekly newsletter. The university's director of communications may pull a few newspaper clips from the front of the file to study. Both practitioners may learn something useful from these samples. The specialist may learn that most of the workers she talked with said they don't read the newsletter because the vocabulary in the newsletter is too complex to be easily understood. The director may learn that, on at least some occasions, her university is described as an expensive private institution.

The samples just described are of the nonprobability type. A *nonprobability* sample is one in which the probability of selecting any sampling element is *not* known. In the preceding examples, we cannot tell how likely it was that any member of the population might be included in or excluded from the sample. This prevents us from determining how *representative* these samples are. Is vocabulary the major reason why assembly line workers don't read the employee newsletter? Is the university frequently described as an expensive private school? Because of the way these samples were drawn, we can't answer these questions. Our knowledge claims about assembly line workers' views of the newsletter and all newspaper articles about the university are of low quality and reliability because of our sampling strategy. The unknown representativeness of the sample and the low quality of knowledge claims about populations are major weaknesses of nonprobability sampling techniques.

On the other hand, the samples just described were easy and convenient to obtain. The samples involved little effort. Both were inexpensive. Each sample was quickly drawn. Convenience, cost, and timeliness are major advantages for nonprobability sampling strategies.

Appropriate Uses of Nonprobability Sampling

Nonprobability samples are useful in scanning and detecting potential problems. The internal communication specialist knows that at least a few workers find the newsletter's vocabulary difficult. This information is especially useful if the internal communication specialist never considered vocabulary a potential problem. When you find something you are not looking for, *serendipity* is at play.

Nonprobability samples are useful precursors to more rigorous sampling and research. The director of communications may be alerted to a potential problem when she sees a few articles calling her university "private" and "expensive." She may then devise a content analysis of the entire clip file for the last three years to rigorously measure the occurrence of such references to the university. The internal communication specialist might add an item about vocabulary to her next readership questionnaire or design a field experiment to test different levels of difficulty. The nonprobability samples play a useful role in helping detect potential problems and serving as the initial step in a series of research activities aimed at measuring the potential problem more precisely and reliably.

Depth interviews, focus groups, and participant observation are all qualitative research techniques described in detail in Chapter 7. These techniques often involve nonprobability sampling. These techniques are useful for detecting emergent and unexpected problems, as precursors to more rigorous follow-up research, and as exploratory research tools. As such, nonprobability sampling plays a useful role in the repertoire of public relations research tools.

Abuses of Nonprobability Sampling

After talking to ten workers in the cafeteria, the internal communication specialist discovers that eight of them said that there are "too many big words" in the employee newsletter. She might be tempted to say that "the majority of the assembly line workers find the newsletter vocabulary above their preferred reading level." Worse, she might report that "about 80 percent of the assembly line workers have problems with the newsletter's vocabulary."

Both statements illustrate a common abuse of nonprobability sampling: estimation of population characteristics from samples of unknown representativeness. You must resist the temptation to make broad knowledge claims from nonprobability samples. Such uses of nonprobability samples lead to misdiagnoses of public relations problems and unreliable and misleading measures of program impact.

As such, avoid nonprobability sampling whenever estimates of entire publics are to be made from the sample. Key research settings where nonprobability sampling is not appropriate include public relations surveys of target publics and program impact measures. While nonprobability sampling may be appropriate in the early exploratory, qualitative research stages of the public relations audit process, the final survey should be based on a census or a probability sample of target publics. Nonprobability samples may also be used in message testing and lab experiments where the impact of public relations activities are studied in a formative evaluation setting. When the impact of the final program is measured in a field setting, however, you need a census or probability sample.

Types of Nonprobability Samples

There are a number of nonprobability sampling techniques.[1] Each technique has useful applications in public relations research.

Convenience sampling is also called accidental sampling. Convenience sam-

---

[1]For further review of nonprobability and probability samples with different examples, see Kenneth D. Bailey, *Methods of Social Research*, 3rd ed. (New York: Free Press, 1987), pp. 87–105.

pling involves selecting any convenient person as a sample element.[2] Criteria used to guide selection do not assure that the sample represents the population of interest.

A practitioner for a major power and gas utility is interested in possible public reaction to a proposed rate increase. He asks his spouse, neighbors, some acquaintances at the bus stop, and his secretary for their reactions to the rate increase. These people provide a quick "seat of the pants" reading of emergent public opinion, but they are not particularly representative of the target public as a whole. The sample is simply a convenient way to start researching the issue of the proposed rate increase—making the survey wording more precise, for instance.

In *quota sampling,* the practitioner selects any convenient person, as long as he or she satisfies a quota requirement. Some key characteristic of the target public is specified; then sample elements are selected to insure that the sample reflects the distribution of that characteristic in the population.[3]

For example, a practitioner wants to sample employees of her organization. The organization is roughly divided equally among clerical, technical, and managerial employees. All three types of employees are to be interviewed about health care benefits and employee communications. The practitioner instructs her interviewers to question thirty employees each. Each interviewer is assigned the quota of ten clerical employees, ten technical employees, and ten managerial employees to interview. Within each quota category, called a *stratum,* interviewers can select any members of the target public at their convenience.

Dimensional sampling is an extended form of quota sampling, where many quota criteria or strata are involved. Generally, an effort is made to insure that at least one individual is included in the sample for every possible combination of the criteria.[4]

Returning to the foregoing example, the health care benefits sample could be modified to include more characteristics of employees relevant to the study. The employees' gender may be an important factor affecting the kind of information employees want about health care benefits. Marital status (single, married, divorced-separated) is also important. In this example, dimensional sampling could involve setting quotas for gender, marital status, and employee category (clerical, technician, managerial). One interviewer might be told to interview a single female employee holding a technical job. Another might be told to interview a married male employee holding a clerical job. As with quota sampling, the interviewer can interview any convenient employee, as long as the employee meets all the quota requirements.

Snowball sampling is a nonprobability technique useful when you can only identify a few members of a target public directly, but members of the target public are likely to know others in that public. A questionnaire is mailed or an

[2]Ibid., p. 93.
[3]Ibid.
[4]Ibid.

interview is conducted with known members of the target public. Respondents are asked to name other people they know who are also members of the target public. In a second wave of information gathering, individuals named by respondents in the first wave are contacted. Successive waves of information gathering can be organized in the same way.[5]

For example, the public relations manager for a business may view single parents as an important public. While a few single parents can be identified through single parent organizations, the vast majority are unknown to the practitioner. Therefore, a mailed questionnaire is sent to known single parents in Wave 1 of information gathering. In addition to other information, the questionnaire asks the respondent to "name five other single parents like yourself" and to provide addresses if known. In Wave 2, single parents named by respondents in the first wave are mailed questionnaires. In this manner, a large sample of single parents can be developed without requiring a comprehensive sampling frame of such parents.

Purposive sampling is also called judgmental sampling. Purposive samples are drawn in a manner that meets the special needs of the research effort.[6] More focused than convenience samples, purposive samples do not use single category or multiple category quotas. Rather, practitioners use their understanding of their information needs and populations to draw samples.

Walter K. Lindenmann of Ketchum Public Relations points out the usefulness of purposive or judgmental samples with hard-to-reach publics:

> *It becomes acceptable to interview only 75 chief executive officers, because nobody can get them and there aren't that many CEOs anyway. Statistical margins of error do not apply to that type of sample. What happens is that people mix up random samples with purposive or judgmental samples. The judgmental sample is used when you are targeting in on special people for a particular purpose.*

For example, a large industrial manufacturer is planning to open a new plant in a new city. In the past, the manufacturing firm has been criticized by active publics claiming that pollutants generated by the company's plants have increased the risk of birth defects in the surrounding communities. Pregnant women are viewed as a potential active public who might oppose the new plant.[7]

The public relations manager wants to take some preliminary readings of public opinion in the new city, especially among pregnant women. She therefore commissions a quick survey of women as they exit maternity clothes stores in the

---

[5]Ibid., p. 95.

[6]Ibid., p. 94.

[7]For a detailed explanation of active publics and factors leading to activism, see James E. Grunig and Todd Hunt, *Managing Public Relations* (New York: Holt, Rinehart and Winston, 1984), pp. 143–59.

new city. This sampling strategy yields a large number of pregnant women from the target city and serves as a useful initial test of the waters of public opinion there.

The five nonprobability samples described here are useful preliminary measures of public knowledge, opinions, and behavior. They are generally quicker and less expensive than the probability sampling techniques described following. However, nonprobability samples are not necessarily representative of the population that the practitioner seeks to understand.

David Clavier, executive director of Husk Jennings Overman Public Relations, argues that nonprobability samples are often the only means available to study difficult-to-reach populations. "You have to accept a non-representative sample as a limitation to your study," he concludes.

As such, you cannot make knowledge claims about the larger publics from which nonprobability samples are drawn. Reliable knowledge claims about larger publics are appropriate only when probability sampling techniques are used.

THE POWER OF PROBABILITY SAMPLING

Probability samples are drawn in such a way that the probability of selecting any particular sampling element is *known*.[8] This allows the use of powerful statistical tools to estimate characteristics of the overall public based on relatively small samples.

For example, Children's Hospital is a nonprofit institution in San Diego providing specialized medical care to children. In an age of rapid commercialization of medical care and aggressive marketing by for-profit hospitals, the managers of Children's Hospital are concerned that parents know that Children's Hospital is a nonprofit organization. Donations and fund-raising are premised on the hospital's nonprofit status. James Boylan, the hospital's vice president who oversees marketing and public relations, wants to know how many of the 250,000 parents in San Diego County are aware of the hospital's nonprofit status.

Boylan has neither time nor money to attempt a census of all 250,000 parents. Using a telephone survey technique called random digit dialing (RDD), Boylan draws a probability sample of households with telephones.[9] (Listed and unlisted numbers are sampled; "parents" are identified by the first screening

---

[8]Sonia R. Wright, *Quantitative Methods and Statistics: A Guide to Social Research* (Beverly Hills, Calif.: Sage Publications, 1979), p. 17. For an easy-to-understand introduction to sampling and statistics, see Frederick Williams, *Reasoning With Statistics: How to Read Quantitative Research,* 3rd. ed. (New York: Holt, Rinehart and Winston, 1986).

[9]For a comprehensive discussion of random digit dialing (RDD), including techniques for generating random digit phone numbers in your community, see James H. Frey, *Survey Research by Telephone* (Beverly Hills, Calif.: Sage Publications, 1983), pp. 67–77. See also Paul J. Lavrakas, *Telephone Survey Methods: Sampling, Selection, and Supervision* (Newbury Park, Calif.: Sage Publications, 1987). See also Appendix F in this book.

question. See Appendix F.) More than 95 percent of households have telephones, so his sample frame closely matches his target public—all parents living in the community. From a sample of 300 parents, he learns that 40 percent of the respondents are aware of the hospital's nonprofit status.

What does he know about the overall public from which the sample was drawn? Boylan knows that any probability sample he draws can overestimate or underestimate the level of awareness in the larger community. But, through probability statistics, Boylan also knows that the actual level of community awareness of the hospital's nonprofit status is *probably no less than 34 percent* and *no greater than 46 percent* among parents in San Diego County.

How does Boylan know this? How confident is he that his sample percentages are "right"? To answer these questions, and to understand the full power of probability sampling, you must first understand how *inferences* about populations can be made from relatively small samples.

STATISTICAL INFERENCE FROM SAMPLES TO POPULATIONS

What is a statistical inference? *An inference is a knowledge claim about a population that is based on a small probability sample drawn from that population.* We infer, in the preceding example, that about 40 percent of the parents in the county (the population of interest) are aware of the hospital's nonprofit status, because 40 percent of the respondents in the sample know about the hospital.

However, we are not sure the actual percentage is exactly 40 percent. The only way to be exact is to ask all 250,000 parents if they are aware of the hospital's nonprofit status. The managers of Children's Hospital don't really care if the percentage is *exactly* right, however. A close *estimate* is all they need to determine if nonprofit awareness is a significant public relations problem or not. A probability sample provides such a good estimate, as long as the sample is large enough to satisfy the need for accuracy.

ACCURACY OF INFERENCES AND SAMPLE SIZE

The Children's Hospital example illustrates how inferences are made from samples to populations and how the sample size affects the accuracy of estimates of populations. Suppose we draw a probability sample of ten parents at random from among all the telephone numbers of parents in San Diego County. A survey of those ten parents might show that seven of them are aware of Children's nonprofit status. The inference from this sample is that 70 percent of San Diego County parents are aware of the hospital's nonprofit status. Intuitively, most of us would be reluctant to accept this inference, because so few parents were surveyed.

Suppose we draw another probability sample of ten parents and surveyed them. The second sample includes only four parents who are aware of the hospital's nonprofit status, while six are not aware. This percentage, 40 percent, agrees with the percentage from the sample of 300 in Boylan's own survey. But again, a sample of ten does not inspire much confidence in our ability to estimate the level of awareness among 250,000 parents throughout the county. You can see that if we drew successive samples of ten parents, and interviewed each parent in the sample, our results would vary considerably.

Figure 6–1 shows the kind of results we found when twelve samples of ten parents were surveyed. In the first survey of ten parents, seven parents are aware that Children's Hospital is nonprofit. In the second survey, four parents are aware of the hospital's status. The results are summarized in Table 6–1.

Figure 6–1   Twelve samples of ten parents each and their awareness of Hospital's nonprofit status.

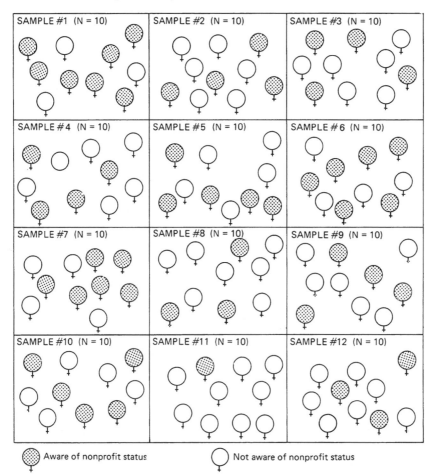

Table 6–1 Summary of Twelve Samples of Ten Respondents Each

Sample 1:	7 parents aware	70% awareness
Sample 2:	4 parents aware	40% awareness
Sample 3:	4 parents aware	40% awareness
Sample 4:	4 parents aware	40% awareness
Sample 5:	5 parents aware	50% awareness
Sample 6:	6 parents aware	60% awareness
Sample 7:	6 parents aware	60% awareness
Sample 8:	3 parents aware	30% awareness
Sample 9:	4 parents aware	40% awareness
Sample 10:	5 parents aware	50% awareness
Sample 11:	1 parent aware	10% awareness
Sample 12:	3 parents aware	30% awareness
AVERAGES	4.3 PARENTS AWARE	43% AWARENESS

The samples differ greatly in the level of awareness they indicate in the target public. Sample 11, for example, indicates that only 10 percent of parents are aware of the hospital's nonprofit status. Sample 1, on the other hand, indicates that fully 70 percent of parents are aware of the hospital's nonprofit status. Our estimate of parents' awareness of nonprofit status basically depends on which ten-person sample we draw. Obviously, a small sample provides unreliable estimates of the target public.

Yet, when we compute the average for all twelve samples, the level of awareness is about 43 percent, only three percentage points higher than the estimate provided by our sample of 300. This example demonstrates an important fact about samples large and small.

The average value for all the samples taken together tends to converge on the actual value in the target public.

The actual value in the population is called a *parameter*.[10] This statistical rule allows us to estimate the accuracy of a sample, based on the size of the sample.

Let's look at the actual Children's Hospital survey results in this new light. Suppose it were financially and logistically possible to do a census of all 250,000 parents in San Diego County and ask them whether Children's Hospital was a for-profit or a nonprofit organization. The results of this census would tell us exactly how many parents are aware of Children's nonprofit status. Suppose our census of the parent population shows that, indeed, 40 percent of all parents in the county are aware of Children's nonprofit status. Figure 6–2 shows an imaginary series of surveys, the distribution of hundreds of samples of 300 as they would fall about the true population parameter of 40 percent. This is the second fact of probability sampling that holds true for all probability samples of all sizes:

[10]Wright, *Quantitative Methods*, p. 16.

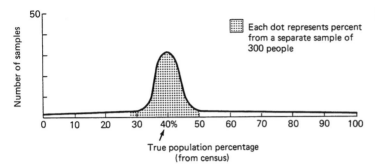

The percentages provided by many samples of the same size drawn from the same population will form a bell-shaped curve around the true population parameter.

As you can see in Figure 6–2, most samples of 300 parents fall very close to the true population value of 40 percent.

As we move further from the population parameter in either direction, the number of samples giving overestimates or underestimates starts to fall off. Extremely high or extremely low estimates occur infrequently. The marks at either of the bell-shaped curve mark off the area that contains 95 percent of all the samples of 300 drawn from the population of parents in San Diego County. We know the width of this area because the bell-shaped curve that many samples form around the true population percentage is *normally distributed.*[11] This is a special term from probability theory that allows us to specify this area containing 95 percent of all samples around the true population value. So here is the third important fact about probability samples:

> *Ninety-five percent of all samples drawn from the same population fall within a specified and known range about the true population parameter. This range can be specified for each size sample.*

What's so special about 95 percent? The 95 percent interval referred to is a *convention,* a number that reflects the level of confidence on which most social scientists like to base claims about populations. To make use of the 95 percent interval, we need to consider what happens when we draw one sample from a population. We never know if our one sample is an overestimate or an underestimate of the true population value.

In Figure 6–3, you see a sample that overestimates the true level of awareness in the Children's Hospital example. That is, the true population percentage is 40 percent, but the one survey highlighted in this example shows 46 percent awareness. This overestimate, however, is within the 95 percent interval.

[11]Ibid., pp. 101–3.

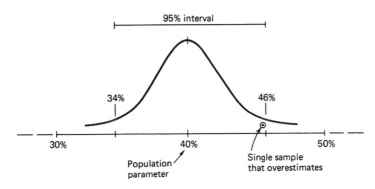

Figure 6–3 A single sample that overestimates true population parameter.

Because of probability theory, we are 95 percent sure that the sample *overestimates* the population parameter by no more than six percentage points. (More about how to look up that information later in this chapter.) In Figure 6–4, we see a sample highlighted that *underestimates* the true level of awareness by six percentage points. But that sample, as well, falls within the 95 percent interval for samples of this size.

So if we combine the information in Figures 6–3 and 6–4 together in a single diagram (see Figure 6–5), we see the real-world problem we face whenever we do an actual survey. We never really do hundreds of surveys as in the imaginary example. The real situation is that we generally draw *one* sample, and then try to estimate the true percentage for the entire population from that *one* sample. In Figure 6–5, our *one* sample of 300 parents indicates that 40 percent are aware of Children's nonprofit status. Is this an overestimate or an underestimate? We don't know. The only way to know for sure is to survey all 250,000 parents in the county.

But we know from probability theory that *if* it is an *overestimate*, we are 95 percent sure that the true population value is no less than 34 percent $(40\% - 6\% = 34\%)$. That is, our sample may be at the upper end of the 95 percent interval for a true population percentage of 34 percent. At the same time, our sample may *underestimate* the true population percentage. Our one sample may be at the lower end of a 95 percent interval for a true population percentage of 46 percent $(40\% + 6\% = 46\%)$.

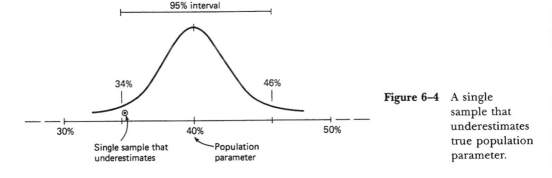

Figure 6–4 A single sample that underestimates true population parameter.

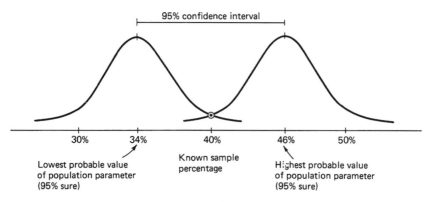

Figure 6-5   A single sample where population parameter is not
                known but inferred.

Regardless of whether we've overestimated the true population percentage or underestimated the true population percentage, we can be 95 percent sure that the true population percentage falls somewhere between 34 percent and 46 percent. We can now make the *knowledge claim* that somewhere between 34 percent and 46 percent of all parents in San Diego County are aware of Children's nonprofit status. This range of numbers is the *95 percent confidence interval,* the margin of error for this sample size.

Where did the six percentage points come from? How do we know what the margin of error, the 95 percent confidence interval, is for a given sample? Fortunately, all the math has been done for us. We simply refer to Table 6–2.

To use the table, we need to know two pieces of information. First we

Table 6-2   Margin of Error Chart For Different Sample Sizes and Different Survey Outcomes to
                Compute the 95 Percent Confidence Interval

| SIZE OF SAMPLE | SAMPLE OUTCOME (PERCENTAGES NEAR . . .) | | | | | | | | |
	10%	20%	30%	40%	50%	60%	70%	80%	90%
100	6	8	9	10	10	10	9	8	6
200	4	6	7	7	7	7	7	6	4
300	4	5	5	6	6	6	5	5	4
400	3	4	5	5	5	5	5	4	3
500	3	4	4	4	5	4	4	4	3
600	2	3	4	4	4	4	4	3	2
700	2	3	4	4	4	4	4	3	2
800	2	3	3	4	4	4	3	3	2
900	2	3	3	3	3	3	3	3	2
1000	2	3	3	3	3	3	3	3	2
1500	2	2	2	3	3	3	2	2	2
3000	2	2	2	3	3	3	2	2	2

Adapted from Earl Babbie, *The Practice of Social Research,* 5th ed. (Belmont, Calif.: Wadsworth, 1986), p. A·32.

need to know the size of our probability sample—300. Next, we need to know the survey results (percent of parents in our survey of 300 aware of Children's nonprofit status)—40 percent. We can now go to Table 6–2 and look up the percentage figure where the row for sample size equals 300 intersects with the column for percentages near 40 percent. The answer is 6. This means that the margin of error, the 95 percent confidence interval, equals 40 percent plus or minus 6 percentage points in either direction—36–46 percent.

Is there a chance that our sample is overestimating or underestimating the population percentage by a greater amount than the confidence interval indicates? Yes! Whenever we use this table to compute the margin of error, we can only be 95 percent sure or *confident* about our findings. There is a 5 percent chance (one time out of twenty) that the true population percentage is actually greater than 46 percent or less than 34 percent in this example. The only way to increase our confidence is to increase our sample size. The only way to be 100 percent sure is to survey all 250,000 parents.

SAMPLE SIZE AND ACCURACY

In Table 6–2, you can see that the accuracy of a sample increases with its size. The sample provides a more accurate estimate of the true population percentage as the sample includes more members of the target public.

But the rate of improvement in accuracy decreases as the sample size grows from 600 to 1,000. Figure 6–6 shows the width of the confidence interval, the *margin of error,* for the sample sizes in Table 6–2. You can see that increasing the sample size from 100 to 200 respondents dramatically reduces the margin of error. This trend continues until the sample size reaches about 600. Then the accuracy—as represented by a shrinking margin of error—doesn't improve much as the sample size increases. This explains why, in major national surveys, samples of 1,000–1,500 are typical. That's because the increased accuracy provided by an even larger sample size is seldom worth the extra expense.

HOW BIG A SAMPLE?

If a probability sample is drawn, how many respondents should be included? As Dr. Walton said in the introduction to this chapter, there is no one "right answer."

If a margin of error of twenty-two percentage points is not too inaccurate, then a sample size of 100 is appropriate. If a smaller margin of error is required, then a larger sample size is required. However, cost is a significant factor. If we think of each interview costing, say, $10 to collect and analyze, then each increase in sample size by 100 respondents increases the basic research cost by $1,000. While a sample of 1,000 provides a slightly more reliable estimate of the population percentage than a sample of 600, the additional $4,000 may not be justified. Whereas the larger sample increases accuracy, you must make a judgment about the cost of the increased accuracy.

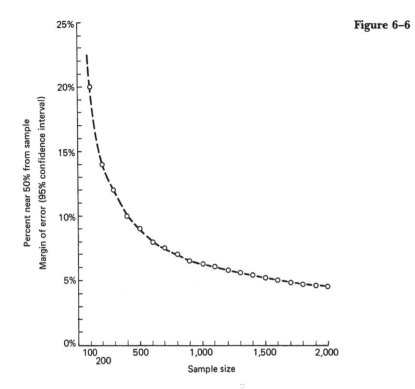

Figure 6–6 Improvement in the margin of error as sample size is increased. Adapted from Earl Babbie, *The Practice of Social Research*, 5th ed. (Belmont, Calif.: Wadsworth Publishing Company, 1989), Appendix G.

HOW LARGE A POPULATION?

Notice that nowhere in Table 6–2 does the size of the population come into play. Surely a sample of 600 can't be as accurate in estimating the population percentage in a nation of 240 million people as it could in estimating the same percentage in a town of 40,000 people! Fortunately, this intuitive argument is wrong. Indeed, once the population exceeds several thousand, the figures in Table 6–2 are valid for *any size* population.

For small populations, consider conducting a census. When the cost of a census becomes too expensive, then shift to a probability sampling strategy and use Table 6–2 to determine the proper sample size. That decision will weight the time and cost of collecting the information against the margin of error required for answering your research question about a population.

TYPES OF PROBABILITY SAMPLES

Random samples are perhaps the ideal form of probability samples, but other probability samples can be used. In some circumstances, these other types of probability samples are more useful or more powerful than a random sample. In the following sections, we discuss each type of probability sampling and illustrate appropriate uses of each method.

Random samples are probability samples in which every element in the target public (population) has an *equal* chance of selection in the sample.[12] A common example of random sampling is to put everybody's name in a hat and draw a sample without looking. Everybody has an equal chance to be included in the sample. In order to draw a random sample, a comprehensive sample frame is generally required. A notable exception is the random sample of telephone subscribers using random digit dialing.[13] This technique permits a random sample of phone numbers without a comprehensive master list of all numbers. (See Appendix F.)

Suppose you want to draw a random sample of 200 from a master list of employees in a corporation that employs 10,000 workers. The names of all employees appear on a computer printout 1,000 pages long with 100 names on each page. Many research methods books contain an appendix of random numbers. (See Appendix G.) These are numbers generated at random by a computer. Numbers taken from these tables can be used as *counters* for selecting sample elements from a sample frame. For example, a list of random numbers can be used to select a page from the employee printout. Then a name from the page can be selected by counting down the page the number of names called for by the counter selected from the random number table. In this way, every employee on the printout has an equal chance of being selected in the sample. For each name selected, each page number and each count of names on the page is selected at random. The sample is random. (If the names are numbered 1 to 10,000, the random number table can be used to select respondent numbers directly. For example, if the table yields 1,741, then go to the employee with that number.)

Systematic samples are similar to random samples and are generally easier to draw. Systematic samples can be used whenever the sample frame is organized in a manner that does not *bias* the sample. To draw a systematic sample, one picks a number from the random number table, then counts down the sample frame indicated by the random number to the name (population element) that serves as the start point. Then skip a specified number of names (population elements) and select a second name. Work through the sample frame, skipping the same number of names after each selection.[14]

Returning to the preceding example, suppose you want to draw a sample of 500 names from the printout of 10,000 employees. To select names at random, you would have to use 1,000 random numbers from the random number table and laboriously look up each name using pairs of random numbers to select first the page, then a name from that page.

Fortunately, you can approximate a random sample by selecting every twentieth name from the printout, starting at some random point. You will end

[12]Bailey, *Methods of Social Research*, pp. 87–88.
[13]Frey, *Survey Research by Telephone*, pp. 58–68.
[14]Bailey, *Methods of Social Research*, pp. 88–90.

up with a sample of 500. First select a number at random between 1 and 20—say 11. Count down to the eleventh name and select that employee as the first sample element. Then skip the next nineteen names and select the twentieth name as your second sample element (the thirty-first name on the printout). The set of nineteen names skipped over is called the *skip increment* or *sampling interval*. Proceed through the list until you draw the sample of 500 names.

This technique is easier to use than random sampling. But serious biases occur when the ordering of the sample frame corresponds with the random start point and the size of the skip increment. For example, many years ago a study of U.S. Army personnel used a sample frame made up of unit rosters.[15] The unit rosters were organized by military rank (sergeants, corporals, and privates). When every tenth name was taken as a sample element, the skip increment exactly matched the location of sergeants on the unit rosters. The systematic sample was devoid of all privates and corporals. When using a systematic sampling strategy, check the sample frame to insure that the ordering of the sample frame does not introduce any biases in your sample. If so, revert to random sampling.

Stratified random samples are used when the target public studied is made up of nonoverlapping subpublics or *strata*. For example, the Children's Hospital survey involved three subpublics or strata of parents. There were parents whose children had never been to a San Diego County hospital, parents who had taken a child to a hospital or hospitals other than Children's, and parents who had taken their child to Children's Hospital. Each subpublic can be viewed as a strata for developing a stratified random sample.[16]

Suppose again that you want to conduct a survey of 10,000 employees, but you know the employees are divided into hourly workers, salaried technical staff, and salaried management staff. The vast majority (7,375) are hourly workers. Another 2,300 are salaried technical staff, while only 325 are salaried managerial staff. All three internal publics are important to your employee communication survey (sample size = 300). Because managerial employees make up less than 4 percent of the work force, a random or systematic sample of 300 will likely yield only ten managerial employees, too few to reliably measure their attitudes toward and use of internal communication.

You can correct for the projected shortfall among managerial respondents by requesting three sample frames from personnel. One printout will list the 7,375 hourly workers. A second will list the 2,300 technical workers. A third will list the 325 managerial employees. You can generate a stratified random sample by sampling 100 respondents from each list, insuring that hourly, technical, and managerial employees appear in equal number in the final sample. Such stratification is useful when key strata or subpublics are likely to be underrepresented in a random or systematic sample. While not every employee has an equal chance of being selected in a stratified random sample, the probability of selec-

[15]Earl Babbie, *The Practice of Social Research*, 5th ed. (Belmont, Calif.: Wadsworth, 1989), pp. 184–6.

[16]Bailey, *Methods of Social Research*, pp. 90–91.

tion within each strata is known and equal. In this manner, stratified random samples are probability samples.

Obviously, your stratified sample is not representative of the true overall public (employees). Managers are greatly overrepresented in the sample, technical workers are overrepresented, and hourly workers are underrepresented. To make valid knowledge claims about the entire public (as opposed to knowledge claims about a particular subpublic or strata), you must first *weight* the individual responses to properly represent the population.

The actual mechanics of weighting can be accomplished by the computer software used to analyze the data. In brief, each managerial respondent is weighted downward by a factor of 0.098. The 100 managerial respondents are treated as if they only account for 10 of the 300 respondents. The technical respondents are weighted downward by a factor of 0.696. The 100 technical employees in the sample are treated as if they only account for 70 of the 300 respondents. The hourly respondents are weighted upward by a factor of 2.2. The 100 hourly employees in the sample are treated as if they account for 220 of the 300 respondents. The weighted responses now represent the different subpublics or strata in proper proportion to their occurrence in the population. Characteristics of the sample (level of awareness of internal communication channels, for example) now represent the overall public (all employees) without bias.

Cluster samples are useful when a comprehensive list of the target public, a comprehensive sample frame, is *not available*. A cluster sample is drawn from a sample frame where clusters of sampling elements are listed. Clusters are sampled at random; then some or all of the sample elements within the selected cluster are sampled.[17]

For example, a practitioner for an activist women's organization wants to sample women active in organizations that support the Equal Rights Amendment (ERA). No comprehensive list of such activist women exists, however. But four national organizations that actively support the ERA have comprehensive lists of all their local chapters throughout the United States. By merging the four chapter lists of the national organizations into a single sample frame, called a *cluster sample frame*, the practitioner now draws a cluster sample. By selecting clusters (chapters, in this case) at random from the sample frame, the practitioner need contact only those chapters selected for the sample. Local chapters can supply membership lists and individuals are sampled from each selected local membership list. Or, the practitioner may elect to conduct a census of each local chapter selected from the cluster sample frame. This sampling strategy differs from stratified random sampling because not every subpublic or strata (local chapters in this example) is included in the final sample.

Because not every strata appears in the final sample, it is important to sample many, many clusters from the cluster sample frame. A good rule of thumb is to sample no more than five sampling elements from any one cluster. In this way, to achieve a final sample size of 200 activist ERA supporters, forty chapters

---

[17]Ibid., pp. 91–92.

would be selected at random from the cluster sample frame. Because chapters may vary in size, the final set of responses may be weighted to correct for the implicit underrepresentation of respondents from large chapters and the overrepresentation of respondents from small chapters.

Sometimes cluster samples involve several sample frames, one nested inside another. For example, in sampling residents in a city, first a random sample may be drawn of census tracts. Second, city blocks are sampled from within each census tract selected. Third, households are sampled from each city block selected. And fourth, a particular respondent is sampled from within each household (second oldest male in household, for example). This is referred to as *multistage cluster sampling*.[18] Multistage cluster sampling, like simple cluster sampling, is a technique for generating a probability sample when no comprehensive sample frame of sampling elements exists.

COMBINING DIFFERENT SAMPLING STRATEGIES

Each of these sampling strategies can be combined to meet special research needs.[19] For example, you might want to conduct face-to-face interviews with respondents in ten cities where your company manufactures its products. You decide to sample census tracts in each of the ten cities. Because each subpublic or strata (cities with manufacturing plants) is represented in the initial sample, the first stage of sampling is stratified. The second stage involves sampling census tracts within cities. You accomplish this by random sampling or stratified random sampling. City blocks within census tracts and households within city blocks can also be sampled at random. Individuals within households can be sampled using dimensional sampling.

As the sampling strategy becomes more complex, sources of bias increase. However, the statistical elegance of the simple random sample often must be subordinated to the administrative pragmatics of conducting meaningful research within a limited budget and time frame.

[18]Babbie, *Practice of Social Research*, p. 194.
[19]Ibid.

CHAPTER 7

MAKING THE OBSERVATIONS

David E. Clavier, PhD, APR, Executive Director, HUSK
JENNINGS OVERMAN PUBLIC
RELATIONS, Jacksonville, Florida.

URPR: What issues do you consider when thinking about the methods you'll use to gather research information?

Clavier: *To do a good job and to put research skills to use, it's important from a purist standpoint to look at all those things that affect reliability and validity. You select the proper observation technique to ask the right questions and get the right answers.*

URPR: Qualitative research techniques like focus groups are growing in popularity. What concerns do you have about qualitative techniques simply confirming your own biases and assumptions?

Clavier: *Before you lock in on any method, you have to try to identify your own bias and biases already inherent in the problem and the process. Otherwise, you're right. You'll get caught either consciously or unconsciously setting up a project that will give you the answer that you want from day one.*

URPR: Tell us about focus groups.

Clavier: *The advantage of focus groups is probably timeliness—the speed of delivery of that technique. You can test a message very quickly and get a lot of good subjective data that can then be used to identify potential major problems or to confirm positive directions that staff predicted but had not confirmed out in the field. Focus groups are a quick way to get a field test. But focus group findings are not the most generalizable. In the hierarchy of research techniques, focus groups would not be on the highest step.*

URPR: Much has been said about quantitative versus qualitative observation techniques. But isn't the real issue the quality of research regardless of technique?

Clavier: *Absolutely. In other organizations, I've heard people say, "I've talked to some people and those people believe that. . . ." They have formed an opinion based on that. But as soon as I hear those words, I turn off. The vagueness creates more questions for me. I need to know more about the people they talked to. Was it a representative sample of the people involved? Was there any bias introduced in the way you talked to them about this issue? If you're using qualitative analysis for major business decisions, you'd better have a good explanation for how you collected the data, where it came from, and whether it's valid.*

URPR: The large sample survey is perhaps the most familiar method of gathering information.

Clavier: *There are many questions for which surveys are inappropriate. However, surveys are still probably one of the most viable forms of communication research that you can use. There are advantages to surveys that are unspoken. It's easy to find and describe results of surveys in a form that people can understand.*

URPR: Large sample surveys are costly. What do you do to get around the cost problem?

Clavier: *One excellent cost-saving method is to piggyback surveys with others in the organization. For one of our clients, we wanted to measure entry in the market for a share of certain services. We needed to know if the images we were trying to project as a new entry in the market were being received and believed. As part of the market data gathering, survey research was involved. So we coordinated with the marketing depart-*

ment to ensure that our measures of key communica-
tion points were included in their survey.

In this chapter, we consider the range of observation techniques for conducting research in public relations. These scientific methods of *observation* are systematic and standard procedures for collecting information.[1] As will become apparent, each observation technique has strengths and weaknesses that make it appropriate for some research questions and settings, but not for others.

When making scientific observations, we need to decide on the unit of observation. The *unit of observation* is the object to be measured. Often, members of publics are the unit of observation. But newspaper articles and television news stories may also be units of observation. Sometimes, organizations may be the unit of observation. Prior to implementing a study, you need to decide on the appropriate unit of observation.

Some methods of observation are *unobtrusive,* meaning that the act of observation in no way effects the unit observed. This is important, because obtrusive measures (also called *reactive measures*) can change the very thing you are trying to observe.[2] For example, if you ask someone if they have ever heard of your company, the very act of asking affects awareness of the company. An important unobtrusive observation technique is content analysis.

CONTENT ANALYSIS

Media relations and placement of mass media messages about the organization make up a large portion of a practitioner's working day. The ubiquitous clip file has long served as a measure of the productivity of the public relations department or firm. For these reasons, the content of messages about your organization is important to describe and analyze. Paradoxically, the more effective you are at placements, the more difficult the task of describing and interpreting that content to members of the management team. That's because the sheer volume of content about your organization makes description and analysis more complex.

Content analysis is the objective, systematic, and quantitative description of the content of documents, including print media and broadcast media coverage.[3] This is a rather strict definition, because it excludes casual and informal content analysis described in Chapters 2 and 6. The purpose of content analysis is to describe the content of documents (including audio and videotapes of broadcast coverage) using quantitative measures.

For example, your organization has received substantial media coverage over the last twelve months on two fronts. First, your Adopt-A-School program

[1]Fred N. Kerlinger, *Foundations of Behavioral Research,* 2nd ed., (New York: Holt, Rinehart and Winston, 1973), p. 478.

[2]Eugene J. Webb, Donald T. Campbell, Richard D. Schwartz, Lee Sechrest, and Janet B. Grove, *Nonreactive Measures in the Social Sciences,* 2nd ed. (Boston: Houghton Mifflin, 1981).

[3]Bernard Berelson, "Content Analysis," in *Handbook of Social Psychology,* ed. Gardner Lindzey (Cambridge, Mass.: Addison-Wesley, 1954), p. 489.

has received considerable coverage, because your company provides extensive support to an inner city school with a large minority enrollment. Second, your factory has received considerable coverage for potential air and water quality violations. How much coverage has each topic received? Are some publications and TV stations emphasizing one topic more than the other? Are the pollution stories receiving more prominent play than the Adopt-A-School stories? How balanced or fair are the pollution stories? What other topics involving your company have received coverage during the last year?

Unit of Observation

To answer these questions effectively, quantitative measures are required. The first step is to determine the unit of observation. One reasonable choice would be to treat each story that mentions your company as the unit of observation. Each story then becomes a *case,* a single unit of observation that can be categorized by a number of variables. In other instances, you might use a smaller unit of observation like each paragraph or sentence in a story. Or you might elect to treat the publication or TV station's news program as the unit of observation. The appropriate unit of observation is dictated by the research question you want to answer.

Manifest and Latent Content

The next step is to identify the relevant variables to observe for each unit. The specifics of measurement are detailed in Chapter 8. In this chapter, the focus is on content analysis as an observation technique. Content can be classified as either manifest or latent. In this example, the topic of the story (pollution, Adopt-A-School, other) is manifest content. When we seek to determine the balance or fairness of the pollution coverage, we are dealing with the *latent* content or underlying meaning of a story.

Whether manifest or latent content is involved, the units of observation are assigned to code categories. *Code categories* are a set of systematic rules for assigning numeric values to different categories of variables.

Coding and Intercoder Reliability

When manifest content is involved, judgments made by the *coder* (the person who reads the articles and assigns values to the variables) are likely to be relatively reliable. When latent content is involved, reliable observation is more difficult. For example, balance is more difficult to reliably observe than story length. Further, some methods of observing balance are more reliable than others. One indication of balance is whether your company spokesperson was quoted in the article. Stories that only quote the regulatory officials monitoring plant pollution, for example, are judged to be unbalanced. Another indication is the coder's personal judgment of whether the story is fair or unfair. This is subjective and therefore may not be a very reliable observation of balance.

Often, however, such evaluations of content are critically important. When that is the case, more than one coder may be required. If the same judgment is made by two or more coders for the same content, we consider the observations made reliable. If coders disagree, our measure is unreliable. Often, a pilot test involving multiple coders will indicate latent content which generates unreliable observations. By discussing differences in judgments among the coders, you can often specify additional *rules* for observing that content. You then retest these observation rules with multiple coders on new content to see if the additional specifications increase reliability. Exhibit 7–1 shows how to calculate intercoder reliability.

Sampling

Chapter 6 provides an extensive discussion of sampling. Those same guidelines apply to content analysis. Sometimes, the amount of coverage permits a census of all relevant documents. Often, the amount of coverage is so extensive that a representative sampling strategy is required.

Other Uses of Content Analysis

Media coverage of your organization is not the only use of content analysis in public relations research. Letters and phone calls to your organization can be important indicators of emerging public relations problems. By developing systematic code categories for such complaints, you can conduct an ongoing content analysis. This can alert you to emerging problems and help you track the success or failure of efforts to alleviate those problems. Organizational records of all kinds also generate documents that can be analyzed. All of these are nonreactive observations that serve as the basis for research on media relations as well as indicators of emerging public relations problems. This brief treatment of content analysis can be supplemented by other references.[4]

QUALITATIVE AND QUANTITATIVE RESEARCH

The debate continues among social scientists and communication scholars over the strengths and weaknesses of quantitative and qualitative research.[5] Indeed, new interest in qualitative research has even affected research in public rela-

---

[4]For a comprehensive review of content analysis, see Robert P. Weber, *Basic Content Analysis* (Beverly Hills, Calif.: Sage Publications, 1985). See also Guido H. Stempel, III, "Content Analysis," in *Research Methods in Mass Communication,* eds. Guido H. Stempel, III, and Bruce H. Wesley (Englewood Cliffs, N.J.: Prentice Hall, 1981), pp. 119–31. A more generic treatment is provided in O.R. Holsti, *Content Analysis for the Social Sciences and Humanities* (Reading, Mass.: Addison-Wesley, 1969).

[5]Clifford G. Christians and James W. Carey, "The Logic and Aims of Qualitative Research," in *Research Methods in Mass Communication,* eds. Guido H. Stempel, III, and Bruce H. Wesley (Englewood Cliffs, N.J.: Prentice Hall, 1981), pp. 342–62.

EXHIBIT 7–1

How to Compute
Intercoder Reliability

A simple formula for computing intercoder reliability is provided by Ole R. Holsti in his book, *Content Analysis for the Social Sciences and Humanities* (Reading, Mass.: Addison-Wesley, 1969). The formula is based on a reliability test where two coders simultaneously code a set of items according to the code category rules. The formula is:

$$\text{Reliability} = \frac{2M}{N1 + N2}$$

M is the number of cases where the two coders agree in their classification. $N1$ is the number of cases coded by coder 1, and $N2$ is the number of cases coded by coder 2.

Suppose you are coding newspaper articles about your company. You code stories using the following code categories, with the following outcome:

1.	Pollution Story Unfavorable Toward Company	30%
2.	Pollution Story Neutral Toward Company	10%
3.	Pollution Story Favorable Toward Company	5%
4.	Adopt-A-School Story Favorable Toward Company	30%
5.	Adopt-A-School Story Neutral Toward Company	10%
6.	Adopt-A-School Story Unfavorable Toward Company	0%
7.	Other	15%

You and another coder code fifty stories and agree in forty-two of the fifty cases. Using the formula:

$$\text{Reliability} = \frac{2(42)}{50 + 50} = 0.84 \text{ or } 84\%$$

Scott* developed a more sophisticated measure of reliability called the *pi* index. This technique takes into account that some intercoder agreement can occur by chance. Here is the formula:

$$pi = \frac{\% \text{ Observed Agreement} - \% \text{ Expected Agreement}}{1 - \% \text{ Expected Agreement}}$$

*W. Scott, "Reliability of Content Analysis: The Case of Nominal Scale Coding," *Public Opinion Quarterly*, Vol. 17 (1955), pp. 321–25.

Percent Expected Agreement is computed by squaring, then summing, the observed outcomes in the preceding list:

$$(0.3)^2 + (0.1)^2 + (0.05)^2 + (0.3)^2 + (0.1)^2 + (0)^2 + (0.15)^2 = 0.225$$

That is, given the foregoing code category outcome, we would expect agreement 22.5 percent of the time by chance alone. Plugging numbers into the *pi* index formula:

$$pi = \frac{0.84 - 0.225}{1 - 0.225} = 0.794$$

This provides a corrected measure of reliability that removes the chance agreement of the coders.

---

tions.[6] These quantitative versus qualitative discussions often involve deep philosophical concerns about the nature of knowledge. But we do not delve into those issues here. Rather, we look at qualitative and quantitative research as different approaches to scientific observation. Then, we outline the strengths and weaknesses of each. Last, we provide examples of the use of each observation technique in the public relations context.

Intensive Observation

Qualitative observation techniques usually involve *intensive observation*. Intensive observation means that only a few cases are examined, but they are examined in great detail. Because only a few units of observation are involved, reliable representative sampling is difficult to achieve. As detailed in Chapter 6, the inferences from small samples inspire little confidence. On the other hand, most qualitative observation techniques gather detailed information from the few cases studied. These techniques are often useful in the detection and exploration phases of defining public relations problems. Each unit of observation is understood in great detail. Such detailed observation is rarely achieved in large-sample quantitative studies.

Further, the units of observation in qualitative research are often studied in naturalistic settings, in *context*. For these reasons, qualitative techniques are frequently employed by researchers using the grounded theory approach to research (see Chapter 5). Grounded theory researchers argue that you are more likely to discover theory by looking at a few cases very carefully, as permitted by qualitative research techniques.

[6]Hy Mariampolski, "The Resurgence of Qualitative Research," *Public Relations Journal*, Vol. 40 (July 1984), pp. 21–23.

For example, your high-tech company is losing top engineers and technicians to competitors. Based on conversations with some of these employees, you suspect that fringe benefits play a role in keeping—and losing—key employees. You conduct a series of focus group studies with about twenty-five of these employees, seeking to explore the role that fringe benefits play in job satisfaction and dissatisfaction. You use the results to suggest several changes in the benefits package. Then you use internal publications to communicate these changes to the employees.

Extensive Observation

Quantitative observation techniques usually involve a large number of units of observation. As such, quantitative techniques are well suited for representative sampling. A sufficient number of observations can be made to permit confidence in the estimates that such samples provide. Because a large number of observations are made, each observation is typically attenuated—few measures are made of each case.

For example, you wish to know how current employees would react to a job sharing plan proposed by an association of women employees who have young children. The proposed plan would allow two employees to share one full-time job, each working part-time. You conduct a survey, sampling 500 employees at random from the 5,000 working for your company. Each is asked only ten questions in a brief telephone interview. That's extensive observation, the brief observation of a large number of cases.

Combining Observation Techniques

Which observation technique—intensive or extensive—is most appropriate? The answer may well be that *both* techniques are appropriate. For example, you might wish to examine stockholder reactions to your company's plan to open a new factory in Korea. While the plan will boost profits, you are concerned about a possible backlash if the move is viewed as taking jobs from American workers. One observation technique you use is open-ended interviews with a small, purposive sample of stockholders. Each interview lasts from one to two hours. This approach emphasizes intensive observation of few cases. Once the qualitative research is complete, you conduct a survey of 400 stockholders, with each interview lasting less than five minutes.

The qualitative, open-ended interviews are a good initial strategy for observing stockholder views in context, across a large number of potential issues. The findings of these qualitative observations suggest key dimensions of the issue—for at least some stockholders. How generalizable are these qualitative findings? To find out, the qualitative findings are used to guide the structuring of the follow-up questionnaire for a large sample of stockholders. The quantitative study is conducted, using an abbreviated, focused, and structured questionnaire to gather information from a large representative sample of all stockholders. The cycle (see Figure 5–1 in Chapter 5) continues if you use focus groups or depth interviews to follow up on survey findings which were unexpected or hard to interpret.

The purpose of the example is to show the logic of inquiry. The intensive, qualitative techniques serve as useful precursors to more extensive, quantitative techniques of observation. Because qualitative techniques of observation are generally more open-ended, they sensitize you to the context of the research question. You are likely to discover new dimensions to the problem and new insights as to how to proceed. At the same time, qualitative findings are incomplete. They are not sufficiently representative to permit estimates about populations.

In the sections that follow, we detail four techniques of qualitative observation—the depth interview, focus group studies, field observation, and Q-sorting. Strengths and weaknesses of each observation technique are considered; examples of appropriate applications in public relations research are provided.

DEPTH INTERVIEWS

This form of observation has roots in the self-psychology of Carl Rogers.[7] A *depth interview* is an open-ended interview in which an individual is encouraged to discuss an issue, problem, or question in his or her own terms. The technique is based on the principle that individuals are the best observers of what's going on within themselves. In applied research settings, depth interviews are sometimes called *individual focus sessions.*

Respondent-Driven Interviews

Depending on the research question, depth interviews tend to be structured by the person interviewed. The interviewee is given a general indication of the issue or topic of interest to the researcher. From that point on, the person interviewed is generally free to explore the issue or question in any manner he or she deems appropriate. You, as the interviewer, encourage such exploration through active listening techniques. When the interview hits a lull, you can facilitate the interview by simply repeating the last statement made by the person being interviewed. The idea is to let the person explore the issue, problem, or question in any direction he or she chooses.

While the ideal depth interview is driven by the person interviewed, you can vary the amount of directing or structuring. Great care should be exercised to insure that any directing of the interview not lead the interviewee away from his or her frame of reference. The strength of this observation technique is that the interviewee—not the interviewer—structures the interview.

---

[7]The orientation of respondent-centered interviews can be most vividly seen and appreciated in client-centered psychological therapy of Carl Rogers and other self-psychologists. See Carl R. Rogers, *Client-Centered Therapy: Its Current Practice, Implications, and Theory* (Boston: Houghton Mifflin, 1951).

Length of Depth Interviews

Depth interviews last from forty-five minutes to several hours. By tape recording the interview, you can engage in active listening. However, you might find note-taking a useful supplement to the recording. You may choose to impose structure on the interview by compiling a number of issues or topics to be probed during the interview. However, the more structure imposed, the less opportunity for discovery of latent issues.

Depth interviews, like other qualitative techniques, are useful during the formative stages of research. They permit you to examine a particular research question in an open-ended fashion. As such, serendipity is at play. In this context, *serendipity* is the unintended discovery of useful information. You are likely to discover dimensions to the research question that were not originally anticipated. Depth interviews are a powerful precursor to the design and execution of quantitative research. In particular, opinion statements made during depth interviews often provide natural-language items for subsequent questionnaire construction.

Depth interviews take considerable time to conduct. As such, they are generally limited to small, purposive samples rather than representative samples that permit estimates of populations. Skill is required to distill the substantive findings from the ideosyncratic and irrelevant material collected in depth interviews. Further, the process of isolating the important from the unimportant in a depth interview is highly subjective. Therefore, the reliability of observations from any particular depth interview is low.

A Precursor to Questionnaire Construction

Say you are charged with conducting a public relations campaign to encourage greater utilization of mass transportation (principally busses) in a large metropolitan community. You have a working theory as to why some people don't use mass transit. Because of extensive freeways, many people believe that it's faster and more convenient to drive by private auto than to use mass transit. At the same time, rapid population growth is increasing traffic congestion and parking inconvenience. Your working theory is that if people were shown that the private auto is inconvenient (traffic and parking), mass transit use would increase.

Prior to a structured survey of nonusers of mass transit, you conduct a number of depth interviews. You ask respondents to describe their transportation habits and whether they anticipate any changes in those habits. In the course of one depth interview, a respondent mentions the freedom afforded by the private automobile. The respondent remarks somewhat paradoxically, "I don't care if I'm stuck in traffic for two hours; I don't want to give up the freedom I have when I drive myself."

The remark unearths a new dimension to nonuse of mass transportation. Autonomy—the driver's control over his or her own destiny—leads *at least some* people to prefer private transportation over mass transit. Further, the inconvenience of the private auto does not offset this desire for autonomy.

Of course, the remark of one respondent does not provide any indication of the intensity or frequency of this concern for autonomy among the population of mass transit nonusers. Greater understanding will require further, quantitative research. However, the depth interview plays the pivotal role of alerting you to the problem or issue. Without the depth interview, you might not have detected the issue of autonomy at all.

FOCUS GROUPS

No observation technique rivals the growing popularity of focus groups in marketing and public relations research. *Focus groups* are focused discussions led by a moderator and involving six to twelve participants. Often working from a moderator's guide of open-ended questions and suggested topics, the moderator guides the group discussion to elicit qualitative data on knowledge, opinions, and behavior of participants regarding the focus topic.

A focus group session may last up to several hours. While focus group discussions can be held anywhere, they are typically held at special research facilities where the discussion can be monitored by observers through two-way mirrors. Further, most focus group facilities permit audio or videotape recording of the discussion. Moderators use stimuli such as posters, videotapes, and graphic handouts to help guide discussions. Appendix C explains how to do focus group studies.

Flexible Observation Technique

Moderators vary considerably in the degree of structure they impose on focus group discussions. As with most front-end, qualitative observation techniques, the focus group discussion is best suited for unstructured exploration of issues on the participant's own terms. Increased structure in focus group discussions usually reflects an attempt to "squeeze" this essentially qualitative technique for information more appropriately gained through quantitative techniques. This technique works best, however, for detecting and exploring public relations problems or issues, and for pretesting program materials before field tests.

Focus groups offer several advantages to the researcher. First, they are quick. Because small, purposive samples are generally used, research firms can use existing sample frames to quickly draw participants of desired characteristics. A screening questionnaire is used to insure that focus group participants qualify for the purposes of the study. A competent supplier can put together a focus group study in seven to ten days. A final report of findings can be generated within a day or two of the discussion. However, more time is required if transcripts of the discussion are made and content analyzed.

Second, focus group studies are inexpensive. Costs range upward from as low as $1,000, depending on the moderator's fees and the special characteristics of the participants. Participants are usually paid for participating in focus group discussions. Studies of the general public require only small incentives or co-ops of $25 or so. Studies of professionals such as doctors and lawyers may require co-ops in excess of $100. Third, the qualitative data provided by focus groups is rich in context and nuances. As such, focus groups are a powerful tool for discovery of issues and dimensions not fully anticipated at the study's outset.

On the other hand, focus groups are weak in external validity. Limited by small, purposive samples, *focus groups are not suited for estimating population characteristics using probability statistics.* This is partially offset by doing multiple focus group studies. However, increasing the number of sessions does not fully correct for the inherent indeterminant representativeness of purposive samples.

A second weakness of this observation technique is dynamics of group discussion. Often, one participant will dominate the discussion and impose a particular point of view on more timid participants. An effective moderator can reduce this problem by containing the dominant participant and soliciting the viewpoints of less dominant participants. A third weakness is the qualitative and subjective nature of focus group findings. In the process of distilling several hours of discussion into a concise report, the researcher may introduce a number of subjective biases into the process. This danger is reduced by the researcher's open-mindedness during the analysis phase and recognition of his or her own biases. Fourth, the synergistic effect of the group may yield perspectives and reactions that do not reflect any individual's point of view or feelings. Rather, the "data" result from the group and the dynamics of group process. Some issues are simply not dealt with by groups.

A Community Relations Application

Suppose your company has invested more than 1 million dollars in community relations efforts since relocating in a new community five years ago. Your working theory is that efforts supporting community beautification and various arts projects have generated a reservoir of goodwill that the company can draw on during hard times of falling profits and assembly line layoffs. However, you followed a low-key approach in communicating these community relations efforts. You counted on the beneficiaries of these efforts to spread the word.

To plan for future community relations efforts, you conduct several focus group studies of community leaders and the general public. In the course of the focus group discussions, you learn that both community leaders and the general public participants are generally unaware of your community relations activities. The moderator shifts the discussion to how participants feel about "tooting your own horn"—aggressively communicating community relations activities to the public. Most participants indicate that they consider such self-promotion acceptable as long as it's done in good taste.

As with depth interviews, the findings in this example are unexpected. That's the power of qualitative research. Further, the research effort should not stop with focus groups. Now you need to determine, through more rigorous quantitative research, the level of awareness of current community relations efforts and the degree of public acceptance of self-promotion. As with the depth interview example, you are alerted to a significant public relations problem which you were not previously aware.

FIELD OBSERVATIONS

Field observations are a qualitative observation technique that puts you among the public you are studying in a naturalistic setting. This label is an umbrella for several techniques, including field studies, certain types of case studies, and participant observation. What these observation techniques share is the researcher's immersion into the daily lives of the publics studied.

An issue inherent in field observations is the level of participation that the researcher engages in while making observations. In participant observation, the researcher is an active member and participant in the activities of the public studied. In other circumstances, the researcher engages in total observation and carefully avoids participation. In either case, the researcher is seeking to understand the public by immersing himself or herself in the activities of this public. Participation in these activities provides special insight into the public studied. At the same time, participation is reactive. By participating in the activity, the researcher is changing the very thing he or she is seeking to study. On the other hand, total observation is often difficult to explain to the people under study. You have to balance the ethical imperative of full disclosure against your desire not to alter the very phenomena you are attempting to study.

A Community Case Study

A useful variant of field observations is the community case study approach. Walter K. Lindenmann, vice president of Ketchum Public Relations, advocates this approach in public relations when the researcher is seeking to analyze and understand a community or neighborhood. In academia, sociologists have conducted community case studies lasting several years. Lindenmann argues that a community case study can be completed in as little as four or five days.[8] In an example, Lindenmann describes how he came to understand Pleasant Gardens, an urban community in transition. As Lindenmann explains:

[8]Walter K. Lindenmann, "Measuring Public Opinion Through Unobtrusive Methods: A Community Case Study Approach." Paper presented to the American Association for Public Opinion Research, McAfee, New Jersey, May 14, 1985.

The community, to a large degree, is an artificial one, held together primarily by geography, by political structuring, and also by the fact that the centerpiece of the neighborhood is a large 500-bed medical complex. . . . I took a room in a motel located within Pleasant Gardens only a few blocks from the hospital. I rented a car and drove throughout the area several times in an effort to become thoroughly familiar with the physical environment. I ate all of my meals in community restaurants and, as I ate, I conducted informal interviews with other persons who were dining there. . . . I found a large number of "home-for-sale" signs throughout the community and decided to conduct informal interviews with area realtors and prospective home sellers to determine the reason for this pattern. I found a small area shopping center and did a series of informal man-on-the-street interviews with community shoppers. I spotted a laundromat frequented by a large number of Spanish-background housewives and conducted informal interviews in there as well. . . . I remained in Pleasant Gardens for only four days, but during that period of time I interviewed informally a total of 65 residents, either individually or in small groups. Rather than write up my interviews, to save time, I dictated the results of my interviewing into a portable tape recorder. During my brief stay in the community, I was able to talk to most of those individuals in political, economic, and social circles who were labeled by their peers as among the most influential in Pleasant Gardens.[9]

The findings of Lindenmann's community case study are a rich, detailed, and intimate understanding of the character and dynamics of Pleasant Gardens. Subsequent public relations research and programs will be enriched by Lindenmann's qualitative understanding of the community.

Contextual Richness

Field observation provides a richness of context unrivaled by other qualitative and quantitative observation techniques. Even in a depth interview or a focus group discussion, the participant is engaging in a research activity that differs from day-to-day living. Having a Pleasant Gardens resident describe the community's dynamics in a focus group setting is not nearly as rich as actually experiencing the community dynamics directly. Regardless of the level of participation, field observations provide context and nuance for understanding publics that few other techniques can rival.

Field observations require the researcher to gain access to the people to be studied. Often this is difficult to achieve in a nonreactive manner. The more

[9]Ibid., pp. 8–10.

immersed the researcher becomes in the public under study, the more his or her behavior will affect the people being studied. A second problem is the richness and extensiveness of the data collected. Through participant observation, the researcher is exposed to literally millions of pieces of information. In reducing that data, through notes or tape recordings, the researcher introduces a host of personal biases and subjective evaluations. As such, the findings of one researcher's field observations may differ considerably from those of another researcher, intrigued by different aspects of the same research question and viewing the situation through a different set of filters.

An Application in Internal Communication

As director of internal communications, you publish a weekly newsletter and a quarterly magazine for employees of your high-tech manufacturing company. You are interested in how effectively your publications communicate with research and development employees. These specialists, technicians, and engineers indicate in a readership survey that—as a group—they were not satisfied with the publications and were not inclined to read them. You want to find out why.

The company's large cafeteria permits different employees to congregate in groups. The research and development employees have taken over a set of tables to one end of the cafeteria. They congregate there, often bringing computer printouts and other work-related materials to the cafeteria. You have a question about word processing equipment that provides you entrée to the R&D tables. Over the next several days, you join the R&D staff for lunch. You listen to the conversations. You develop an understanding of their attitudes toward their jobs, their perceptions of the company, and—most important—their feelings about internal communication. Their offhand comments about the newsletter and magazine help you identify problem areas and opportunities. More important, you see these internal communication problems and opportunities in the context of these specialists, technicians, and engineers in their natural work setting.

Q-SORTING AND Q-METHODOLOGY

Q-methodology is a technique that mixes intensive data collection with quantitative data analysis. Q-sorting requires subjects to sort opinion statements about an issue, organization, or other object along a "most like me" to "most unlike me" continuum. Q-methodology uses Q-sorting as an observation technique and factor analysis as an analytic technique.

How Q-Sorting Works

Figure 7-1 shows the responses from one subject who arranged the Q-statements from "most uncharacteristic of me" (-5) to "most characteristic of

(A) SELF

uncharac- teristic −5	−4	−3	−2	−1	0	+1	+2	+3	+4	charac- teristic +5
10	22	1	8	14	21	7	15	2	11	5
32	28	4	9	17	27	13	20	3	19	47
48	44	6	12	18	35	25	23	16	29	49
	46	24	38	33	37	31	30	34	41	
		26	42	40	39	36	52	53		
				50	43	51				
					45					
					54					

(B) IDEAL

uncharac- teristic −5	−4	−3	−2	−1	0	+1	+2	+3	+4	charac- teristic +5
36	10	6	2	4	7	17	3	1	5	29
48	26	24	8	13	16	21	19	11	9	31
50	30	28	12	20	18	23	25	15	33	45
		32	14	22	27	35	43	51		
		44	40	38	34	37	45	53		
				46	41	39				
					42					
					54					

From Steven R. Brown, *Political Subjectivity: Applications of Q-Methodology in Political Science* (New Haven, Conn.: Yale University Press, 1980), p. 17.

Figure 7–1 Example of the structure of a Q-sort for the subject's actual and ideal self. From Steven R. Brown, *Political Subjectivity: Applications of Q-Methodology in Political Science* (New Haven, CT: Yale University Press, 1980), p. 17.

me" (+5). The subject, a congressman, sorted the statements two ways. At the top, he sorted the statements as they best described himself. At the bottom, he sorted the same statements as they described his ideal. The numbers in the figure identify specific Q-statements. The Q-statements are a set of self-referent opinion statements. They might include statements like "Nuclear power puts an incredible burden on future generations to care for radioactive waste" or "I balance the risks of nuclear accidents against the higher standard of living that nuclear power provides." Subjects sort the statements on a −4 to +4 or −5 to +5 scale, where the negative scores are "most unlike me" and positive scores are "most like me." As illustrated in Figure 7–1, only a few statements are permitted in the extreme piles. Many more statements fall in the middle piles, indicating that the subject has no strong feelings about those statements one way or the other.

Subjects sort from sixty to eighty statements. The resulting Q-sort is a model of the subject's belief system about the issue or topic under study. Q-statements can be thought of as different colored tiles of opinions. The completed Q-sort can be viewed as a mosaic that the subject has constructed of his or her own belief system, using different self-referent statements. Using Q-factor analysis, similarly organized Q-sorts are grouped together by the computer. Some Q-statements are consensus items—they are scored the same by subjects in different groups. Other statements are discriminating items—they point out differences in beliefs between groups of subjects.

Models of Belief Systems

Q-sorting permits subjects to construct models of their belief systems. While these belief systems are inherently subjective, the description of them by the Q-sort is objective. Further, Q-factor analysis groups different subjects together based on objective similarities in their structure. Thus, data reduction and analysis is not as vulnerable to the unrecognized biases of the researcher. At the same time, the Q-sort itself is a very rich, intensive model of the subject's opinions, beliefs, and values about a particular issue. Thus, Q-methodology possesses much of the richness of other qualitative techniques.

Q-sorting is limited by data analytic techniques (Q-factor analysis) to small, purposive samples. As such, Q-methodology is weak on generalizability. Second, the process of sorting Q-statements can take over an hour, so the technique is not suitable for getting a "quick fix" on a person's opinions. Third, the technique is usually administered face-to-face, so that subjects can learn the sorting technique from the researcher. This reduces its usefulness when the target public is geographically dispersed. For a more detailed explanation of Q-methodology, see William Stephenson's *The Study of Behavior*[10] or McKeown and Thomas's *Q-Methodology*.[11]

An Application in Consulting

Your public relations firm is approached by a Japanese corporation which is considering opening a manufacturing plant in a medium-sized city in the U.S. midwest. The city has experienced economic decline and high unemployment during the last decade, so new jobs would be welcome. However, the factory would be run by a Japanese management team. How would the community leadership react to foreigners owning and operating one of the largest factories in town?

You start your Q-study by conducting depth interviews with business and

[10]William Stephenson, *The Study of Behavior: Q-technique and Its Methodology* (Chicago: University of Chicago Press, 1953).

[11]Bruce McKeown and Dan Thomas, *Q-Methodology* (Newbury Park, Calif.: Sage Publications, 1988).

labor leaders, politicians, and ministers. From these interviews, you distill about seventy statements that you feel capture the range of opinions about the proposed Japanese factory. Then you carefully select twenty-four leaders representing the range of vested interests in the community. Each community leader sorts the seventy statements, constructing a model of his or her beliefs about the proposed factory. These Q-sorts are then factor analyzed, so that people with similar Q-sorts are grouped together. Consensus and discriminating items are identified.

Three groups emerge from the factor analysis, representing three belief systems about the proposed factory. One group, the economic growth group, is generally favorable. Made up of business and labor leaders, they see the factory as providing jobs for the unemployed and enhancing other community businesses through wages. Another group, the doubtfuls, are less positive. Made up of leaders from the not-for-profit sector, they see value in new employment opportunities but question whether the Japanese company will provide support for the arts and other cultural institutions. The third group consists of strong locals who see foreigners as a threat to the community's way of life.

One consensus item reflects an emerging public relations problem. All three groups agree with the statement: "The Japanese aren't going to put anything back in the community the way an American firm would." This suggests that the Japanese firm should undertake an aggressive community relations program to convince their reluctant American neighbors that the company is a good corporate citizen with an obligation to the community.

Research efforts should not stop with the Q-study. Follow-up research, perhaps using a large-sample survey, is needed to determine frequency and intensity of each belief system in the larger population. Discriminating items from the Q-study can be converted into opinion measures on the questionnaire. In this way, the rich belief system models from the Q-study can be used to supplement and interpret findings from the large-sample survey.

THE QUESTIONNAIRE

The questionnaire is the "work horse" observation technique of public relations research. As part of a cross-sectional or longitudinal survey, the questionnaire provides information easily assimilated by other members of the management team. The survey questionnaire is a known commodity. The *questionnaire* is a written, structured series of questions or probes that collect information from publics. The questionnaire guides interviewers conducting face-to-face interviews or interviews over the telephone. (Those filled in by the interviewer are sometimes referred to as *interview schedules*.) Some questionnaires, called self-administered questionnaires, are handed to respondents who fill them out. Mailed questionnaires are a special type of self-administered questionnaire with special concerns that don't plague other forms of self-administered questionnaires.

Face-to-Face Interviews

The questionnaire guides face-to-face interviews. Because a trained interviewer is collecting and coding the data directly, relatively complex branching instructions can be used. Figure 7–2 provides an example of such complex branching or "skip" instructions to the interviewer, based on responses to previous questionnaire items. The major advantage of the face-to-face interview is the rapport that the interviewer builds with the respondent. Another advantage is that the interviewer can show the respondent graphic materials or physical ob-

Figure 7–2   Example of complex branching or "skip" instructions to interviewers for face-to-face or telephone survey.

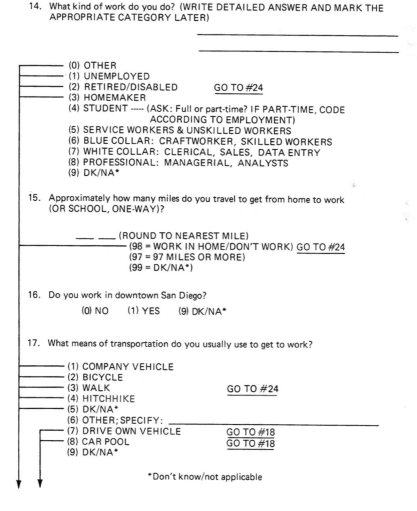

14. What kind of work do you do? (WRITE DETAILED ANSWER AND MARK THE APPROPRIATE CATEGORY LATER)

```
(0) OTHER
(1) UNEMPLOYED
(2) RETIRED/DISABLED        GO TO #24
(3) HOMEMAKER
(4) STUDENT ----- (ASK: Full or part-time? IF PART-TIME, CODE
                   ACCORDING TO EMPLOYMENT)
(5) SERVICE WORKERS & UNSKILLED WORKERS
(6) BLUE COLLAR: CRAFTWORKER, SKILLED WORKERS
(7) WHITE COLLAR: CLERICAL, SALES, DATA ENTRY
(8) PROFESSIONAL: MANAGERIAL, ANALYSTS
(9) DK/NA*
```

15. Approximately how many miles do you travel to get from home to work (OR SCHOOL, ONE-WAY)?

```
___ ___ (ROUND TO NEAREST MILE)
        (98 = WORK IN HOME/DON'T WORK) GO TO #24
        (97 = 97 MILES OR MORE)
        (99 = DK/NA*)
```

16. Do you work in downtown San Diego?

     (0) NO   (1) YES   (9) DK/NA*

17. What means of transportation do you usually use to get to work?

```
(1) COMPANY VEHICLE
(2) BICYCLE
(3) WALK                   GO TO #24
(4) HITCHHIKE
(5) DK/NA*
(6) OTHER; SPECIFY: _____
(7) DRIVE OWN VEHICLE      GO TO #18
(8) CAR POOL               GO TO #18
(9) DK/NA*
```

*Don't know/not applicable

jects that can help the respondent recall information or respond to stimuli. Generally, respondents find it more difficult to refuse a face-to-face interview and to terminate such an interview in the middle.

Disadvantages of face-to-face interviews include cost and time. Of all the techniques for collecting questionnaire data, the face-to-face interview is the most expensive. Further, getting the interviewer and respondent together is a time-consuming process. Another disadvantage is that the physical presence of the interviewer may negatively affect the respondent's willingness to answer sensitive questions or prompt socially desirable responses designed to impress the interviewer.

Telephone Interviews

The telephone interview is a low-cost alternative to the face-to-face interview. The principal advantage of the telephone interview is cost. On a per-respondent basis, the telephone survey is substantially less expensive. In contrast to most face-to-face interviews, telephone interviews can be completed back-to-back. For this reason, telephone survey research projects can be completed in a fraction of the time of a comparable face-to-face study. Sometimes the anonymity of the telephone interview permits the interviewer to obtain responses to sensitive questions. Cost and time factors, as well as computer-aided random digit dialing (RDD), are rapidly making the telephone interview the most popular method of observation using structured questionnaires.

There are several disadvantages to telephone surveys. Because the telephone interview is wholly dependent on the spoken word, the interviewer is restricted in the type of questions that can be asked. No visual aids or other handouts can be given to the respondent. One major limitation is the number of response categories that can be provided to the respondent and recalled. Generally, when the responses are provided in the question ("How do you feel about deregulation of the nuclear power industry. Do you *favor, oppose,* or feel *neutral* about deregulation?"), you are generally limited to three or four choices. More choices may only confuse respondents, who can only remember a few categories when they are provided aurally. This limitation does not apply to face-to-face or self-administered questionnaires. Because of social customs surrounding the use of the telephone, a phone interview is generally shorter than face-to-face interviews. Some researchers, using skilled interviewers, are able to conduct telephone interviews lasting twenty minutes to an hour.[12] We have found that, with inexperienced interviewers, questionnaire length should be restricted to ten minutes or less. Generally, refusals and early terminations of interviews are more likely with telephone surveys than face-to-face interviews. In a study of 182 telephone surveys, a median refusal rate of 28 percent was encountered.[13] This figure was computed as the percent of households contacted who refused to be interviewed.

The speed and complexity of telephone surveys is enhanced by the use of computer-assisted telephone interviewing (CATI). Different CATI systems offer different capabilities. Sophisticated systems provide the interviewer with the questionnaire on the screen of a video display terminal. The interviewer asks the question and types the answer (usually a numeric response) into the computer. In this manner, the survey data are immediately entered into the data base. At the same time, the computer can evaluate the answer and branch in complex ways to different sections of the questionnaire. The principal advantages of this technique are the elimination of interviewer errors with skip questions and branching instructions, as well as instant capture of responses in a machine-readable form. The disadvantage is the preplanning and the hardware-software expense of such systems. The disadvantages of CATI systems are likely to be reduced as software becomes more user friendly.

Self-Administered Questionnaires

Self-administered questionnaires are handed to the respondent directly and filled out by the respondent. Often, these questionnaires are administered to groups of respondents who have been brought together for the purpose of completing the survey. An example is an employee communication survey where questionnaires are administered to groups of employees assembled to, among other things, complete the questionnaire. There are several advantages to self-administered questionnaires. First, the respondent can see the questionnaire items, including long lists of responses. This allows you to ask questions that are precluded in telephone interviews. Second, because you can be there, you can clear up any questions or ambiguities while the respondents are completing the questionnaires. Visual aids and other stimuli can be used to supplement information in the questionnaire. Because of the context of most self-administered and group-administered interviews, the response rate is generally high and the refusal rate low. These same social constraints permit the use of questionnaires longer than would be effective in a mailed questionnaire.

---

[12]James H. Frey, *Survey Research by Telephone* (Beverly Hills, Calif.: Sage Publications, 1983), pp. 48–49.

[13]Frederick Wiseman and Phillip McDonald, "Noncontact and Refusal Rates in Consumer Telephone Surveys," *Journal of Marketing Research,* Vol. 16 (November 1979), pp. 478–84. The average refusal rate was calculated as the percent of contacted households who refused to participate in the survey. Noncontact households are excluded from this calculation.

There are also disadvantages to self-administered questionnaires. Because you do not control the data collection, nor can you clarify and elaborate on confusing items in one-on-one fashion, respondent errors of various forms reduce data quality. A good rule for self-administered questionnaires is *keep it simple.* Avoid complex branching or skip instructions. Simplify questionnaire items. A major problem with self-administered questionnaires is respondent failure to complete all items relevant to them. Attractive page layout and instructional graphics can improve the quality of the data collected. The same social constraints that boost response rates for self-administered questionnaires can also affect the respondent's answers to sensitive questions. Assure the respondent of the confidentiality of his or her responses. The most glaring disadvantage of self-administered questionnaires is that this approach can only be used when you have direct access to the respondents, either individually or in groups. In many research situations, this observation option is not available.

Mailed Questionnaires

The mailed questionnaire is a variation of the self-administered questionnaire. The questionnaire is mailed to the respondent for self-administration. Then the completed questionnaire is mailed back. The major advantages to mailed surveys are low costs and ease of administration to geographically dispersed publics. Through specialized mailing lists, you can survey very small publics (households making more than $50,000 a year, medical doctors, etc.) that otherwise might not be available. Costs of mailed surveys include purchase or maintenance of mailing lists, duplicating, and mailing expenses. Generally, response rates are improved by providing a stamped return envelope or a business reply envelope. As with other self-administered questionnaires, simplicity of the instrument is essential to the quality of data collected. Respondents of mailed surveys have considerable privacy in completing the questionnaire. Further, they can refer to records and other documents in providing information.

The major disadvantage with mailed surveys is that they can be ignored. Mailed surveys generally experience the lowest response rates of any interview or questionnaire technique. Response rates for mailed surveys are affected by many factors. Major factors include the content of the questionnaire, the length of the questionnaire (the shorter the better), the sponsoring organization, and the target public studied. Babbie describes a 50 percent response rate as adequate, 60 percent as good, and 70 percent as very good.[14] However, Babbie's comments are based on the pragmatic limitations of mailed surveys and their low response rates. Low response rates still affect the representativeness of the sample. Other disadvantages include restricting the length of the questionnaire and slow turnaround time.

Other questionnaire design issues are considered in Chapter 8 and Ap-

[14]Earl Babbie, *The Practice of Social Research,* 5th ed. (Belmont, Calif.: Wadsworth Publishing, 1989), p. 242.

pendix D. For even more detailed discussion of questionnaire design, see Converse and Presser's *Survey Questions: Handcrafting the Standardized Questionnaire.*[15]

An Application in Plant Automation

Suppose your company manufactures large electrical motors and generators. In an effort to meet foreign competition, your company is initiating a five-year robotics program, converting many assembly line positions over to robots. A tentative agreement has been reached with the worker's powerful union leadership: no layoffs, generous early retirement for some assembly line workers, retraining and continued employment for the rest. How will the rank-and-file workers feel about the changes? What role can internal communications play in facilitating the change?

You start by holding focus group and depth interview studies with management, stockholders, the union leadership, and selected rank-and-file workers from different specialized parts of the assembly line. In addition, you conduct some field observations by joining some assembly line workers for their regular brown-bag lunches near the assembly line. To further immerse yourself in the lives of the rank and file, you join the employee's bowling league. Using all of these qualitative observations, you meet with key managers to design the survey. Managers don't help you write questionnaire items. Rather, they help write research objectives. These objectives specify what research questions need to be answered by the survey. For each research objective, you ask the management team to specify how that information will be used.

Once you've reached consensus on research objectives, you return to your qualitative research reports to begin constructing the instrument. You use as much of the natural language as possible from your qualitative research when developing questionnaire items. You include items (responsive to research objectives) that were not anticipated prior to the qualitative, front-end research efforts. You consider the various options for administration of the questionnaire: face-to-face, telephone, mailed, or group administered. You opt for the mailed questionnaire option. Anticipating a low response rate, you devise incentives for participation and extensive follow-up for nonresponding employees.

Once the instrument is developed, you circulate the draft to other managers. Then you meet with them individually to solicit their feedback. Inevitably, managers seek to add more items to the instrument. You ask them to specify the research objective that the new items address, as well as the uses planned for that information.

Once consensus is reached on the rough draft of the questionnaire, you conduct a pilot test. You have several groups of employees gather in groups and fill out the questionnaire. Then you go over the questionnaire item-by-item with

---

[15]Jean M. Converse and Stanley Presser, *Survey Questions: Handcrafting the Standardized Questionnaire* (Beverly Hills, Calif.: Sage Publications, 1986).

these respondents. You find some items are unclear; other items are misinterpreted. Several important changes are made in the final instrument.

Next, a representative sample of 800 employees is drawn systematically from current personnel records of the 10,000 employees. The questionnaire is mailed to the employee's home. In the cover letter, you explain that responses are completely anonymous. There is no identifying information on the questionnaire. The employee is offered an incentive of two hours of additional vacation time for completing the questionnaire. The vacation time is authorized through a special personnel card given to the employee when he or she returns the completed questionnaire in a sealed return envelope. After three weeks, you check the number of nonresponses, indicated by the number who have not picked up their vacation cards. A postcard is sent to these households. After another week, nonresponding employees are contacted by phone.

After one month, you have obtained completed questionnaires from 720 of the original 800 employees in the sample. You decide that the responses rate (90 percent of the original sample) is adequate and that the few nonresponses do not threaten the representativeness of the final sample. You conclude the data collection phase of your study. Now you are ready to compile and organize the data. The details of these tasks are described in Chapter 9.

CHAPTER 8

TAKING THE MEASUREMENTS

Larissa A. Grunig, PhD, Assistant Professor, College of Journalism, UNIVERSITY OF MARYLAND, College Park.

URPR: Explain the process of operationalization.

Grunig: *Operationalizing is a trade-off between the kind of rich data that you can elicit by looking at the concept in its broadest sense and what you get when you take it down to something that can be measured with some degree of accuracy. We may be interested in knowing how many people read our publication. But in operationalizing the concept of readership, we are going to lose a lot of that information. Say, for example, that readership means any employee—not that employee's family or outsiders from the community—who reads the publication a certain number of times or a certain number of articles. When we do that, we may not have the rich data you would get if you counted any possible reader or any amount of readership. What we are doing is pinning down the concept so that we can measure it over and over again and not be talking about apples and oranges. Other people interested in studying the same phenomenon can compare their results with ours.*

URPR: Contrast reliability and validity.

Grunig: *Are we asking the questions in such a way that if we asked the question later and the situation had not changed, we would get the same answers? That's reliability. A valid measure is one that taps into the concept we are really interested in knowing about. So if I have a measurement of attitude—say—toward one's work environment, I really should be measuring that rather than—say—the concept of how much one likes one's boss. For that reason, we use scales that have been developed and tested before and found to be both reliable and valid. We don't want to reinvent the wheel.*

URPR: The kind of analysis you can do on research data is dictated by the level of measurement of the variables. Explain why level of measurement is such an important issue.

Grunig: *Any information can be expressed at different levels, from discrete naming of categories—blue-eyed people versus brown-eyed people—on up through very sophisticated levels of measure that include ratio and proportion. The higher the level of measurement, as one progresses up through these levels, the more powerful the kinds of statistical tests that are appropriate. More powerful predictions are possible.*

URPR: As a practical matter, how can practitioners take advantage of high-level measures?

Grunig: *It's better to ask the questions that elicit the measurements that you really want. In most cases, these are* **counts** *and* **amounts,** *rather than the more general categories such as "often," "sometimes," "rarely," or "never." So if you are interested in how often someone is reading a publication, don't attempt to use a five-point scale from "always" to "never." Instead, ask a question that really gets at what you want to know, such as "How many of the last twelve issues of this publication have you read?"*

In this chapter, you will learn how a concept is reduced, through the process of operationalization, to measures of observable aspects of that concept. Once a concept has been operationalized, we're concerned about that measure's validity and reliability. How we operationalize a concept also affects the types of statistical analyses we can perform. The higher the level of measurement, the more options we have. Finally, you will be introduced to several techniques for measuring variables, including counts and amounts, summated scales, Likert-type scales, semantic differential scales, and factor scales.

OPERATIONALIZATION

Operationalization is the process of connecting an abstract concept to observable phenomena in the real world. Operationalization always involves a loss of richness. A relevant example is the concept of communication satisfaction. A theoretical proposition states that as an employee's satisfaction with communication within an organization increases, the employee's job satisfaction also increases.[1]

Let's first consider the concept of communication satisfaction. As a relatively abstract concept, it applies to a number of forms and types of communication within an organization. An employee may be satisfied or dissatisfied with communication with his or her supervisor. Communication satisfaction also involves the organization's communication climate—informal, horizontal communication through the grapevine—and satisfaction with media quality, the formal channels of communication. In all, communication satisfaction has eight different components or dimensions that contribute to its richness as a concept.[2]

The concept of communication satisfaction is one building block of theory. The proposition that communication satisfaction leads to job satisfaction is part of a theory. Other propositions may specify conditions under which the first proposition is true. Together, the propositions make up a theory of communication and job satisfaction.

Figure 8-1 illustrates the process of operationalizing a concept. This figure uses an example of a practitioner seeking to link one form of communication satisfaction to job satisfaction. Jim McBride is public affairs officer for Kaiser Permanente in San Diego. Kaiser Permanente is one of the oldest and largest health maintenance organizations (HMO) in the United States. As editor of the employee newsletter, McBride is interested in satisfaction with the publication itself, as well as the relation between newsletter satisfaction and job satisfaction.

Concepts, Constructs, and Variables

McBride starts with employee communication satisfaction, the more abstract *concept* from which a theory of communication and job satisfaction is built. Communication satisfaction is an abstraction that includes the many aspects or dimensions of satisfaction. For the purposes of his research, McBride is interested in one dimension of communication satisfaction. For his particular research purposes, McBride introduces the construct of newsletter satisfaction. A

[1]For a comprehensive overview of the relationship between communication and job satisfaction, see Cal W. Downs, "The Relationship Between Communication and Job Satisfaction," in *Readings in Interpersonal and Organizational Communication,* eds. Richard C. Huseman, Cal M. Logue, and Dwight L. Freshley, 3rd ed. (Boston: Hallbrook, 1977), pp. 363–76.
[2]Ibid., pp. 369–70.

LEVEL	*EXAMPLE*
CONCEPT	Communication satisfaction—individual satisfaction that come from successfully communicating to someone or in successfully being communicated with.
CONSTRUCT	Newsletter satisfaction—the degree to which the employee newsletter is perceived as a credible, interesting, and useful source of information about the organization and its employees.
VARIABLE(S)	Newsletter evaluation set (FROM QUESTIONNAIRE . . .) Do you agree that the *San Diego Coverage* is a good source of information about Kaiser Permanente programs and policies? 　　[4] ALWAYS 　　[3] USUALLY 　　[2] SOMETIMES 　　[1] NEVER How interesting is the San Diego employee newsletter? 　　[4] ALWAYS 　　[3] USUALLY 　　[2] SOMETIMES 　　[1] NEVER Now I would like your reaction to the information in the San Diego employee newsletter. Do you find it useful? 　　[4] ALWAYS 　　[3] USUALLY 　　[2] SOMETIMES 　　[1] NEVER

The left margin shows an arrow labeled **ABSTRACT** (at top) pointing up and **CONCRETE** (at bottom) pointing down.

Figure 8-1   The operational process.

construct is a concept invented or adopted for a specific research purpose.[3] In this example, McBride invents newsletter satisfaction as a construct to link his employee newsletter to the broader theory of communication and job satisfaction. A construct is invented in a manner that permits its measurement. As such, the invention of constructs is a useful link between the relatively abstract original concept (communication satisfaction) and phenomena we can measure in the real world.

Operationalization is complete when a series of measurement activities are specified for a particular concept. A *variable* is a characteristic or treatment that can vary along a continuum, which assumes different values for different units of analysis (people, placements, organizations, etc.).[4] A variable may be a characteristic, such as sex of the respondent, which has only two values (male or female), or income, which has many values along a continuum. A variable may

---

[3]Kerlinger, Fred N. *Foundations of Behavioral Research,* 2nd ed. (New York: Holt, Rinehart and Winston, 1973), p. 29.

[4]Kenneth D. Bailey, *Methods of Social Research,* 3rd ed. (New York: Free Press, 1987), p. 40.

also be a treatment, such as printing the employee newsletter versus disseminating the same information through a videotape. In each instance, the variable can assume more than one value.

Multiple Measures

McBride has several strategies for measuring the variable he names the *newsletter evaluation set.* By interviewing employees, he can determine how useful they consider the information to be, how interesting they consider the information to be, and how credible they consider the newsletter to be as a source of information. Taken together, these measures triangulate on the abstract construct of newsletter satisfaction. They can be combined to form an index that measures newsletter satisfaction.

The use of multiple measures of constructs helps capture more of what is meant by the construct. All other things being equal, it's better to develop multiple measures of constructs rather than relying on a single measure. McBride captures much of what is meant by newsletter satisfaction when he measures the newsletter's usefulness, interest, and credibility as perceived by employees. Combined, these separate measures make an index that provides a better indicator of the construct McBride sought to measure. As we seek to operationalize abstract concepts, we inevitably capture only part of the information embodied in the original concept. When we look at any variable, then, we should ask: To what extent does the operational measurement really capture the construct of interest? When we ask that question, we are concerned with the *validity* of the variable and the operationalization process.

Types of Validity

There are three ways to argue the validity of a variable which supposedly measures a construct. They are face validity, criterion validity, and construct validity.[5] Primary to all validity arguments is face validity. *Face validity* is the judgment that a variable indeed measures what is meant by the construct. The argument is semantical, resting on the link between what we define a construct to mean and the operations we conduct to measure it. Closely related to face validity is *content validity,* the degree to which the variable captures the various subparts of the construct's definition.

Returning to McBride's measurement of newsletter satisfaction, we define the construct as the degree to which employees regard the newsletter to be useful, interesting, and credible. McBride can argue the face validity of his newsletter evaluation set by showing that he has measured how employees regard the usefulness, interest, and credibility of the newsletter. Since this is what we mean

---

[5]For a more detailed explanation and other examples, see Earl Babbie, *The Practice of Social Research,* 5th ed. (Belmont, Calif.: Wadsworth Publishing, 1989), pp. 122–24. See also Bailey, *Methods of Social Research,* pp. 67–69.

by newsletter satisfaction, McBride's newsletter evaluation set has face validity. Note that we cannot prove face validity, only make a judgment based on the linkage between abstract meaning and the concrete operations we use to capture that meaning in the real world. Looking at how frequently an employee reads the newsletter would have little face validity as our definition of newsletter satisfaction now stands. However, if our definition of newsletter satisfaction included the statement that such satisfaction is indicated by high frequency of reading, then measures of reading frequency would have face validity.

Criterion validity is an argument that a new measure is a valid measure of a construct because it correlates with an established, face-valid measure of the construct. When the two measures of the construct are available at the same time, *concurrent validity* is argued. If the criterion measure occurs at some future time, *predictive validity* is argued. For example, we have an established, standardized intelligence test which we use as a criterion to assess the validity of a new, shorter intelligence test. If individuals taking both tests get similar relative scores, then we argue the criterion (concurrent) validity of our new test. On the other hand, a test like the Scholastic Aptitude Test (SAT) is supposed to measure a student's future success in college. If the SAT correlates with a student's future success in college, measured perhaps by grade point average and probability of graduating, then we can argue its criterion (predictive) validity. In each instance, we link the variable to an established, face-valid criterion variable.

Figure 8–2 illustrates the three types of validity through a single example. The construct is intelligence. The Stanford-Binet IQ test is an established and accepted face-valid measure of the construct. We've developed a short form of the test. We administer both tests to a representative group of subjects. Because

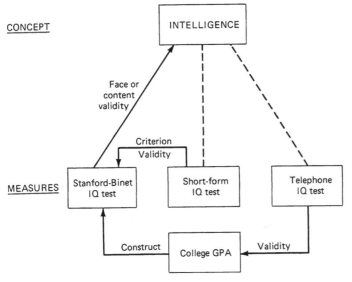

Figure 8–2 An illustration of face, criterion, and construct validity.

the Stanford-Binet IQ test scores correlate with scores on the new, shorter test, we argue concurrent criterion validity.

Construct validity links the new measure to a criterion variable through a third variable. Returning to the example in Figure 8-2, we do a survey of college graduates, measuring their intelligence through a short set of items over the phone. We do not want to have these same people also complete the Stanford-Binet IQ test. We would need to meet them face-to-face, which is impractical. We know from prior research that scores on the standardized IQ test are correlated with college grade point average (GPA). Therefore, we will ask our respondents about their college GPA. If college GPA correlates with telephone IQ scores, then we argue construct validity for our telephone IQ test.

Reliability

Closely related to the validity of a measurement is its *reliability,* its ability to provide consistent results when measuring the same attribute several times.[6] McBride would regard his newsletter evaluation set as a reliable measure if it yielded the same results when one person completed those questionnaire items several times. This is not the same as saying the newsletter evaluation set accurately assesses newsletter satisfaction. That's validity. Reliability is indicated by intercoder reliability, stability, and equivalence.[7] As in content analysis, *intercoder reliability* or reproducibility means that different researchers using the same measures will get the same results when they measure the same object. *Stability* means that, if measuring an object that does not change over time, the same results are yielded. A questionnaire item asking for your city of birth is unstable if you provide different responses to the question in separate administrations of the questionnaire. *Equivalence* is an indication of reliability when multiple measures are used to triangulate on a construct. The items that make up the newsletter evaluation set should yield similar results for any given employee.

Computing Reliability

As with the newsletter evaluation set, the reliability of scales or indices can be computed. This allows you and others using your scale or index to assess how the items in the scale, taken together, reliably measure an attribute or characteristic. For example, three items make up the newsletter evaluation set (see Figure 8-1). McBride adds the responses to these items together, creating an additive scale. If this additive scale is a reliable measure, then people giving a positive response to the usefulness question should also give a positive response to the credible question. If not, the additive scale is unreliable. The computation of

---

[6]Roger D. Wimmer and Joseph R. Dominick, *Mass Media Research: An Introduction,* 2nd ed. (Belmont, Calif.: Wadsworth Publishing, 1987), pp. 59–61.

[7]Ibid., p. 60.

reliability coefficients is done by a computer, because it involves computing all possible correlations or covariances among all the measures.[8]

Tension Between Reliability and Validity

Babbie notes that a certain tension exists between reliability and validity. The most valid measure may not be the most reliable.[9] For example, McBride might obtain a more valid measure of an employee's satisfaction with the newsletter through an open-ended depth interview. After an hour of unstructured discussion about the newsletter and other aspects of internal communication, McBride would have a rich, face-valid indication of that employee's satisfaction with the newsletter. As indicated in Chapter 7, however, such qualitative techniques of observation may not be as reliable as more structured efforts to collect data. The newsletter evaluation set may be more reliable, but may not be as valid as the more qualitative observation technique. Figure 8–3 illustrates distinctions to be made about the reliability and validity of a measurement.

LEVELS OF MEASUREMENT

Social scientists and statisticians classify all variables as one of four types: nominal, ordinal, interval, and ratio. Nominal level variables generally result from qualitative observations. From a statistical perspective, this is the lowest level of measure. Only limited statistical analyses can be performed on nominal level variables. As one moves from lower-level nominal variables to ordinal, interval, and ratio level variables, a wider range of analytic tools become appropriate. In the sections that follow, each level of measure is defined and examples provided from public relations research.

Nominal Level Variables

A *nominal* level variable is one that has categories that are mutually exclusive and exhaustive. That is, a nominal variable classifies each unit of observation into one and only one category. Further, a nominal variable has a category for all possible measurement outcomes. For example, you might want to measure the news magazine preferences of your employees as part of a study of internal publications. You might ask: "Which news magazine do you read *most* often?" The possible responses include: (1) *Time* (2) *Newsweek* (3) *U.S. News & World Report* (4) Other. This nominal variable is mutually exclusive; there is only one magazine that you can read "most often." It's exhaustive because the "other" category allows the respondent to answer the question, regardless of which magazine he or she reads most often. (There is also a category called "not applicable" for

---

[8]See, for example, SPSS, Inc., *SPSS-X User's Guide* (New York: McGraw-Hill, 1983), pp. 717–32.
[9]Babbie, *Practice of Social Research*, p. 125.

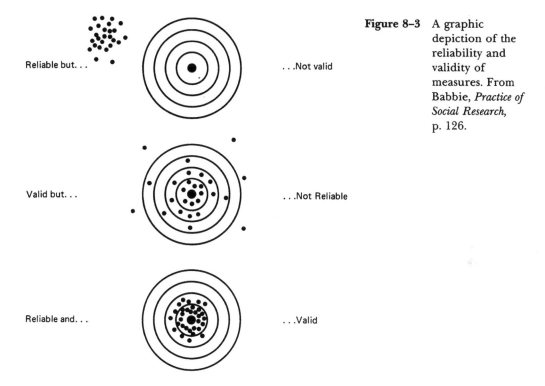

Reliable but... ...Not valid

Valid but... ...Not Reliable

Reliable and... ...Valid

Figure 8-3 A graphic depiction of the reliability and validity of measures. From Babbie, *Practice of Social Research,* p. 126.

respondents who don't read any news magazines; these responses are not included in subsequent statistical analysis.)

In the example, numbers have been assigned to news magazines. However, these numbers are simply stand-ins for the magazine name itself. We err if we treat respondents naming *U.S. News* as having high scores on the news magazine preference variable. The high number that we assigned to *U.S. News* was an arbitrary choice. Likewise, it's a mistake to think that people naming *Newsweek* have twice as much news magazine preference as do *Time* readers. While numbers are used to represent the names of magazines, these numbers can't be treated like numbers that measure our weight or our income.

Another example is provided by the *PR Reporter* "Annual Survey of the Profession," a mailed questionnaire sent to U.S. and Canadian public relations practitioners. Practitioners are asked to identify their employer's industry category. Choices include (1) public relations firm (2) ad agency (3) other consulting (4) bank, and so forth. The last category is: (23) other. As with news magazines, the numbers assigned to various industry categories are arbitrary.

Ordinal Level Variables

Like nominal variables, the categories of ordinal variables are mutually exclusive and exhaustive. In addition, the categories of ordinal variables are ordered. That means that higher-numbered categories have more of the attribute than lower-numbered categories. Typically, ordinal variables involve the rank ordering of categories. For example, you are doing a readership study of the internal newsletter you edit. You want to know which topics your readers consider most interesting to read about in the newsletter. You have identified several topics through focus group studies—news about plans for the organization, personal news about coworkers, news about company policy changes, news about employee benefits, news about promotions, and news about company-sponsored recreation activities. You also include an "other" category. You ask your survey respondents to "rank these topics from *most* interesting to *least* interesting to *you.*" You have them assign a 7 to the most interesting topic, a 6 to the next most interesting topic, and so on. Each category, such as news about promotions, can be treated as a separate variable with each respondent giving that variable a score between 1 and 7. The category with the highest score among all respondents is the one deemed most interesting.

Another example of an ordinal level variable is provided by a consumer relations questionnaire that probes attitudes toward oil companies. Respondents are asked to indicate their level of education by marking one of the following categories: (1) less than high school (2) high school graduate (3) some college (4) college graduate (5) some postgraduate (6) post-graduate degree. Each category represents a higher level of education, but the distance between a 1 and 2 on the scale is not the same as the distance between 5 and 6.

Let's consider a third ordinal variable to appreciate an important characteristic of ordinal measures. The five employees of your company's public relations department are assigned numbers, based on their order of hire in the department. Sara Henderson and Lara Dowd are both hired the same week; Sara was hired two days before Lara. Sara is assigned a 5 on the order of hire variable; Lara is assigned a 4. Due to corporate downsizing, no further hires are made in the department for five years. After five years, Patrick Jones is hired. Patrick is assigned a 3 on the order of hire variable. Two years later, during rapid expansion of the company into new product lines, Eric McDonald is hired. A month later, Larry Steinberg is also hired. Eric is assigned a 2, while Larry is assigned a 1 on the order of hire variable.

Note that the difference between a 5 and a 4 on this measure is two days. The difference between a 4 and a 3 is five years. The difference between a 3 and a 2 is two years, while the difference between a 2 and a 1 is one month. The distances between points on an ordinal level measure are not equivalent. Figure 8–4 illustrates this point.

Interval Level Variables

Categories for interval variables are mutually exclusive, exhaustive, and ordered. In addition, the distances between points on an interval variable measure are equal. The difference between 1 and 2 on an interval measure is the same as the difference between 3 and 4. For example, you run an experiment to see if entertainment-oriented public service announcements (PSAs) are preferred

ORDER OF HIRE VARIABLE

```
1 month        2 years                              5 years              2 days
I---I----------------I-----------------------------I---I
1    2                3                              4   5
Larry Eric           Patrick                        Lara Sara
```

Figure 8–4 The nonequivalence of distances between points on an ordinal variable.

to more traditional information-oriented PSAs. Subjects in both groups are exposed to the same one hour of television programming. Inserted where commercial ads usually appear, each group is exposed to fourteen sixty-second PSAs. In one group, all the commercials have been replaced with entertainment-oriented PSAs. In the other group, all the commercials are replaced with information-oriented PSAs. After exposure, subjects in both groups are asked: "In the next hour of TV viewing, how many *more* PSAs would you like to see?" The more PSAs a subject would like to see, the higher the score on the PSA Preference Scale. Subject A wants to see one more PSA, so his response is 1. Subject B wants to see two more PSAs in the next hour, so her response is 2. Subject C's response is a 3. The difference between Subject A (1) and Subject B (2) is the same as the difference between Subject B (2) and Subject C (3): one PSA. Since PSAs are roughly equivalent to each other, we can describe the intervals between points on the PSA Preference Scale as equal.

Note that if a subject says she doesn't want to see any more PSAs, her score is 0. But zero doesn't mean the complete absence of preference for PSAs. It just means that after watching over a dozen PSAs in the previous hour, she doesn't want to see any more PSAs. Zero, then, does not mean the complete absence of the attribute being measured. Zero is simply an arbitrary numeric designation. This interval variable is similar to measures of temperature using the Centigrade or Fahrenheit scales. Zero degrees Centigrade and zero degrees Fahrenheit do not mean the complete absence of heat. They are simply arbitrary points on the scale. That's why we can talk about temperatures below zero. Objects below zero still contain some heat that can be measured. Centigrade and Fahrenheit measures of temperature are interval level scales.

Sometimes the intervals on a measure are equal-appearing. That is, the points on the measure appear to be separated by intervals of equal size. For example, in a consumer relations survey conducted for an oil company, respondents were asked "how important is it that an oil company is doing a good job to ensure adequate energy supplies for the future?" Each respondent was to provide an importance score for that item, using the following scale:

```
NOT AT ALL                                                      VERY
IMPORTANT                                                  IMPORTANT
  1     2     3     4     5     6     7     8     9     10
```

Since points on the scale seem to be separated by equal-appearing intervals, you can argue that the scale is an interval level measure. Note also that zero does not appear on this scale.

Ratio Level Variables

Ratio variable categories are mutually exclusive, exhaustive, ordered, and have equal intervals between points on the scale. In addition, zero on a ratio level measure means the complete absence of the attribute measured. For example, you might ask employees in an internal communication readership study: "How many minutes did you spend reading the last issue of the employee newspaper?" Called the Last Issue Exposure Scale, this variable elicits answers in terms of minutes. If the respondent did not read the last issue of the newsletter at all, then the answer is 0. If the respondent read the last issue for ten minutes, the answer is 10. Zero, for this ratio variable, means no exposure to the last issue at all, the complete absence of the attribute you are measuring.

Returning to measures of temperature, there is a scale that measures heat on a ratio level scale. Called the Kelvin scale, zero is equal to the absolute absence of heat (molecular motion) in the object measured (-273 degrees Centigrade). The intervals on the Kelvin scale are the same size as on the centigrade scale. The only difference is that zero is arbitrary on the centigrade scale (objects at 0 degrees Centigrade still have heat) but absolute on the Kelvin scale (0 degrees Kelvin means the object is without any heat at all).

Figure 8–5 illustrates the different levels of measures, provides definitions, and gives examples of each.

Why Levels of Measure Are Important

Often, in public relations research, you will examine the relationship between two variables. Do employees who frequently read the employee publication have a clearer understanding of the organization's mission than do employees who don't read? Do people who see our corporate advertisements have a more positive image of the company than people who do not see the ads? The statistics used to examine these relationships are considered in detail in Chapter 11.

When studying relationships, your concern is not simply that two variables are related to each other in the sample. For example, a sample of 200 employees shows that publication readership is related to a clearer understanding of the organization's mission. However, you are not just concerned with the 200 employees sampled. You want to know if readership and understanding of mission are related for *all* employees. Inferential statistics help us to determine if the relationship in the sample is true for the entire population.

Regarding level of measure, nominal level variables permit the use of a set of analytic tools called nonparametric statistics. *Nonparametric* statistics are

LEVEL OF MEASURE	DEFINITION	EXAMPLES
RATIO	• Mutually exclusive • Exhaustive • Ordered • Equal intervals • True zero	"How many *minutes* did you spend reading last Friday's employee newsletter?" (0 = DIDN'T READ) NUMBER OF MINUTES: _____ _____ _____
INTERVAL	• Mutually exclusive • Exhaustive • Ordered • Equal intervals	"How *important* is it for oil companies to take an active role in protecting the environment?" 5 = Extremely important 4 3 2 1 = Not important at all
ORDINAL	• Mutually exclusive • Exhaustive • Ordered	"Rank order the following oil companies in terms of your *trust* in each company. (5=most trusted, 4=next most trusted) _____ AMOCO _____ EXXON _____ MOBIL _____ SHELL _____ TEXACO
NOMINAL	• Mutually exclusive • Exhaustive	"Which source do you *most* depend on for information about new company policies?" (1) Grapevine (2) Newsletter (3) Supervisor (4) Other

Figure 8–5   Definitions and examples of levels of measures.

relatively insensitive at detecting relationships in the population. For example, a sample of 200 employees indicates that two nominal level variables are related in the sample. We use a nonparametric statistic to see if the relationship in the sample holds for all employees. (The alternative explanation is that the sample is not representative of the population; the relationship in the sample is the product of sampling error.) The nonparametric statistic indicates that the relationship probably does not hold for the population as a whole. Our conclusion may be wrong, however. As shown in Chapter 11, the power or sensitivity of our statistic may be too weak to detect a relationship in the population—even when one actually exists.

If the two variables were either interval or ratio level measures, we could use both nonparametric and parametric statistics to examine the relationship. *Parametric* statistics are more sensitive than nonparametric statistics at detecting relationships in the population. By using higher levels of measure, we are permitted to use a whole range of more sensitive statistics denied to nominal variables.

Ordinal variables are a special case. Strictly speaking, ordinal variables are limited to nonparametric statistics. However, empirical studies have shown that parametric statistics can be used successfully on ordinal level variables.[10] Labowitz suggests that treating ordinal variables as if they are interval variables has several advantages, including the use of more powerful parametric statistics.[11] Such practice is more appropriate when there are many response categories in the ordinal level variable.

The Highest-Level Imperative

When operationalizing a construct for purposes of measurement, you should be guided by the highest-level imperative. The imperative states that each variable should be measured at the highest possible level of measure. Sometimes, with concrete variables like eye color and sex, nominal-level measures are necessary. When operationalizing more abstract constructs, however, you have wide latitude in how you will capture real-world manifestations of such constructs. When that is the case, always seek to measure the construct at the interval or ratio level. This increases the number of analytic tools you can use to interpret your data.

Often, measuring a construct using higher-level variables captures more of the richness of the construct. For example, we seek to measure employee job satisfaction as part of our internal readership study. We could measure job satisfaction using a nominal level variable: "Are you satisfied with your present job?" The response categories are either "yes" or "no." At the other extreme, an interval/ratio level measure might ask: "How satisfied are you that your job gives you the chance to do the things you feel you do best?" The response categories range from zero ("not satisfied at all") to nine ("extremely satisfied"). This measure would be coupled with other indicators of job satisfaction. The point is that the interval/ratio measure captures more information about the construct we are measuring than does the nominal measure. See Exhibit 8–1 for a detailed example.

MEASUREMENT TECHNIQUES

Measurement techniques involve the assignment of numerals to the characteristics or attributes of objects or treatments according to rules.[12] We just considered different levels of measures in terms of the rules that apply to assigning numbers to variables. In this section, we consider some of the common techniques for measuring variables in public relations research.

---

[10]Sanford Labovitz, "The Assignment of Numbers to Rank Order Categories," *American Sociological Review,* Vol. 33 (June 1970), pp. 515–24. See also Q. McNemar, *Psychological Statistics* (New York: John Wiley, 1962).

[11]Labovitz, "The Assignment of Numbers," p. 523.

[12]Wimmer and Dominick, *Mass Media Research,* p. 51.

EXHIBIT 8–1
Information Value and Levels of Measure

The following variables were developed to measure the level of exposure of the employee public to a particular article in the company newsletter. A variable is provided for each level of measure. Note how higher level measures in this example provide more information about the public's exposure to the article.

NOMINAL: ____ Read article   ____ Did not read article

ORDINAL: ____ Nonreader—did not remember article
____ Noted reader—remembered seeing article
____ Associated reader—read some of article and remembered topic
____ Read-most reader—read half but not all of article and recalled major points
____ Read-all reader—read all of the article and recalled major points and detailed content

INTERVAL: How much of the article did you read?

NONE						ALL
1	2	3	4	5	6	7

RATIO: What percent of the article did you read? ____%

OR

Use this marker to indicate how far into this article you remember reading.

COLUMN INCHES: ____   OR   ____ PERCENT

Counts And Amounts

The most direct way to measure many constructs is to directly count or to estimate the amount of its real-world occurrence. For example, you seek to measure the frequency of readership of your internal newspaper. One approach is to count how often, in a specified time period, a respondent in a readership survey has read the publication at all. That's counting. Another approach is to ask respondents what percent of the last issue they read. That's an estimate of amount. You could also ask them how many articles they read in the last issue, or estimate how many articles they typically read in the internal newspaper. That's counting. Asking them to indicate in an article where they stopped reading and then noting column inches would be measuring amount.

Each of the aforementioned counts and amounts is a ratio level variable. As such, they permit a wide range of statistical tools to be used in their interpretation. They satisfy the highest-level measurement imperative.

Self-reported measures that count or estimate amounts are no better than the respondent's ability to reliably estimate such behavior. For example, we might ask you in a survey to count how many times you mentioned public relations during the last three months. Most of us would have a difficult time reliably answering that question. Often, this problem can be reduced by restricting the time frame. You might ask employees how many times they read the company's weekly newsletter over the last month. This would be more reliably answered than asking the same employees to estimate how many times they read that same weekly newsletter over the last year.

Many constructs don't easily render themselves to measures involving counts and amounts. For example, you may ask respondents how strongly they agree or disagree with the statement: "XYZ Company provides equal promotion opportunities to all its employees." There are ways to measure opinions such as this, but such measures don't involve counts. However, many constructs *can* be measured using generally reliable counts and estimates of amounts. Often, you will have to use your imagination and creativity to devise such measures. But that effort will provide you with a ratio level measure that permits you to use a wide range of analytic tools.

Additive Indices

Additive indices (sometimes called additive scales) take a series of individual measures of a construct and add them together to create a single measure. As indicated in the operationalization section of this chapter, multiple measures of a construct allow you to triangulate on that construct, capturing much of its conceptual richness through multiple indicators. Additive indices are one way to combine such multiple measures together into a single measure.

Scales and indices are often used interchangeably, but we distinguish between the two.[13] *Indices* are multiple measures that add a series of individual items together. Each item is treated as contributing equally to the index. For example, your company has three channels through which to communicate to employees. They are a weekly newsletter, a monthly magazine, and a half-hour videotape program (updated weekly) shown in the employee cafeteria. You ask employees how many minutes they spent watching the videotape last week, how many minutes they spent reading the last issue of the newsletter, and how many minutes

[13]Babbie, *Practice of Social Research*, p. 391.

they spent reading the last issue of the magazine. The three responses are added together to create an index of exposure to employee communications.

Scales, on the other hand, take into account the relative intensity of the items making up the multiple measures. For example, you want to measure employee dissatisfaction in an (anonymous) employee survey. One indicator is whether the employee complains to spouse or friends about his or her job. A second indicator is whether the employee has ever filed a formal complaint through the boss or through the union. A third indicator is whether the employee is actively looking for employment elsewhere. Each indicator is more intense than the one mentioned before it. Simply adding them together would treat each indicator as equal, which they are not.

There are several useful references that can guide you in constructing such scales.[14] But these detailed procedures for constructing and validating scales make them somewhat unwieldy. Indices, on the other hand, are relatively easy to construct. By assuming that items making up the index are equivalent, they are simply summed together.

When constructing an additive index, items of like measures should be used. In the preceding index example, exposure to all three employee media was measured using a common indicator: minutes of exposure. Let's reconsider that same example, using different measures of exposure for each medium. Suppose you asked employees how many articles they read in last week's newsletter. Since the newsletter only contained eight articles, responses range from zero to eight. You asked employees what percent of the last magazine they read. Responses range from zero (percent) to 100. You ask employees how many minutes they spent watching the videotape program last week. Responses range from zero (minutes) to a high of thirty-five. If we add these together in their present form, the index is overwhelmed by the magazine measure. An employee reading the magazine exclusively might score 100 on the employee communications exposure index. An employee reading the newsletter exclusively (100 percent of the last issue) would only score eight on the index (all eight articles were read).

When nonequivalent measures are combined in an index, normalizing the variables provides a useful technique for making the measures equivalent. *Normalization* is a mathematical process where the mean (average) for that variable is subtracted from the respondent's score, then the result is divided by the standard deviation for that variable. This operation puts all the variables on the same scale. Each normalized variable has a mean of zero and a standard deviation of 1. As such, they can be added together to form an index. Each variable contributes equally to the total index score.

---

[14]Ibid., pp. 408–11. See also Kerlinger, *Foundations of Behavioral Research,* pp. 491–511. Another useful source is Pamela L. Alreck and Robert B. Settle, *The Survey Research Handbook* (Homewood, Ill.: Richard D. Irwin, 1985), pp. 129–57. This book provides an overview of eleven different scaling techniques. A useful source for developing your own measures is Marlene E. Henerson, Lynn L. Morris, and Carol T. Fitz-Gibbon, *How To Measure Attitudes* (Beverly Hills, Calif.: Sage Publications, 1978).

Likert Items

Likert items are measures of agreement or disagreement with opinion statements. Typical are five-point and seven-point scales ranging from "strongly disagree" to "strongly agree." For example, you wish to evaluate the effectiveness of several message points made in a series of corporate advertisements about your company. One opinion statement states that your company "has always cared about and protected the environment." Subjects exposed to the commercials are asked to indicate whether they: (1) Strongly Disagree (2) Disagree (3) Neutral-Unsure (4) Agree (5) Strongly Agree. Table 8–1 provides further examples of Likert items measuring job satisfaction.

Table 8–1 Likert Items Measuring Employee Satisfaction With Company Training

ITEM	STRONGLY AGREE	AGREE	UNDECIDED/ NEUTRAL	DISAGREE	STRONGLY DISAGREE
The training I received to perform my present job was adequate.	5	4	3	2	1
I would like to see more specialized, state-of-the-art technical training programs offered by the company.	5	4	3	2	1
I am well aware of the training programs available to me in the company.	5	4	3	2	1
The training offered by the company is helpful for general personal development.	5	4	3	2	1
The company provides me with ample training to advance my career.	5	4	3	2	1
My management provides me the opportunity to participate in company training programs.	5	4	3	2	1

NOTE: The second item indicates a negative attitude toward company training, whereas the other items are all expressions of positive attitudes. To create an additive index, you would need to reverse the responses (strongly disagree equals 5, disagree equals 4, etc.) *before* adding item scores together.

Reprinted with permission from *Employee Opinion Survey Results 1982*, by Southern Company Services, Atlanta, Georgia, p. 17.

Several such Likert items can be summed together to create an additive index called a Likert-type index. Because the items all use the same five-point, agree-disagree scale, they can be summed without normalization. The advantage of such a Likert-type index is that it reduces the data into a more manageable form. The index combines a series of opinion statements about the company into an index that measures an underlying attitude toward the company.

Semantic Differential

Another technique for measuring attitudes toward stimuli is the *semantic differential*. This measurement procedure uses paired adjectives of opposite meaning—called anchoring adjectives—to evaluate people, messages, issues, organizations, and the like. For example, we might choose to evaluate the image of your company, XYZ Corporation. Respondents to a survey are asked to rate XYZ Corporation using the following items:

Responsible	__:__:__:__:__:__	Irresponsible
Traditional	__:__:__:__:__:__	Innovative
Fair	__:__:__:__:__:__	Unfair
Wasteful	__:__:__:__:__:__	Efficient

Respondents are asked to mark the blank between the colons for each pair that reflects their opinion of XYZ Corporation. The multiple measures permit you to develop a profile of the company. Further, you could have respondents rate competitors in the same manner, and compare XYZ Corporation to other companies.

Note that the more favorable responses (from the company's perspective) are on the left side for the first and third items (responsible, fair) while the more favorable response is on the right side for the second and fourth items (innovative, efficient). The reason for reversing the order of favorable items is to reduce *response set,* the tendency for respondents to habitually mark the same side of the scale rather than carefully mark their responses.

Generally, you select sets of anchoring adjectives relevant to the object you are trying to evaluate. For instance, if you were measuring respondent attitudes toward a particular corporate advertising commercial, you might use anchoring adjectives like interesting-boring, convincing-unconvincing, informative-uninformative, and so forth. You might use a different set of anchoring adjectives if you were evaluating satisfaction with the employee newsletter.

While sets of anchoring adjectives vary across measurement settings, many anchoring adjectives seem to measure a common construct. In a study of many anchoring adjectives, three basic constructs were discovered. The *evaluative* dimension is made up of anchoring adjectives like good-bad, nice-awful, and helpful-unhelpful. The *potency* dimension is made up of adjectives like big-little, strong-weak, and powerful-powerless. The *activity* dimension is made up of adjectives like fast-slow, noisy-quiet, and alive-dead.[15] These dimensions consistently emerge when anchoring adjectives are factor analyzed in different research settings. Factor analysis is discussed following as a tool for constructing scales.

Factor Scales

An additive index (an index made up of Likert-type items or an index made of semantic differential items) is a multi-item measure of the same construct. Therefore, each item making up the index is assumed to be a reliable and valid indicator of the single construct being measured. That is, the index is assumed to be *unidimensional,* in that items making up the index measure a single construct. Often, however, this assumption is not justified.

One way to determine the unidimensionality of an index is through a statistical procedure called factor analysis.[16] The statistical procedure is sufficiently complex to be left to computers. Briefly, you decide which items in a questionnaire you wish to use to construct a factor scale. These items are then subjected to factor analysis. If the items constitute a unidimensional measure of a single construct, the factor analysis procedure will yield a single factor. This is true if the items in the set are all strongly related to each other. (They should be, since they each measure the same construct.) The factor analysis procedure groups items together, based on their relationships or intercorrelations.

A single factor solution means that all items were sufficiently intercorrelated to form a single group measuring a single construct. Often, however, the factor analysis generates multiple factors, multiple groups of items. By examining the items that are grouped together on a single factor, the nature of the construct measured by those items can be inferred. Multiple factors mean that several dimensions of the construct are involved in the item set.

For example, the Metropolitan Transit Development Board is charged with regional planning for mass transportation. They conduct a telephone survey of citizens who do not regularly use mass transportation. Thirteen items, identified through depth interviews, measure attitudes toward mass transit. While the thirteen items all measure opinions of mass transportation, the item set is thought to include more than one construct, more than one set of attitudes. The factor analysis bears this out. Five factors emerge, meaning that at least five major attitude clusters are present in the item set. Items that are grouped together through factor analysis can be combined in additive indices to measure each of the attitudes.

These attitudes toward mass transportation are illustrated in Table 8–2. The first factor consists of opinions about the safety of busses and bus stops, the first two items at the top of the table. The items have high factor loadings on

---

[15]David R. Heise, "The Semantic Differential and Attitude Research," in *Attitude Measurement,* ed. Gene F. Summers (Chicago: Rand McNally, 1970), p. 237.

[16]SPSS, Inc., *SPSS-X User's Guide,* pp. 647–62. See also Babbie, *Practice of Social Research,* pp. 450–53.

Table 8–2 Items Measuring Attitudes of Nonusers Toward Mass Transportation

| | FACTOR LOADINGS | | | | |
ITEM	FACTOR 1	FACTOR 2	FACTOR 3	FACTOR 4	FACTOR 5
I feel unsafe at the bus stop in the evening.	.90				
I feel unsafe riding the bus during the evening.	.88				
I don't want other people to think of me as a bus rider.		.80			
I generally don't like being around the type of people who ride the bus regularly.		.72			
I don't want to give up the freedom of my car.		.45			
The bus times don't fit my schedules.			.77		
Riding the bus or trolley takes too long.			.71		
I don't know how to use public transportation.	.20		.25		.24
Bus drivers tend to be rude to passengers and car drivers.				.70	
Buses are not kept mechanically safe.	.24			.66	
Riding the bus costs too much.				.44	−.26
In my community, covered bus stop shelters are a better idea than bus stop benches.				−.21	.77
Having advertising on bus stop shelters is OK if it pays for the shelter.					.69

NOTE: Factor loadings of less than 0.20 have been deleted from this table for clarity. Ideally, high factor loadings appear on only one factor, meaning that item measures a single construct. When an item loads heavily on two or more factors, it measures more than one construct. For example, note the item: "I don't know how to use public transportation." While this item loads most heavily for factor 3, it also loads on factors 1 and 5.

factor 1. Factor 2 consists of three items dealing with the low social status of bus riding and the symbolic importance of the automobile. Factor 3 consists of attitudes about the convenience of mass transportation, while factor 4 involves negative opinions about bus operations. Factor 5 involves opinions about bus shelters. The *factor loadings* are measures of the strength of the relationship between each item and the construct that the factor embodies. A high factor loading means an item is a strong indicator of the construct.

The indices created from the factor analysis are called *factor scales*. Because of the factor analysis, each scale is unidimensional. For example, factor 1 is concerned solely with opinions about personal safety and mass transit. Items identified as better measures of the construct (based on high factor loadings) are given greater weight in each respondent's *factor score,* the number generated by the factor scale for each respondent. For example, the opinion "I don't want other people to think of me as a bus rider" would be given greater weight in the scale for factor 2 than the opinion "I generally don't like being around the type of people who ride the bus regularly." This is because the first opinion has a higher factor loading (0.80 versus 0.72) than the second opinion. This procedure insures that the intensity of the original variables are reflected in the composite measure provided by factor scores. Because factor scales are unidimensional and capture the relative intensity of the items that make them up, they are classified as true scales.

Off-the-Shelf Measures

Often, you will develop measures of key variables that are specific to the research question you seek to answer. However, there are many occasions when you need not reinvent the wheel. Many variables that you seek to measure have already been tested and used before. Indeed, indices or scales may already have been developed with proven reliability in past research.

There are several advantages to using such off-the-shelf indices and scales. First, the construction of indices and scales involves considerable pilot testing and revision of the original measures. Second, use of an established measure permits comparisons to other studies and other findings. If your findings differ from those of prior studies, you can eliminate differences in operationalization as a confounding factor. Third, if reliability coefficients are known from prior research, you have increased confidence in that measure's reliability for your study.

Some scales and indices are proprietary. An example is SRI International's Values and Life-styles (VALS)™ psychographic typology. Your organization can become a member of the VALS™ program directly, or you can hire the services of one of the public relations or advertising agencies licensed to use the program. An abbreviated thirty-item set can be used to classify respondents into the VALS™ typology.

Other measures are not proprietary. A good source of common social measures (job satisfaction, for example) is Delbert Miller's *Handbook of Research Design and Social Measurement.*[17] The International Association of Business Communicators Foundation maintains a communication bank of useful publications. Documents on readership surveys and employee opinion surveys contain many

---

[17]Delbert C. Miller, *Handbook of Research Design and Social Measurement,* 4th ed. (New York: David McKay, 1983). See also Henerson and others, *How To Measure Attitudes,* pp. 40–56.

examples of questionnaire items appropriate to public relations research. However, no information is provided on the reliability of different measures.

You can develop a network of professional contacts to share scales and indices developed for public relations research purposes. While you may not be willing to share all the results of research, the sharing of measurement techniques (including their reliability) benefits the individual practitioner and the profession.

CHAPTER 9

==

COMPILING AND ORGANIZING DATA

Charlotte M. Vogel, President, THE RESEARCH GROUP, New York.

URPR: You've got back a stack of completed questionnaires. How do you approach compiling and organizing the data?

Vogel: *I would sit down at that point and make notes on the field work while it's fresh. Note the beginning and ending dates of your data collection. Note your response volume by period. Did questionnaires come in more at the beginning or at the end? Compare the questionnaires that came in at the beginning and at the end. You might find interesting patterns. Note any problems you had getting responses, including number of refusals—and why. If the questionnaire was pretested, you shouldn't have many problems. But if you do, you should note them right away. All questionnaires need to be checked for completeness and accuracy. Number each questionnaire.*

URPR: When should you make a decision about hand tabulation or computerization of research data?

Vogel: *That decision should have been assessed when you did your data analysis plan, when you first designed the questionnaire. What do you want to do with each question? What do you want to do with the overall survey? We block out our charts and tables in blank form. We know the kinds of comparisons we may want and the kinds of questions we want to answer. It's not efficient from an economic and time standpoint to make the decision after the data have been collected.*

URPR: What factors go into the decision to either hand tabulate or computerize research data?

Vogel: *That depends on what you want to do with the data. If you need to compare several variables, that's very time-consuming by hand. You need to consider how many variables you have. How complex and long is the questionnaire? How many questionnaires are there? Some analysis really can't be done by hand. You really have to have a computer. If you haven't planned and budgeted for that, you're up a creek. On the other hand, if you have a relatively short questionnaire or simple analysis, if you have the staff and time, then it makes sense to do it by hand.*

URPR: Explain the advantages and disadvantages of computerized analysis of research data.

Vogel: *Advantages and disadvantages are not always clear-cut. Cost advantage, for instance, has to be weighed on a case-by-case basis. A disadvantage of computerization is you tend to remove yourself from the process. Many people assign mystical capabilities to computers to make judgments. But you really need to stay involved. You don't always save as much time as you thought you would. You need to stay involved with the inputers and the people doing the analysis to make sure that the judgments made make sense. If you just hand it over, you're losing quality control. An advantage of computerization is that you can group and play with the data in different ways. If you've done it by hand, you're stuck. If your data analysis and word processing are on the same computer, computerized data analysis makes it easier to write the final report. You can usually pull your tables right off the computer. It's time-saving, and you are able to do more with your report.*

URPR: Open-ended questions pose special problems for analyzing data.

Vogel: *Sometimes people without a lot of experience put many open-ended questions into a questionnaire. Open-ended questions are easier to write at the front end. When it comes time to analyze the data, enormous amounts of time and energy are needed, requiring your real involvement. If you have a lot of open-ended questions, it may not make sense to do them by computer. Often, relatively little will be done quantitatively with open-ended questions.*

In this chapter, you will learn that compiling and organizing data starts with a data analysis plan developed during the basic design and questionnaire construction phases. Key to your data analysis plan is a decision to either hand tabulate the data or computerize the data for tabulation and analysis. You will also learn how to field edit and reduce data for hand tabulation or computerization. Finally, you will learn how to assess the quality of data prior to analyzing the information.

THE RESEARCH PLAN

The *research plan* is a written document that specifies what information your organization needs and how that information will be used. One part of the research plan, the *data analysis plan,* details the strategy for collecting and analyzing research data. The research plan specifies *research objectives,* the outcomes you hope to achieve through your study. Research objectives, like public relations program objectives (detailed in Chapter 2), do not describe the process. Rather, research objectives specify what you hope to learn from your research efforts. Written research objectives guide decisions about research project design (see Chapter 5), modes of observation (see Chapter 7), and the operationalization of constructs (see Chapter 8).

Information Needs and Applications

Whereas program goals and objectives respond to a written problem statement and situation analysis, research objectives are a response to written information needs and projected applications of findings. Before you write research objectives, specify the kind of information that your organization does not have and hopes to learn from the research project. To put these information needs in context, project how you will use that information to identify problems and make decisions about programs. (See Chapter 5.)

There are two reasons for specifying information needs, projecting applications of information, and detailing research objectives. First, such planning makes the process of research design, data collection, and data analysis rational. For example, in designing a questionnaire, you often want to ask more questions than the questionnaire can accomodate without losing respondents. How do you

ask whether XYZ Corporation contributes a lot, a little, or hardly anything to the betterment of the community. The categories should be numbered as follows: (1) Hardly Anything (2) A Little (3) A Lot. To preserve directionality, higher numbers were assigned to categories that indicate more of the attribute (community betterment in this case); lower numbers were assigned to categories indicating less of the attribute.

Edge Coding

This technique eases entry of data into a computer. *Edge coding* is the assignment of variables to specific positions or columns in a data file during the construction of the questionnaire. This process is illustrated in Figure 9–1. In

Figure 9–1   An illustration of an edge-coded questionnaire and computer data entry.

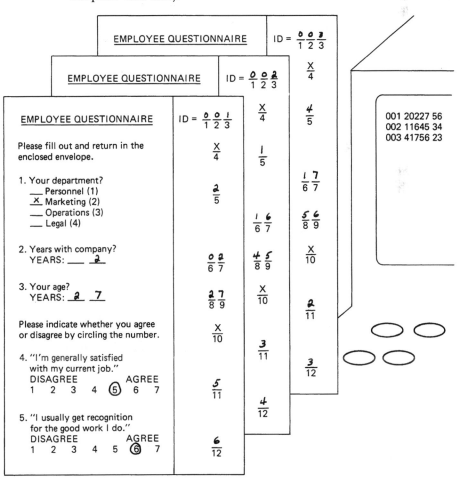

the middle of Figure 9–1, three completed employee questionnaires are shown. The questionnaire on top is for respondent 001 (an arbitrarily assigned respondent identification number), a twenty-seven-year-old employee from the marketing department where he or she has worked for two years.

An edge code scheme was implemented during questionnaire construction and printed on the questionnaire. The respondent identification number is assigned to columns 1–3 in the data file. Column 4 is left blank, designated by a preprinted "X" in the edge code. Question 1 asks what department the employee works for. Respondent 001 works for marketing, which is precoded as a 2. Respondent 002 works for personnel, precoded as a 1. Responses to Question 1 are always recorded in column 5 in the data file.

On the right of Figure 9–1 is a computer terminal, with the data from the three questionnaires appearing on the screen. The first line of data is from respondent 1. The identification number appears in columns 1–3 on the screen. Column 4 is blank. Column 5 displays the numeric code for department, a "2" for respondent 001. Study this example carefully to see how information is transferred from the main body of the questionnaire to the edge code area, and from there into the computer.

Columns 4 and 10 have been left blank on purpose. Note how they form an even blank column on the computer screen. A common error when entering data is multiple keystrokes for a single numeral. When this happens, a number will appear in the next blank column, since all numbers in the set where the error occurred will be off by a keystroke. This signals the person entering the data that an error has been made in the last set of numbers entered, provides a quick visual check of entry of data in their proper columns, and eases correction of errors.

Data Reduction

Edge coding is used to reduce errors. Data are transferred to the edge of the questionnaire in a manner that permits quick checks for accuracy. This process of converting verbal responses to questionnaire items into numeric codes for data entry is called *data reduction*. When a questionnaire is extensively pilot tested, when questions are closed-ended and categories precoded, the data reduction process is relatively accurate. Open-ended responses require greater judgment on the part of the coder. Therefore, such coding is prone to higher levels of error. Once data reduction is complete, the data can be entered directly into the computer. The use of designated blank columns insures that data are arrayed in their proper columns in the data file. (This, however, does not insure that each number is the right number; it simply insures that the variables are arrayed in their proper columns in the data file.)

With open-ended questions, you often cannot anticipate exactly how many responses will be given. Therefore, it's hard to know how many digits to assign to such a variable in the edge code scheme. For example, you might ask respondents in the employee survey in Figure 9–1 what steps they would take to open channels of communication between themselves and top management. Such an open-ended probe could generate many unanticipated responses. A single-digit code for that variable can accomodate up to nine unique responses, plus a code for missing responses for that variable.

If more than nine categories of responses are anticipated, assign two digits to such a variable. For example, in Figure 9–1, two digits have been assigned to respondent age and years with the company. Responses up to ninety-eight years can be captured for both variables. (The value "99" is reserved for coding people who don't answer that question.) When variables generate categorical answers, you will not want more than two digits assigned to that measure. That's because there is little quantitative analysis that you can do on large numbers of categories. If there are seventy-five categories, for example, generally there will be few respondents giving any one response. Three-digit and four-digit variables are only appropriate for ratio-level measures (counts and amounts). Examples include household income (coded to the nearest thousand dollars) and number of employees. Keep in mind that there is a cost in assigning extra digits to variables in the edge-coding scheme. If you plan to survey 600 respondents, the assignment of two digits rather than one digit to a variable means 600 *extra* keystrokes when inputting data into the computer.

Data Transmittal Forms

Sometimes, you wish to analyze data that has not been precoded. To analyze the data on a computer, a mechanism called a *data transmittal form* is used to transfer information from the original document into the computer. A data transmittal form is a sheet with preprinted lines corresponding to lines of data in the data file, marked off with the appropriate number of columns (usually eighty columns). See Figure 9–2 for an example of a data transmittal form. The top three lines of data in Figure 9–2 are taken from the three questionnaires shown in Figure 9–1. The six lines of data in the middle of the form are from the questionnaires in Figure 9–4. In order to transfer information from the original document to the data transmittal form, a codebook is usually required.

Response Rates

When you conduct a survey, you will not be 100 percent successful obtaining data from every sample member. When compiling and organizing data, you must estimate how successful you were at collecting data from sample members. There are four figures you calculate to estimate how representative your final sample is. To calculate these figures, you need to track outcomes of your attempts to collect data from sample members. The four figures are the completion rate, the response rate, the refusal rate, and the noncontact rate. The *completion rate* is the percent of original sample members who complete the questionnaire. This rate is generally low, since the original sample drawn from the sample frame may include some members who are not eligible, not actually members of

```
         1         2         3         4         5         6         7         8
12345678901234567890123456789012345678901234567890123456789012345678901234567890
 1 001 20227 561425171 431542216 991327543 151437267 994317261 211711149 312563217
 2 002 11645 341527799 214726511 743215777 615143516 231542777 625416371 231514216
 3 003 41756 231171726 117325164 231547212 611431511 239999999 917321572 114321161
11 2071 876543532 76547754325434 24354311125439 31247156911231 14732154614127 12137
12 2072 544365543 54324421445553 42424442133342 442
13 2081 876758899 54342214456654 24456654323444 54317261143211 65456111321472 61531
14 2082 543234455 65432345666672 55322345564332 644
15 2091 976899779 77654235666346 54324564466433 55417321357652 31543212114654 32116
16 2092 247144776 76546775443134 77654339999999 655
```

Figure 9–2 Data transmittal form with data.

the target population. This figure is most useful for planning purposes, for making sure that the original sample drawn contains enough eligible respondents to permit completion of the required number of questionnaires. For example, you want to conduct a telephone survey of the community near your factory using random digit dialing. From prior surveys, you know that the completion rate is 20 percent of the original sample. In order to complete 500 interviews, you will need an original sample of random digit telephone numbers of 2,500.

Calculation of the remaining rates requires you know the final number of eligible respondents, or *valid* sample size. That number is computed by subtracting ineligible respondents from the original sample size. For example, some questionnaires mailed to a sample of employees of your company may be returned because the employee has left the firm. These sample members are no longer part of your target population (the currently employed), so they are removed from the sample of eligible respondents. The *response rate* is the percentage of the valid sample that complete the questionnaire. The higher this figure, the more confidence you have that your completed questionnaires are representative of the population from which the original sample was drawn.

The *refusal rate* is the number of eligible people from the valid sample who refuse to complete the questionnaire or completed only a few of the introductory items to the survey. In telephone surveys, these latter sample members are people who hang up early in the interview. A study of 182 telephone surveys indicated an average refusal rate of 28 percent.[1] Others have reported refusal rates of 20–25 percent.[2] Refusal rates are lower for face-to-face surveys, but such studies are relatively expensive. Refusal rates for mailed surveys are higher—up to 50 percent—but mailed surveys are cheaper.

A final figure is the *noncontact rate* (NCR), which is calculated by dividing the number of (presumably) eligible respondents not contacted by the valid sample size. This figure is important in telephone surveys, where many potentially eligible respondents are not reached despite several attempts.

To keep track of the data needed to compute these rates, you need to maintain a response rate log during data collection. Figure 9–3 shows one such log, used in random digit telephone surveys. A tally is kept of each phone number attempted and the final outcome for that number. The top three numbers are ineligible respondents and are subtracted from the original sample size to provide the valid sample size. The formulas and step-by-step procedures for computing response, completion, refusal, and noncontact rates are provided in Appendix H.

Codebooks

A *codebook* details the assignment of variables to designated columns in the data file. An edge-coded questionnaire serves as its own codebook, since it

[1]Frederick Wiseman and Phillip McDonald, "Noncontact and Refusal Rates in Consumer Telephone Surveys," *Journal of Marketing Research*, Vol. 16 (November 1979), pp. 478–84.
[2]James H. Frey, *Survey Research by Telephone* (Beverly Hills, Calif.: Sage, 1983), p. 41.

Number of phone numbers attempted: _____
   (Initial sample size)

		Valid numbers?
Number of disconnects	A. _____	NO
Number of no answers (at least three attempts)	B. _____	NO
Number of ineligible numbers (business, government numbers, non-English speakers, nobody in household is member of target public)	C. _____	NO
Number of no answers with insufficient attempts (all interviews completed at other numbers before three attempts of these numbers)	D. _____	YES
Number of refusals	E. _____	YES
Number of hangups (within first two pages of questionnaire)	F. _____	YES
Number of completed interviews	G. _____	YES
TOTAL (should equal number of attempts)	H. _____	

NOTE: The valid sample size is computed by subtracting the sum of A, B, and C from the total numbers attempted, the original sample size. These are the valid phone numbers that make up the valid sample size. Divide G by the valid sample size to compute the response rate. Divide the sum of E and F by the valid sample size to compute the refusal rate. Divide D by the valid sample size to compute the noncontact rate (NCR). Divide G by the total numbers attempted to compute the completion rate.

Figure 9–3   Response rate log for a random digit telephone survey.

has already assigned variables to specific columns in the data file. The only information missing is the assignment of computer recognizable names to each variable in the questionnaire. When the original document has not made such assignments, the codebook is used to a) sequentially identify variables from the original document, b) assign computer recognizable names to each variable, c) assign numeric codes to each value of each variable, and d) designate the column or columns in the data file where that variable will be recorded.

To enter data into the computer, you examine the original document and the codebook. You locate the first variable in the original document. Using the codebook, the numeric value or response for that variable is determined. That number is then marked on the data transmittal form in the column designated for that variable in the codebook. This process is repeated for each variable in the original document. Because of the number of steps involved, the probability of human error is relatively high. However, certain types of information cannot or were not collected using edge-coded questionnaires.

For example, assume that the telephone receptionists at your organization have used a standardized form for several years to record telephone complaints about your company. The form records the date of complaint, the name and phone number of the complaining party, a series of yes-no questions about the complaint, and a brief written description. You want to examine the volume and nature of complaints quantitatively. So you develop a codebook that assigns the date of complaint and the various yes-no responses to specific columns in the data file. All variables are assigned names compatible with the computer software you are using. (SPSS-X, for example, restricts variable names to eight characters.) Exhibit 9–1 shows a portion of a typical codebook.

BASICS OF COMPUTERIZATION

This introduction will not attempt to discuss all issues relevant to the revolution in data analysis precipitated by computers. For our purposes, it's sufficient to say that computers have profoundly impacted the ease, speed, and cost of analyzing survey and other types of public relations research data. Today, most organizations have access to computing resources, ranging from large mainframe computers to minicomputers to micro- or personal computers (PCs). Even PCs have the capacity to analyze public relations research data using a variety of statistical software packages.[3]

The Data File

The best way to understand computerized data analysis is to understand how data are arranged in the computer. Since data you collect will eventually be organized in a data file, picturing the organization of the data file facilitates compilation and organization of data. The data file is a matrix, consisting of rows and columns of numbers. The rows of the data file correspond to cases. *Cases* are the data collected from (or about) a particular unit of analysis. In a survey, the cases are the respondents who completed the questionnaire. In content analysis, cases may consist of words, paragraphs, or entire stories from the clip file. Sometimes, organizations serve as the unit of analysis; each case in the data file corresponds to a specific organization studied.

For each case studied, several variables are collected. Each variable is assigned a specific position in the case. For example, Figure 9–1 shows a questionnaire where cases are employees surveyed and variables include an identification number, department of employment, years with the company, age, satisfaction with current job, and recognition for good work done. The six variables may be assigned convenient but meaningless names like *V1, V2, V3, V4, V5,* and *V6.* Or, depending on the computer software, meaningful *mnemonics* ("names" that help you remember the variables they stand for) can be assigned. For example, ID, DEPT, YEARSCO, AGE, JOBSAT, and RECOG could be assigned to the six variables just mentioned. Printouts of analyses will include these mnemonics to remind you which variables have been analyzed.

---

[3]Two common software packages available for use on large personal computers are SPSS-PC and StatPac. The dominant software application package for large mainframes is SPSS-X. Other major application packages for large mainframes include SAS and BMD.

EXHIBIT 9–1
A Typical Codebook
for a Survey Questionnaire

RECORD[1]	COLUMN(S)[2]	VARIABLE NAME[3]	QUESTIONNAIRE ITEM & VALUES[4]
1	79	ENVIRON	XYZ Corp. has shown strong leadership in protecting the environment. (DISAGREE) (AGREE) 1 2 3 4 5 6 7 9=DON'T KNOW/NOT ASKED
1	80	HARMONY	XYZ Corp. should do more to promote racial harmony in this community. (DISAGREE) (AGREE) 1 2 3 4 5 6 7 9=DON'T KNOW/NOT ASKED
		END OF RECORD 1. START RECORD 2.	
2	1–3	ID	Respondent identification number. 001–675 (range of valid identification numbers)
2	4	RECORD	DATA file record number. 1–2 (range of valid record numbers)
2	6	ETHNIC	Do you consider yourself to be a member of a minority group? (IF YES) Which one? 1=NOT MINORITY 2=BLACK 3=HISPANIC 4=NATIVE AMERICAN 5=ASIAN-PACIFIC ISLANDER 6=OTHER 9=DON'T KNOW/NOT ASKED
2	7–8	AGE	How old are you? (RECORDED TO NEAREST YEAR) 18–98 (range of valid ages in years) 98=OLDER THAN 98 YEARS 99=REFUSED OR NOT ASKED

[1]RECORD is the "card number" in the data file for each respondent. A record usually represents eighty columns or digits of information.

[2]COLUMN is the designated location of a variable within a line (record) of data. Column 1 is the first digit in a record; column 80 is the last digit in a record.

[3]VARIABLE NAME is a name assigned to a variable that is compatible with the computer software. These variable names are SPSS-X compatible.

[4]QUESTIONNAIRE ITEMS AND VALUES includes the actual wording of the questionnaire items and all the response categories for that variable. The "missing value" code is also specified.

Cases and Records

A single case may take up one line or several lines in a data file. A line of data is called a *record,* a holdover from the days of computer punch cards when each line of data corresponded to a card or record. Generally, a record of data (one line on the terminal screen) in a large mainframe computer can include up to eighty columns or digits of information. Often, long questionnaires will require more than eighty digits to store all the information collected. Under such circumstances, a second or third line of data—additional records—will be required for each case in the data file. Typically, each line of data will be identified by an identification number for the particular case and a record or line number.

For example, a survey of 600 stockholders of a corporation requires two lines of data—two records—for each case (respondent) in the survey. The first line of data for the respondent assigned identification number 324 might start with the code "3241." This code means that the line of data is from the questionnaire for respondent 324 and that this is line 1 or the first record of data for this respondent. The second line of data would start with the code "3242," meaning that the line contains the second line of data for respondent 324. You assign blanks periodically in your edge code scheme to ease error detection and correction during data entry. For example, you may assign blanks to columns 5, 15, 30, 45, and 60 in your first line of data. For this reason, you will assign blanks to columns 5, 15, 30, 45, and 60 in your second line of data, so that the blanks will "line up" on the computer terminal screen. Figure 9–4 illustrates part of a questionnaire requiring two lines of data and a computer screen displaying data for several cases in the data file. Note that the information on the bottom half of the questionnaire appears in the second line of data on the terminal screen.

The data file is stored in a form understandable by the computer on either disk, magnetic tape, punched cards, or punched tape. Punched cards, once the standard storage medium for computer data, are rapidly falling into disuse because of improvements in magnetic disk and tape storage systems.

In-House Computer Analysis

Should you (or others in the public relations department) conduct computerized data analysis yourself or subcontract for computer services from a research firm or computer service bureau? The answer you give today may change tomorrow, as computer hardware and software continue to develop. Wimmer and Dominic argue that anyone interested in media research (including public relations research) must understand computer analysis.[4] However, as Charlotte Vogel argues, bringing complex computer analysis inside the public relations department or firm may not be the best use of a practitioner's time and energy.

---

[4]Roger D. Wimmer and Joseph R. Dominick, *Mass Media Research: An Introduction,* 2nd ed. (Belmont, Calif.: Wadsworth Publishing, 1987), p. 409.

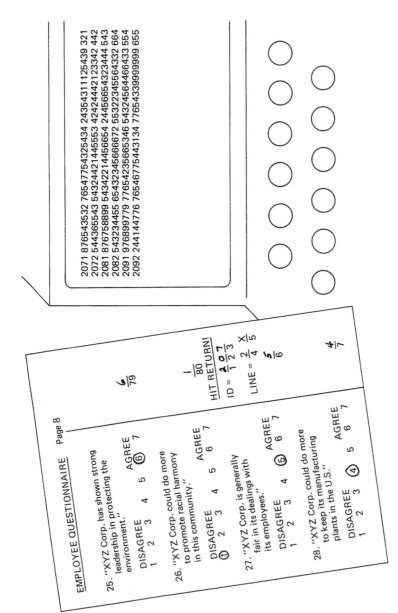

EMPLOYEE QUESTIONNAIRE   Page 8

25. "XYZ Corp. has shown strong
    leadership in protecting the
    environment."

    DISAGREE   AGREE
    1   2   3   4   5   ⑥   7

26. "XYZ Corp. could do more
    to promote racial harmony
    in this community."

    DISAGREE   AGREE
    ①   2   3   4   5   6   7

27. "XYZ Corp. is generally
    fair in its dealings with
    its employees."

    DISAGREE   AGREE
    1   2   3   4   ⑤   6   7

28. "XYZ Corp. could do more
    to keep its manufacturing
    plants in the U.S."

    DISAGREE   AGREE
    1   2   3   ④   5   6   7

$\frac{6}{79}$

$\frac{1}{80}$

HIT RETURN!

ID = $\frac{2}{1}\frac{0}{2}\frac{7}{3}$ $\frac{X}{5}$

LINE = $\frac{2}{4}\frac{}{5}$

$\frac{5}{6}$

$\frac{4}{7}$

2071 876543532 765477543254334 2435431112542439 321
2072 544365543 543244214455533 42424442123342 442
2081 876758899 54342214456654 244566543423444 543
2082 543234455 654323456666672 553223456564332 664
2091 976899779 77654235665346 54324564466433 554
2092 244144776 76546775443134 77654339999999 655

Figure 9–4 A partial questionnaire requiring two data lines and display of part
of a data file on a terminal screen.

The *advantage* of in-house computer analysis is that computer costs of conducting research can be absorbed in the ongoing personnel expenses of the department. The cost of the computer itself must be justified, but such justification, once established, need not be rejustified for every research project. Whenever an outside research firm or service bureau is used, the expense must be justified on a case-by-case basis. As David Clavier of Husk Jennings Overman Public Relations argues, budgeting research expenses is difficult in a corporate setting, because it's not tangible like personnel and equipment.

The *disadvantage* of in-house computer activities is that such efforts tax the frequently limited time and energy resources of the public relations staff. In-house research analysis requires that you become familiar with much of the minutiae (technical detail) of computers, software, data storage, system expansions, upgrades, and so forth. You can avoid much of that minutiae by contracting for computer analysis services.

In a larger sense, however, familiarity with computer analysis is necessary whether you do the analysis yourself or you have an outside firm do it for you. To effectively use outside computer services, you have to specify precisely how the information needs and the research objectives of your organization are to be met by the data analysis. To simply turn over the analysis to an outside firm, Charlotte Vogel argues, is to sacrifice quality control. Further, it's difficult to make sense of the computer analysis without being close to the data and the judgments made in the data reduction process.

ORGANIZING CONTENT ANALYSIS DATA

In Chapter 3, we discussed applications of content analysis in public relations research. Chapter 6 concerns the sampling of content for analysis. Chapter 8 outlines the issues related to unit of analysis and operationalization. In this chapter, we consider how content data are organized for analysis. First, we organize content data for analysis using computers. In the final section of this chapter, we consider hand tabulation of content data, as well as hand tabulation of other forms of data.

Unit of Analysis

In content analysis, selection of the unit of analysis requires closer scrutiny than does such selection for other types of public relations research. Generally, the smallest content unit of analysis is the word. An intermediate unit is the sentence or paragraph. Even larger is an entire item—an article or story in a newspaper, magazine, television, or radio. And larger still is the complete issue of a newsletter, newspaper, or broadcast program. A census of such items occurring during a specified period of time can be conducted, or a sample can be drawn. Each unit of analysis constitutes a case. Each case consists of one or more records (lines of data) in the data file.

Variables

For each unit of analysis, one or more variables are measured. In content analysis, variables consist of several types. One variable type is the simple presence or absence of an attribute. For example, Children's Hospital in San Diego discovered through a survey of parents that most were not aware of the hospital's nonprofit status. Since awareness of nonprofit status is important for raising money, the hospital sought to include the hospital's nonprofit status in media placements. Articles or stories about Children's Hospital are evaluated to determine if nonprofit status information is present or absent. The article or story is the unit of analysis, the case in the data file.

Presence of Content Type

The presence or absence of nonprofit status information in articles about Children's Hospital is one variable measured for each case, each article, or each story. The nonprofit variable is assigned a specific location in the data file for each case or unit of analysis studied. Another related problem for Children's Hospital is public confusion of Children's Hospital with another hospital located adjacent to Children's Hospital. Many people think the two separate hospitals are owned and run by the same corporation. Articles about Children's Hospital are analyzed to determine the presence or absence of information about Children's independent corporate status. This measure constitutes another variable for each article about Children's Hospital. As such, a specific location (or column) is assigned to this variable in the data file.

Frequency

A second category of variables collected through content analysis includes measures of frequency—a count. For example, a single story might include several references to the hospital's nonprofit status. Rather than simply indicate the presence or absence of such information in the article, a measure of frequency would indicate how many times nonprofit status information appeared in the article.

Amount

A third category of variables includes measures of the amount of coverage dedicated to a specific content category. For example, Children's Hospital is the officially recognized trauma center for children in its region. The hospital carefully monitors media coverage that publicizes its role as the Regional Pediatric Trauma Center because such publicity tends to enhance the hospital's reputation for state-of-the-art care. Each article about Children's Hospital is analyzed to determine if its role as a trauma center is mentioned. If so, the number of column inches dedicated to the trauma center is recorded. If the center is not mentioned, a figure of zero (no column inches dedicated to the center) is recorded.

The same measurement strategy can be applied to broadcast coverage of Children's Hospital. Instead of column inches, however, the unit of measure is the amount of time dedicated to the trauma center. This variable is measured in seconds. A value of zero seconds is recorded if the story does not mention the trauma center at all.

Intensity

A fourth strategy measures the intensity of statements about an issue. For example, Children's Hospital is concerned about public awareness of its non-profit status because this perception affects fund raising activities of the hospital. Articles or stories about the hospital may simply mention that the hospital is nonprofit. For fund-raising purposes, this is a low intensity statement. If the article or story also mentions that, as a nonprofit, Children's Hospital solicits private support, that's a middle-level intensity statement. If the article or story mentions that such private donations are necessary for Children's to offer many of its special services, that's a high-intensity statement. A coding scheme is developed to assign higher numbers to more intense statements of relevance, lower numbers to statements of lesser intensity.

Prominence

A fifth measurement strategy indicates the prominence of a particular content category. For example, an article appearing on the front page of a newspaper is more prominent than one on the inside pages. An article with a large headline is more prominent than one with a small headline. A story with video on the evening newscast is more prominent than one without video. A story reported by a broadcast reporter in the field is more prominent than a story read by the anchor. Measures of prominence constitute an additional attribute or variable of content.

Each case, then, can be evaluated according to a number of variables. These variables include measures of the presence or absence of content categories, frequency of such categories, amounts of categories, intensity of categories, and prominence of categories. Each variable is assigned a specific position or column in the data file.

Data Reduction

Data reduction in content analysis can be performed several ways. Which way is best depends on the complexity of the categorization scheme. When the unit of analysis is small (for example, the sentence) and the categories simple (the presence or absence of a few attributes), then data can be coded directly on to a data transmittal form. The assignment of variables to specific locations in the data file is accomplished through a codebook. Coders can refer to the codebook as needed, but with practice they will have little need to do so. When the unit of analysis is large (for example, an entire article) and the categorization scheme complex, a content analysis form similar to an abbreviated questionnaire is used. The form identifies each variable and the categories for each variable. Numbers are precoded for the specified categories. Edge coding may be used to facilitate data entry. A form is developed for each specific content analysis study undertaken. A separate form is completed for each case in the data file.

HAND TABULATION OF DATA

In the age of microprocessors and statistical software, many see hand tabulation of research data as an unacceptable approach to compiling data. In discussing hand tabulation, Dr. Larissa Grunig of the University of Maryland says that "I can't see that it's even a choice these days; if you have access to a computer, you should use it." The attractiveness of computerization becomes obvious the first time you have to retabulate data by hand. For example, you hand tabulate employee satisfaction with internal communication by respondent gender. You want to see if female employees are more satisfied with internal communication than male employees. Hand tabulation requires that you go through all the completed survey questionnaires, noting whether internal communication satisfaction is high or low and whether the respondent is male or female. If this is the only analysis you will do on these data, hand tabulation may be as quick or quicker than coding that same information and entering it into a computer. However, any advantage disappears when you conduct further analysis.

For example, you become curious as to whether the employee's department is related to satisfaction with internal communication. Again, you must go through the entire stack of questionnaires, retabulating each respondent as either satisfied or not satisfied and as belonging to one of the several departments in your organization. If the data were already entered into the computer, the machine could accomplish this analysis in seconds with just a few lines of instructions from your terminal.

When an index is created from several questionnaire items, tabulation occurs in several steps. First, each respondent must be assigned an index score by tabulating the responses to several items within each respondent's questionnaire. Next, index scores for each respondent are tabulated for the sample as a whole.

Despite the clear advantages of computerization, there are times when hand tabulation of research data is advantageous or necessary. Hand tabulation is advantageous when the research data is highly qualitative in nature. For example, you record a focus group study and have the discussion transcribed. You review the transcript, tallying favorable comments about a particular message strategy you were testing as well as unfavorable comments. You group similar comments together, allowing you to build multiple categories of favorable and of unfavorable comments. Because the tabulation is dynamic, and because categories emerge from the transcript comments themselves, the completed hand tabulation may be sufficient for your purposes. Hand tabulation may also be advantageous when the number of cases and the number of variables are few and the analysis is simple. And, obviously, hand tabulation is necessary when you have no access to a computer. Get one, or get access to one, if you plan to use research as part of how you do public relations.

Figure 9–5 provides examples of univariate (one variable) and bivariate (two variables) tally sheets for hand tabulation. At the top, a hand tabulation has been made of a single variable, a measure of how useful employees consider the employee newsletters to be. A tally mark was made for each respondent in the

Figure 9–5 Examples of univariate and bivariate tally sheets.

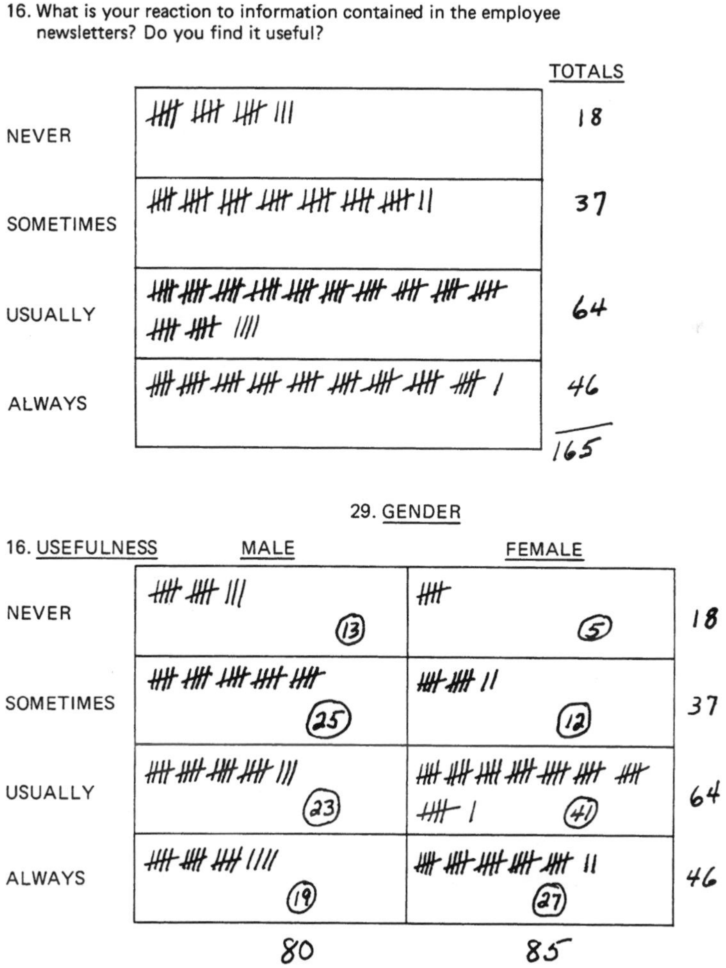

16. What is your reaction to information contained in the employee newsletters? Do you find it useful?

		TOTALS
NEVER	⊦⊦⊦ ⊦⊦⊦ ⊦⊦⊦ |||	18
SOMETIMES	⊦⊦⊦ ⊦⊦⊦ ⊦⊦⊦ ⊦⊦⊦ ⊦⊦⊦ ⊦⊦⊦ ⊦⊦⊦ ||	37
USUALLY	⊦⊦⊦ ⊦⊦⊦ ⊦⊦⊦ ⊦⊦⊦ ⊦⊦⊦ ⊦⊦⊦ ⊦⊦⊦ ⊦⊦⊦ ⊦⊦⊦ ⊦⊦⊦ ⊦⊦⊦ ⊦⊦⊦ ||||	64
ALWAYS	⊦⊦⊦ ⊦⊦⊦ ⊦⊦⊦ ⊦⊦⊦ ⊦⊦⊦ ⊦⊦⊦ ⊦⊦⊦ ⊦⊦⊦ ⊦⊦⊦		46
		165

29. GENDER

16. USEFULNESS	MALE	FEMALE	
NEVER	⊦⊦⊦ ⊦⊦⊦ ||| (13)	⊦⊦⊦ (5)	18
SOMETIMES	⊦⊦⊦ ⊦⊦⊦ ⊦⊦⊦ ⊦⊦⊦ ⊦⊦⊦ (25)	⊦⊦⊦ ⊦⊦⊦ || (12)	37
USUALLY	⊦⊦⊦ ⊦⊦⊦ ⊦⊦⊦ ⊦⊦⊦ ||| (23)	⊦⊦⊦ ⊦⊦⊦ ⊦⊦⊦ ⊦⊦⊦ ⊦⊦⊦ ⊦⊦⊦ ⊦⊦⊦ ⊦⊦⊦	(41)	64
ALWAYS	⊦⊦⊦ ⊦⊦⊦ ⊦⊦⊦ |||| (19)	⊦⊦⊦ ⊦⊦⊦ ⊦⊦⊦ ⊦⊦⊦ ⊦⊦⊦ || (27)	46
	80	85	

block corresponding to his or her answer. At the bottom, the relationship between perceived usefulness and gender is tallied. Questionnaires were divided
into a male stack and a female stack. Then, the answers to Question 16, the usefulness measure, were tallied again. Responses from the male pile of questionnaires
were tallied in the left column; responses from the female pile were tallied in the
right column. Using this information, a test of statistical significance such as the
Chi Square test (see Appendix I) can be used to determine if the relationship in
the sample of 165 (females find the newsletters more useful) can be generalized
to the entire employee population.

CHAPTER 10

DESCRIBING THE FINDINGS

John V. Pavlik, PhD, Associate Director for Research and Technology Studies, GANNETT CENTER FOR MEDIA STUDIES, Columbia University, New York.

URPR: The questionnaire data are in the computer and the computer analysis program is debugged. Describe what you do next.

Pavlik: *A frequency distribution is the right place to start. You describe the results and look at how the data are distributed. That's the first thing you need to examine. First you want to look at how the table is labeled. What is the variable? What are the response categories? After identifying what's in the table, I would look at the frequency and the percent in each category. I would look at the valid percentage, because this percentage indicates the percentage after we have sorted out missing cases. I would also highlight the number of valid cases and missing cases.*

URPR: Most statistical application packages will provide you with a number of summary statistics, in addition to the frequency distribution table.

Pavlik: *Under certain circumstances, depending on the type of data, there might be things to look at in the summary statistics. For example, the mean, the mode, and the standard deviation are sometimes useful statistics. But when the variable is nominal, these summary statistics aren't as important as the table itself. Just the percentages turn out to be the most useful.*

URPR: Describe the usefulness of measures of central tendency for nominal level variables and for higher level measures.

Pavlik: *The mode indicates which answer was given most often. That can be useful with nominal level data, as well as any higher-order data—ordinal, interval, or ratio. The mode can often be very useful in interpreting results or summarizing them to an audience. For ordinal, interval, and ratio levels, the median tells us the value at the midpoint of the distribution. Statistically, about half the cases are less than the median value, while the other half of the cases are greater than that. This is a good measure of central tendency when the distribution is highly skewed.*

URPR: Give us an example.

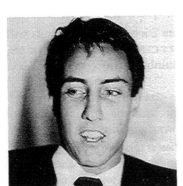

Pavlik: *Take income as an example. Often, income is highly skewed. There is a limit to how low income can go. A person can't have less than zero income. On the other hand, income can go extremely high. Say you have a sample of 500 people. Fifty percent of them have an income of less than $40,000. But then there's a small minority that make more than a million dollars. The shape of the distribution is highly skewed. There's a heavy concentration at one end, but there is a small number whose income is extremely high. Visualize this distribution as having a large lump at the lower end and then stretching out to a million at the upper end. What this does is inflate the mean or average income. Maybe you'll get a mean income level of $100,000. But in reality, only 10 percent of the actual subjects—50 out of the 500—had income of $100,000 or more. The median might indicate that half of the people have incomes of more than $40,000, while the rest have incomes over $40,000. The mean can be somewhat misleading if it is a highly skewed distribution. Under such circumstances, the median or mode can be more useful.*

URPR: Discuss measures of dispersion.

Pavlik: *It's useful to look at how data are clustered, through measures of central tendency—the mean, median, and*

> *mode. At the same time, you want to look at measures of dispersion—how widely spread the data are. Measures of range and skewness are helpful. If the data are not highly skewed, the three measures of central tendency should be close to the same value.*

URPR: Explain the 95 percent confidence interval.

Pavlik: *The 95 percent confidence interval is very useful but underused. You don't see it reported a lot. But it's simple to use. If you have a higher-order variable, then you construct a 95 percent confidence interval, which gives you a range that you're 95 percent confident that the true population parameter lies within.*

URPR: An example might help.

Pavlik: *Let's say we have a mean on our income measure of $30,000. We construct a confidence interval from the standard deviation or take it directly from the frequency distribution printout. Let's say the confidence interval ranges from $28,000 to $32,000. You're 95 percent sure that the true population mean falls between $28,000 and $32,000.*

Chapters 10 and 11 show you how to analyze public relations research data. In this chapter, you learn how to describe research findings one variable at a time. In Chapter 11, you learn how to measure relationships between variables. In the chapters that follow, you will learn how to use research findings to test for causation, to report research findings, and to change organizational behavior.

UNIVARIATE ANALYSIS

When you examine one variable at a time, you are conducting *univariate analysis.*[1] For example, the Office of Communications at San Diego State University publishes a quarterly magazine called *SDSU Report*. The publication goes to alumni and opinion leaders in the community. Marsha Gear, editor of *SDSU Report,* wants to measure reader reactions to the magazine. Do they read the magazine and, if so, how often? What parts of the magazine do they prefer? What additional features would readers like to see included in the magazine? To find out, Gear draws a random sample of names and phone numbers from the 75,000-member subscription list. Telephone interviews are conducted with 519 readers on the *SDSU Report* mailing list.

Table 10–1 displays the answers to one question in the survey asking respondents to indicate their favorite section of the magazine. Table 10–1 is a

---

[1]Earl Babbie, *The Practice of Social Research,* 5th ed. (Belmont, Calif.: Wadsworth, 1989), p. 369.

Table 10–1   Frequency Distribution of the *SDSU Report* Favorite Section Variable

FAVORITE				WHICH SECTION IS YOUR FAVORITE?	
VALUE LABEL	VALUE	FREQUENCY	PERCENT	VALID PERCENT	CUM PERCENT
CAMPUS	1	58	11.2	12.8	12.8
PEOPLE	2	93	17.9	20.5	33.3
CALENDAR	3	76	14.6	16.8	50.1
AZTEC (SPORTS)	4	66	12.7	14.6	64.7
ALUMNI	5	72	13.9	15.9	80.6
CLASS NOTES	6	88	17.0	19.4	100.0
UNSURE OR NON-READER	9	66	12.7	MISSING	
	Total	519	100.0	100.0	

MEAN	3.585	STD ERR	.080	MEDIAN	3.000
MODE	2.000	STD DEV	1.706	VARIANCE	2.911
KURTOSIS	1.309	S E KURT	1.996	SKEWNESS	.027
S E SKEW	.115	RANGE	5.000	MINIMUM	1.000
MAXIMUM	6.000	SUM	1624.000		

NOTE: In this and subsequent tables in this chapter, the format of the frequency distribution closely follows the format of the SPSS-X output of the FREQUENCIES procedure.

frequency distribution for the variable FAVORITE. (FAVORITE is the computer name for the variable in the data file.) By examining the distribution of answers, we can begin to understand how the 519 respondents answered the question. Some researchers describe this scanning as "letting the data talk."

The purpose of the frequency distribution is to help us manage the information obtained from the survey. Rather than examining each of the 519 questionnaires one at a time, the frequency distribution allows us to examine each variable in considerable detail. Once we know how respondents answered the question, we can make decisions about programs. In this case, the answers help Gear adjust the amount of editorial copy dedicated to each section, based on reader preferences. This question provides baseline data against which subsequent issues of the magazine can be evaluated.

Valid Cases

At the bottom of Table 10–1, you see that of the 519 respondents in the survey, only 453 are valid cases for this variable. That's because some people were not asked or were unable to answer the question. For this variable, respondents who indicated that they never read *SDSU Report* (49 of the respondents) were not asked the question; another 17 respondents were unsure. As such, this is a *contingency question,* an item asked only of a subset of the original sample (readers). The missing cases, 66 for this variable, are *excluded* from all subsequent computer computations of statistics. As indicated in Chapter 9, missing cases must be assigned a special code (9 was arbitrarily assigned for this variable) and the computer program must include instructions that identify that code as a missing case or missing value code.

Interpreting the Table

The table displays the number of people giving each answer in the FREQUENCY column.[2] For example, fifty-eight people indicate that the "Campus" section (news about faculty and staff at the university) is their favorite. Another ninety-three people indicate that the "People" section (short features about students, faculty, and alumni) is their favorite. The next column displays the percentage of people giving each answer, based on the total number of people in the sample. That is, 11.2 percent of the total sample say that the "Campus" section is their favorite, while another 17.9 percent say that the "People" section is their favorite. Some 12.7 percent of the respondents didn't answer this question but were included in the calculation of this column of percentages.

The next column displays percentages calculated using only the people who answered the question. Called the VALID PERCENT in the table, this number gives us a better understanding of the responses from among those people who answered the question. That is, 12.8 percent of the respondents who answered the question said the "Campus" section is their favorite, while another 20.5 percent of the respondents answering the question said the "People" section is their favorite.

The CUM PERCENT column displays the accumulation of valid percentages. For this variable, we see that 33.3 percent of the respondents answering the question consider either the "Campus" or "People" sections their favorites. This figure was computed by adding together the valid percentage of those naming the "Campus" section (12.8 percent) and the valid percentage of those naming the "People" section (20.5 percent). Examining this column further, we see that 50.1 percent of respondents named either the "Campus," "People," or "Calendar" sections their favorites.

Levels of Measure

FAVORITE is a nominal variable. Numbers are arbitrarily assigned to the different response categories of nominal variables. Many calculations are inappropriate when numbers are assigned arbitrarily to different answers to a ques-

---

[2]SPSS, Inc., *SPSS[x] User's Guide* (New York: McGraw-Hill, 1983), pp. 265–78. (Other software may give this column a different label.)

tion. Therefore, most of the statistics below the table are meaningless for this variable.

Note, however, that the computer provided us these meaningless numbers anyway—because we asked for them. When we wrote the computer instructions, we directed the SPSS-X program to compute all the available statistics for this variable. Many of these statistics are only appropriate for higher order measures, but the computer program does not recognize the FAVORITE variable as a nominal level measure. Therefore, the computer calculates the statistics in ignorance, including those without meaning for this variable. Because of the computer's ignorance, *you* must provide intelligence when interpreting these statistics.

Central Tendency and Dispersion

Before examining the statistics in Table 10–1, you need to know about measures of central tendency and dispersion. Measures of *central tendency* are statistics that summarize the point in the distribution where the "typical" case occurs. Measures of central tendency include the mean, the median, and the mode. Measures of *dispersion* are statistics that summarize the degree to which the distribution is concentrated (most respondents gave the same or similar answers) or scattered (respondents gave many different answers). Measures of dispersion include the variance, the standard deviation, and the range.

Summary Statistics for Nominal Variables

Some of the statistics below the frequency distribution table are appropriate for a nominal level variable. The mode, for example, is the most frequently given answer to the FAVORITE question. Of the three ways to summarize central tendency just mentioned, the mode is the only one appropriate for a nominal-level variable. In this case, the mode is 2, meaning that the largest number of respondents answering the question said the "People" section is their favorite. The range tells us that values for this variable span a five-point scatter, from a low of 1 (the minimum) to a high of 6 (the maximum). The range, minimum, and maximum are useful indicators of dispersion for nominal variables such as this one.

Summary Statistics for Higher-Order Variables

When a variable is ordered and points on the measure are equal distances apart, there are a number of summary statistics that describe the central tendency and dispersion of the distribution. These statistics are explained best through the use of an example.

In the same readership survey, respondents were asked how many minutes they spend reading *SDSU Report*. This information is important, because length of time spent reading the magazine can be used by the public relations staff to make decisions about the length and number of articles, style of writing, and the mix of graphics and type. Table 10–2 shows the distribution of responses.

The frequencies and percentages in Table 10–2 show patterns of readership. For example, the frequency and valid percent columns indicate that respondents tend to give answers to the question in five-minute blocks. That is, many respondents indicated that they read *SDSU Report* for five minutes, ten minutes, fifteen minutes, and so forth. The cumulative percentage column indi-

Table 10–2 Frequency Distribution of the *SDSU Report* Reading Time Variable

MINUTES	*GENERALLY, HOW MANY MINUTES DO YOU SPEND READING* REPORT?				
VALUE LABEL	*VALUE*	*FREQUENCY*	*PERCENT*	*VALID PERCENT*	*CUM PERCENT*
LESS THAN MINUTE	0	3	0.6	0.7	0.7
	1	1	0.2	0.2	0.9
	2	8	1.5	1.8	2.7
	3	12	2.3	2.7	5.4
	4	7	1.3	1.6	7.0
	5	59	11.4	13.3	20.2
	6	2	0.4	0.4	20.7
	7	7	1.3	1.6	22.2
	8	3	0.6	0.7	22.9
	10	112	21.6	25.2	48.1
	12	6	1.2	1.3	49.4
	13	2	0.4	0.4	49.9
	15	82	15.8	18.4	68.3
	17	6	1.2	1.3	69.7
	18	1	0.2	0.2	69.9
	20	52	10.0	11.7	81.6
	22	1	0.2	0.2	81.8
	25	4	0.8	0.9	82.7
	30	52	10.0	11.7	94.4
	40	6	1.2	1.3	95.7
	45	5	1.0	1.1	96.9
	60	13	2.5	2.9	99.8
	85	1	0.2	0.2	100.0
DEPENDS ON ISSUE	88	23	4.4	MISSING	
UNSURE OR NON-READER	99	51	0.6	MISSING	
	TOTAL	519	100.0	100.0	

MEAN	15.924	STD ERR	.585	MEDIAN	15.000
MODE	10.000	STD DEV	12.341	VARIANCE	152.296
KURTOSIS	5.732	S E KURT	1.996	SKEWNESS	2.039
S E SKEW	.116	RANGE	85.000	MINIMUM	0
MAXIMUM	85.000	SUM	7086.000		

cates that about 20 percent of those answering the question spend five minutes or less. Nearly 50 percent read for ten minutes or less. Fewer than 20 percent spend more than twenty minutes. That is, more than 80 percent spend twenty minutes or less reading *SDSU Report*. Because there are so many more response categories than in Table 10–1, it's more difficult to manage all the information in the table. That's why the summary statistics at the bottom are so useful.

The mean, median, and mode are useful measures of central tendency for this ratio-level variable. As indicated by the mean, the average number of minutes spent reading *SDSU Report* is 15.9 minutes. However, as in Dr. Pavlik's example at the beginning of this chapter, the distribution is skewed. Nearly half the cases cluster in the 0–10 minute range. At the upper end, less than 1 percent of respondents fall in the 80–90 minute range. For this reason, the median is a better measure for some purposes than the mean. The median, 15.0 minutes, is the mathematically determined point that cuts the sample in half. Half the respondents spend fifteen minutes or less reading *SDSU Report*. The other half spend more than fifteen minutes.

The mode indicates the most frequently occurring response. The response most commonly given is ten minutes. You can verify this number by examining the frequency column. The modal answer will have the highest frequency value (excluding missing cases).

There are several measures of dispersion applicable to higher-order variables. As with nominal level variables, the range, minimum, and maximum are useful. For this variable, the values range from a minimum of zero minutes (respondent spends less than a minute reading *SDSU Report*) to a maximum of eighty-five minutes.

NORMAL DISTRIBUTION

The variance and the standard deviation indicate dispersion or scatter. To understand these statistics, it's necessary to consider the normal distribution assumption. The *normal distribution* is a theoretical distribution based on an infinite number of cases. A variable in a single sample may not be perfectly *normal*. That is, such a variable from a single sample may not be shaped like the ideal normal distribution displayed in Figure 10–1. The normal distribution in Figure 10–1 is perfectly symmetrical, meaning that the part of the curve greater than the mean is shaped the same (actually a mirror image) as that part of the curve less than the mean. Its bell shape is precisely defined by a mathematical formula.

An actual distribution, like the one for the number of minutes spent reading the *SDSU Report* displayed in Table 10–2, may only approximate a normal distribution. Figure 10–2 displays the distribution of minutes spent reading the *SDSU Report*. Since 445 valid cases is considerably fewer than the infinite number of cases idealized in Figure 10–1, it's not too surprising that the two distributions are different.

The bars in Figure 10–2 provide a *histogram* of the distribution of the

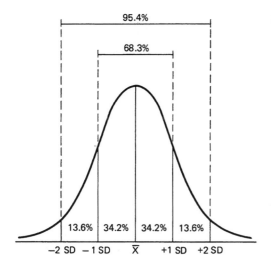

Figure 10–1   The normal distribution.

reading time variable. The number of minutes reported reading the *Report* are grouped into five-minute categories. The height of each bar indicates how many respondents fell into that category. The dashed line is an *idealization* of the distribution. This graphic representation of the "ideal" distribution assumes a very large number of respondents.

The clustering of cases at the five-minute, ten-minute, fifteen-minute, and twenty-minute points on the scale are a product of the way people estimate time

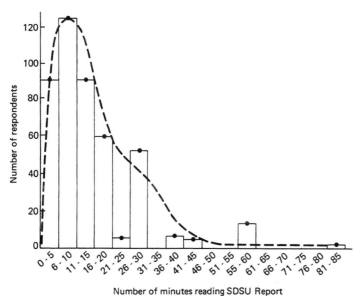

Figure 10–2   Histogram and graphic representation of length of reading time.

spent reading a magazine. A reader who typically spends an average of nineteen minutes reading the magazine may likely report spending twenty minutes. The same answer may be given by readers who typically spend twenty-two minutes reading *SDSU Report*. This clustering, a form of measurement error, is not likely to disappear as the number of cases increases. Respondents are likely to estimate reading time in five-, ten-, and twenty-minute clusters, regardless of sample size. So the idealized dashed line in Figure 10–2 is also an idealization of the respondent's more accurate estimation of reading time.

The Importance of Normal Distributions

In Chapter 11, you will learn about several statistical procedures that assume that the variables you analyze are normally distributed. Before you use such statistics, you should check variables to see how much they differ from the normal distribution. Note that few distributions in samples are perfectly normal. Statistical procedures that assume variables are normally distributed are generally robust enough to work on variables that are not perfectly normal. When you use such statistics, you need to know that the variables are not normally distributed. Two statistics provided with the frequency distribution help you assess how "normal" variables are. These statistics are kurtosis and skewness.

Kurtosis

The *kurtosis* statistic indicates whether the distribution is flat or peaked relative to the normal distribution.[3] When the kurtosis value is zero, the distribution is perfectly normal, in the strict statistical sense of the word, as in the top curve in Figure 10–3 (curve A). When the distribution is peaked, as in Table 10–2 and Figure 10–2 for the reading time variable, the kurtosis value is a positive number which increases as the distribution becomes more peaked. A positive kurtosis distribution is illustrated for an imaginary variable in the bottom curve (curve C) of Figure 10–3.

On the other hand, if the distribution were flat when compared to the normal distribution, the kurtosis value would be negative. The curve in the middle of Figure 10–3 (curve B) illustrates a negative kurtosis distribution for an imaginary variable. The kurtosis value becomes even larger—in the negative direction—as the distribution becomes flatter.

Skewness

Skewness indicates how lopsided the distribution is. If the skewness value is zero, the distribution is perfectly symmetrical.[4] The distribution to the left of

[3]Norman H. Nie, C. Hadlai Hull, Jean G. Jenkins, Karin Steinbrenner, and Dale H. Bent, *Statistical Package for the Social Sciences*, 2nd ed. (New York: McGraw-Hill, 1975), p. 185.
[4]Ibid., pp. 184–85.

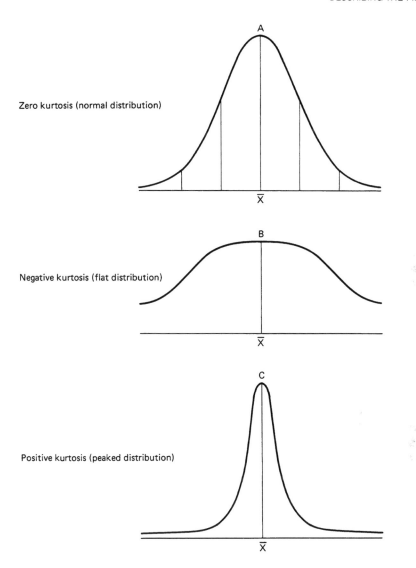

Figure 10-3 Examples of positive and negative kurtosis distributions.

the mean is a mirror image of the distribution to the right of the mean. That is, an equal number of cases fall to the left and to the right of the mean. Therefore, the median (the point that divides the number of cases in the distribution into two equal halves) is equal to the mean. The normal distribution in Figure 10–1 is symmetrical, with a skewness value of zero.

In the Table 10–2 example, the 2.039 value of the skewness statistic (a positive skew) indicates that the distribution is lopsided, with many cases falling to the left of the mean and fewer cases falling to the right of the mean and spread out over a larger range of numbers. The distribution of the magazine reading time, as illustrated in Figure 10-2, is said to have a "long tail" to the right.

This longer "tail" to the right of the distribution *inflates* the mean. That is, no respondent reads the magazine less than zero minutes. That's only fifteen minutes from the median, the midpoint of the distribution. But some respondents read the magazine for nearly ninety minutes, seventy-five minutes from the midpoint of the distribution. These extremely high reading times inflate the mean and, for some purposes, make the median a better indicator of central tendency. At the bottom of Table 10-2, you see that the mean is higher than the median, inflated by readers who spend over an hour reading a magazine that takes the "typical" reader only fifteen minutes to read.

Figure 10-4 illustrates positive and negative skewed distributions for two idealized, imaginary variables. The distribution at the top of Figure 10-4 illustrates a positive skewed distribution. Note that the mean is higher than the median, just as in the case of the magazine reading time variable. The distribution at the bottom of Figure 10-4 shows a negative skewed distribution.

An example of a negatively skewed distribution is shown in Table 10-3.

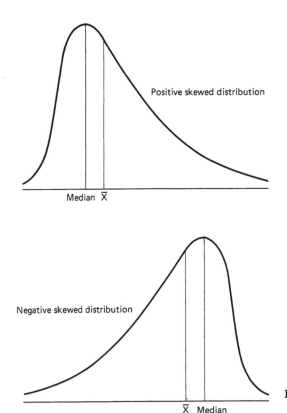

Figure 10-4 Positive and negative skewed distributions.

Table 10–3 Frequency Distribution of Number of Issues Read Variable (Last Two Years)

NUMREAD		NUMBER OF LAST EIGHT ISSUES READ			
VALUE LABEL	VALUE	FREQUENCY	PERCENT	VALID PERCENT	CUM PERCENT
NONE	0	2	0.4	0.4	0.4
	1	15	2.9	3.3	3.8
	2	32	6.2	7.1	10.9
	3	31	6.0	6.9	17.7
	4	80	15.4	17.7	35.5
	5	19	3.7	4.2	39.7
	6	37	7.1	8.2	47.9
	7	13	2.5	2.9	50.8
ALL ISSUES	8	222	42.8	49.2	100.0
UNSURE OR NONREADER		68	13.1	MISSING	
	TOTAL	519	100.0	100.0	

MEAN	5.933	STD ERR	0.110	MEDIAN	7.000
MODE	8.000	STD DEV	2.346	VARIANCE	5.502
KURTOSIS	−1.047	S E KURT	1.996	SKEWNESS	−0.617
S E SKEW	.115	RANGE	8.000	MINIMUM	0
MAXIMUM	8.000	SUM	2676.000		

Respondents in the survey were asked how many of the last eight issues of *SDSU Report* they read. Respondents could read no more than eight issues over the two-year period, and nearly half (49.2 percent) of the readers read all eight. A histogram and an idealized curve of that distribution (which assumes a larger sample size) is shown in Figure 10–5. As you can see, the "tail" is now to the left. Note also that the median is *higher* than the mean. That is, the mean is *deflated* by the extreme cases to the left in the "tail" of the distribution. This is consistent with the idealized negative skewed distribution in Figure 10–4.

Measures of Dispersion

The kurtosis and skewness statistics are useful when measures of dispersion are considered. In addition to the range, the minimum, and the maximum variance and standard deviation are appropriate measures of dispersion for higher-order measures such as the magazine reading time variable. The *variance* is a measure of the scatter of cases about the mean, computed by subtracting the value of each case from the mean, squaring that difference, and taking the average of all those differences. The higher the variance, the more widely dispersed or scattered the cases about the mean. The *standard deviation,* the square root of the variance, is another way of expressing dispersion or scatter.

If the distribution is normal, as in the bell-shaped curve in Figure 10–1,

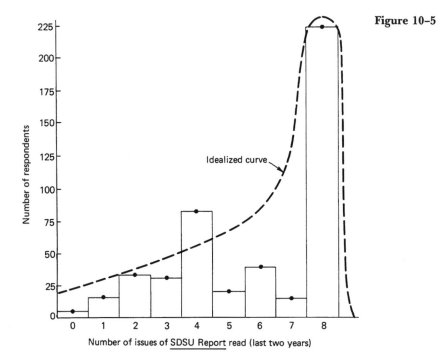

Figure 10-5 Histogram and idealized curve of number of issues of *SDSU Report* read during last two years.

then 68.3 percent of the cases fall within one standard deviation above and below the mean; 95.4 percent of cases fall within two standard deviations above and below the mean.[5] Because the distribution of minutes spent reading *SDSU Report* only approximates a normal distribution (it's skewed to the left and "flat" over most of the distribution), the standard deviation provides only an approximation of the number of cases falling within a standard deviation of the mean.

The Confidence Interval

In Chapter 6, the 95 percent confidence interval was considered in detail for percentages of a sample. Using statistics at the bottom of Table 10-2, the 95 percent confidence interval can be computed for the mean of this higher-order variable. To make this calculation, you use the standard error.

The *standard error* is the measure of the dispersion of many sample means if we were to conduct many readership surveys similar to the one just described. That is, if we went out and surveyed another 519 respondents, we would likely get a different mean from the new sample, when compared to the one obtained from the present survey. If we repeated this process of sampling 519 respondents over and over again, we would obtain a distribution of sample means, one sample

[5]Sonia R. Wright, *Quantitative Methods and Statistics: A Guide to Social Research* (Beverly Hills, Calif.: Sage, 1979), p. 102.

mean from each sample. Figure 6–2 in Chapter 6 provides an illustration of such a distribution of many sample values from many different surveys *with the same number of respondents.*

The distribution of these sample means is normally distributed about the mean of means, the *grand mean* we would get if we took the mean from each sample and computed the average mean from all the studies. The standard deviation of these sample means is the *standard error.*[6] About 95 percent of the sample means fall within 1.96 standard errors of the mean of means. As indicated in Chapter 6 for percentages, this mean of means converges on the true population mean.[7] If we repeated the sampling an infinite number of times, the mean of means would equal the true population mean.

Computing the Confidence Interval

Knowing the sample size and the dispersion within the sample, the computer calculates the standard error.[8] Some statistical software computes the 95 percent confidence interval for you. If not, simply multiply the standard error by 1.96. *Subtracting* the resulting value from the sample mean establishes the lower limit of the 95 percent confidence interval. *Adding* the resulting value to the sample mean establishes the upper limit of the 95 percent confidence interval. Here are the formulas:

Lower Limit = Mean − (1.96 × Standard Error)
Upper Limit = Mean + (1.96 × Standard Error)

For this example, the mean is 15.92 and the standard error is 0.585. (See MEAN and STD ERR at the bottom of Table 10–2.) Plugging these numbers into the formula:

Lower Limit = 15.92 − (1.96 × 0.585) = 14.77
Upper Limit = 15.92 + (1.96 × 0.585) = 17.07

That is, we can now state that we are 95 percent sure that the average length of time spent reading the *SDSU Report* among its 75,000 readers falls somewhere between 14.77 minutes and 17.07 minutes. We cannot be precisely sure of the exact average without surveying all 75,000 readers. But we can estimate the length of time spent reading the *SDSU Report* for the entire population of 75,000 readers through the confidence interval.

[6]Nie and others, op. cit., p.184.
[7]This is one implication of the Central Limit Theorem. For an explanation of this theorem, see Wright, op. cit., pp. 98–99.
[8]The standard error is calculated by dividing the standard deviation of the sample by the square root of the sample size.

CHAPTER 11

TESTING RELATIONSHIPS

Mary Ann Ferguson, PhD, Associate Professor and Director, Communication Research Center, College of Journalism and Communications, UNIVERSITY OF FLORIDA, Gainesville.

URPR: What kind of errors do researchers make when measuring relationships between variables?

Ferguson: *One error I often see is violation of the major assumptions of the statistics. Some are quite serious. The student or practitioner of public relations is probably not going to know which ones are serious and which are not. It's not at all unusual to have a student use a Pearson correlation to correlate two nominal variables [an inappropriate use of that statistic]. And they're so proud of what they've got! Another common error in statistical analysis is using a general test like ANOVA and the F-test to assert difference in groups without any kind of contrast tests. Just because the F-test is significant, it doesn't mean that all groups differ. Or to use a Chi-Square value to assert differences between groups without any test within the cells. With Chi-Square, there may be only a couple of cells that are different. For the rest of the cells, there may be no difference.*

URPR: There is a trade-off between the more powerful multivariate statistical procedures and the more understandable utility statistics like the Chi-Square. The more complex and interesting the analysis, the harder it is to explain.

Ferguson: *What I like to do is go to the highest level of analysis. I might use regression models, correlation coefficients, or whatever's appropriate. If the relationship is interesting and significant—and we underline **interesting** in applied research—I try for the client's sake to move it down to a more simple analysis. I might do a crosstab. Once I'm convinced I have an interesting and significant relationship, I try to find the most simple way to present that relationship.*

URPR: When using the Pearson correlation coefficient, you are only able to detect simple, linear relationships. What about testing for nonlinear relations? Do you classify or categorize your metric data and use crosstabs? Or do you do something else?

Ferguson: *The best thing to do is look at a plot. The problem with classification is that there may well be a nonlinear relationship there. But by the choices you make in classifying the data, you may miss it entirely. The relationship may all be in the upper, right cell of your crosstab table. You miss it if you've collapsed too much information.*

URPR: What advice do you have as we begin this chapter on using data to test for relationships?

Ferguson: *One thing I tell my students is spend as much or more time with the descriptive statistics as with the inferential statistics. They should come to learn the data at more than just a cognitive level. I get earthy and tell them to "gut the data," come to feel it at a gut level. To learn what the data really mean. To draw lots of pictures and graphs, to understand what their data look like. Use histograms, plots, or whatever else you can to understand the data.*

In this chapter, you will learn the meaning of *relationships* between variables. You also will learn about five commonly used statistical tests of relationships: Chi-Square, *F*-test, *t*-test, Pearson correlation, and Kendall's tau correlation. These statistical procedures are not all that are available, but they give you the basic statistical tools needed to analyze quantitative data. These statistical procedures describe relationships between variables in probability samples and test for the presence or absence of relations in populations from which these samples are drawn.

THE MEANING OF RELATIONSHIPS
BETWEEN VARIABLES

What does it mean to say that two variables are related to each other?

First, variables are related if they measure the same construct. For example, you ask a probability sample of employees if they agree or disagree: "Articles in the magazine are about things that interest me." You also ask if they agree or disagree: "Articles in the magazine are enjoyable to read." You've selected these items as separate measures of the construct "reader satisfaction." Because both items are designed to measure the same single construct, you expect that employees who agree with the first statement will tend to agree with the second. Those who disagree with the first, you reason, should also disagree with the second. They co-vary together. This means that the two variables tend to go together, that they are correlated or associated with each other. In short, they are related.

Reliability Coefficients

As Chapter 8 explains, researchers generally like to use multiple measures of key constructs, to triangulate on the construct by combining several different real-world measures. When three or more measures of a construct are combined in an index or scale, Cronbach's *alpha coefficient* provides a measure of how reliably the variables measure some construct. Cronbach's alpha ranges from zero (wholly unreliable index) to one (perfectly reliable index). An alpha reliability coefficient of 0.90 or better indicates a highly reliable index or scale. Indices or scales with alpha coefficients as low as 0.70 are still useful measures of constructs. Items are selected for inclusion in an index or scale, based on the strength of their relation, correlation, or association with other items in the index or scale.

Cause and Effect

Second, variables are related if a change in one variable *causes* a change in another variable. For example, we increase the number of placements about our corporation in newspapers and on television, emphasizing our company's commitment to product quality. We survey potential consumers of our products *before* and *after* we implement our communication strategy. In both surveys, we ask potential consumers if they agree or disagree with the statement that our company "has a strong commitment to the quality of products it produces." Before the program, only 25 percent agree. After the program, 50 percent agree. From this, we might conclude that the increase in communication about our product quality has "caused" an increase in the perception among potential consumers that we're committed to product quality. As indicated in Chapter 5, there are other rival explanations for this outcome. Our evaluation design would have to incorporate control groups or other strategies to make sure that the program is the only truly plausible explanation for the change in perceived commitment to product quality. We discuss the issue of causality in greater detail in Chapter 12.

Independent and Dependent Variables

In this example, the messages about product quality in the media make up the independent variable. Our working theory is that the *independent* variable will influence (cause a change in) the dependent variable. The *dependent variable* is consumer perceptions of our company's commitment to product quality. The value of the *dependent* variable (low versus high commitment to product quality) is theorized to depend on or be influenced by the magnitude or value of the independent variable.

Which variable is independent and which is dependent in a relationship is a decision you make. Your decision rests on your understanding of what variable is *causally antecedent* in the relationship. For many statistical procedures, we designate a variable as independent because we see that variable influencing (causing a change in) the dependent variable—and not the other way around. That is, we theorize that the value of the independent variable is not dependent on (is independent of) the value of the dependent variable.

For example, we know that parents with brown eyes have a high probability of bearing children with brown eyes. (Let's leave out mixed parentage where parents differ in eye color.) Parents with blue eyes are more likely than brown-eyed parents to have blue-eyed children. In a survey of students in your public relations research methods course, ask each student his or her eye color and the color of the eyes of both parents. You find that parent eye color is related to child's eye color. (See Table 11–1.)

Is parent eye color *caused* by the child's eye color? Certainly not! We theorize the opposite: Parent eye color influences child eye color. Why? First, we know that parent's eye color was determined *first;* it happened before the child's eye color occurred, before the child was born. Second, theories of genetics and heredity suggest the direction of causality in the relationship. *Direction of causality* is used to determine which variable is independent and which is dependent. Note, however, that there is nothing inherent in the aforementioned survey of students that determines causality. That is an important fact to remember about cross-sectional survey research: You can't tell which variable is independent and which is dependent from the survey results. You determine the direction of causality—specifying the independent and dependent variables—based on your understanding of the theoretical connection between the two variables.

Table 11–1 is a simplified example of a *contingency* or *crosstabulation* table. Traditionally, the independent variable is displayed as columns in a contingency

Table 11–1 Relationship Between Parent Eye Color and Child's Eye Color

		Color of Parents' Eyes	
		BROWN	*BLUE*
Child's Eye Color	*Brown*	90%	30%
	Blue	10%	70%
		100%	100%

table. The dependent variable is displayed as rows in the table. In Table 11–1, percentages in the table are computed for each column, totaling 100 percent for each column. When contingency tables are generated by statistical software, you may get many percentages for each cell, each using a different computation strategy. The problem is that you may be overwhelmed by the numbers!

Table 11–2 provides a quick introduction to computer-generated contingency or crosstabulation tables. This table is the long version of Table 11–1, with all possible percentages included for a sample of 200 people. In each cell, four numbers appear. The top number is the number of people in each cell. The second number is the percentage of people in each cell computed for the *row*. The third number is the percentage of people in each cell computed for the *column*. The last number is the percentage of people in each cell computed for the *entire sample* of 200.

To interpret contingency tables, the most common way is to compare column percentages across columns. If the percentages differ, the two variables are related. If they are the same, the two variables are not related. In this example, we see that among the brown-eyed parents, only 10 percent of their children have blue eyes. Among blue-eyed parents, fully 70 percent have a blue-eyed child. We can see the same strong relationship by comparing row percentages. Among brown-eyed children, fully 81.8 percent have brown-eyed parents. Among blue-eyed children, only 17.6 percent have brown-eyed parents. Any way you look at Table 11–2, children are more likely to have the same eye color as their parents. The two variables, parental and child eye color, are related.

If you find Table 11–2 and this explanation confusing, please stop now and read Appendix K, "How to Interpret a Contingency Table." This appendix provides a detailed, step-by-step explanation of how to make sense of contingency tables. You will need to know how to interpret contingency or crosstabulation tables to make sense of the rest of this chapter.

Prediction

Sometimes variables are related to each other but we don't know why. That is, we have no theoretical explanation for this relationship; we simply observe that two variables are related to each other. For example, the Office of

Table 11–2 A Guide to Interpreting Computer-Generated Contingency Tables
(Relationship Between Parent and Child Eye Color)

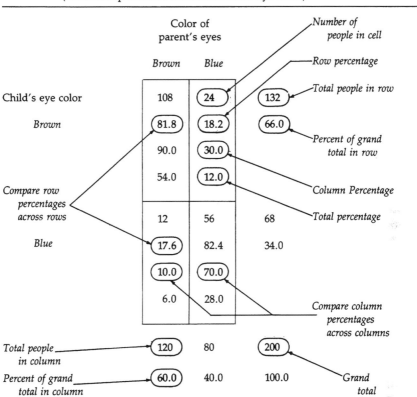

Communication, San Diego State University, conducts a survey of a random sample of alumni, faculty, staff, and community influentials. These individuals make up the 75,000 recipients of *SDSU Report.* The survey shows that involvement in extra-curricular activities was more common among alumni who started college many years ago than among alumni who started college a few years ago. That is, the year the respondent started college (the independent variable) is *negatively correlated* (related, associated) with involvement in extra-curricular activities (the dependent variable). The *higher* the year college started (1980 versus 1970), the *lower* the respondent's involvement in extracurricular activities.

If we want to *predict* whether alumni were involved in extracurricular activities while attending the university, we could make a better prediction if we know what year they started college. For example, among all alumni, only 38.8 percent participated in extracurricular activities. (See the column for all decades combined in Table 11–3.) The remaining 61.2 percent were not involved in such activities.

If you know nothing else about the respondent, you would predict that the respondent was *not* involved in extracurricular activities. That's because,

Table 11–3 Relationship Between Participation in Extracurricular Activities and Year Attendance at University Began

Involvement in extracurricular activities	Decades university attendance began		For ALL decades combined
	1910–1969	*1970–1986*	
Not involved	37.3%	66.3%	61.2%
Involved	62.7%	33.7%	38.8%
	100.0%	100.0%	100.0%

when all decades of college attendance are combined, the majority of respondents were *not* involved in extracurricular activities. You would be right 61.2 percent of the time. However, as indicated in Table 11–3, involvement in extracurricular activities is dependent on (related to, correlated with) the year alumni began studies at the university. Among those starting at the university prior to 1970, 62.7 percent were involved in extracurricular activities. Among those starting at the university from 1970 to the present, only 33.7 percent were involved in extracurricular activities.

This example illustrates two points. First, when two variables are *related* (correlated, associated), we can do a better job of *predicting* the value of one variable by knowing the value of the other variable. In this example, we can improve our prediction as to whether alumni participated in extracurricular activities by knowing the years they started attending the university. If alumni started at the university prior to 1970, we predict that they *did* participate. We would be right 62.7 percent of the time. Without that information, our best prediction would be that alumni did *not* participate in extracurricular activities, but we would be right only 37.3 percent of the time. We improve our prediction by 25.4 percentage points by knowing that these alumni attended the university prior to 1970. A relationship between two variables permits us to improve our prediction of the value of the dependent variable by knowing the value of the independent variable. If two variables are not related, knowing the value of the independent variable does nothing to improve prediction of the value of the dependent variable.

The second point is more subtle. Our prediction is not driven by any theory that explains *why* year of starting college makes a difference in participation in extracurricular activities. Knowing when someone started college helps *predict* but does not *explain* participation in extracurricular activities.

Explanation

Another example from the same survey illustrates a relationship that is both explained and predicted by theory. In this example, we test the theory that exposure to the content of *SDSU Report* is related to a positive image of San Diego

State. Respondents are asked how frequently they read *SDSU Report*—frequently or infrequently. Later in the questionnaire, they are asked if they agree or disagree with, or feel neutral about, the statement that San Diego State is a high-quality, comprehensive university. Because much of the content of the magazine deals with university activities and events that portray its high quality and comprehensive character, it's plausible to predict that exposure to such messages will lead to agreement with the opinion statement.

Crosstabulation A at the top of Table 11–4 shows survey results for a relatively strong relationship between the two variables in the sample. Among

Table 11–4 Three Different Relationships Between Opinion of University As High Quality and Frequency of Reading *SDSU Report*

CROSSTABULATION A: "STRONG" RELATIONSHIP IN SAMPLE

"SDSU is high-quality comprehensive"		Frequency of reading magazine		ALL RESPONDENTS
		INFREQUENTLY	FREQUENTLY	
	DISAGREE	5.0%	2.3%	3.6%
	NEUTRAL	14.5%	8.1%	11.2%
Chi-square = 8.35, d.f. = 2	AGREE	80.5%	89.6%	85.2%
SIGNIFICANCE = .0153	TOTAL	100.0%	100.0%	100.0% (N=501)

CROSSTABULATION B: "WEAK" RELATIONSHIP IN SAMPLE

"SDSU is high-quality comprehensive"		Frequency of reading magazine		ALL RESPONDENTS
		INFREQUENTLY	FREQUENTLY	
	DISAGREE	3.9%	3.3%	3.6%
	NEUTRAL	11.4%	11.0%	11.2%
Chi-square = 0.12, d.f. = 2	AGREE	84.7%	85.7%	85.2%
SIGNIFICANCE = .9413	TOTAL	100.0%	100.0%	100.0% (N=501)

CROSSTABULATION C: PERFECT "NULL" RELATIONSHIP

"SDSU is high-quality comprehensive"		Frequency of reading magazine		ALL RESPONDENTS
		INFREQUENTLY	FREQUENTLY	
	DISAGREE	3.6%	3.6%	3.6%
	NEUTRAL	11.2%	11.2%	11.2%
Chi-square = 0.00, d.f. = 2	AGREE	85.2%	85.2%	85.2%
SIGNIFICANCE = .9999	TOTAL	100.0%	100.0%	100.0% (N=501)

respondents who frequently read *SDSU Report,* 89.6 percent agree that San Diego State is a high-quality, comprehensive university. Only 80.5 percent of the infrequent readers agree. Knowing that respondents are frequent readers of *SDSU Report,* we can *predict* that they will agree the university is high quality and comprehensive. We will be right more often than if we did not know about the readership of *SDSU Report.*

More importantly, we have evidence supporting the theory that exposure to the content of *SDSU Report* leads to a positive opinion of the university. Note, however, that there are alternative explanations—rival theories—for this relationship. For example, one could theorize that some respondents already held positive opinions of the university for other reasons. These positive respondents then seek out more information about the university. That is, positive opinion of the university motivates reading *SDSU Report,* not the other way around. The two variables are *related,* but we have not determined the *direction of causality.* You will learn more about determining direction of causality in Chapter 12.

When No Relationship Exists

Many variables are not related. That is, the value of one variable exerts no influence on (does not cause) the value of another variable. Crosstabulation C at the bottom of Table 11–4 illustrates what we would expect if *SDSU Report* readership exerted no influence on opinions of San Diego State. This table isn't what a survey would actually show. Rather, this table is constructed to show what a table would look like if two variables are not in any way related in a sample.

Crosstabulation C (Table 11–4) indicates that exactly 85.2 percent of the infrequent readers and exactly 85.2 percent of the frequent readers regard San Diego State as a high-quality, comprehensive university. These percentages are the same as the combined percentage for both frequent and infrequent readers. In other words, it doesn't make any difference whether one reads *SDSU Report* or not, in terms of viewing the university as high-quality and comprehensive. Frequent and infrequent readers feel exactly the same about the quality and comprehensiveness of the university.

The Null Hypothesis

Crosstabulation C (Table 11–4) shows what we would expect if the null hypothesis is true. The *null hypothesis* is the prediction that two variables are not related—that the value of the dependent variable does not depend on the value of the independent variable. We use the null hypothesis to make inferences from samples to populations. Inferential statistics are usually interpreted in terms of the null hypothesis. Inferential statistics allow us to determine the probability that *no* relationship exists in the population (the null hypothesis), despite observing *some* relationship in the sample.

The Research Hypothesis

The null hypothesis is the opposite of the *research hypothesis*—a statement that says two variables are related to each other. In this instance, the research hypothesis says that exposure to the content of *SDSU Report* is positively related to the opinion that the university is high-quality and comprehensive. That is, people with high levels of exposure to *SDSU Report* have a high opinion of San Diego State. Persons with lower exposure hold lower opinions.

There are two types of research hypotheses. The first type indicates that two variables are related to each other and also indicates the *direction* of that relationship. The foregoing research hypothesis is an example of this type of hypothesis. Hypotheses that specify the *direction* of the relationship call for a "one-tailed" test of the relationship. The second type simply states that two variables are related, but the direction of the relationship is not predicted. For example, a research hypothesis predicts that salaried employees and hourly employees will have different scores—on the average—on a job satisfaction survey. The hypothesis doesn't predict that salaried employees will do better or that hourly employees will do better. It simply predicts that salaried employees, as a group, will score differently than hourly employees as a group. This type of hypothesis calls for a "two-tailed" test of relationship.

The middle crosstabulation, crosstabulation B, in Table 11–4, exhibits the results we might find in a sample drawn from a population where the null hypothesis is true. (These are not actual data from the survey; they were simulated to make a point about the null hypothesis.) We rarely see two variables that are wholly unrelated in a sample survey, as in crosstabulation C. Random fluctuations in the sample (sampling error) are more likely to generate results like crosstabulation B. In fact, let's state that as a "rule" about data collected in the real world:

> *Two variables will appear related to each other to some degree in a large sample, whether the null hypothesis is true or false.*

Of course, there will be times when this isn't true. You might analyze two variables in a sample and get results like those in crosstabulation C (Table 11–4). Usually, however, you will get results more like those in crosstabulation B, even when the null hypothesis is true.

In crosstabulation B, 85.7 percent of the frequent readers of the magazine hold a positive opinion of San Diego State, whereas 84.7 percent of infrequent readers hold a positive opinion. Among 260 frequent readers in the survey, 1 percent more agree with the opinion statement than among the 241 infrequent readers. The one percentage-point difference indicates a weak relationship between the two variables in the sample. Is this weak relationship indicative of a genuine relation between the two variables in the population of 75,000 people mailed the magazine? Or is the relationship in the sample an illusion created by sampling error? To find out, we use *inferential statistics*.

AN INTRODUCTION TO THE
CHI-SQUARE STATISTIC

One inferential statistic commonly used in public relations research and through-out the social sciences is the Chi-Square statistic. This statistic is popular because it can be used on nominal-, ordinal-, interval-, and ratio-level variables. That is, it's hard to misuse the Chi-Square statistic. The Chi-Square statistic performs a very useful function. It provides a probability statement about the truth of the null hypothesis. The Chi-Square statistic tells us how likely it is that the null hypothesis (no relation between two variables) is true for the *population*, despite some relationship in the *sample* we analyze.

In the typical research methods book, the next page or two would explain how to compute the Chi-Square statistic. As a practical matter, however, you rarely need to hand calculate any inferential statistic. You use a mainframe computer or a small personal computer and off-the-shelf application software (such as SPSS-X) to compute inferential statistics. (If you really want to know what's going on inside the "black box" of the computer, study Appendix I. In that appendix, you can learn to do what statistical application packages do: compute Chi-Square—and compute the Chi-Square for yourself.)

Rather than overwhelm you with arithmetic and mathematical symbols, let's develop a conceptual understanding of this statistic. The Chi-Square statistic is computed by examining a particular sample outcome, like crosstabulation A in Table 11–4. The Chi-Square statistic determines how much the real-world sample deviates from the outcome we would expect under the condition of the null hypothesis. What outcome would we expect if the two variables are not related to each other? That null outcome, shown in crosstabulation C for this example, shows *no relation* between frequency of reading *SDSU Report* and agreement with the opinion statement.

To compute the Chi-Square statistic, the computer looks at each of the six boxes or cells in crosstabulation A and crosstabulation C in Table 11–4. How many people are there in the upper, left-hand cell? Crosstabulation C, the expected outcome under the null hypothesis, says that 3.6 percent of the infrequent readers should disagree with the opinion statement. That's if the two variables are unrelated to each other in the population. What we actually find in our sample of 501 respondents is shown in crosstabulation A. We see that 5.0 percent of the infrequent readers disagree with the opinion statement, somewhat greater than the 3.6 percent we would expect under the null hypothesis. The *observed* values in crosstabulation A differ from the *expected* values under conditions of the null hypothesis in crosstabulation C. The Chi-Square statistic is computed by adding up the differences in each cell of the table for frequent and infrequent readers. (For a more precise explanation, refer to Appendix I.) The more the observed value differs from the value expected under the null hypothesis (no relation), the larger the Chi-Square statistic. The larger the Chi-Square statistic, the less likely the null hypothesis is true.

Strong Relationship

In crosstabulation A, we see that the Chi-Square statistic equals 8.35. The size of the Chi-Square increases as the relationship between two variables becomes stronger. The relatively strong relationship in the sample is reflected in a relatively large Chi-Square value.

Weak Relationship

In crosstabulation B, we see that the values in each cell deviate a little bit from the values in crosstabulation C, from values we would expect under conditions of the null hypothesis (no relationship). For example, the null hypothesis says that 3.6 percent of the infrequent readers should disagree with the opinion statement. Table 11–5 shows that 3.9 percent of the infrequent readers actually disagree with the opinion statement. While the 0.3 percentage-point difference is small, these tiny deviations occur in several cells of the table. When added together, we see these deviations from the null hypothesis total 0.12, the value of the Chi-Square statistic. Since the observed values differ little from what we would expect to see if the null hypothesis is true, the Chi-Square statistic is small.

Null Relationship

In crosstabulation C, the values in the table exactly match what we would expect to observe under conditions of the null hypothesis (no relationship). Therefore, there is no difference between the observed value and the value ex-

Table 11–5 Negative Relationship Between Perception of University as High Quality and Frequency of Reading *SDSU Report*

		Frequency of reading *SDSU Report*		
		INFREQUENTLY	*FREQUENTLY*	*FREQ. & INFREQ. READERS COMBINED*
"University is high-quality & comprehensive"	*DISAGREE*	2.3%	5.0%	3.6%
	NEUTRAL	8.1%	14.5%	11.2%
	AGREE	89.6%	80.5%	85.2%
		100.0%	100.0%	100.0%
Number of respondents =		241	260	501

Chi-square = 8.35   d.f. = 2   SIGNIFICANCE = 0.0153

pected under the null hypothesis for each cell in the table. When we add up all these zeros, the Chi-Square statistic equals zero.

Degrees of Freedom

The Chi-Square statistic becomes larger when we add more cells to the table. For example, we could measure frequency of readership by asking respondents if they read *SDSU Report* always, often, sometimes, or almost never. Since there are four values to the readership variable and three values (agree, neutral, disagree) to the opinion variable, the table would have twelve cells ($3 \times 4 = 12$). Since the Chi-Square statistic adds up differences between the expected and observed value in *each* cell, we would expect the Chi-Square statistic to be larger for large tables and smaller for small tables, *even if* the null hypothesis is true. Therefore, to interpret the Chi-Square statistic, we need to know how big the table is that generates the statistic. The size of the table (number of cells) is indicated by a statistic called *degrees of freedom*. The bigger the table (more rows or columns), the more degrees of freedom. In the three crosstabulations in Table 11–4, there are three rows (agree, neutral, disagree) and two columns (infrequent, frequent). This represents two degrees of freedom. (See Appendix I to compute the degrees of freedom by hand.)

Significance

Knowing the Chi-Square statistic and the degrees of freedom statistic, we can compute how likely it is that the null hypothesis is true for the population. In the days before inexpensive computers and application software, you would use the Chi-Square statistic and the degrees of freedom to look up the probability of the null hypothesis being true in the appendix of a methods textbook. (We provide one in Appendix J.) Fortunately, now the computer computes this probability for us. That value is shown for each of the three crosstabulations in Table 11–4 as the SIGNIFICANCE statistic. In crosstabulation A, where the Chi-Square statistic is 8.35, the probability of the null hypothesis being true is 0.0153. This means that there is only a 0.0153 chance of the null hypothesis being true for the population of 75,000 recipients of *SDSU Report,* given the relationship we observed in *this* sample of 501 recipients. We can convert this probability statement to a percentage by moving the decimal point two places to the right:

0.0153

That is, there is a 1.53 percent chance that there is *no* relationship in the population between frequency of reading *SDSU Report* and the opinion that San Diego State is a high-quality, comprehensive university.

What is the probability that the research hypothesis is true, that frequency of readership and agreement with the opinion statement *are* related to each other in the population? To find out, we subtract the probability (in percent form) of the null hypothesis being true from 100 percent:

$$100 - 1.53 = 98.47$$

That means that there is a 98.47 percent chance that the two variables are related to each other among all 75,000 recipients of *SDSU Report*.

Examine crosstabulation B in Table 11–4. The Chi-Square statistic is 0.12—much smaller than the 8.35 in crosstabulation A and closer to the 0.00 in crosstabulation C. SIGNIFICANCE equals .9413. Converted to percentage form, there is a 94.13 percent chance that the two variables are *not* related to each other in the population, *given* the weak relationship detected in *this* sample. That is, the relationship in our sample is *probably* (about a 94 percent chance) due to sampling error. However, there is a *slight* chance (about 6 percent) that there *is* a relationship in the population. The weak relationship in the sample may not be a product of sampling error. There's always a chance of a relationship in the population which our sample has missed. As we said in Chapter 6, the only way to be 100 percent sure is to survey all 75,000 recipients of the *SDSU Report*.

Examine crosstabulation C. This is the exact outcome we would expect if the two variables are wholly unrelated to each other in the population. The Chi-Square statistic is zero. The computer says that there is a 0.9999 chance of the null hypothesis being true in the population, given *this* outcome in a sample of 501 respondents drawn from that population. Converting this probability into percentage form, we see that there is a 99.99 percent chance that there is no relationship in the population, since there is no relationship in the sample.

Why aren't we 100 percent sure that there's no relationship in the population? There *is* always a remote chance that there is some relationship in the population. Our sample of frequent and infrequent readers simply failed to detect such a relationship. Results in crosstabulation C might *possibly* be (but are not *likely* to be) the product of *sampling error* in which the true relationship in the population does not show up in the sample.

Examining the Relationship in the Table

At this point, you might conclude we've told you more than you need to know about the Chi-Square statistic. After all, if the SIGNIFICANCE value tells us the probability of no relationship in the population, who needs the rest of the table? Table 11–5 indicates the problem with this simplified approach to analyzing the Chi-Square statistic. As in crosstabulation A, there is a high probability that the two variables are related to each other in the population. So we conclude that those who read the *SDSU Report* more frequently are more likely to view San Diego State as a high-quality, comprehensive university. Right?

Wrong! Remember, our *research hypothesis*—the relationship predicted by our theory—states that there is a *positive* relationship between the two variables.

As reading *SDSU Report* increases, positive opinion toward the University (high-quality, comprehensive) also increases. Examine the percentages in Table 11–5. Among *infrequent* readers, 89.6 percent view the University as high-quality and comprehensive. Among *frequent* readers, only 80.5 percent view the University as high-quality and comprehensive. In *this* sample, there is a *negative* relationship between frequency of reading *SDSU Report* and opinion of the university. These simulated data illustrate why you must understand the relationship *within the sample* before making inferences about the population. In this example, there is a relationship between reading *SDSU Report* and opinion of the university, but the relationship is opposite that of the research hypothesis. The Chi-Square statistic indicates that this negative relationship probably holds true (about a 98 percent chance) for the other 74,500 recipients of *SDSU Report* as well. Our research hypothesis is soundly rejected, based on Table 11–5.

DECISION RULES AND STATISTICAL SIGNIFICANCE

To make inferences from samples to populations, we use the probability that the research hypothesis is true for the population. In crosstabulation A, we are 98.47 percent sure that the research hypothesis is true for the population as well as the sample. In crosstabulation B, there is only a 5.87 percent chance that the research hypothesis is true in the population. Social scientists usually set a *cutoff* point to decide whether a relationship is significant. Whenever the probability of the research hypothesis being true falls below the cutoff point, we decide that the relationship is not significant. Any probability equal to or greater than the cutoff point is considered statistically significant.

Statistical Significance versus Practical Importance

A statistically significant relationship may be of no practical importance. For example, in a sample of 9,000 employees of a large corporation, we find that those who read the employee newsletter tend to have a more positive attitude toward the company than employees who do not read the newsletter. However, the difference is small. Among newsletter readers, 40.9 percent have a favorable attitude toward the company. Among newsletter nonreaders, 40.1 percent have a favorable attitude toward the company. Because of the large sample size, this 0.8 percent difference is statistically significant. But managers of employee communication may regard the difference as of no practical importance.

At the same time, a relationship that is deemed not statistically significant may be of some practical importance. Suppose medical researchers tested a new vaccine that reduces the chances of contracting the AIDS virus. They conduct an experiment on a sample of 150 individuals at risk to contract AIDS. After two years, the incidence of AIDS among those receiving the vaccine is lower than among those not receiving the vaccine. However, the sample size is small. The medical researchers are only 80 percent sure that the relationship between the vaccine and reduced occurrence of AIDS can be generalized to the population. The 80 percent probability of the research hypothesis being true in the population (the vaccine reduces chances of contracting AIDS) may not meet the cutoff point originally established by the researchers. However, the 80 percent probability that the vaccine works is of enormous practical importance.

Decision Rules

Decisions about significance can be made with regard to the null hypothesis or the research hypothesis. When the decision is based on the probability of the null hypothesis being true, we refer to this probability as the *alpha* level. If the alpha level is higher than a certain level, we conclude that the null hypothesis is true. Social scientists commonly use an alpha level of 0.05. That is, if the alpha level (the probability of the null hypothesis being true) is greater than 0.05, we accept the null hypothesis and reject the research hypothesis. If alpha is 0.05 or less, we accept the research hypothesis and reject the null hypothesis. This means that if there is only a 6 percent chance that the null hypothesis is true in the population, we accept the null hypothesis anyway. The relationship predicted by the research hypothesis is rejected. This puts very stringent requirements on research hypotheses. We want to be *very* sure that a relationship exists in the larger population before we call a relationship in our sample statistically significant.

The 0.05 alpha level can alternately be described as the 95-percent decision rule. In other words, the research hypothesis is not accepted unless we are 95 percent sure that the predicted relationship in the sample generalizes to the larger population from which the sample was drawn. If we are only 94 percent sure that the hypothesized relationship exists in the population, we reject the research hypothesis. There are other decision rules, such as the 99-percent decision rule (alpha = 0.01). This decision rule is used in large samples and when many tests of significance are planned. The 90-percent decision rule (alpha = 0.10) is often used when samples of less than 100 cases are analyzed.

The use of decision rules has been criticized by evaluation researchers.[1] As in the AIDS example, a relationship deemed not statistically significant according to a stringent decision rule may still be of great practical importance. This is especially the case when the number of cases studied is small.

To some degree, the use of yes-no decision rules may be a product of an earlier era when the precise alpha level for a particular relationship was extremely difficult to calculate. Today, computers allow us to calculate the alpha level (probability of no relationship in the population) to four digits in seconds. Given this technology, there seems little value in only reporting that a relationship is "not significant at alpha = 0.05 level," especially when the computer tells

---

[1]Anne L. Schneider and Robert E. Darcy, "Policy Implications of Using Significance Tests in Evaluation Research," *Evaluation Review,* Vol. 8 (August 1984), pp. 573–82.

us that there is a 93.75 percent chance that the hypothesized relationship does exist in the population.

> *We recommend that you report the actual probability of the research hypothesis being true in the population, as well as acceptance or rejection of the research hypothesis according to a decision rule.*

Type I and Type II Error

Whenever you make inferences from samples to populations, you always risk making the wrong inference. That's because samples never allow us to be 100 percent sure about the presence or absence of relations in the population. There are two decisions we can make. We can *accept* the research hypothesis (reject the null hypothesis); we are confident that the relationship in the sample is also true for the population from which the sample was drawn. We can *reject* the research hypothesis (accept the null hypothesis); we are not confident the relationship in the sample is also true for the population.

In both cases, we could be wrong. When we are wrong, we make an *inferential error*. When we accept the research hypothesis, but we are wrong (the null hypothesis is actually true), we commit *Type I error*. When we reject the research hypothesis, but we are wrong (the null hypothesis is actually false), we commit *Type II error*. These types of error are shown in Table 11-6.

Decision rules are designed to minimize Type I errors. For example, the 95-percent decision rule (alpha = 0.05) means that there is only a 5 percent chance that we will accept the research hypothesis (reject the null hypothesis) when the null hypothesis is actually true for the population. Even the more lenient 90-percent decision rule (alpha 0.10) means that we only have a one in ten chance of accepting the research hypothesis when it's not true for the population. A Type I error is sometimes called a *false positive* conclusion.

It's harder to éstimate the probability of making a Type II error—of

Table 11-6 A Diagram of Type I and Type II Errors

	Null hypothesis is actually . . .		
DECISION . . .	*TRUE*	*FALSE*	
REJECT NULL	Type I error	Correct decision	Data show *relation*
ACCEPT NULL	Correct decision	Type II error	Data show *no* relation
	Variables are *not* actually related	Variables *are* actually related	

Adapted from Sonia R. Wright, *Quantitative Methods and Statistics: A Guide to Social Research* (Beverly Hills, Calif.: Sage, 1979), p. 105. Reprinted by permission of author.

reaching a *false negative* conclusion. Sometimes even a large sample and a powerful inferential statistic may fail to detect a weak relationship in the population. However, we do know that the stricter the decision rule (the lower the alpha level), the more likely we are to make a Type II error. So decision rules involve trade-offs. If we set a strict decision rule (alpha=0.001, for example), we reduce the probability of making a Type I error but increase the probability of making a Type II error.

STATISTICAL POWER

Whereas increasing the decision rule (say from 95 percent to 99 percent) reduces the possibility of Type I error, increasing the *power* of a particular statistical test reduces the possibility of Type II error. That is, increasing the *power* of an inferential statistical test increases our probability of detecting a relationship if one actually exists in the population.[2] Cohen recommends that researchers seek a coefficient of statistical power equivalent to 0.80.[3] That means that when we draw samples to detect a particular relationship using a particular statistical tool, we should seek to have an 80 percent chance of finding a significant relationship in that sample, given that such a relationship truly exists in the population.

Effect Size

To figure out the power of a particular statistical test for a particular sample, we have to know how strong a relationship we are interested in detecting. As indicated, some relationships are too weak to be of any practical importance. Since larger samples are required to detect weaker relationships, there is a trade-off between the cost of sample size and the detection of weak relationships. The strength of a relationship between two variables *in the population* is called the *effect size*. We never know what the actual effect size is in the population, unless we do a census. But we may decide that we aren't interested in detecting a small effect size. So we draw a sample with an 80 percent chance of detecting a medium or large effect size, if such an effect size actually exists in the population. If we increase the decision rule (say from 95 percent to 99 percent), we reduce the chance of concluding that a relationship exists in the population *when one actually does*. We reduce the chance of Type I error—the null hypothesis is actually true, but we reject it. However, if we increase the decision rule, we decrease the power of the test. That is, we decrease our chances of finding a significant relationship in our sample, even if one actually exists in the population. We increase the chance of Type II error—the null hypothesis is actually false, but we accept it.

[2]Jacob Cohen, *Statistical Power Analysis for the Behavioral Sciences,* 2nd ed. (Hillsdale, N.J.: Lawrence Erlbaum Associates, 1988).
[3]Cohen, *Statistical Power.*

Selecting Sample Size for Power

When we conduct research, let's agree that we want to select a sample large enough so that we have an 80 percent chance of detecting a relationship in the population when one actually exists. To make that decision, we need to know what *statistic* we will use (some statistical procedures are inherently more powerful than others), what *decision rule* we will use (stringent decision rules reduce power), and what *effect size* we are interested in detecting (small effect sizes are harder to detect than large effect sizes). Appendix E includes tables for determining sample sizes for different decision rules and different effect sizes for the Chi-Square statistic and the Pearson correlation coefficient.

ANALYSIS OF VARIANCE

Again consider our measure of frequency of reading the *SDSU Report*. Respondents were asked how often they read the magazine. Their responses to the question were classified as frequent or infrequent. This is not a very precise measure of reading frequency or exposure. A better measure of exposure to the magazine was also included in the questionnaire. Respondents were told that eight issues of *SDSU Report* had been issued over the two years prior to the survey. Of those, respondents were asked, how many did you read? This is a count that allows us to more precisely measure the construct of exposure and permits a wider range of statistical analysis.

In this section, you learn how to use analysis of variance to test relations between two variables. We conduct an analysis parallel to the one at the beginning of this chapter, involving frequency of readership and opinion toward San Diego State as a high-quality, comprehensive university. This time, however, we will use a *metric* variable to measure exposure to *SDSU Report*. Our metric variable ranges from zero (no exposure to *SDSU Report* over the last two years) to eight (exposure to all eight issues of the magazine). As indicated in Chapter 8, this is a ratio-level variable. Generally, interval-level and ratio-level variables are considered metric measures. However, research by Labovitz indicates that ordinal-level measures can be treated like interval-level measures for purposes of statistical analysis.[4] That is, we can treat ordinal-level variables as metrics for purposes of statistical analysis, though we should report that our measure is, in fact, ordinal.

Mean as Measure of Central Tendency

One key characteristic of a metric variable is that the mean (or average) is a meaningful measure of central tendency. That's important when using the

[4]Sanford Labovitz, "The Assignment of Numbers to Rank Order Categories," *American Sociological Review*, Vol. 33 (June 1970), pp. 515–24. See also Q. McNemar, *Psychological Statistics* (New York: John Wiley, 1962).

analysis of variance procedure, because this test compares means. In this case, we compare the mean level of exposure to *SDSU Report* among respondents who *agree*, who *disagree*, and who feel *neutral* about San Diego State as a high-quality, comprehensive university. That is, we construct a table in which the mean level of exposure (on a zero to eight scale) is computed for each subsample. That analysis is shown in Table 11-7.

The top of Table 11-7 shows the mean level of exposure to *SDSU Report* among respondents who agree, who disagree, and who feel neutral about the opinion statement. Among those who agree, the mean or average level of exposure to *SDSU Report* is 6.1 issues during the last two years. Among those who disagree, the mean level of exposure is only 3.9 issues during the last two years. The exposure of those who feel neutral fall between those means, with a mean of 5.7 issues during the last two years. These means are based on a sample of 441 respondents who answered both questions, drawn from the population of 75,000 *SDSU Report* recipients.

Clearly, respondents in the sample who agree San Diego State is a high-quality, comprehensive university are exposed to *SDSU Report* more often than those who disagree. Can this be generalized to the population? Is this relationship true for the 75,000 recipients of *SDSU Report?* Or, is this difference in mean levels of exposure only a product of sampling error?

Intuitively, we might think that the greater the difference in means between groups, the more likely the difference reflects true differences in the population. Small differences in means are more likely caused by sampling error. However, difference in means is not enough information to make a decision about

Table 11-7 Analysis of Variance of Exposure to *SDSU Report* Broken Down By Opinion of San Diego State as High Quality and Comprehensive University

		DESCRIPTION OF SUBPOPULATIONS			
Value Label	Sum	Mean	Standard Deviation	Sum of Squares	Cases
Disagree	63.0	3.93	2.67	106.9	16
Neutral	268.0	5.70	2.42	269.8	47
Agree	2299.0	6.08	2.26	1928.5	378

		ANALYSIS OF VARIANCE			
Source	Sum of Squares	D.F.	Mean Square	F	Sig.
Between groups	74.195	2	37.097	7.048	.0010
Linearity	61.433	1	61.432	11.672	.0007
Dev. from linearity	12.762	1	12.762	2.425	.1201
Within groups	2305.225	438	5.263		

the statistical significance of the relationship. That's because the scatter of cases in the sample, as measured by the standard deviation, must also be considered. Recall from Chapter 10 that the standard deviation is a measure of dispersion of cases about the mean.

Figure 11–1 illustrates the problem. Suppose that we conduct a survey of 200 respondents and find out that those who *disagree* with the opinion statement about the university were exposed to an average of 2.7 issues of *SDSU Report* during the last two years. Among those who agree with the opinion statement, the mean is 3.2 issues. The top portion of Figure 11-1 shows the case in which standard deviations for both groups (those who agree and those who disagree) are large. That is, while the average is higher among those who agree, many who agree have levels of exposure lower than those who disagree. There's a good chance that the difference in means in this sample is the product of sampling error. The two groups are so scattered that they tend to overlap. We don't see a clear pattern of two separate groups with meaningfully different means.

Figure 11–1   Examples of significant and nonsignificant differences in means where difference in means is equal but standard deviations differ.

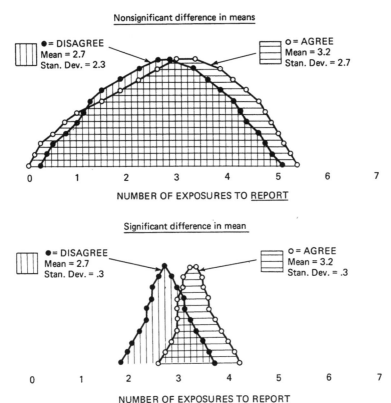

Nonsignificant difference in means

●= DISAGREE
Mean = 2.7
Stan. Dev. = 2.3

o = AGREE
Mean = 3.2
Stan. Dev. = 2.7

NUMBER OF EXPOSURES TO REPORT

Significant difference in mean

●= DISAGREE
Mean = 2.7
Stan. Dev. = .3

o = AGREE
Mean = 3.2
Stan. Dev. = .3

NUMBER OF EXPOSURES TO REPORT

The bottom portion of Figure 11-1 shows a different survey outcome. The means are exactly the same as in the top survey. However, in this case, the standard deviations are small for both groups. The difference *between* the groups is greater than the differences *within* the two groups. As the difference between groups becomes much larger than the difference within the groups, we can be more confident that the relationship can be generalized to the population from which the sample was drawn.

Within-Group and Between-Group Differences

Analysis of variance compares the variation or scatter within groups with the difference between groups. At the bottom of Table 11-7, the F statistic is computed. The F statistic is an inferential statistic like the Chi-Square statistic. The F statistic allows us to make inferences about differences in means between groups (agree, neutral, disagree) in the larger population from which the sample is drawn. The greater the difference in means between groups and the less the scatter of cases within groups, the larger the F statistic becomes.

Degrees of Freedom

As with the Chi-Square statistic, we can assess the probability of the null hypothesis being true for the population, given a particular relationship in the sample. Also like the Chi-Square statistic, we need to know the number of degrees of freedom to interpret F values. In analysis of variance, there are two measures of degrees of freedom. One measure is the number of *groups* used when comparing means. In the Table 11-7 example, there are three groups (agree, neutral, disagree). The between-group degrees of freedom equals two—the number of groups minus one. The within-group degrees of freedom is 438—the total sample size (441) minus the number of groups (3). Here's the way to report the findings in Table 11-7:

$F = 7.05; d.f. = 2, 438; p = 0.001.$

Significance

The significance (sometimes called the p-value) for the F statistic has the same meaning as it does for the Chi-Square statistic. That is, significance is the probability that there is *no difference* in means in the population, despite some difference observed in means in the sample. The p- or significance-value is the probability that the null hypothesis is true.

In this case, we observe in our sample that those who agree with the opinion statement have a higher level of exposure to *SDSU Report* than do those who are neutral or who disagree with the opinion statement. The analysis of variance procedure and the F statistic indicate that this relationship in the sample can be generalized to the larger population with a 99.9 percent level of confidence. In other words, there is only one chance in a thousand that these differences in means in our sample are due to sampling error.[5]

Notice that we are more confident in generalizing our relationship to the population than we were with the Chi-Square statistic. With the Chi-Square statistic, we were only 98 percent sure that frequency of exposure is positively related to agreement with the opinion statement in the larger population. With the F statistic, we are 99.9 percent sure. That's partly because we did a better job of measuring exposure for analysis of variance than we did for the Chi-Square analysis. The other reason is that the F statistic is a more *powerful* statistic than the Chi-Square statistic. The F statistic is more likely to detect a significant relationship in a sample than is the Chi-Square statistic, given that such a relationship actually exists in the population. This is why we always seek to measure constructs at the highest level of measure. Higher-level measures (metrics) permit us to use more powerful statistical tools.

Linear Relationships

Note in the analysis of variance part of Table 11–7 that there is a separate F statistic computed for linearity and for deviation from linearity. This is a statistical test to determine if a straight-line or linear increase in level of agreement is related to a consistent increase in level of exposure to the magazine. In this case, the relationship is strongly linear ($F = 11.7$; $d.f. = 1$, 438; $p = 0.0007$). That is, as level of agreement increases from disagree to neutral to agree, the mean number of exposures also goes up. (We discuss the issue of linearity in greater detail in the section on the Pearson correlation coefficient later in this chapter.)

Nonlinear Relationships

A linear relationship isn't the only possible outcome. For example, in the same survey of *SDSU Report* recipients, respondents were asked how much they would be willing to donate to the university in the future. In Table 11–8, analysis of variance for this metric variable is provided for those who agree, disagree, and who feel neutral about San Diego State as a high-quality, comprehensive university. The table indicates that among respondents who disagree with the opinion statement, the mean level of projected donations is $61.11. Among those who agree, the mean level of projected donations is $27.64. Those who feel neutral are only willing to donate an average of $12.84 to the university. That is, willingness to donate is greater among those who disagree and those who agree than among those in the middle group—those who feel neutral about San Diego State.

The relationship between willingness to donate and agreement with the opinion statement is *nonlinear,* more resembling a U-shaped curve than a straight

[5]As Professor Ferguson noted at the beginning of the chapter, we would want to test the difference in means between each of the three pairs of means. The overall difference in means is statistically significant, but differences between any two pairs of means may not be. (For example, the neutral and agree means are not very different from each other.)

Table 11–8   Analysis of Variance of Amount Willing to Donate Broken Down By Opinion of San Diego State as High-Quality and Comprehensive University

DESCRIPTION OF SUBPOPULATIONS

Value Label	Sum	Mean	Standard Deviation	Sum of Squares	Cases
Disagree	1100.0	61.11	187.32	596527.8	18
Neutral	732.0	12.84	31.36	55073.6	57
Agree	11885.0	27.64	54.68	1282779.1	430

ANALYSIS OF VARIANCE

Source	Sum of Squares	D.F.	Mean Square	F	Sig.
Between groups	32532.2	2	16266.1	4.221	.0152
Linearity	1472.7	1	1472.7	.382	.5367
Dev. from linearity	31059.5	1	31059.5	8.060	.0047
Within groups	1934380.5	502	3853.3		

line. This is indicated by the test for linearity and deviation from linearity in the analysis of variance table. There is no significant linear relationship between willingness to donate and the opinion statement ($F = 0.38$; $d.f. = 1, 502$; $p = 0.537$). However, there is a significant nonlinear relationship ($F = 8.06$; $d.f. = 1, 502$; $p = 0.005$) that we can generalize to the larger population at a 99.5 percent level of confidence.

Theories that explain nonlinear relationships are generally more complex than those explaining linear relationships. Our simplified theory for the linear relationship in Table 11–7 is that exposure to *SDSU Report* leads to a more positive opinion of the university. Our theory for the nonlinear relationship in Table 11–8 is that individuals who feel that the university *is* high-quality and comprehensive give money to keep it that way. Individuals who believe that the university is *not* high-quality and comprehensive are willing to donate (even more) funds to make it so. These two groups give money to the university for entirely different reasons. Only the neutrals—who don't feel one way or the other—are relatively unwilling to donate money to the university.

THE *t*-TEST

Sometimes we want to compare the difference in means of two separate variables measured for the entire sample, rather than compare the difference in means of one variable for different subsamples, as with analysis of variance. The *t*-test provides a useful tool for testing for significant differences in means between two variables.

For example, in the *SDSU Report* readership survey, respondents were asked how often they read the different sections—sports section, alumni news section, and class notes. Respondents indicate they read each section often (3), sometimes (2), or almost never (1). Like Labovitz, we can treat these variables as metrics, even though they are properly classified as ordinal measures.[6] As a result, we can compute the mean for each variable. The higher the mean, the more often that section is read. When means are examined for the three variables, the sports section posts a 1.96 average on the three-point scale. The alumni news section posts a 2.06 average, while the class notes section posts a 2.32 average.

These differences in means in our sample may be the product of sampling error. Do these differences actually exist in the population? Among all *SDSU Report* readers, is the class notes section read most frequently, followed by alumni news and the sports section? Using procedures similar to analysis of variance, the *t*-test compares means, generating a *t*-value for each of the three possible comparisons of means. The larger the *t*-value, the greater the difference in means and the more likely the difference is due to actual differences in the population, not sampling error. Table 11–9 shows the *t*-tests for the three comparisons. Using the 95-percent decision rule (alpha=0.05), we conclude that the differences exist in the population from which the sample was drawn. It's unlikely that these differences in means are caused by sampling error.

CORRELATION COEFFICIENTS

Sometimes with metric variables, we are interested in whether the two variables are correlated or associated with each other. In the *SDSU Report* readership survey, for example, university practitioners want to know if a person's household income influences how much that person is willing to donate to the university. The working theory is: The greater the household income, the more likely the individual has discretionary money to support the university. In other words, we expect that those with higher household incomes intend to give more money to the university than those with lower household incomes. Prior to conducting our analysis, we decide to use the 99-percent decision rule to decide if the relationship between income and future donations is statistically significant. That is, we accept the research hypothesis as true if—and only if—we are 99 percent sure that the relationship in our sample is true for the population as well.

Recall respondents were asked if they would donate money to the university in the future and, if so, how much. There were twenty-three separate responses to this second question, ranging from $0 to $800. Elsewhere in the questionnaire, respondents were asked to give an estimate of their annual household income. There were sixty-five different responses to this question, ranging from a low of $3,000 to a high of $200,000. A crosstabulation table for these two variables would have 1,445 cells in the table (23 rows × 65 columns). Most of the

[6]Labovitz, "The Assignment of Numbers."

Table 11–9   *t*-Test of Difference in Means for Readership Frequency of Class Notes, Alumni News, and Sports Sections of *SDSU Report*

[Readership Frequency: OFTEN = 3   SOMETIMES = 2   ALMOST NEVER = 1]

VARIABLE	NUMBER OF CASES	MEAN	STAN. DEV.	STAN. ERROR	*t* VALUE	D.F.	SIG.
Alumni News		2.06	.75	.035			
	460				2.05	459	.04
Sports		1.96	.84	.039			

VARIABLE	NUMBER OF CASES	MEAN	STAN. DEV.	STAN. ERROR	*t* VALUE	D.F.	SIG.
Class Notes		2.31	.77	.036			
	460				6.96	459	.00
Sports		1.96	.84	.039			

VARIABLE	NUMBER OF CASES	MEAN	STAN. DEV.	STAN. ERROR	*t* VALUE	D.F.	SIG.
Class Notes		2.06	.75	.035			
	461				6.53	460	.00
Alumni News		1.96	.84	.039			

cells would have no numbers in them. Even if our sample were large enough to fill all the cells with five or more cases (the minimum required per cell to compute a meaningful Chi-Square statistic), we would never be able to make sense out of our results. There would be too many columns and rows to compare!

Categorizing Metric Data

One analysis strategy is to create categories for the income variable and categories for the donation variable. By looking at the cumulative percentages for the income variable, about a third make $30,000 or less a year. Roughly another third make between $31,000 and $49,000. The upper third make $50,000 or more a year. Regarding future donations, about half indicated that they would give nothing to the university. Another quarter indicated that they would give between $5 and $25, while roughly another quarter would give $30 or more.

By creating new, categorized versions of the income and donation variables, we can use crosstabulation and the Chi-Square statistic to test the relation between household income and size of donations to the university. Table 11–10 shows the results.

Table 11–10   Relationship Between Categorized Future Donations to the University and Categorized Household Income

Amount Willing To Donate in Future	Annual Household Income			FOR ALL INCOMES
	$3K–$30K	$31K–$49K	$50K & UP	
NONE	57.5%	45.9%	49.3%	51.4%
$5–$25	28.1%	31.2%	20.9%	26.3%
OVER $25	14.4%	22.9%	29.7%	22.3%
	100.0%	100.0%	100.0%	100.0%
Number of respondents =	146	109	148	403

Chi-Square = 12.39   d.f.=4   SIGNIFICANCE = 0.0146
Pearson Coefficient = .1243   SIGNIFICANCE = 0.0062
Kendall's tau b = .1014   SIGNIFICANCE = 0.0117

Among low-income respondents, only 14 percent are willing to donate more than $25 to the university in the future. Among middle-income respondents, 23 percent are willing to donate more than $25 to the university. Among high-income respondents, 30 percent are willing to give more than $25 to the university. Within our sample, the higher-income respondents are willing to donate larger amounts of money to the university.

Can we generalize this relationship in our sample to the 75,000 recipients of *SDSU Report*? Remember, we decided to use the 99-percent decision rule (alpha=0.01) to determine if the relationship is statistically significant. Using this decision rule, we *reject* the research hypothesis and accept the null hypothesis. While the relationship comes close to statistical significance, we are less than 99 percent sure that the relationship in the sample is true for the whole population as well.

Loss of Richness of Data

One reason why the relationship is not statistically significant may be that there is no relationship in the population. But we really didn't give our research hypothesis a fair test! When we created our low-income category, we lumped people making $3,000 a year into the same category as people making $30,000 a year. For our statistical analysis, we treated the $3,000-a-year and the $30,000-a-year respondent as making the same "low" income. We threw away information when we collapsed data into a few categories. This weakened our ability to detect a relationship.

Power

More importantly, we used a procedure with low statistical power. The Chi-Square statistic is not particularly powerful at detecting relationships in samples, given that such relationships actually exist in the population. A more powerful statistical procedure is the Pearson correlation coefficient.

The Pearson correlation coefficient (r) is a number that ranges from −1 to zero to +1. Before applying this statistical procedure to income and university donations, let's first consider the Pearson correlation coefficient in some detail. In Figure 11–2, the relationship between *exposure* to public relations messages about an organization and *knowledge* about the organization is illustrated for different values of Pearson *r*. Each graph in Figure 11–2 shows the relationship between exposure and knowledge. *Exposure* is measured by counting the number of messages an individual is exposed to. Knowledge is measured through a multiple-choice test. The score on the *knowledge* scale is the number of answers that the individual gets right on the test. Each variable is measured on a scale ranging from 0 (no exposure and no right answers on the test) to 100 (exposure to all the messages and all the answers right on the test).

Figure 11–2 An illustration of the Pearson product-moment correlation coefficient.

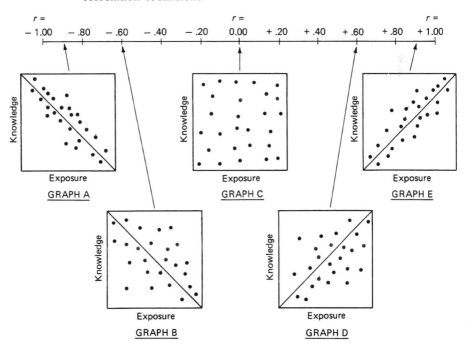

Zero Correlation Coefficient

When two variables are unrelated to each other, the Pearson correlation coefficient is zero. Graph C in Figure 11–2 shows what a zero correlation relationship looks like. There is no pattern to the data. Exposure to messages about the organization is unrelated to knowledge about the organization. Zero means the absence of a *linear* relation between the two variables.

Positive Correlation Coefficients

Two variables may be *positively* related to each other. For any one person, a high score on one variable usually means a high score on the other variable. Two graphs in Figure 11–2 (Graphs D and E) indicate a positive relationship between exposure and knowledge. That is, the Pearson correlation coefficient for these graphs is a positive number greater than zero and less than one. The higher the coefficient, the stronger the linear relation between the two variables. Graph E shows a larger effect size than does Graph D. The Pearson coefficient for Graph E, therefore, is greater than the coefficient for Graph D. Graph E shows a strong, positive straight-line relationship between exposure and knowledge. As exposure increases, knowledge increases. The same is true for Graph D, but the effect size is not as large. In Graph D, level of exposure is not as strong a predictor of level of knowledge—when compared to Graph E.

Negative Correlation Coefficients

Two variables may be negatively related. For any one person, a high score on one variable usually means a low score on the other variable. Graphs A and B in Figure 11–2 illustrate two negative relationships between exposure and knowledge. Suppose the messages about the organization are *wrong*. (The organization has fallen victim to a disinformation campaign!) As exposure to these inaccurate messages goes up, knowledge about the organization (as measured by *right* answers on the knowledge test) goes down. The Pearson correlation coefficients for Graphs A and B are negative numbers between zero and minus one. The effect size in Graph A is larger. Graph A shows a strong, negative straight-line relationship between exposure and knowledge. As exposure increases, knowledge decreases. The same is true for Graph B, but level of exposure is not as strong a predictor of level of knowledge—compared to Graph A.

Effect Size for Pearson Coefficients

Effect size is the strength of the relationship *in the population*. When computed for sample data, the correlation coefficient estimates how strong the relationship is in the population from which the sample is drawn. A positive or negative correlation of 0.10 (the sign shows the direction of the relationship, not the strength) indicates a small effect size, a weak relationship. A positive or negative correlation of 0.30 is considered a medium effect size, a moderate relationship. A positive or negative correlation 0.50 is considered a large effect size, a strong relationship.[7] In Appendix E, you see how smaller sample sizes can be used to detect large effect sizes using the Pearson correlation coefficient.

Restrictions

The Pearson correlation coefficient has three restrictions you should consider when using Pearson r. First, recall from Chapter 10 that kurtosis and skewness are statistics that indicate how much a sample distribution differs from a normal distribution. The Pearson coefficient, as a parametric statistic, assumes that variables are normally distributed. Before computing Pearson r, check the skewness and kurtosis of the variables you are testing. Second, Pearson r should only be computed for relations between two metric variables, preferably interval or ratio level measures. As Labovitz demonstrated, however, the Pearson coefficient can be used cautiously (and with full disclosure) on ordinal-level data as well.[8] Third, the Pearson coefficient tests only for *linear* or straight-line relationships. Nonlinear relationships, like the one in Table 11–8, cannot be detected by Pearson r. For the relationship in Table 11–8, the Pearson correlation coefficient is not significant, even though a strong nonlinear relationship is detected by the F statistic.

Inferences

The Pearson correlation coefficient can be used to make inferences from samples to populations. The null hypothesis is that the Pearson correlation coefficient is zero ($r = 0.00$) in the population. Given a particular correlation in a sample, what's the probability that the true relationship in the population is zero? Generally, the larger the coefficient (either positive or negative), the more likely the relationship exists in the population. The larger the coefficient, the less likely the coefficient is generated by sampling error. The closer the coefficient is to zero, the more likely it's caused by sampling error.

Example

Returning to the relationship between income and the amount of money respondents are willing to give to the university, we can test the relationship again using the Pearson correlation coefficient. Let's use the same categorized variables for income and donation size that we used with the Chi-Square test, so we can compare results. The Pearson correlation coefficient between the two variables in Table 11–10 is $+0.12$. The "plus" means that the relationship is posi-

---

[7]Cohen, *Statistical Power.*
[8]Labovitz, "The Assignment of Numbers," p. 522–23.

tive—the size of donation increases with the respondent's income level. The *p*-value—or significance statistic—of the Pearson correlation coefficient is 0.0062. That means that there is only a 0.62 percent chance of the null hypothesis being true. The probability of the research hypothesis being true for the entire population is 99.38 percent. Using the 99-percent decision rule, the research hypothesis is *accepted,* whereas with the Chi-Square statistic, the research hypothesis is *rejected.* Since the data were precisely the same for both tests, the difference in statistical significance is strictly due to the greater statistical *power* of the Pearson correlation coefficient.

Using Full Metrics

Recall that one problem with the preceding Chi-Square test is that we collapsed data into categories in order to generate an interpretable contingency table and a meaningful Chi-Square statistic. In our retest using the Pearson coefficient, we used those same categorized variables. However, with Pearson coefficients, we don't need to collapse data. We can meaningfully analyze all sixty-five responses to the income question and their relation to all twenty-three responses to the donations question, retaining the richness of the original data. When the Pearson correlation coefficient is computed using the original measures of income and future donations, the coefficient equals + 0.15 rather than + 0.12. With the new coefficient, the significance or *p* value is 0.001, meaning we can accept the research hypothesis with a 99.9 percent level of confidence, rather than a 99.4 percent level of confidence.

Clearly, when testing for linear relations between two metric variables, the Pearson correlation coefficient is superior for two reasons. First, the Pearson correlation coefficient is inherently more powerful than the Chi-Square test. We are more likely to detect a significant relationship with the Pearson correlation coefficient, when compared to the Chi-Square test, whenever such a relationship actually exists in the population. Second, we can use the full range of metric variables with the Pearson correlation coefficient, whereas such data must be collapsed into categories to use the Chi-Square test. Collapsed data lacks the richness of the original metric.

Kendall's Tau

Recall the restrictions just mentioned for the Pearson coefficient. One restriction was that only interval and ratio level variables should be used. While there is empirical evidence that such restrictions are excessive and unnecessary, you can elect to use a nonparametric correlation coefficient—Kendall's *tau.*[9] Kendall's tau is appropriate for ordinal-level data, such as the categorized income and future donations variables. Like the Pearson coefficient, Kendall's tau ranges

---

[9]Kendall's tau is only one nonparametric correlation coefficient that permits inferences from samples to populations. Another is the Spearman rho coefficient.

from -1 (perfect negative relationship) to zero (no relationship), to $+1$ (perfect positive relationship). Like the Chi-Square and Pearson coefficient, tau is an inferential statistic. However, Kendall's tau has less statistical power than the Pearson coefficient. For example, Kendall's tau for the relationship between the categorized income and donations variables is $+0.10$ with an alpha level of 0.011, meaning that we are 98.9 percent sure that the relationship exists for the population as a whole, rather than the 99.4 percent level of confidence provided by the Pearson coefficient.

MAKING CHOICES ABOUT STATISTICAL PROCEDURES

When making decisions about which statistics to use to test relations between two variables in a sample—and make inferences to populations—you need to consider two issues. The first issue is the levels of measure of your two variables. The second issue is the nature of the relationship you seek to test. Table 11-11 provides a guide to making decisions about levels of measure, the nature of the relationship, the recommended statistical procedures, and the limitations of such uses.

When analyzing two nominal-level variables, you are limited to contingency tables and the Chi-Square statistic. You need to collapse variables into a small number of categories. This insures an adequate number of cases per cell (a minimum of five *expected* cases per cell is recommended) to facilitate interpretation of the percentages in the table. This test tells whether the subpopulations defined by the independent variable differ—in percentages—from each other in terms of the dependent variable.

When analyzing ordinal variables, you are in a controversial area where researchers and statisticians often differ in statistical analysis strategies. To test for a linear, straight-line relationship, the Pearson correlation coefficient is recommended.[10] However, ordinal measures violate the underlying assumptions of this parametric statistic, so you need to report that you have used ordinal data in your Pearson correlation test when the results are presented to others in the organization or to a client.

Kendall's tau also tests for linear relations for ordinal-level data. Because tau assumes only ordinal-level measures, there is no question about the appropriateness of the test. Kendall's tau, however, is not as powerful as the Pearson correlation coefficient in detecting relationships in samples drawn from populations in which such relationships actually exist.

You may want to compare differences in the means of two or more ordinal-level variables and to infer that the differences in sample means indicate a true difference in means in the population. You can use the t-test. However, some

---

[10]Labovitz, "The Assignment of Numbers."

Table 11–11   Guide to Selecting Statistical Procedures for Different Levels of Measure and Different Purposes

LEVEL OF MEASURE	PURPOSE	STATISTICAL PROCEDURE	LIMITS
Nominal by nominal	To test for relationship and make inferences to the population	Chi-Square	1
Ordinal by ordinal	To test for *linear* relationship and make inferences to the population	Pearson corr. (*r*)	2
Ordinal by ordinal	To test for *linear* relationship and make inferences to the population	Kendall's tau	None
Ordinal by ordinal	To determine if the means of the variables differ in the population	*t*-test	3
Interval-ratio by all levels	To test for both *linear* and *nonlinear* relations and make inferences to the population	F-test	4
Interval-ratio by interval-ratio	To determine if the means of the variables differ in the population	*t*-test	None
Interval-ratio by interval-ratio	To test for *linear* relationship and make inferences to the population	Pearson corr. (*r*)	None
All levels by all levels	To test for *nonlinear* relationships and make inferences to the population	Chi-Square	1

Limits:

1. Chi-Square requires that there be no fewer than five expected cases per cell of the contingency table from which the statistic is computed. If not, you should collapse data into fewer categories.
2. Ordinal measures violate the underlying assumptions of this parametric statistic. Indicate ordinal level measures were used in reports of findings of such analysis.
3. Some critics may challenge whether the mean is a reasonable measure of central tendency for ordinal level variables.
4. Analysis of variance requires that the criterion variable be one for which the mean is a reasonable measure of central tendency. The other variable must fall into a discrete number of categories but may be of any level of measure.

may challenge your use of the mean as a meaningful measure of central tendency for ordinal-level variables.

When one of the two variables is interval or ratio, you can use the analysis of variance procedure and the F-test to see if the mean of the interval-ratio variable differs significantly across categories of the other variable. The other variable may be an interval or ratio measure, or it may be nominal or ordinal. However, it must be categorical. The relationship between the two variables is tested by determining the probability that the means differ in the population from which the sample was drawn.

When both variables are interval or ratio measures, a wide range of parametric statistics are applicable. We consider only three here. To determine if the difference in sample means of two variables differ from each other in the population, use the t-test. However, the two variables ought to share a common scale, such that you compare apples with apples, oranges with oranges. For instance, the mean income level will always be greater than mean age level in nearly all samples of adults.

When you want to determine if a linear relation exists between two variables, the Pearson correlation coefficient provides a powerful test and helps you make inferences to the population from which the sample is drawn. When you need to test for nonlinear relationships between two interval-ratio measures, first examine a plot or scattergram of the relationship. Then collapse data into categories, if necessary, and use the crosstabulation procedure and the Chi-Square statistic to make inferences to populations from which samples are drawn.

In Chapter 12, you will use the procedures you learned in this chapter to examine causal relations between variables. In this chapter, you learned how to use a variety of statistical procedures to examine relationships between variables in samples and to make inferences from samples to the populations from which those samples are drawn. Knowing two variables are related is one step in determining causality. If variables are *not* related, then it's unlikely that one causes the other. However, if two variables *are* related, the first may cause the second, or the second may cause the first, or both may be caused by other variables. Chapter 12 shows how to unravel what causes what. In Chapter 13 and 14, you will learn how to take the information you've learned from testing relationships and determining causes and apply that information. Specifically, you will learn how to report research findings and how to use research information to change organizations.

CHAPTER 12

TESTING FOR CAUSATION AND CHANGE

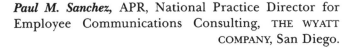

Paul M. Sanchez, APR, National Practice Director for Employee Communications Consulting, THE WYATT COMPANY, San Diego.

URPR: How do you explain causal relationships to your clients?

Sanchez: *First, present the data in as understandable a fashion as possible. We try to avoid drawing conclusions about causal relationships until we have the client comfortable with what the information represents. This is particularly true in a fast-paced organization where the CEO looks at a profile line or a couple of percentages and says, "Oh my God, we've got to do X, Y, and Z!" As ready as a rocket, ready to go and do something! That is the worst possible kind of interpretation of a causal relationship in the data. Some management groups are all too ready to interpret the data at the most superficial level. The researcher's role is to make sure that there is a deliberate analytical phase so the full import of the data is made apparent.*

Once that is done and the client sees the "weight" of the information, then you start looking for the causal relationships. For example, if the employees feel this way, then what does that mean in terms of their behavior? This part of the analysis has to be entered into deliberately after *you have looked at all the data, refined all the data, and examined the paradoxes. Only then are you ready to move into that causal kind of analysis. And that's really where the "art" of this science is.*

URPR: Wouldn't the scientist say that all of this is a scientific process?

Sanchez: *It is scientific process to gather the data, look at the data, study the coefficients of the relationships among the variables, but the assumption—for example—that the perceptions you measured are directly the result of X, Y, or Z factor is only as good as the interpreter's experience and understanding of the situation. That is where the "art" is. You can do the whole process scientifically—you can systematically gather the data, you can use tested questions, you can use good analytical procedures like SPSSx$_{tm}$, you can make sure you do everything right. But when you get to looking at that relationship and understanding the nuances in the data, that is when you need a very seasoned, experienced person who can look beyond the mere numbers.*

Even more "artful" is attempting to predict what will happen in the future. Talking about "causal relationships" suggests that you can examine the facts as they are now, or you can try to make a case about what will happen in the future. And here I use "artful" to mean that the actual interpretation calls for even more experience, understanding, and wisdom from the practitioner.

URPR: How do you handle the problem of people going "too far" with the results—putting interpretations on the findings that simply cannot be justified?

Sanchez: *The first thing we do is put data into the context of national or regional data. We say, "Let me show you what that item looks like in the context of national or regional information." Putting findings in context with hard data solves four-fifths of the problems. The other one-fifth usually represents an existing condition—meaning that somebody has an objective they want to achieve and they commission a research proj-*

ect in the hopes that the findings will support their hypothesis. Then they prosecute that position, trying to get the data to support it whether they are really there or not. In this case, our role is to be as honest as we can and to say, "You just can't draw that conclusion. You are trying to make two plus two equal five, and that just doesn't add up." In other words, we point out that there is no legitimate way to draw that conclusion from the research data.

URPR: Programs typically include many activities. How do you separate their effects—determining which activity or activities caused the change or made a difference?

Sanchez: *The scientist may want to isolate the variables, but in complex organizations you are not always able to do that. You can't afford not to try, however. Even in the most controlled scientific experiment in social science, often the best we can do is identify the major forces operating. Given all that we understand about this sort of empirical research, management is not concerned about crossing all the t's and dotting the i's of methodological purity. Rather, they are concerned about getting information that is useful to them for solving some of their problems. The important result is that management have a body of information to work with. In the absence of research, they don't have anything. I don't think you can afford not to do it, even if you can't always satisfy the purist on this issue of causal inference.*

After gathering and analyzing data, you need to link the findings back to the original questions and motivations driving the research. Usually this means answering questions about whether or not the program *caused* something to happen, and if so, by how much did it *change*? To do so, you make "causal inferences" about the relationships between program activities and the outcomes stated in program objectives and goals. Certainly your bosses or clients will want evidence that program expenditures "produced" results. Never mind that the research was done under less-than-ideal conditions. Most likely, you will have to make summative statements about program "effects."

Questions about if and how programs "worked" call for answers based on evidence, not simple assertions that the program produced desired changes. Persuasive answers require evidence from research designed to rule out nonprogram causes. Answers about program effects must also pass the scientific test of cause-and-effect relationships. The evidence comes from real-world settings of public relations programs, however, not from controlled laboratory experiments where it is usually easier to isolate causal relationships.

Field experiments complicate attempts to obtain "conclusive" evidence of cause-and-effect relationships. Natural, uncontrolled settings and multiple program "treatments" introduce complexity and open the way for plausible alternative explanations of effects attributed to the program. As a result, in order to understand and explain the relationships between program activities and observed outcomes, you need knowledge and experience beyond scientific research methods. No research book—alas, not even this one—can substitute for the sense of understanding and practical knowledge that comes with years of experience. Making causal inferences about program effects draws on all of your knowledge, not just the imperatives of scientific interpretations of cause-and-effect relationships. To demonstrate causal relationships, however, you need an understanding of the logic and causal imagery of experimental science. The same logic and imagery apply to program evaluation research.

In other words, you should know the constraints inherent in the scientific method before you unabashedly claim that your program "caused" something to change. But, that making causal inferences is risky business does not mean you cannot draw cause-and-effect conclusions from your research. No doubt, it was your desire to draw such conclusions that motivated the research in the first place. Rather, you simply need to know the limits and rules, so you can more appropriately interpret, qualify, and report the findings. This chapter discusses the concepts and issues of causal inference you will use when interpreting research findings.

ESTABLISHING CAUSE AND EFFECT

Notions of cause and effect portray *sequences* of events using the assumption that antecedent conditions "produce" subsequent conditions. But, of course, few things are that simple. What if you did not observe the order of occurrence? What if all your measures were taken at the same time—as in a survey? What is to keep somebody from pointing to other possible "causes" of what you call "program effects"? How will you demonstrate the cause-and-effect relationships needed to answer questions about program impact? Strictly speaking, you cannot, but few really operate by such a strict interpretation of the scientific method.

Researchers use assumptions about causation to help explain their observations. In essence, causal relationships are working assumptions or hypotheses that can never be fully verified or tested empirically. As frustrating as that may be, you must understand that philosophers of science have debated the concept and conditions of causality for almost three centuries without resolving all the questions. Rest assured that the unresolved issues of causal inference will not be answered in the pages that follow! There are, however, some generally accepted and widely used criteria for demonstrating cause-and-effect relationships that you can apply to public relations programs.

Requirements for Causal Interpretations

Researchers generally agree on three major requirements for demonstrating a causal relationship.[1] Logically, for something to be viewed as a "cause," it must occur before whatever it is supposed to produce. It must also be empirically related to the hypothesized "effect." And finally, alternative explanations of what could produce the "effect" must be ruled out.

First, then, look at the sequence of events to determine if a public relations activity can be considered as causally related to some observed condition. Temporal sequence alone, however, does not prove causality. The direction of influence must make sense. You should be able to construct a logical explanation of which caused the other, incorporating the sequence of events as part of the causal model. It makes sense, for example, for Monsanto public relations specialists to suggest that the information campaign increased support for field testing biotechnology products and increased confidence in Monsanto's participation in such tests. On the other hand, it makes little sense to suggest the reverse causal model—that public support for field testing and increased confidence in Monsanto "produced" the information campaign.

Laboratory and field experiments clearly have an advantage over cross-sectional surveys when it comes to demonstrating temporal order. In experimental designs, you can control when "treatments" are administered—demonstrating convincingly that they preceded the hypothesized "effect." Interpreting survey data obtained simultaneously calls for assumptions about the direction of influence based on theory. So the working theories used to develop program strategies provide the theoretical basis for suggesting causal relationships between program activities and phenomena measured after the program. Your design helps demonstrate the order of occurrence. In effect, without some idea about the order of things—what causes what—you are limited to noncausal interpretations of relationships.

Second, demonstrate that differences in the "causal" factor are, in fact, associated with differences observed in the "effect." Some researchers say that the two factors must be correlated—or vary together—thus demonstrating a linkage. The Monsanto biotechnology information campaign provides an example: The survey data show that those who saw the campaign expressed more support for both field testing and Monsanto than did those not exposed to the campaign materials. This adds strength to the case for suggesting a cause-and-effect relationship, but it is not an iron-clad argument. Some who did not see the campaign materials, for instance, also expressed support for field testing and for Monsanto. You can-

[1]Earl Babbie, *The Practice of Social Research,* 4th ed. (Belmont, Calif.: Wadsworth Publishing Company, 1986), pp. 55–58.

not say, then, that exposure to the campaign is a *necessary* condition for producing such public support in all cases. Likewise, some of those exposed to the campaign did not support field testing or Monsanto's involvement in such tests when asked these questions in the follow-up surveys. Exposure to the campaign, then, clearly is not a *sufficient* condition for producing public support in all cases. Monsanto public relations specialists would have the strongest case for demonstrating a causal relationship if they could show that the information campaign is both necessary and sufficient for producing public support of field testing and Monsanto involvement. Seldom is this possible in public relations programs, however, because many different factors influence public knowledge, predispositions, and behaviors related to organization-public relationships. Research, however, helps isolate the influence you can attribute to public relations.

A related consideration is the direction of influence. In other words, for a causal intepretation to apply, the relationship between two variables must be asymmetric. This means that a change in one is associated with a change in the other, but not vice versa. Consider, for example, the influence exposure to the Monsanto campaign has on public perception that the company is concerned about environmental impact of its operations. The hypothesized direction is:

Campaign   ————→   Increased number in community who think Monsanto is
exposure   concerned about environmental impact of its operations

Surveys conducted in test and control communities prior to the campaign would show similar levels of agreement with the opinion statement. The pre- and post-campaign comparisons between communities provide evidence that the direction of influence supports the hypothesis. Even within the campaign community, those most exposed to the campaign show a greater tendency to *change* their opinion when compared to others in the community not exposed to the campaign. And finally, the evidence does not support, and few would suggest, that the reverse causal model is the most plausible explanation.

If you only have data from one survey, however, then you will have greater difficulty demonstrating the direction of influence—the asymmetry of the relationship. Survey results show a correlation between the two measures, but cannot empirically demonstrate—strictly speaking—the direction of the relationship. To demonstrate direction of influence, you need repeated measures from an experimental design or a panel design. Using only cross-sectional survey data, you must use persuasively strong logical or theoretical arguments to defend causal interpretations of correlational data.[2]

Third, rule out all plausible alternative causes. This requirement effectively rules out the possibility of scientifically "proving" causal relationships in the real world. In the hypothetical Monsanto example, the temporal sequence is relatively

---

[2]Morris Rosenberg, *The Logic of Survey Analysis* (New York: Basic Books, Inc., Publishers, 1968), pp. 10–13.

easy to establish—using pre- and post-campaign surveys. Public support for field testing and Monsanto increased *after* the information campaign. And, it is relatively easy to show a correlation between exposure to the campaign and increased public support—simply put, those who saw the campaign were more supportive than those not exposed to the campaign. It is all but impossible, however, to demonstrate that the information campaign is the *only* plausible cause of the increased support.

Could something else have occurred in the test communities coincidental to the information campaign? Sure. Could people in the test communities have figured out that they were participating in an experiment, which in turn influenced their answers on the surveys? That also is a possibility—sometimes referred to as the *Hawthorne Effect*.[3] Could there have been a selection or sampling problem? After all, not everybody was interviewed. Sampling problems caused by high refusal rates, small samples, and faulty selection procedures are always concerns. Some of these concerns are controlled for by using control groups and placebo "treatments" for comparison with the treatment group.

Ruling out plausible alternative causes also requires consideration of what are known as *spurious relationships*. In a spurious relationship—or more properly, a spurious interpretation—what appears to be a causal relationship between two events actually reflects two coincidental effects caused by a third unobserved factor. For example, assume that Monsanto appoints a new plant manager at its location for announced field tests of genetically improved products. Word spreads through the community that the old plant manager has been replaced by a highly respected scientist. As part of his strategy for establishing community support for Monsanto's field tests, the new manager initiates an information campaign such as the one used in previous examples. The new plant manager "causes" two things to occur in the plant community—a new information campaign and increased public support. Some observers, however, might attribute the increased public support to the information campaign, even though the apparent relationship really is an accidental coincidence. The relationships would appear as follows:

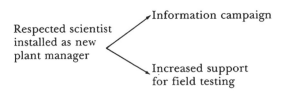

To avoid making spurious interpretations of relationships, build a strong explanation of how the independent variable affects the dependent variable. In

---

[3]The term *Hawthorne Effect* comes from a classic experiment on working conditions that demonstrated how knowledge of their participation in an experiment influenced employee reactions to new arrangements in the work setting. Researchers now use the term to represent any effect that might result from people being aware that they are subjects in a research project.

other words, have a working theory to explain the relationship. The empirical approach, however, is to hold constant or remove the third variable you suspect as the extraneous cause of the observed relationship. If the relationship disappears or does not appear, then you have evidence that the third variable indeed is the common cause of the two variables of interest. For example, assume that in another similar plant community the information campaign is introduced without changes in plant management, but support for field testing does not increase significantly. The comparison between communities suggests the possibility that the new plant manager caused the increased public support *and* the information campaign. The campaign did not produce increased support when applied without the new plant manager.

If you apply similar tests by controlling for other possible causes—and the original results are confirmed—then you add support to the interpretation that the observed relationship between two variables is a causal relationship. In natural program settings, however, you can never rule out all the possible extraneous causes of the two variables you hypothesize as being causally related. Here again, the best available evidence and a sound theory of how one influences the other reduce the plausibility of alternative explanations. Such arguments supported by data tend to be more persuasive than wild speculation about other possible causes and calls to control for all possible contaminating variables.

Notice also that experimental designs with control groups and placebo programs are powerful ways to help isolate program effects and rule out plausible alternative causes. In the real world of public relations research, such treatment versus control comparisons are indeed persuasive.

Direct versus Indirect Causes

The relationship between two variables is a *direct causal relationship* if and only if a change in the independent variable brings about a subsequent change in the dependent variable, *and* all the other possible influences in the model have been controlled for or do not change. An *indirect causal relationship* exists if and only if a change in one variable brings about a change in a second variable only when a third variable also changes or is introduced. Three types of indirect causal relationships deserve attention—those involving *intervening* variables, those with *antecedent* variables, and those modified by *conditional* variables. These third variables are sometimes referred to as *test factors.*

An intervening variable is one that occurs *between* the independent and dependent variables. Indirect causal relationships with intervening variables take the following form (continuing with the hypothetical Monsanto example):

| Increased awareness of biotechnology's potential for increasing world food supplies | Increased willingness to have field tests in community | Increased support for Monsanto involvement in field tests |

According to this theoretical model, a person's willingness to have field tests in his or her community is a result of increased awareness of biotechnology's potential for increasing world food supplies. Once willingness to have field tests generally increases, then support increases for Monsanto in particular to conduct field tests. Increased awareness of biotechnology's contribution to helping solve world food problems leads to increased support for Monsanto field testing only among those—but not necessarily all—who became generally more favorable of field testing in their communities. At the same time, the evidence would have to show that support for Monsanto field tests did not occur without the preceding sequence shown in the model.

Indirect causal relationships with antecedent variables suggest that something precedes the independent variable in the causal sequence. Antecedent variables, then, come before both the independent and dependent variables in the causal chain. The search for antecedent variables could mean tracing back many steps in a chain of causally related phenomena. In our hypothetical Monsanto program, for example, suppose that we hypothesize that concern about famine and hunger in developing countries is an antecedent variable. The causal model would be:

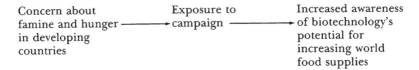

Concern about famine and hunger in developing countries ⟶ Exposure to campaign ⟶ Increased awareness of biotechnology's potential for increasing world food supplies

In other words, concern about famine and hunger in the world is why people pay attention to the Monsanto campaign. Those not concerned about such conditions in developing countries simply don't notice the campaign messages. Those who happen to attend to messages, however, do learn about biotechnology's potential for increasing food supplies. The campaign messages are the independent variable being manipulated in this grand field experiment, with increased awareness of biotechnology's potential contribution to food supplies as the dependent variable being "caused" by the exposure to the messages. In this model, that exposure tends not to occur except for people with the predisposition of being concerned about famine and hunger. Notice, however, this model differs from the model of a spurious relationship. When exposure to the Monsanto campaign does not occur, there is no increase in awareness of biotechnology's potential for increasing world food supplies—even among those concerned about world famine and hunger.

A conditional variable enhances or impedes the effect of the independent variable on the dependent variable. The effect remains, although the strength of the effect is influenced by the conditional variable. For example, level of media dependency could enhance the campaign's impact on awareness of biotechnology's potential for increasing world food supplies. In effect, the extent to which a person depends on the mass media for news and information has an impact on the relationship between the independent and dependent variables—

acting much like a catalyst does in a reaction between two chemicals. The causal model looks like this:

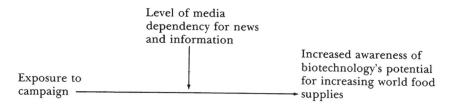

Level of media
dependency for news
and information

Exposure to
campaign

Increased awareness of
biotechnology's potential
for increasing world food
supplies

Concern about famine and hunger may or may not be a necessary condition for campaign impact on awareness of biotechnology's potential for increasing food supplies. In other words, given lower levels of concern—even to the point of disappearing entirely—the campaign may still have an impact, albeit a lesser impact, on awareness. Unlike an intervening variable, a conditional variable does not have to be present for there to be a relationship between the independent and dependent variables.

The Elaboration Process

The process of introducing third variables to more fully understand the relationship between independent and dependent variables is the process of *elaboration* (first discussed in Chapter 5). This involves using test variables, or control variables, to search out antecedent, intervening, and conditional variables that directly or indirectly affect the relationship between independent and dependent variables. Without such tests, you may miss the real causal relationship or misread the strength of the relationship.

After you detect a relationship between two variables, elaboration involves segmenting or stratifying the sample on the basis of third variables. The partial tables generated by these segmentations yield multiple tests of the original relationship. In effect, each subsample created by the breakdown on the third variable becomes another test of the relationship—a replication. The elaboration process is nothing more than a search for a better understanding of the conditions under which relationships occur.

Unfortunately, there is no universal set of variables we can suggest as test factors. You will have to use your understanding of the situation under study. Use your "hunches" and working theories about third variables that might influence or play a role in the observed relationship between two variables. The logic is rather straightforward:

- First, decide if the basic, two-variable (zero-order) relationship is asymmetrical (logically or theoretically)—meaning that one variable (independent) "causes" the other variable (dependent).
- Second, segment or stratify the sample on the basis of measures made on a third variable.

- Third, calculate the relationship between the original two variables for each of the subsamples—these new values are the partial relationships.
- Fourth, compare the original two-variable relationship with the partial relationships to discover a pattern that will add to your understanding of the nature of the relationship between the independent and dependent variables.

If the relationship stays the same for all the subgroups created by the stratification using values of a third variable, then the test variable has no impact. This means the original relationship is *confirmed* or replicated. For example, imagine splitting the treatment community sample on the basis of whether or not respondents expressed concern about world famine (before the program began). If you found no differences in the patterns of post-program awareness, then the original relationship remains unchallenged. As Table 12-1 shows, the relationship between exposure to the program and levels of awareness for those concerned about world famine and those not concerned about world famine is essentially the same. Controlling on the basis of the test variable makes no difference—the original relationship is confirmed.

If the relationship in some subsamples disappears while remaining strong in other subsamples, then you have evidence of the conditions under which the two variables are causally related. This means the original relationship is *specified.* For example, again assume that you split the sample based on whether or not respondents are concerned about world famine at T_1. If only those who expressed a concern about world famine are affected by the campaign, then you have specified one of the conditions necessary for campaign impact detected at T_2. (See Table 12-2.) In effect, controlling for the third variable indicates one of the conditions affecting the campaign's impact on public awareness.

If the relationship disappears in all subsamples, then you have identified an antecedent or intervening variable—depending on how you interpret the order and direction of influence in the causal model. For example, Table 12-3 illustrates how the apparent relationship between exposure and awareness does not hold when controlling on T_1 concern for world famine. Notice that when the sample is divided into the "concerned" and "not concerned" subsamples, significant differences in the levels of awareness disappear. In other words, within the two conditions there is no difference in the levels of awareness for those exposed to the campaign and those not exposed to the campaign.

Of course, another interpretation is possible if the relationship disappears when "controlling" on the basis of the third variable—the relationship between the first two variables is spurious, or not real. In other words, the third variable causes coincidental changes in the other two variables, which are otherwise not linked in any way.

Some conditional variables suppress or distort the real relationships between independent and dependent variables.[4] A suppressor variable exerts an influence on the relationship between the independent and dependent variables,

---

[4]Rosenberg, *Survey Analysis,* pp. 84–104.

Table 12–1   Zero-Order Relationship Confirmed or Replicated

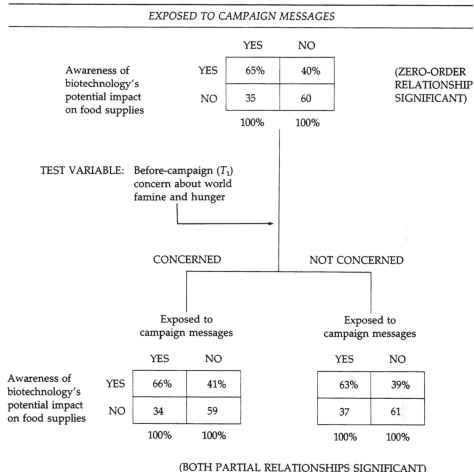

EXPOSED TO CAMPAIGN MESSAGES

		YES	NO	
Awareness of biotechnology's potential impact on food supplies	YES	65%	40%	(ZERO-ORDER RELATIONSHIP SIGNIFICANT)
	NO	35	60	
		100%	100%	

TEST VARIABLE: Before-campaign (T_1) concern about world famine and hunger

CONCERNED   NOT CONCERNED

Exposed to campaign messages   Exposed to campaign messages

		YES	NO		YES	NO
Awareness of biotechnology's potential impact on food supplies	YES	66%	41%		63%	39%
	NO	34	59		37	61
		100%	100%		100%	100%

(BOTH PARTIAL RELATIONSHIPS SIGNIFICANT)

such that the relationship seems to not exist. For example, assume that some community members believe that world famine and hunger are caused by divine will as an early warning of the Armageddon prophesy. Monsanto's message strategy apparently alerts believers to what they see as prophesy. Unfortunately for Monsanto, believers feel that to reduce famine and hunger is to resist divine will. Exposure to the messages actually reduces their support for biotechnology field tests. At the same time, other community members increase their support for biotechnology field tests. The overall effect on the total community—believers and nonbelievers combined—is no apparent change in awareness. However, when believers and nonbelievers are studied separately, a strong positive effect is evident for nonbelievers, and a strong negative effect is isolated for those subscribing to the Armageddon scenario.

Table 12–2 Zero-Order Relationship Specified

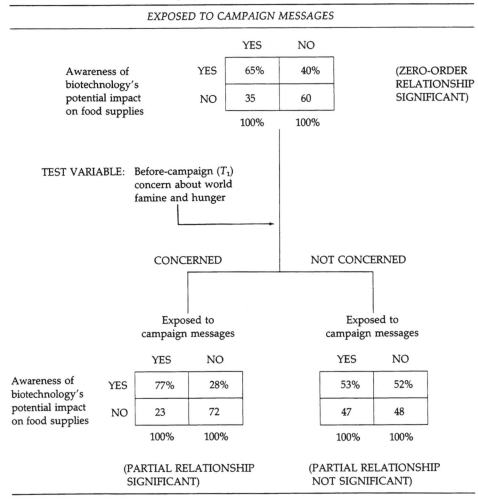

EXPOSED TO CAMPAIGN MESSAGES

		YES	NO	
Awareness of biotechnology's potential impact on food supplies	YES	65%	40%	(ZERO-ORDER RELATIONSHIP SIGNIFICANT)
	NO	35	60	
		100%	100%	

TEST VARIABLE: Before-campaign (T_1) concern about world famine and hunger

CONCERNED   NOT CONCERNED

Exposed to   Exposed to
campaign messages   campaign messages

Awareness of biotechnology's potential impact on food supplies		YES	NO		YES	NO
	YES	77%	28%		53%	52%
	NO	23	72		47	48
		100%	100%		100%	100%

(PARTIAL RELATIONSHIP   (PARTIAL RELATIONSHIP
SIGNIFICANT)   NOT SIGNIFICANT)

In the case of a distorter variable, the effect would be—as the name suggests—to distort or reverse the direction of a relationship. A true positive relationship appears as a negative relationship, until the test variable is controlled. For example, what if the results from a community survey showed that those exposed to the campaign express *lower* levels of support for field testing rather than the expected higher levels? You might be tempted to conclude that the campaign reduced support for field testing! When you examine your media placements and where respondents said they saw campaign messages, however, you notice that most respondents were exposed to your messages through thirty- and sixty-second spots on a local independent television station. The majority of adjacent programming consisted of fundamentalist televangelism. You hypothesize

Table 12–3 Zero-Order Relationship Spurious (Antecedent Variable Controlled)

EXPOSED TO CAMPAIGN MESSAGES

		YES	NO	
Awareness of biotechnology's potential impact on food supplies	YES	65%	40%	(ZERO-ORDER RELATIONSHIP SIGNIFICANT)
	NO	35	60	
		100%	100%	

TEST VARIABLE: Before-campaign (T_1) concern about world famine and hunger

CONCERNED   NOT CONCERNED

Exposed to campaign messages   Exposed to campaign messages

Awareness of biotechnology's potential impact on food supplies		YES	NO		YES	NO
	YES	70%	68%		27%	25%
	NO	30	32		73	75
		100%	100%		100%	100%

(BOTH PARTIAL RELATIONSHIPS NOT SIGNIFICANT)

that perhaps the people most frequently exposed to your messages are those who see world famine as Biblical prophesy. You reexamine your data, this time splitting the sample on the media measures. As expected, those who saw the message in the nonsectarian newspaper show greater levels of support for biotechnology field testing—compared to those not exposed to messages. Apparently, those exposed to the messages on the televangalism station distorted the generally positive impact of campaign messages to a negative reaction.

Such testing and interpretation increase your understanding of the complex chain of causal relationships. If you do not explore the nature of an apparent causal relationship by introducing test variables, you can end up with an incomplete and simplistic interpretation. The more you understand about the conditions under which the causal relationship exists, the more exact and powerful your interpretations can be. Rosenberg concludes, in his classic book on interpreting survey data:

> *Properly conducted survey research tells us* **whether** *independent variable A is related to dependent variable B. The introduction of test factors helps to tell us* **why** *(or why not) the two variables are related. Test factors thus afford important new knowledge and help in filtering out erroneous conclusions.* . . . [5]

In effect, the elaboration process attempts to unravel the chain of causal relationships and to increase your understanding of complex circumstances. Nobody said it would be easy. And it is unrealistic to assume that the important relationships among key variables are simple and direct. Most likely, you will deal with many variables, with causal sequences, and working theories that change with each new insight gained from the elaboration process.

DEMONSTRATING PROGRAM EFFECTS

Strictly speaking, you cannot scientifically *prove* that your program "caused" some observed "change" or "effect." And in the real world of public relations programs, you can't eliminate this problem by simply getting better technical advice or by spending more money. The issue remains the gap between what is possible in naturalistic settings and the nature of evidence needed in any research effort to "prove" something. Because programs occur in uncontrolled settings, random assignment is usually not possible, and both the program and conditions change over time, "pure" science is seldom possible.

Instead, you *interpret* evidence as either supporting or refuting working theories and hypotheses about causal relationships and models—offering plausible causal inferences based on the evidence. The intent is to demonstrate that your program produced results that would not have occurred without the program. By following the generally accepted principles of research design, measurement, and data analysis, you can make convincing causal inferences about such program impact.

Rather than give up because perfect research and scientific proof are not possible in dynamic program settings, Rossi and Freeman propose the "good enough rule." This means you "should choose the best possible design, taking into account practicality and feasibility."[6] The good enough design should produce the evidence you need to support your interpretation that the program caused observed changes. The idea is that reasonable people will accept interpretations based on the best available evidence obtained under controlled conditions using the scientific methods outlined in Chapters 5 through 8.

[5]Ibid., p. 100.
[6]Peter H. Rossi and Howard E. Freeman, *Evaluation*, 3rd ed. (Beverly Hills, Calif.: Sage Publications, Inc., 1985), pp. 189–90.

Not surprisingly, a plausible and convincing causal interpretation must specify the nature of program outcomes and the extent to which they can be attributed to the program—*what* changed as a result of the program. Objectives spell out intended program outcomes, but program effects must be separated from changes brought about by nonprogram influences. This calls for longitudinal designs or control group comparisons using one of the experimental designs. Additionally, the elaboration process can add understanding of the conditions under which observed changes can be reasonably credited to the program.

Using comparison groups and the elaboration process also helps identify *who* the program affects. It is even possible to miss a program impact if you don't test all your hunches about who might be and who might not be affected. For example, recall that in an earlier example we used a hypothetical causal model suggesting that respondents' concern about famine and hunger before the program affected the degree to which the information campaign increased awareness about biotechnology's potential for increasing food supplies. To assess the impact of this test variable—concern about famine and hunger—you would divide the sample into subsamples using test variable responses from the first survey. Figure 12–1 illustrates data from a hypothetical treatment community in the biotechnology information program field experiment. (In this example, we simply split the subsample of those exposed to the program into equal subsamples by dividing at the median score on the concern about famine and hunger measure.)

In this example, concern for famine and hunger has a profound impact on how people responded to the information campaign. For some reason yet to be explored using the elaboration process, those with little concern experienced a *decrease* in awareness. As the program planners' working theory predicted, those concerned about famine and hunger became more aware after the campaign. Notice, however, if we had not divided the sample into the high and low concern subsamples, the average level of awareness for all of those in the exposed subsample did not change during the campaign—the same as for those not exposed to campaign messages. Limiting the analysis to a simple direct causal model would have yielded evidence supporting a "no-effect" conclusion. By controlling on the level of concern for famine and hunger, the evidence suggests an interaction

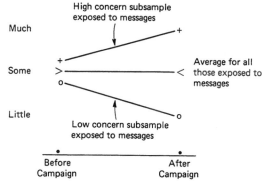

Figure 12–1   Illustration of cause-and-effect relationship controlling for test variable.

effect between the test variable and exposure to campaign messages. In other words, some responded to the campaign with increased awareness, whereas the campaign had an adverse effect on others' awareness. The elaboration process helps uncover cause-and-effect relationships masked when the answers from many types of people under all kinds of conditions are combined in the analyses.

Rosenberg uses the concept of *block-booking* to illustrate this masking problem.[7] The term originated in the movie business: In order to get a popular film, movie theater owners used to have to rent "blocks" of films containing some that might not be as desirable.

The analogy applies, in that anytime you select respondents on the basis of one or more attributes—say the independent variable in your causal model or a test variable—you undoubtedly introduce or may not eliminate variance on other variables. In other words, even though people share one characteristic— such as gender, age, family income level, type of employment, concern about world famine, etc.—they may have little in common on other variables. (Random assignment to treatment and control groups eliminates the problem, because the variance introduced by uncontrolled variables is—in theory—evenly distributed between the two groups.)

You may not find the real program effect or you may not truly understand how the program affects different people unless you take into account the variance resulting from block-booking. These variables are the test variables used in the elaboration process. For example, if we had compared only the treatment groups with the control group in the situation used to illustrate Figure 12–1, we could have concluded that the program had little or no effect—as illustrated in Figure 12–2. Recall that even in the treatment group the post-program average awareness for all those exposed was the same as before the program. The comparison with the control group levels would suggest a nonsignificant difference between treatment and placebo conditions. (Notice here that the appropriate test of program effect is a comparison of the *changes* observed in the two groups. In other words, is the change O_2-O_1 in the treatment group greater than the change

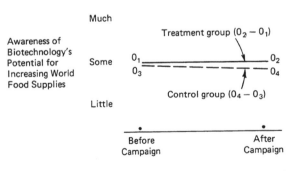

Much

Awareness of Biotechnology's Potential for Increasing World Food Supplies

Some

Little

Treatment group $(O_2 - O_1)$

O_1 ———————————— O_2

O_3 — — — — — — — — O_4

Control group $(O_4 - O_3)$

Before Campaign

After Campaign

(TEST FOR PROGRAM EFFECT: Is $O_2 - O_1$ greater than $O_4 - O_3$?)

Figure 12–2 Illustration of non-equivalent control group design.

[7]Rosenberg, *The Logic of Survey Analysis*, pp. 26–27.

O_4-O_3 in the control group?) By controlling for the level of concern about world famine and hunger, we were able to demonstrate how the program did have an impact on some people in the treatment community.

In the end, sophisticated techniques can't substitute for thinking about what caused something to happen. Methods can't substitute for a good theory of what happened. Research then tests your ideas about causal relationships and adds the weight of evidence to your interpretations.

SEARCHING FOR THE REAL CAUSES

Determining *what is having an effect* requires knowledge of program content that could have produced observed changes and understanding of the mechanism or process linking program content to the changes. Too often in public relations program evaluations, our working theories are too simple and general.

Rather than simply noting gross number or amount of placements, amount read, or time spent, you first need to quantify portions of media content that could be causally related to observed changes and the amount of that specific content read or attended to. Then, you must show that awareness changes occurred for those people who read or attended to the particular portions of the total message content—or at least that their awareness levels changed significantly more than for those not exposed to the specific messages. For example, in the hypothetical Monsanto case, if you cannot demonstrate a difference in awareness changes for different levels of campaign exposure, then you have weak evidence to support your working theory linking exposure to the intended changes. Reeves summarizes the dilemma this way:

> *Attributes of communication that could produce change are numerous and can be found in all parts of a message—sentence structure, pictures, typography, headlines, choice of words, etc. Further, the effect could be dependent on multiple messages or several exposures to the same one. Choosing the appropriate dimensions to analyze might be tough, but ignoring the problem is an admission that we don't know what caused a change.*[8]

Rosenberg raises the possibility of more than one cause, referring to their relationship to the dependent variable as "conjoint influences."[9] In this causal model, there are two or more independent variables. The challenge is to untangle the intertwined influences so that you have a better understanding of their relative impacts. To what extent do the "causes" have separate impacts? Which "cause" makes the greatest contribution to the observed change? Does the

[8]Byron Reeves, "Now You See Them, Now You Don't: Demonstrating Effects of Communication Programs," *Public Relations Quarterly,* Vol. 28, No. 3 (Fall 1983), p. 19.
[9]Rosenberg, *The Logic of Survey Analysis,* pp. 160–94.

presence of one independent variable modify the impact of other "causes"? To find out, you can create tables with one independent defining the columns, the other independent variable defining the rows, and the value in each of the cells representing the dependent variable. If there aren't too many categories for each of the independent variables, you should be able to identify and interpret conjoint influences. (For more on how to interpret such a table, review Appendix K on interpreting contingency tables and the discussion on analysis of variance in Chapter 11.)

Of course, the most efficient way to isolate program effects is to randomly assign subjects to treatment and control conditions. In most public relations program situations, however, it is not possible to isolate the treatment subjects from the placebo subjects. More typical program evaluation designs employ intact groups—plant groups, work teams, departments, communities, etc.—in the treatment and control conditions. The persuasiveness of your treatment-control comparison depends on how convincing you can be that the intact groups were comparable on all important dimensions other than the program treatment.

SERENDIPITY AND EX POST FACTO INTERPRETATION

Sometimes the elaboration process uncovers completely unexpected relationships. Can you use such findings as evidence of causal relationships? In other words, once you know the answer, can you go back and write the question? In strict hypothesis-testing, the answer is probably, no. In fact, however, some of the most important scientific discoveries resulted from unanticipated results or inconsistencies in data. Researchers often refer to such findings as *serendipity*.

The problem centers on how such results are interpreted and reported. If you do nothing more than "data snooping" and then report findings as if you had hypothesized such relationships before looking at the data, then you engage in pseudoscience. However, if you use unexpected findings as the basis for suggesting possible explanations that can be tested, then you are being sensitive to all that your research may uncover. To ignore serendipitous findings would be to miss much of what can be learned. Researchers sometimes describe this as "letting the data talk to you."

Use replication to confirm an unexpected finding. In other words, either in other samples or within subsamples, look for the same relationship or pattern in the data. Consistency in the findings adds to one's confidence in the empirical generalization, but it does not confirm your *interpretation* of why the relationship exists. That will call on your ability to draw upon and apply theory. As Rosenberg points out, "...the strength of the interpretation rests upon the theoretical or deductive foundations which underpin it."[10]

---

[10]Ibid., p. 238.

Tentative explanations typically draw on working theory or educated hunches about what is happening. Unfortunately, such ex post facto interpretations are often presented as having been "tested" by the data. More appropriately, serendipitous and ex post facto generalizations should be presented as tentative conclusions awaiting systematic investigation and external confirmation. Such findings become one step in an incremental research process, not the conclusion. In this view, scientific inquiry is a cyclical process with no beginning or end. (Recall the spiral of science discussed in Chapter 5.)

This discussion is not intended to minimize the importance of serendipitous findings and ex post facto interpretations. To the contrary, we see these as both necessary and desirable approaches in the search for causal interpretations. By being sensitive to findings—even those that are inconsistent with the working theories and models that guided your program—you will contribute to your own and others' understanding of what works and why things work or don't work in the real world.

In the short term, pressures for accountability and performance evaluations generate concern about what did or did not work. In fact, "Did the program work?" is often the only question asked that calls for any semblance of a causal interpretation. In the long run, however, you need to know a great deal more about causal relationships in order to generalize and apply your knowledge to other program situations. It is this quest for professional understanding that motivates the application of science to testing for causation and change. The next challenge is to interpret and report the findings so others can share your understanding.

CHAPTER 13

INTERPRETING
AND REPORTING
THE FINDINGS

Ann H. Barkelew, APR, Vice President–Corporate Public Relations, DAYTON-HUDSON CORPORATION, Minneapolis.

*I always look at the results first. In other words, to put the research into perspective and to shorten my time, I look at the conclusions first and then go back to study the details. So that is also how I report research to other managers—giving them the major findings first and then filling in the details that led up to those final results. I start with a cover memo stating the bottom line result and then attach a tally sheet or some type of summary breakout. At a follow-up meeting, we work **together** to come to some conclusion and **jointly** make recommendations. But managers have to "buy in" on the results before you can move to the point of making recommendations based on the research.*

Gary L. Schmermund, Senior Vice President, LOUIS HARRIS & ASSOCIATES, INC., New York.

I have heard year after year, time after time, "How do you get management to listen?" The answer is, "Have something to say." Management will listen if it's not just dribble.

Years ago at AT&T, we used to put out a book that would take six months to generate. By the time it came out, the data were six to eight months old. It cost a fortune to mail out. And nobody looked at it! We finally got smart. We put out twelve pieces that went out sequentially to different people. It is the same data base, but it was parceled out to whom it was relevant. We began doing a better job of connecting the research to the consumer of the information, rather than according to the organization chart.

Jerry W. Cooper, APR, Manager–Public Affairs, Planning and Administration, AMOCO CORPORATION, Chicago.

What we've tried to do the last few years is to overcome a problem. From a research standpoint, we were coming up with good information, with what we thought was useful information. We were coming up with papers that we would distribute, from which nothing would happen. The problem was not coming up with the research; the problem was how do you make it useful in the corporation. So we have changed the way we do things. First, we're not turning out as much. We are concentrating somewhat less on methodology. And we are concentrating more on how we can get more people in the corporation involved in the process so they buy in on the use of the information too. The ways we are doing that is getting more people involved at the different steps along the way and reporting our research results lower down in the organization.

David E. Clavier, PhD, APR, Executive Director, HUSK JENNINGS OVERMAN PUBLIC RELATIONS, Jacksonville, Florida.

It is important to have research results on paper. Major decisions, based on research, should not be made on hearsay. Findings have got to be in that form anyway, just because of the nature of corporate decision making. You would never have a business plan only in somebody's head. You would have something down on paper so that people could review it and reflect on it.

From the standpoint of a corporation, a research report should be short and concise. The executive summary has the short answers to the key questions and gives the key findings. The executive summary then alludes to the research design, the methodologies, the samplings, and any of the qualifications, but by no means should it be a lengthy document. If it is, it ought to be sectioned out adequately, so that anyone can get to it quickly. The amount of information most business people are inundated with in any given day precludes them from spending an awful lot of time looking at the answer to one research question.

Walter K. Lindenmann, PhD, Vice President-Director of Research, KETCHUM PUBLIC RELATIONS, New York.

Research has to be easy to understand. Research reports should be as brief and straight to the point as possible. One area in particular makes me nervous. I've had trouble with other researchers on this one. How far should you go in the report? Some researchers will put actual recommendations into a report. They will write an actual program. I don't think it's appropriate for them to do that because they don't really know all of the dimensions of the client's problems.

*What I do is detail the findings and then provide an executive summary of highlights. I **may** have a section called "Implications of the Findings." But, my stance is, that section—from the researcher's standpoint—should **only** be attributable back to the data base and not to anything else.*

At the risk of stating the obvious, we begin this chapter by pointing out that you do research in public relations so the results can be used. First, that means findings have to be translated into a form decision makers can apply to their management problems. Second, if the research is to be used, the results must get into the hands of decision makers. Third, the applied nature of research means that decision makers must understand the report of findings and their interpretations. This chapter addresses *interpreting* and *reporting* research findings. In Chapter 14, we discuss strategies for *applying* research findings in organizations.

DOING "SCIENCE" IN THE "REAL WORLD"

Clearly, our approach in the first twelve chapters was based on the imperatives of science and scientific methods of inquiry. Public relations programs, however, occur in the real world—a trite but meaningful term for the dynamic environment of organization-public relationships. All too often, practitioners offer the real-world setting as an excuse for not doing research—pointing out that the constantly changing setting makes scientific research nearly impossible. Certainly, the real-world setting lacks the control possibilities of the laboratory. Consider some factors that illustrate the complexity of the research task in public relations.

Changes in the Setting

Scientists design and conduct research to control for alternative explanations of cause-and-effect relationships. They attempt to isolate effects caused by the experimental treatment from those caused by confounding nontreatment influences. Evaluation research in public relations programs seldom enjoys such control over and isolation from non-program events. The ever-changing real-world setting often complicates—sometimes precludes—isolation of program effects. Imagine the scrambling that accompanies steep downturns in the stock market. Mountains of research data and volumes of planned program strategies are disgarded as crisis management and reactive communication take the place of carefully crafted, research-based programs. Or, recall how news coverage of the Bhopal, India, Union Carbide plant disaster affected public perceptions of chemical plant safety . . . and Union Carbide. Imagine how press coverage of the accident, the more than 2,500 fatalities, and subsequent lawsuits affected Union Carbide's investor relations program. Now, imagine yourself in the midst of conducting an evaluation of the company's community and investor relations programs! Research in the real world lacks the tidy controls possible in the scientist's laboratory.

Changes in Organizational Goals

Priorities change for more reasons than we can list here. Obvious examples include changes in organizational leadership; catastrophic accidents; new threats from competitors, protest groups, or government agencies; financial restructuring due to bankruptcy, merger, takeover or leveraged buy-out; and changes in products, services, or programs. For example, before the Chernobyl nuclear power station accident released high levels of radioactive matter, the Atomic Industrial Forum (Maryland) program goal was to increase public awareness of future demand for electricity and the uncertainty of imported oil as an energy source. During the first week after the Chernobyl accident, AIF got more than 1,200 media calls—about the same number received in a typical *year*. The industry trade association changed its goal to increasing public knowledge of the safety factors built into U.S. nuclear power plants.[1] When such changes in organizational goals and priorities occur, old criteria for assessing public relations program effectiveness must also change. Old benchmark measures no longer fit the criteria mandated by new goals. Impact measures designed for the old program are scuttled as attention and resources are directed to new concerns.

Changes in Publics

Even the best-researched and most skillfully implemented program may have to be scrapped or revised if target publics change. If this happens, there goes the benchmark research! Newly organized community groups, a suddenly active consumer group, and an employee group pushing for unionization are just three examples of emergent, active publics that can throw off even the best-planned program evaluation. New publics cause program resources to be redirected, shift the focus of program strategies, and even divert the attention of

---

[1]Mark Jacobs, "Closing the Generating Gap: Chernobyl, the Nuclear-Power Industry, and Public Support," *Public Relations Journal*, Vol. 43, No. 5 (May 1987), pp. 19, 22–23, and 39.

decision makers. Naturally, these publics seem to emerge just as pretest or benchmark measures were in place to do some really "scientific" evaluation research on the originally targeted publics!

Changes in Program Strategies

What happens when the program no longer resembles what the research was intended to help evaluate? Program goals and objectives are originally based on benchmark situation analysis research. These outcome statements become unrealistic when the budget is cut, key personnel leave the staff, or technical "glitches" significantly alter program delivery. Numerous real-world problems cause such major program modifications that the original evaluation research design and methods must also be modified.

Changes in Program Outcomes

What if unanticipated consequences of the program are not detected because the research instruments do not measure these variables? What if those unintended effects turn out to be more interesting or more important than original intended outcomes? Examples include unanticipated "backlash" reactions, misinterpretations, and overreactions. A well-planned formal evaluation, using highly reliable measures of specific *intended* program effects, may have to be scrapped if program evaluators detect unanticipated outcomes through informal observation.

At this point, you might ask, "Why do research if things change and compromise the results?" You do research because there is no other, more reliable way to gather useful information over the long haul. Most research conducted in the real world suffers from flaws and, therefore, so do research findings. You can't avoid changes encountered in the dynamic settings in which public relations is practiced. Research done in public relations programs will always be somewhat equivocal.

Real-world conditions and resulting limitations on research, however, do not reduce the importance of research findings as inputs for management decision making. Interpreting and reporting the research calls for objectivity and recognition that the research report will be used along with information from many other sources. As Gary Schmermund at Louis Harris & Associates told us:

> One should not do a research project with the anticipation that the research is going to provide "the answer"—that whatever the research shows, that's what we're going to do. To me, research provides the public relations function **input**. It's part of the decision information upon which management must act. It is a management tool—not the only tool—that represents a systematic collection of information to be added to the pile of not-so-systematically-collected information. I mention this, because far

too often the less experienced may think that management just sits there waiting on the research to give the answer. It just doesn't happen that way.

In other words, you must be realistic about what research can do and cannot do in real-world settings. Further, you don't get points for having done research under adverse conditions, nor are you excused from the imperatives of science. Instead, you are charged with the task of providing good data, suggesting reasonable interpretations of the findings, and defending your conclusions—even though you had to do the research under less than ideal conditions. You should have a clear picture of your role and know what others expect from the research.

GENERAL GUIDELINES FOR REPORTING RESEARCH FINDINGS

The public relations program setting complicates the research task, but does not nullify the findings—as long as you report only what you can support with the data and avoid overstating what you have learned. In other words, limit what you attribute to the research and qualify your interpretations by making explicit the bases for conclusions drawn from the findings. Here are our suggestions for interpreting and reporting the findings:

Clarify Your Role

How you and others see your role in part determines *what, to whom,* and *how* you report. Are you expected to serve as the "expert" responsible for both reporting the results and telling others what they mean? Are you to limit your role to that of a "technician," gathering and reporting data that others will interpret and factor into decision making? Or, are you seen as a "problem-solving facilitator," collaborating with other members of the management team to interpret, report, and apply the findings? As in other aspects of your public relations work, you will assume one or more of these roles—depending on the problem situation, your other roles in the organization, and how others see your role in decision making. Because situations and expectations vary, your effectiveness in interpreting and reporting research findings will depend in part on how sensitive you are to your role in the process.

Stick to the Research Questions

Focus the research report on the main questions you originally wanted to answer. Report the findings without subjective prejudice and "let the chips fall where they may." In other words, keep before you at all times the purposes for which you did the research. Remember that the results are intended to help you and others make *better* decisions. To help others put the findings in context, remind them up front about why the research was done. Readers or listeners should understand what motivated the research in the first place and how the results were intended to be used.

State Limits of Findings

Make explicit anything about the setting, goals, publics, program, and outcomes that limit or qualify the research findings. Both you and the audience for your research report must be sensitive to the constraints imposed by the real-world setting. As David Clavier at Husk Jennings Overman Public Relations, Jacksonville, Florida, reminded us:

> *The limitations of a research project become the backdrop for explanation and description of the results. Because two years from now when you're not there or you don't remember, somebody will use that research to form a new decision. They will have forgotten some of the major qualifications on how you did that research. So documenting qualifications and limitations is pretty important.*

Use Tables and Graphs to Display Complex Information

You can put a lot of information into a well-designed table or graph. In fact, we recommend constructing the tables and graphs *before* you write anything about the findings. You then organize the report around the tables and graphs, using just enough text to support and explain each. As you design each table and graph, keep in mind that some "readers" turn to these first to get a quick idea of the results. Others will read *only* the tables and graphs! This means that the tables and graphs should be so clearly constructed that they can stand alone. With this in mind, you need meaningful titles; complete labels for rows, columns, and other parts of the presentation contents; and footnotes explaining symbols, statistics, and other elements of the display. (See Exhibits 13–1 and 13–2.) Of course, don't let tables and graphs stand alone, because some readers will overlook them or miss their importance. In the narrative, summarize the major findings and refer the reader to specific illustrations.

Some research report writers use the tables to structure their reports. In their book on technical and scientific writing, Zimmerman and Clark suggest that you begin with the tables and use them to outline the narrative for technical reports based on data analyses.

> *By developing your visuals before you organize your manuscript, you can let your manuscript support, explain, and interpret the*

EXHIBIT 13–1
Anatomy of a Frequency Table

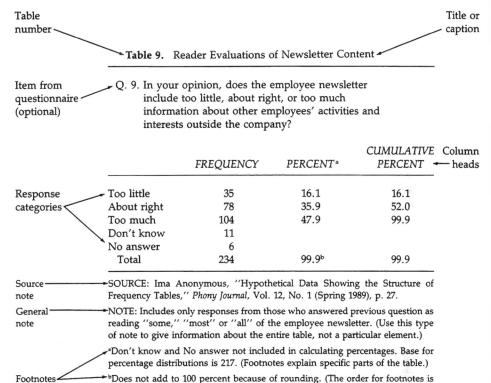

Table number

Title or caption

Table 9. Reader Evaluations of Newsletter Content

Item from questionnaire (optional)

Q. 9. In your opinion, does the employee newsletter include too little, about right, or too much information about other employees' activities and interests outside the company?

Response categories	FREQUENCY	PERCENT[a]	CUMULATIVE PERCENT
Too little	35	16.1	16.1
About right	78	35.9	52.0
Too much	104	47.9	99.9
Don't know	11		
No answer	6		
Total	234	99.9[b]	99.9

Column heads

Source note

SOURCE: Ima Anonymous, "Hypothetical Data Showing the Structure of Frequency Tables," *Phony Journal*, Vol. 12, No. 1 (Spring 1989), p. 27.

General note

NOTE: Includes only responses from those who answered previous question as reading "some," "most" or "all" of the employee newsletter. (Use this type of note to give information about the entire table, not a particular element.)

[a]Don't know and No answer not included in calculating percentages. Base for percentage distributions is 217. (Footnotes explain specific parts of the table.)

Footnotes

[b]Does not add to 100 percent because of rounding. (The order for footnotes is from top to bottom, left to right.)

visuals. You may find that writing about the illustrations helps you clarify your interpretation of the information they present.[2]

Number the tables in the order they appear in the report. Notice that our style in this book calls for a new sequence for each chapter, with each illustration number incorporating both the chapter and position in the order of presentation. (This approach works well when more than one person or group contributes different parts of the report.) To avoid this compound numbering system, simply number the illustrations in order of presentation, without regard for

[2]Donald E. Zimmerman and David G. Clark, *Guide to Technical and Scientific Communication* (New York: Random House, Inc., 1987), pp. 147–48.

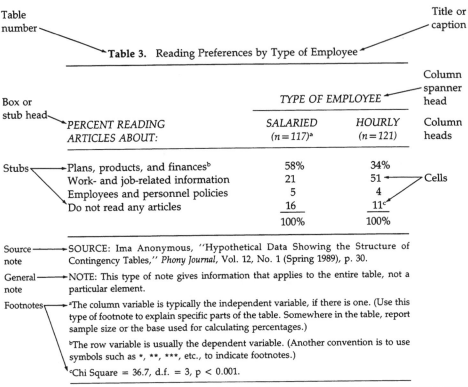

EXHIBIT 13–2
Anatomy of a Contingency Table

Table number

Title or caption

Table 3. Reading Preferences by Type of Employee

	TYPE OF EMPLOYEE	
PERCENT READING ARTICLES ABOUT:	*SALARIED (n = 117)[a]*	*HOURLY (n = 121)*
Plans, products, and finances[b]	58%	34%
Work- and job-related information	21	51
Employees and personnel policies	5	4
Do not read any articles	16	11[c]
	100%	100%

Box or stub head

Column spanner head

Column heads

Stubs

Cells

Source note — SOURCE: Ima Anonymous, "Hypothetical Data Showing the Structure of Contingency Tables," *Phony Journal,* Vol. 12, No. 1 (Spring 1989), p. 30.

General note — NOTE: This type of note gives information that applies to the entire table, not a particular element.

Footnotes — [a]The column variable is typically the independent variable, if there is one. (Use this type of footnote to explain specific parts of the table. Somewhere in the table, report sample size or the base used for calculating percentages.)

[b]The row variable is usually the dependent variable. (Another convention is to use symbols such as *, **, ***, etc., to indicate footnotes.)

[c]Chi Square = 36.7, d.f. = 3, p < 0.001.

chapter or section of the report. Notice that tables and figures are different. Tables generally present numbers without illustrative support. Figures, on the other hand, use diagrams, bar graphs, lines, etc., to represent the relationships among elements and numbers. Common practice numbers tables in sequence and separately numbers figures in sequence of presentation. For example, Chapter 3 presents two tables (Table 3–1 and Table 3–2) and three figures (Figure 3–1, Figure 3–2, and Figure 3–3).

Notice that we use exhibits to present supplemental information or illustrations that do not fit as either tables or figures. Chapter 3, for example, contains "Exhibit 3–1. Examples of Using Research to Monitor and Adjust Programs"— Ann Barkelew's description of how she uses research for those purposes at Dayton-Hudson Corporation. In research reports, such information or other supplemental materials would most likely be attached to the main report as appendices.

Use Statistics to Summarize Information

The descriptive and inferential statistics outlined in Chapters 10 through 12 efficiently condense large amounts of information. They replace what would be pages of words needed to convey the same interpretations of research findings. Statistics also help your audience determine how much confidence to put in your findings and how much attention to give various findings. Increasingly sophisticated managers understand the statistics commonly used in marketing, quality control, and operations. Most will be comfortable seeing measures of central tendency, association, and probability in public relations research reports.

If you want to determine if two or more sets of measures are related ("go together"), then use either a nonparametric or parametric correlation method to represent the strength of the relationship. If you want to find out if a difference exists between measures taken from two or more groups, then compute statistical significance and confidence level to help judge the relative importance of the differences you observe. In other words, use the statistics discussed in the previous chapters to help others interpret and understand your findings.

Write to a Busy Reader

Research on how managers make decisions shows something other than a thorough, analytical, and rational decision maker. First of all, managers spend about three-fourths of every working day *talking*. In other words, much of what they learn and pass on is in conversation, not writing. Second, they spend about one-third of their time in scheduled meetings. Third, they devote the rest of their time to a wide variety of activities, but each commands only short attention—under ten minutes on average. Fourth, managers themselves do not schedule or initiate the majority of their conversations and activities.[3] So much for any hopes you had that management would spend hours poring over your detailed and expertly prepared research report! You will know your managers better than any generalizations made here, but the rule of thumb is to report your research as if the recipient of the information is very busy and will spend little time with the report.

Relate Research Findings to Pressing Decisions

In the hurried environments in which many managers work, many will ignore research reports that are too much, too technical, too complex, or too distant from pressing business. So a primary requirement of your research report is to show your audience how the findings are valid and useful. If the research was

---

[3]Lee Sproull and Patrick Larkey, "Managerial Behavior and Evaluator Effectiveness," in *The Evaluator and Management*, ed. by Herbert C. Schulberg and Jeanette M. Jerrell (Beverly Hills: Sage Publications, Inc., 1979), pp. 91–94.

designed to answer a series of specific questions, then try reporting the relevant findings under each question. This question-and-answer format efficiently presents the data and interpretations for each of the questions that motivated the research. If the questions originally addressed managers' real needs and concerns, then the findings should represent valuable information for decision making.

Put esoteric and interesting findings that don't directly relate to current or future decisions in appendices, or in a separate and later section of the report. Position them as supplements to the major and usable findings. Report them sparingly, as they can easily add too much detail to your report, resulting in information overload and confusion.

Some researchers give into another temptation—going into great detail about the research design and methods. They assume that this information establishes credibility for the researcher and increases confidence in the findings. A little information in these sections usually goes a long way. Report only what you think the audience needs to know in order to understand and evaluate the findings. Put the detailed explanations and descriptions in appendices or in a separate *technical report*, if there are potential consumers of such background information.

Keep in mind that the research report must make the research findings relevant to the needs and concerns of your audience. If not, your work and the report itself will lose the battle for managers' attention. You did the research in the first place to help them make better decisions. Construct the report to attract their attention and keep their interest, so they have an opportunity to use your findings.

Use Easy-to-Read Presentation to Increase Readership

Potential users will miss even the most relevant information lost in a sea of words or blurred by drab presentation. All too often, researchers use passive voice and stilted language. Use your best writing and communication skills to increase readership and interest. And although a standard report outline dominates, use a presentation order that gives your audience the information they need without making them wade through unnecessary details.

For example, some report writers begin by summarizing the findings. A study of National Aeronautics and Space Administration (NASA) managers, indicated that 79 percent read the summary section of technical reports to help them decide what reports to read. The next most frequently read section was the conclusion section (69 percent), followed by the abstract (53 percent), title page (46 percent), and introduction (41 percent).[4] Assuming that many in the audience

---

[4]T.E. Pinelli and others, "Report-Reading Patterns of Technical Managers," *Technical Communication*, Vol. 31, No. 3 (1984), pp. 20–24, as reported in Zimmerman and Clark, *Guide to Technical and Scientific Communication*, p. 147.

have little time to seek information they need from your report, put the most important findings up front. "Here's what you wanted to know from this research" captures the spirit of the section that summarizes findings.

For example, here are the first two paragraphs in a summary report of the United States Telephone Association's nationwide survey of residential customers:

> *"An overwhelming majority of survey respondents (84%) rated the overall quality of their present local phone service as either excellent (30%) or good (54%). Only one-sixth considered their current service fair (12%) or poor (4%).*
>
> *"When asked to compare the quality of their present local service with that of two years ago, a similar majority (83%) judged their service to be at least as good as it was two year ago. More than half (67%) said their service was "about the same," 16% thought it was better and 13% felt it was not as good."*

The sections that follow highlight other major findings using a similar presentation style. The summary report *ends* with a brief description of how the research was conducted and the major purposes of the study. This summary reverses the usual order for research report content, but it effectively and efficiently presents key findings to a large audience. For the limited audience that needs more information about the study and results, prepare a detailed technical report following a more traditional sequence. Begin by discussing the study's purpose; include sections outlining the methods and findings; and end with appendices detailing technical aspects of the study.

To help readers and increase readership, use headings to highlight important findings. Keep headings and subheads short, but make them informative. For example, instead of "Style and Presentation Aids" as the heading for this section, we added a verb to give it "power" and told you why you should pay attention to style and presentation. Here are examples to illustrate this point in writing headings for research reports:

> *Business and Public Consumer Survey Results*
> says less than
> *Business and Public Consumer Survey Results Compared*
> says less than
> *Business Community and Public Disagree on Consumer Issues*

Informative headings help convey important findings, build interest, and motivate readership.

Finally, write the research report using your best writing and communication skills. Research terminology seduces many writers, tempting them to use technical language to establish themselves as research experts. Your research has value, however, only if the management team reads (or hears), understands, and relates the findings to management concerns. Others regard you and your research as valuable only when these three conditions are met.

ELEMENTS OF RESEARCH REPORTS

We told you earlier that the content of research reports varies from situation to situation, depending on audience needs. In the sections that follow, however, we outline the major components of research reports and offer suggestions for preparing the report. We use the traditional research report model, recognizing that you may need to adapt the order and content in a particular situation.

Cover Letter

Some refer to the letter that accompanies written research reports as the transmittal letter. Whatever you chose to call this letter, it serves the purposes of directing the report to the intended reader(s) and generating initial interest in reading what you learned from the research. You may also need to remind the reader what problem or information needs the research addresses, or you may need to refer to the relevant ongoing project to put the report in context. The cover letter typically uses formal business letter style for external distribution and formal memo style for internal distribution.

Title Page

While working on this book, we reviewed many research reports. Formats vary, but most title pages include: a) the title of the study, b) the date or period of the study, c) for whom the study was conducted, d) who conducted the study, and—if relevant—e) acknowledgement of funding sources, cooperating agencies, or cosponsors. Some use code numbers for easy filing and referencing. In other words, the title page rather completely tells readers what the study is about, for whom it was done, who did it, when it was done, and who else was involved.

Executive Summary

This short element of the report—essentially an abstract of report highlights—plays a major role for many. Remember, some readers may read only this part of your report. Most reports we reviewed kept this element to one or two pages, but reports of large, complex studies included up to four pages of executive summary. Highlight the major findings in this section, along with your interpretations and conclusions. To help readers follow up on points you want them to study in more detail, use specific page references. Above all, keep this section brief and get right to the major issues that motivated the research. Gary Barton at Monsanto emphasizes the need for brevity:

We work to get the findings down to three or four "needle-moving things" for an executive summary. You have to get down to those three or four major questions that you really need to know. The rest are just sort of interesting sidelines.

Table of Contents and Lists of Illustrations

Placement of these lists before or after the executive summary is a matter of choice. Most reports we studied included table of contents and lists of illustrations after the summary. The amount of detail in the table of contents varies with the length and complexity of the report. Typically, the table of contents includes part, chapter, or section titles; one or two levels of headings and subheads; and a listing of appendices. Keep in mind that the purpose is to help readers find major sections of the report, not to serve as a topical index. Lists of tables, figures, and exhibits should show page numbers and exact titles. Again, the purpose of these lists (a separate list for each category) is to help the reader find specific parts of the presentation. (In addition to Exhibit 13–3, use the table of contents and lists of illustrations at the beginning of this book as models.)

Background and Purpose of Study

Some refer to this as the research problem section. The goals of this section are to put the study in perspective, to make the motivations explicit, and—in some cases—justify the research project. Here also, you unequivocally state the research questions answered and the hypotheses tested. The following excerpts from a Monsanto research report section entitled "Fear of Chemicals/Program Description" illustrate how this section provides both the context and purpose of the research:

> *Public fears and suspicions about chemicals increased signifi-cantly during the early part of 1985 in the aftermath of the Union Carbide Bhopal tragedy and subsequent accidents in the U.S. . . . .*
>
> *To test the effectiveness of a local advertising and public rela-tions program designed to deal with this issue on the local level, Monsanto Platform selected two plant cities in which to under-take a series of activities during July, August and September. . . . .*

This section of the research report makes clear that the research is de-signed to assess the impact of the advertising and public relations activities using specific criteria related to the program objectives. In other words, after reading this section, your audience will have a clear picture of the information needs that motivated the research.

Other parts of the background and purpose section spell out the target

=====

EXHIBIT 13–3
Example of a Research Report
Table of Contents

TABLE OF CONTENTS

SOURCE: Technical Report, *1986 National Telephone Customer Behavior & Opinions Survey*, conducted for United States Telephone Association by the Gallup Organization, Inc., Princeton, N.J. Used with permission.

public(s), define the major concepts in the study, and describe the conditions that make the study important to the organization. In addition, this part of the report positions the research in relation to existing knowledge and other research efforts.

    The review of literature section is not something that only scholarly researchers have to write. Part of your mission in this section is to spell out what ideas and models guided the research. Some refer to this as the conceptual framework for the study. The question is not whether or not a research project was based on theory; the issue is the extent to which you make explicit the thinking that guided the research. Readers also need to know what was learned in other similar studies. In short, this review includes discussions of both the theoretical basis of the study and the empirical evidence already available from previous research.

After reading this part of the report, your audience should have a good understanding of *why* the research was done, what problem(s) the research will help solve, what you hoped to learn from the study, how the information will be used, and who will use the findings. In addition, your audience will understand the concepts and models used in the study, as well as see how your study fits with existing knowledge on the topic.

Naturally, not all research reports include all these elements. Rather, you should match content to audience needs and intended uses. The technical report of a research project, however, includes complete descriptions of the background work and thinking that went into the study. However, this is not the kind of con-

---

EXHIBIT 13–4
Elements of a Research Report

I. **COVER LETTER**

II. **INTRODUCTORY MATERIAL**
    A. Title Page
    B. Executive Summary
    C. Table of Contents
    D. Lists of Tables and Figures

III. **MAIN BODY OF REPORT**
    A. Background and Purpose of Study
        1. Research question or problem
        2. Public(s) and concepts studied
        3. Review of related theory and research
    B. Methods
        1. Research design and setting
        2. Samples or subjects
        3. Data collection
        4. Analysis techniques
    C. Findings
    D. Conclusions and Recommendations

IV. **ATTACHMENTS**
    A. References or Bibliography
    B. Appendices

tent one "makes up" after the study in order to provide a cosmetic veneer of thoroughness. If a study is simply descriptive research, not intended to find relationships or to test working theory, then report it as such. "Padding" the background and purpose section serves no purpose.

Methods

Simply put, this section describes what you did. The major purpose is to give readers information they need to understand how you did the study and to decide how much confidence to put in the findings. Another purpose is to provide the detailed description one would need to replicate the study or compare studies. To meet those needs, this section typically describes four aspects of the study:

1. *Research design and setting.* Describe the type of study conducted and the conditions under which the research was done. Outline what was done, where it was done, when it was done, and what happened that might affect the results. Was the study a cross-sectional survey, field experiment, or exploratory focus group study? Give readers information about laboratory settings, plant locations, test and control communities, and other conditions needed to understand the design and setting of the research. (Review Chapter 5.)

2. *Samples or subjects.* First, clearly identify the populations (publics) you sampled. Whereas most readers will look at the number of subjects studied or number of respondents included in samples, they usually should be more concerned with how they were selected. How representative are the subjects or respondents? What was the sampling frame? What was the refusal, response, completion, and participation rates? How do those in the study differ from those not included? Surely, sample size is important information to include in this section, but readers should have full information about how individuals were selected or included in the study. (Review Chapter 6.)

3. *Data collection.* This is where you tell readers how you made the observations and measured the variables under study. Describe how you developed and refined the data collection instrument, tracing the evolution from depth interviews or focus groups to pilot tests. Include copies of the actual interview schedules, survey questionnaires, coding sheets, and other observation tools used in the study. Pay particular attention to how you operationalized the major variables—showing exact wording of questions. If you decide that a long questionnaire or interview schedule does not add that much to the main body of the report, include it as an appendix and refer to it in the narrative. Describe who did the observations, how they were trained for the task, and the checks you used to maintain quality control during data collection. (Review Chapters 7 and 8.)

4. *Analysis techniques.* This information may not deserve a separate section if nothing extraordinary was done in the analysis. If the table footnotes provide the information, then there is no need to describe commonly used statistical tests applied to the data. Use this section to explain why you used nontraditional approaches, how you collapsed categories to create tables, or why you used partic-

ular measures or analysis techniques. Again, other than a brief description, you may want to include much of the technical information in an appendix rather than run the risk of serious eye-glazing among readers.

A special case of research reporting deserves attention in this discussion of what to report about research methods. As we pointed out in Chapter 1, mass media frequently report the results of public relations research—all too often paying little attention to the methods used. Exhibit 13–5 presents the American Association for Public Opinion Research guidelines for what should be included in public reports of survey results.

Findings

Sometimes called the results section, this section is probably the most important part of your research report. Use tables, graphs, and charts to efficiently present large amounts of information in understandable form. Tie the

---

EXHIBIT 13–5
Standards for Minimal Disclosure
for Reporting Opinion Polls

Good professional practice imposes the obligation upon all public opinion researchers to include, in any report of research results, or to make available when that report is released, certain essential information about how the research was conducted. At a minimum, the following items should be disclosed:

1. Who sponsored the survey, and who conducted it.
2. The exact wording of questions asked, including the text of any preceding instruction or explanation to the interviewer or respondent that might reasonably be expected to affect the response.
3. A definition of the population under study, and a description of the sampling frame used to identify this population.
4. A description of the sample selection procedure, giving a clear indication of the method by which the respondents were selected by the researcher, or whether the respondents were entirely self-selected.
5. Size of sample and, if applicable, completion rates and information on eligibility criteria and screening procedures.
6. A discussion of the precision of the findings, if appropriate, estimates of sampling error, and a description of any weighting or estimating procedures used.
7. Which results are based on parts of the sample, rather than on the total sample.
8. Method, location, and dates or data collection.

SOURCE: Used with permission from March 1986 Code of Professional Ethics and Practices, American Association for Public Opinion Research, Princeton, New Jersey. (Other sections presented in Appendix A.)

presentation of the *objective* findings to the research questions or hypotheses, showing how the evidence turned out for each. The goal in this section is to present the findings in such a way that readers will have an opportunity to see the evidence themselves and draw conclusions based on the complete and unbiased results. If you do not include complete tables or all the details of the findings, then attach them as appendices and refer to them in the narrative. In some reports, this is the final section, leaving interpretation and conclusions based on the findings to subsequent meetings and discussions. Whether or not you should go beyond the straight presentation of findings depends on how you and others see your role in the decision-making process. Others' expectations of you in the researcher role help determine the appropriateness of drawing conclusions and making recommendations.

Conclusions and Recommendations

If you go beyond *reporting* the findings and venture to draw conclusions and make recommendations, make sure you have the franchise, as well as the client's perspective on the problem situation. This section doesn't just end the report; it makes suggestions about how the program should be conducted and gives directions for strengthening the continuing program research effort. In this concluding section you also remind readers about any limitations on the findings and caution against going beyond what the findings support. But most of all, you draw together various findings and suggest the implications for the public relations program and the organization's ability to fulfill its mission. In a sense, this is the "call to action."

References

Many points in the report can be strengthened by citing credible and authoritative sources. Sometimes a direct quote is the most effective way to emphasize or explain, which means you will need to use footnote references. In this text, we use the numbered footnote style, listing footnotes at the bottom of each page on which they are referenced. In many research reports, however, numbered footnotes are used only to present supplemental information or extended explanations of issues or concepts mentioned in the narrative. To cite sources, essential information is included in parentheses in the narrative. Here are examples of this approach, known as "APA style" because it is recommended by the American Psychological Association for research publications:[5]

> "...*By making a deep and abiding commitment to research*"
> (*Center, 1980, p. 22*).
> or

---

[5]*Publication Manual of the American Psychological Association*, 3rd ed. (Washington, D.C.: American Psychological Association, 1983).

> *Center (1980) says that a profession not practiced on the basis*
> *of a body of knowledge is like "an inverted pyramid" (p. 22).*

A list of references at the end of the report includes the complete citation for each of the footnotes. For example, the preceding footnotes refer to this item in the reference list:

> CENTER, A. (1980).   State of the Art: Is the Pyramid
> Upside Down? *Public Relations Journal, 36* (7), 20–
> 22.

Notice that APA style differs significantly from the approach used in this book. Each has its pluses and minuses, so the one you use depends on personal preference or the dictates of convention where you work. Regardless of which style you use, keep the appropriate manual handy.[6]

Appendices

Use appendices to attach supplemental materials and detailed information referred to in the narrative. Information included here may either be nonessential and of interest to only those wanting to dig deeper into some aspect of the report, or be so large that it would disrupt the narrative flow if placed in the main body of the report. Appendices are usually labeled and presented in alphabetical order and given a descriptive title. For example, if you wanted to attach a copy of the survey questionnaire and to provide a very detailed description of the research methods as the first two appendices in the report, the labels and titles might be:

> *APPENDIX A. The Questionnaire*
> *APPENDIX B. Technical Details and Methodology*

The complete list appears in the table of contents, as illustrated in Exhibit 13–3.

In conclusion, remember that getting research results to potential users quickly may be more important than taking time to create an attractive presentation. At AT&T, for example, research results are distributed quickly to the four or five levels of managers most likely to use the results. Ed Block contrasts this timely reporting with an earlier approach:

> *We would do this elegant research—beautifully done and beauti-*
> *fully reported—but we were so absorbed in the process by which*
> *it gets assembled, reported, and distributed that it never got used.*

So whether you use the written report or oral presentation, organize the content and develop the illustrations to help make the information *useful* to decision makers. If and how research findings get used are topics of the next chapter.

[6]A good reference for the style used in this book is Kate L. Turabian, *A Manual for Writers of Term Papers, Theses, and Dissertations,* 4th ed. (Chicago: The University of Chicago Press, 1973).

CHAPTER 14

USING THE FINDINGS FOR ORGANIZATION CHANGE

Paul M. Sanchez, APR, National Practice Director for Employee Communications Consulting, THE WYATT COMPANY, San Diego.

There is always some resistance to change, particularly if you are dealing with sensitive topics such as the quality of supervision, the efficacy of management, or the freedom to act—any of these things which relate to how people function within organizations. If you are going to try to move into new territory, there is a built-in resistance to change. You have to understand that. We see case after case of well-intentioned programs grinding to a halt because someone underestimated the resistance to change.

*In the change environment, people will look for ways to discredit the research information. They will say, "Yeah, but it doesn't apply to me because of thus and so." Or, "Yeah, but I didn't take the survey." Or, "Yeah, but these questions apply to another part of the business." Or, "Yeah, but . . . ." That is why—from the public relations point of view—we must attend to research methodology, to the correctness of the procedures, because if there is any flaw the detractors will seize upon it and ask, "What kind of confidence can we have that this **really** represents the views of our publics?" In almost every research project, there is this kind of denial that you have to deal with. So be prepared*

for the kind of resistance that takes the form of attacking the validity of the research.

The procedure that I follow is:

*1. **Provide feedback.** You must get the information back into the organization in an understandable way. The worst thing is to do a "data dump" in which people are left floundering in mountains of unconnected minutia. They aren't given a way to relate the information to their work lives or facilitate any sort of action planning. So first, get the information fed back in a useful way.*

*2. **Get commitment.** You have to get commitment to an action plan that says, "We will do something with this information." Two things must be in place: First, procedures for dealing with the information—a systematic process for getting the information into the action planning and priorities. This helps avoid the problem of leaping to solve problems before deciding how to process and digest information. In countless examples I have seen, if you don't have an established process, understandable things happen—inefficiencies, double-backs, people doubting the utility of the endeavor, confusion, disorganization—a whole litany of unfortunate things. Our approach is to get commitment as to how the information will be used **before** we ever get to actual problem solving. Second, we get to setting the priorities for which issues we will attack. So another part of getting commitment is the act of prioritizing what problems are most important to the organization. This will therefore establish the order in which the issues will be addressed.*

*3. **Relate actions to research.** I can't say this strongly enough. In an organization where you are trying to make the research serve an important purpose internally, you have to go back and link the actions to what people told you in the surveys. If you decide to put lights in the parking lots, for example, you have to point out that you did so because in the survey people said they were concerned about parking lot security. Or, we are now telling you what the mission of this organization is because we heard that new employee orientation did not provide that information. You have to let people know that their opinions were considered— that what they said in the survey counted for something and was factored into the planning process.*

*4. **Plan for measuring efficacy of actions.** Develop plans for measuring how well the survey response actions worked—some sensing mechanism for detecting perceived accomplishment. One way is to repeat the survey. I find that management groups in most organizations are data-hungry. Most managers find survey information seductive. When they look at a research report, they*

see how useful the information is. It is necessary, however, to build in an evaluation step to ensure the follow-up. I find that I don't have to "sell" this phase. First of all, since management pays for the research, they genuinely want to know if the responses are working—if they are useful. When the results have strategic implications for the organization, the last worry we have is whether the information will be studied and used. And that usefulness is an evaluations measure.

The fact is that organizations will act at their own pace and in their own time, but I have rarely seen research that did not have a long-term effect on an organization. Now it may take two years before the results get throughout the organization, but the research will have an effect.

One of the compelling aspects about being involved in research with organizations is that you can look back and say, "This made a significant difference in this organization's life."

We saved the biggest and most difficult task for the last chapter—using the research findings for program and organizational changes. What does it mean when we say "using the research findings"? What factors influence how and how much the research findings are used? What roles do public relations practitioners play in the utilization of research findings in bringing about organizational change? These are some of the topics of our final chapter. After all, what good does it do to design and conduct research if even the most compelling findings are not used?

THE MEANINGS OF RESEARCH UTILIZATION

The usual notion of using research deals with the extent to which the findings lead to tangible changes in programs, policies, procedures, structures, and organizational behavior. In other words, research produces observable impact on decisions. Decisions yield changes that can be documented and would not have occurred without the research findings. However, researchers often have been frustrated holding to this limited impact notion of research utilization.[1]

The assumptions of the impact notion include: Use of the findings is positive and nonuse is negative. Use should lead to immediate and observable changes. Empirical evidence is compelling. Research evidence can overpower other forces in the decision-making process. In the sections that follow, we expand on the impact notion of research utilization and build a broader notion of how research findings can be used in public relations.

[1]Research utilization in public relations was the topic of Broom's San Diego State University graduate seminar, spring semester 1987. We acknowledge the contributions to this chapter of seminar participants Geoffrey Anderson, Mark C. Baker, Richard Curtis, Grant DuBois, and Larry Nuffer.

Instrumental Versus Conceptual Uses

Instrumental use includes the most commonly applied test for utilization—the findings are applied in decision making or problem solving. Impact can be documented and traced back to the research findings. This may be the purest form of knowledge for action. For example, Ann Barkelew's description of employee research at Dayton-Hudson Corporation illustrates instrumental use:

When one of our companies was having trouble, they did an informal caucus group—like a focus group—to determine what kinds of things employees were nervous about. Based on that session, they put together posters and a video tape of the CEO explaining the new program thrust. The strategy helped people at every level feel more responsible for the business of the company.

We do employee attitude surveys every other year ... and we really pay attention to the results of those surveys. For example, I remember one year we learned that employees felt that one piece of our benefits program was not as good as what other companies offered. That caused personnel to take a new look at that portion of the benefits program.

Naturally, direct impact on decisions is the grand prize when doing research. Unfortunately, studies in other fields suggest that such instrumental utilization may not be the major outcome of applied research. The more common use is informing managers, thus reducing the uncertainty associated with decision making.[2] In other words, the outcome is enlightenment, not direct and observable impact in the short term.

Conceptual use represents knowledge for understanding, meaning that research findings lead to changes in awareness, knowledge, or understanding. In the short term, you might not observe any change or direct impact on decisions. That does not mean, however, that the research findings were not utilized. Rather, the application may be indirect, diffused, or delayed, but utilization nevertheless. For example, Sandra Fuhrman, public policy specialist at Southwestern Bell Corporation, St. Louis, describes how research findings can have cognitive rather than instrumental impact:

When public relations presents relevant research on an issue at hand, it is often the first time that some operations people have seen the relevant public attitudes. You tend to be cloistered at the headquarters level because you don't have as much direct interaction with customers. Time and bureaucracy necessarily remove many decision makers from the customer base and so the research is often the first exposure to what customers think.

[2]Michael Q. Patton and others, "In Search of Impact: An Analysis of the Utilization of Federal Health Evaluation Research," in Carol H. Weiss (ed.) *Using Social Research in Public Policy Making* (Lexington, Mass.: Lexington Books, 1977), pp. 141–63.

Sociologists talk about counterparts to these two forms of utilization— referring to "enlightenment" and "advisement" models of sociological practice.[3] Traditionally, sociologists publish their findings in journals and books (enlightenment model), but stay out of the immediate application of findings to solving problems or formulating policies. Emerging, however, is a professional model of sociological practice that calls for researcher participation in the entire process— from identifying the problem to formulating the program solutions (advisement model). The desire that research findings have an impact on policy formulation motivates this change in roles in sociology. Likewise, public relations researchers see a need to link findings to decision making. According to Roger Sennott at Market Development, Inc., San Diego:

> *There is a lot of good research that absolutely never gets used. There is a link that has to be made between what the research said and what is going to be done. Researchers don't deal with that, typically. And others don't really understand the research enough to make the bridge. It's a messy area. Those who succeed in research are very good at making that linkage.*

The linkage between research findings and utilization is neither simple nor direct, however. Scholars studying the utilization of research have suggested scales that typically run from "considered and rejected" to "implemented." Larsen and Werner combined scale categories to form three summary categories for assessing utilization:

(1) *No utilization* (considered and rejected, nothing done),
(2) *Interest in idea* (under consideration, steps being taken, partially implemented),
(3) *Utilization* (implemented as presented, adapted to fit user's needs).[4]

Notice, however, that these levels of use and nonuse do not address how effective the research proved to be in its application. Utilization and effectiveness are clearly different aspects of the application of research findings.

Figure 14–1 summarizes our review of the literature on research utilization. Our "use meter" incorporates both impact and conceptual uses of findings—indicating direction and level of utilization after the findings are reported. The meter analogy suggests that the needle can go either way after the findings are reported and that use and nonuse represent continuous scales with an infinite number of levels.

Also worth noting is the possibility that some people receiving the report

---

[3]Mark van de Vall and Herbert J. Ulrich, "Trends in Data-Based Sociological Practice: Toward a Professional Paradigm?" *Knowledge: Creation, Diffusion, Utilization*, Vol. 8, No. 1 (September 1986), pp. 167–84.

[4]Judith K. Larsen and Paul D. Werner, "Measuring Utilization of Mental Health Program Consultation," in *Utilizing Evaluation: Concept and Measurement Techniques*, ed. James A. Ciarlo (Beverly Hills: Sage Publications, Inc., 1981), p. 85.

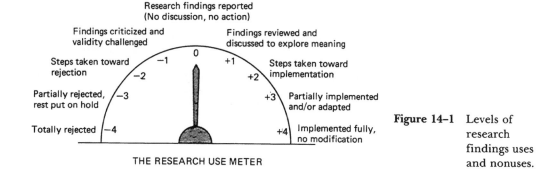

Figure 14-1 Levels of research findings uses and nonuses.

may be predisposed to one direction on the scale while others want to go the other direction. Imagine how critical your ability to report research results are when the use meter needle is on "0." Southwestern Bell's Fuhrman accurately describes how even knowledge of research methods comes into play at this stage:

> *When we make presentations, there are naturally a lot of questions thrown at you about the results, but also about the methods. So we have to learn very fast about the technical side of research. I've been asked some very pointed questions about methodology. Your credibility is shot if you can't tell somebody how the research was done and why it was done that way.*

So one's ability to address concerns about methods can affect the direction and distance the use meter needle moves. Before exploring other factors that affect research utilization, however, we need to address a third notion—symbolic use.

Symbolic Uses

If instrumental use means the findings directly affect decisions and conceptual use means the findings inform, then symbolic use means the findings delay, justify, or persuade. In fact, some refer to this type of utilization as *persuasive* use. In this model of utilization, research findings substitute for making a decision or taking action, support one's position, legitimate a favored policy or program (or to discredit those not supported), or add weight to one's argument for or against another's proposition.

Clearly, these uses—some would call them misuses—differ from the instrumental use that leads directly to program or organizational change. The key difference is that symbolic uses involve using research findings to support positions *already* held or decisions *already* made. Examples include building a case to postpone actions, supporting opinions or decisions, or strengthening an argument. In his seminal books on evaluation research, Suchman outlines these uses as "evaluative 'abuse' or pseudo-evaluation":

1. *Eye-wash*—an attempt to justify a weak or bad program by selecting only . . . those parts of the program that appear successful.
2. *White-wash*—an attempt to cover up program failure or errors by avoiding any objective appraisal. . . . To solicit "testimonials" which divert attention from the failure.
3. *Submarine*—an attempt to "torpedo" or destroy a program regardless of its worth in order to get rid of it . . . when opponents are "sunk" along with their programs.
4. *Posture*—an attempt to use evaluation as a "gesture" of objectivity and to assume the pose of "scientific" research. This "looks good" . . . and is a sign of "professional" status.
5. *Postponement*—an attempt to delay needed action by pretending to seek the "facts." Evaluation research takes time and, hopefully, the storm will blow over by the time the study is completed.
6. *Substitution*—an attempt to "cloud over" or disguise failure in an essential part of the program by shifting attention to some less relevant, but defensible, aspect of the program.[5]

The distinctions among the three major uses of research findings are not always clear. For example, if management is persuaded by the research evidence to change a policy, procedure, or program, then the effect is instrumental use. If the research evidence supports a strategic decision already implemented, then the effect is conceptual use. If the results of an objective program evaluation are used to justify a favored option, then the effect is symbolic use. Pelz suggests that symbolic uses "may in fact be even more prevalent than conceptual use, with instrumental use appearing rarely."[6]

Canadian evaluation research specialist Leonard Rutman sees conceptual uses as the primary outcome of program evaluations. In his view, management is an iterative process of "muddling through" and "disjointed incrementalism." Ideally, research findings get fed back fast enough to be used for making improvements in the program—an instrumental use. He points out, however, that evaluation findings cannot overcome political and organizational factors that affect decision making. His conclusion: "All that can be realistically expected from program evaluation is that it adequately informs the decision makers on the choices that confront them."[7]

Decision Analysis Uses

Herein lies probably the major use of research findings—choosing among alternative actions based on what was learned from program evaluations. The choices depend on the answers to a) was there impact, and if so, b) to what

[5]Edward A. Suchman, *Evaluation Research* (New York: Russell Sage Foundation, 1967), p. 143.
[6]Donald C. Pelz, "Some Expanded Perspectives on Use of Social Science in Public Policy," in *Major Social Issues: A Multidisciplinary View*, eds. J. Milton Yinger and Stephen J. Cutler (New York, Free Press, 1978), p. 352.
[7]Leonard Rutman, *Planning Useful Evaluations: Evaluability Assessment* (Beverly Hills, Calif.: Sage Publications, Inc., 1980), pp. 29-30.

extent can the impact be attributed to the program? Pitz and McKillip refer to the formal *process* for making choices as "decision analysis."[8] Figure 14–2 illustrates how research findings can be used in a public relations program decision analysis.

Decision analysis helps indicate the points in the process where research findings are used. Decision makers use research findings for instrumental, conceptual, and symbolic purposes at each junction in the process, even if they are not fully aware of the process. According to Weiss and Bucuvalas, many decision makers do not think of their work as a series of decisions or choices, and even disavow that they make decisions:

> *They see little opportunity for rational calculation—and little need for it. They seldom engage in explicit formulation of problems, seldom undertake directed searches for information, seldom canvass the range of alternatives available, or calculate the relative merits of each alternative.*[9]

As a result, these authors conclude that the major contribution of research is to increase decision makers' understanding of events and concepts, thus indirectly affecting their actions and choices. They also point out that the impact may be greater than documented, as disclaimers of decision-making power may be a way of avoiding responsibility.[10]

Figure 14–2   Using evaluation findings in decision analysis.

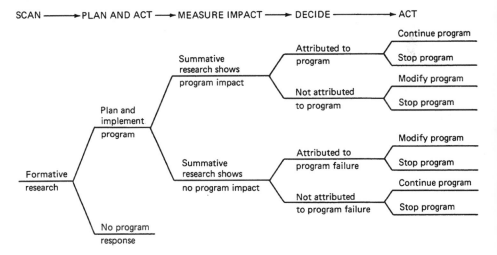

[8]Gordon F. Pitz and Jack McKillip, *Decision Analysis for Program Evaluators* (Beverly Hills, Calif.: Sage Publications, Inc., 1984), p. 14.

[9]Carol H. Weiss and Michael J. Bucuvalas, *Social Science Research and Decision-Making* (New York: Columbia University Press, 1980), p. 266.

[10]Ibid., pp. 267–71.

Decision analysis models, such as the one in Figure 14–2, make those decisions explicit and isolate the opportunities for using research in the decision-making process. The decision points also make explicit the need to monitor program implementation as well as program impact, for eventually decision makers must determine if program failure resulted from inadequate implementation of a potentially effective program or from a truly ineffective program. In other words, did the observed failure result from poor operations or from a faulty working theory?

The stakes are high for decision makers. Clearly, every decision to select one course of action is also a decision not to select one or more alternatives in a decision tree. Notwithstanding personal, parochial, and partisan interests, research provides information needed to reduce uncertainty when selecting among choices available to program managers. Widespread use of computers and interactive information retrieval decision support systems make research findings increasingly important in decision making.

In conclusion, research on uses of research findings indicate that the primary uses are conceptual and indirect, not direct change in programs and organizations. Use of research findings is not limited to the usual notion of direct impact on the course of events and decisions. The more realistic view suggests that research findings have indirect and conceptual consequences. This does not minimize the impact of research, however. Rather, it suggests a cautionary and realistic set of expectations for those who conduct research. The challenge is to maximize both instrumental and conceptual uses in program management.

FACTORS AFFECTING UTILIZATION

Given a broader view of research utilization, what factors help or hinder use? Based on their review of evaluation research utilization studies, Leviton and Hughes identified five clusters of factors that affect research utilization: a) relevance, b) communication between researcher and user, c) implications for short-term actions versus long-term change, d) credibility of researcher and findings, and e) user commitment and researcher advocacy.[11]

Relevance

The first and most obvious consideration, of course, is whether or not the research meets decision makers' needs. As Harold F. Leiendecker, Opinion and Communication Research, Exxon Corporation (retired), told us:

> *Work on issues for which your management is having a tough time deciding what to do. Management would welcome informa-*

[11]Laura C. Leviton and Edward F.X. Hughes, "Research on the Utilization of Evaluations: A Review and Synthesis," *Evaluation Review*, Vol. 5, No. 4 (August 1981), pp. 525–48.

tion on those issues. If you want to make research useful, you do research on those kinds of issues.

Relevance is not a simple matter, however, as it involves both the decision maker's needs and the timeliness of the information. Sometimes the information needed simply cannot be gathered in time to make pressing decisions. Timeliness, therefore, may be a bigger issue for immediate instrumental use situations, and less an issue for long-term conceptual use.

Deshpande and Zaltman found that market research users were more likely to use findings from "confirmatory" research than they were from "exploratory" research.[12] Confirmatory research provides information on the correctness of current ideas and decisions already made—similar to what we discussed as symbolic use. On the other hand, findings from research intended to explore new products, markets, and directions—what to do next or which choice to make—are judged less relevant by managers. In the marketing context, research findings about already-held positions are seen as more relevant than findings about risk-laden new directions. This means that managers are more likely to use research that helps them come to closure on decisions they are struggling with than they are to use research that helps them break new ground.

> *RECOMMENDATION 1:* To increase utilization of research findings, show how research findings relate to potential users' current concerns, policies, procedures, and practices before discussing long-term relevance.

Communication Between Researcher and User

Siegel and Tuckel point out two major reasons for maintaining communication between researcher and potential users: The first reason is to make sure the research addresses issues or problems important to users. Users simply cannot be left out of the process until the findings are reported with the expectation that the research will reflect their interests and perspective. They have to participate in the evolutionary thinking that produces the conclusions. Secondly, communication must be maintained in order to increase the level of interest and commitment to the project. It's a variation on that old truism that the greater the level of participation throughout the process, then the greater the likelihood that users will be committed to seeing that the findings are accepted and used.[13]

For example, when Rothman studied managers' use of evaluation re-

---

[12]Rohit Deshpande and Gerald Zaltman, "A Comparison of Factors Affecting Researcher and Manager Perceptions of Market Research Use," *Journal of Marketing Research*, Vol. 21 (February 1984), pp. 36–37. See also Deshpande and Zaltman, "Patterns of Research Use in Private and Public Sectors," *Knowledge: Creation, Diffusion, Utilization*, Vol. 4, No. 4 (June 1983), p. 568.

[13]Karolynn Siegel and Peter Tuckel, "The Utilization of Evaluation Research: A Case Analysis," *Evaluation Review*, Vol. 9, No. 3 (June 1985), pp. 323–24.

search, he found that participation of field staff, management, and middle-level personnel in the research process increases utilization. He summarizes his findings as follows:

> *Utilization of research is facilitated when relevant operational*
> *people participate in defining the research problem . . . in carry-*
> *ing out the research . . . in the formulation of recommendations.*[14]

Glaser and Taylor report a study comparing successful and unsuccessful research projects—in which success means the studies led to observable results—to identify what made the difference. In the successful cases, researchers found close communication throughout the research project between those doing the research and those who would be using the results. They found direct and informal communication more effective than the usual formal channels of bureaucratic hierarchies.[15]

Effective communication, of course, should be a natural for a public relations practitioner doing research. Unlike applied researchers in many other fields, you possess the communication skills needed to effectively report research in written and oral presentations. The steps are the same as for any communication effort—identify target audiences—stakeholders with an interest in the research results; specify their concerns and match report content to their frame of reference and concerns; and select appropriate media for each audience—oral and written technical reports, internal executive summaries, and external summary reports. (Review Chapter 13 for a more detailed discussion of reporting research results.)

> *RECOMMENDATION 2:* To increase utilization of research findings, maintain frequent and direct participation of and communication with potential users and other stakeholders throughout the research project.

Implications for Short-term Actions Versus Long-term Change

Weiss and Bucuvalas found that decision makers apply "frames of reference" for deciding to consider or reject research results: a) relevance to their concerns, b) "truth," and c) "utility."[16] The utility test concerns the implications

[14]Jack Rothman, *Using Research in Organizations: A Guide to Successful Application* (Beverly Hills, Calif.: Sage Publications, Inc., 1980), pp. 69–74.

[15]Edward M. Glaser and S. H. Taylor, "Factors Influencing the Success of Applied Research," *American Psychologist*, Vol. 28, No. 2 (February 1973), pp. 140–46. Also summarized in Leviton and Hughes, "Research on the Utilization of Evaluations," *Evaluation Review*, pp. 536–37.

[16]Carol H. Weiss and Michael J. Bucuvalas, "Truth Tests and Utility Tests: Decision-Makers' Frames of Reference for Social Science Research," *American Sociological Review*, Vol. 45, No. 2 (April 1980), pp. 302–13. See also, Weiss and Bucuvalas, *Social Science Research and Decision-Making* (New York: Columbia University Press, 1980).

and conclusions drawn from the research results. Potential users look for how the findings can be translated into either immediate actions or used to challenge the status quo. According to Weiss and Bucuvalas, the users' frame of reference is:

1. Action orientation. Does the research show how to make feasible changes in things that can feasibly by changed?

and/or

2. Challenge to the status quo. Does the research challenge current philosophy, program, or practice? Does it offer new perspectives?[17]

The two uses in the utility test represent alternative functions, meaning that the implications are different. Action orientation implications facilitate utilization when the study offers minimal (if any) criticism or challenge to current thinking. Challenge to the status quo implications facilitate utilization when prescriptions for action are left out of the report. In other words, when immediate actions are suggested, it does not add to a study's usefulness to include findings indicating the need for major changes in direction. On the other hand, when the major implications are for new direction, it does not add to the study's usefulness to indicate what immediate steps are recommended. In the first case, decision makers' needs for immediate answers are being met by the research, so they are not attuned to long-term changes in direction. In the latter case, decision makers receptive to research findings suggestive of major changes and the long-term perspective are not as receptive to recommendations for the immediate actions. (Recall the earlier discussions of instrumental and conceptual uses.)

> *RECOMMENDATION 3:* To increase utilization of research findings with implications for immediate action, leave out recommendations for long-term changes in philosophy, program, or practice. Select another report and setting for considering challenges to the status quo.

> *RECOMMENDATION 4:* To increase utilization of research findings with implications for long-term changes in philosophy, program, or practice, leave out recommendations for immediate action steps. Pick another report and setting for suggesting implementation strategies.

Siegel and Tuckel's comparison of the two uses suggests that research implications calling for incremental rather than global changes meet with less resistance and are therefore more likely to be used. They also say that conclusions and recommendations must be direct derivatives of the findings. The connection

---

[17]Ibid., p. 311.

between the data and conclusions must be obvious, otherwise users can discount the results as being nothing more than subjective judgments rather than the products of objective analysis.[18]

> RECOMMENDATION 5: To increase utilization of research findings, report only implications that are logically derived from and supported by the data.

Credibility of Researcher and Findings

As Sandra Fuhrman of Southwestern Bell Corporation reminded us, the wrong answers to questions about the methods used can discredit both researcher and findings. In fact, this is not an uncommon strategy for those not pleased with the findings and implications. So utilization of research findings depends on the researcher passing a credibility test and the methods passing a rigor test. Unless both pass, findings may be rejected.

Potential users of research findings use screening questions such as: Can I trust the results? Are the methods scientifically correct and rigorously applied? Will the results stand up to challenges from others? Weiss and Bucuvalas outline the truth test decision makers use to judge the credibility of research findings:

1. Research quality. Was the research conducted by proper scientific methods?
   and/or
2. Conformity to user expectations. Are the results compatible with my experience, knowledge, and values?[19]

When they tested the extent to which the truth test determines whether or not research results are used, they found that research quality is less important when results are consistent with the user's expectations. As you would expect, when results do not conform with potential users' prior knowledge or expectations, then research quality is a greater factor in determining likelihood of use. In effect, the weight given research quality depends on the degree to which findings are consistent with user expectations.[20]

For example, Deshpande and Zaltman found that marketing managers use "surprise"—unexpected findings—as a reality test to decide whether or not to use certain research results. Managers seldom express this as a concern, however, because they are reluctant to tell researchers that they do not believe findings are inconsistent with their own perceptions and expectations. Instead, managers select something in the research report to criticize.[21] They point out in a

---

[18]Siegel and Tuckel, "The Utilization of Evaluation Research," pp. 315–16.
[19]Weiss and Bucuvalas, "Truth Tests and Utility Tests," p. 311.
[20]Ibid.
[21]Deshpande and Zaltman, "Factors Affecting the Use of Market Research Information: A Path Analysis," *Journal of Marketing Research*, Vol. 19 (February 1982), p. 25.

later study that managers frequently pick on the quality of the research itself or the report instead of attacking the findings directly.[22]

These same researchers compared research use in public and private settings, finding that managers in both prefer research reports of "vague specifics" that avoid conclusions that are "cut and dried and pointing to only one possible direction for action."[23] Some managers say they prefer getting only the raw data so they can draw their own conclusions. Apparently, managers want options and a role in interpreting the data with an eye to perceived political and economic feasibility—room to maneuver, in other words. Managers' desires for open-ended reports may signal that they have been left out of the process. As noted earlier, keeping them involved in a collaborative research process should minimize resistance to conclusions and recommendations in the report.

> *RECOMMENDATION 6:* To increase utilization of research findings, use researchers with established credibility and integrity, and avoid using people seen by potential users as having a vested interest in the results.

> *RECOMMENDATION 7:* To increase utilization of research findings, use research designs and methods that conform to rigorous scientific standards and technical soundness.

> *RECOMMENDATION 8:* To increase utilization of research findings, emphasize corroborating information over information that contradicts users' expectations and frames of reference, minimize negative surprises, and avoid early closure on politically sensitive recommendations.

Advocacy of Research Results

Scientists have traditionally sought truth and avoided the role of advocate, but applied researchers must either take on the role or have a key manager as advocate in order to increase the impact of their research. Leviton and Hughes summarize the findings from several studies on the impact of advocacy of research utilization:

> *... Persistent advocacy by a key individual is essential in getting research findings used.... Commitment of an individual decision*

[22]Deshpande and Zaltman, "A Comparison of Factors Affecting Researcher and Manager Perceptions of Market Research Use," *Journal of Marketing Research*, Vol. 21 (February 1984), p. 37.
[23]Deshpande and Zaltman, "Patterns of Research Use in Private and Public Sectors," pp. 569–60.

*maker determines whether evaluations are used.... The impact
of specific individuals on organizations is seldom as powerful as
in the case of research utilization.*[24]

Paul Sanchez at The Wyatt Company illustrates the role of such an advocate in getting research used:

> *We worked with a large national retail organization for more
> than two years while the people in the organization worked to
> develop a strategy based on our survey information. They devised
> a program that had three major objectives coming from the
> survey.*
>
> *It took the CEO to enliven that process. The CEO had a vision
> of where he wanted that organization to go, but he could not do
> it without achieving those objectives. The survey gave him an
> entire arsenal of information. Once he said, "This is the way
> we're going to go," he then directed the various groups to get on
> with it.*

Whereas you must maintain objectivity and follow the rules of scientific
inquiry while conducting the study, be prepared to take on the role of advocate
once the findings and conclusions are presented. In fact, because some form of
utilization is the ultimate outcome of public relations research, you must plan
and encourage utilization from the beginning. Again, Paul Sanchez describes his
approaches to getting research findings used:

> *I use models. One is what I call the **single-agent model**. This is
> when the survey sponsor or someone else is appointed and empow-
> ered by the CEO to deal with the survey. For example, that might
> be the director of organizational development, the director of com-
> munications, or the director of public relations—any way, that
> single agent is vested with the responsibility to work with the
> survey data, to clarify, and to resolve issues. So in this model,
> we work with this agent who will probe, process, come to some
> conclusion, and report back to the CEO or the management com-
> mittee.*
>
> *The other model is the **participative model**. There is a distri-
> bution of responsibility based on some logical connection to the
> research need. For example, if the research deals with a policy
> problem that requires a high level of authority, then you involve
> people horizontally at a pretty high level in the organization to
> get the results applied across the entire organization. A second
> version of the participative model drives vertically into the orga-*

[24]Leviton and Hughes, "Utilization of Evaluations," pp. 541–42.

nization to get people to participate in analyzing the information and identifying the issues at their level. People examine the results from their more local perspective and report their interpretations back up the organization. The results are then integrated at a central administrative focal point. In this model, the analysis undertaken in this dispersed form stimulates a "bubble-up" process with recommendations for action and solutions for problems.

In short, the researcher-advocate does not attempt to impose or manipulate, but does encourage and facilitate utilization of the research findings. Rather than playing a passive role as conveyor of information, however, assuming the role of active participant and advocate can spell the difference between nonuse and use. In other words, your role extends well beyond the presentation of findings.

> *RECOMMENDATION 9:* To increase utilization of research findings, enlist the sponsorship of key managers in encouraging serious consideration and use of what was learned from the research.

> *RECOMMENDATION 10:* To increase utilization of research findings, devote the time and effort required to persuade potential users to consider the findings and help them to learn from and/or take actions based on what was learned.

Clearly, if you follow all or most of these recommendations for increasing utilization of public relations research findings, you could play an active role on the management team. This would elevate public relations to the management-level role suggested by the open systems model—helping organizations solve problems of adapting to changing environments. As John Koten at Ameritech, Chicago, points out, "We in public relations are a vital part of the organizational change process—as much as the designer, the inventor, the engineer, the marketer, the salesperson, or the deliverer of the product."

OPEN SYSTEMS PLANNING AND ORGANIZATIONAL CHANGE

Research intervenes and disrupts. As Paul Sanchez at The Wyatt Company puts it:

> *A survey is always a symbolic opening of a discussion. If you aren't going to respond in some way—closing the loop, as it were—then you are probably going to frustrate the basic reasons for doing the survey in the first place.*

His observation reminds us that research itself builds expectations of change, so the intervention cannot be made without plans for "closing the loop"—effecting organizational change. Intervening for the purpose of organizational change calls for a combination of organization development and strategic planning skills. Following are steps for working with the management team responsible for strategic planning and organizational change. Each step calls for a solid foundation of public relations research findings:

1. *Analyze current environmental conditions.* Identify the conditions, groups, and organizations and the demands, problems, and opportunities they create.
2. *Analyze current responses.* Describe the ways your organization now responds to these situations.
3. *Analyze values, priorities, and purposes.* Establish agreement on current organizational guidelines, goals, and mission.
4. *Predict trends and conditions.* Predict likely changes in the environment and future conditions if the organization continues current responses to its environment.
5. *Define an ideal future.* Create scenarios that represent ideal future states, including changes in organizational goals and missions, external conditions, and responses.
6. *Compare current and ideal states.* Determine gaps between the conditions predicted in Step 4 and the ideal states outlined in Step 5.
7. *Establish priorities.* Assign priorities to the gaps between projected and ideal conditions.
8. *Develop plans of action and communication.* Plan how to move the organization and its publics toward ideal states by narrowing the gaps identified and ranked in Steps 6 and 7. Schedule follow-up actions and evaluations.[25]

Note that the emphasis on using research in this section focuses on organizational change, not changes only in the publics. Grunig says this is a departure from the usual concept of public relations' role, and few organizations practice such a two-way symmetrical model, "because their worldview of public relations does not include that model and they seldom have public relations personnel with the expertise to practice it."[26] He calls the most commonly practiced version the "one-way press-agentry model," with the one-way "public-information" model most frequently used in government. Research is not a part of public relations practiced as one-way press agentry and public information. When two-way public relations is practiced as the dominant model, it tends to be asymmetrical. More information flows *out* from the organization than into it—in an attempt to manipulate, dominate, or neutralize publics. Research is used to make the outwardly-directed communication more effective, not to help the organization itself adapt.

Grunig's research leads him to conclude that the model of public rela-

[25]Adapted from Michael I. Harrison, *Diagnosing Organizations: Methods, Models, and Processes* (Beverly Hills, Calif.: Sage Publications, Inc., 1987), pp. 113–14.
[26]James E. Grunig, "Symmetrical Presuppositions As a Framework for Public Relations Theory," paper presented to Conference on Communication Theory and Public Relations, Illinois State University, Normal, Illinois, May 1987, p. 23.

tions practiced is chosen by the dominant coalition—its power elite—based on goodness of fit with organizational culture and the expertise of the public relations director. The need for research skills as a requisite for participating in organizational change is implied in Grunig's conclusion that:

> *The more expertise that the public relations director has to practice the more sophisticated, two-way models, the more likely he or she is to be in the dominant coalition—where he or she can influence culture, the strategic public chosen, and the situational model to be applied.*[27]

In effect, using research for organization change calls for applying feedback and feedforward notions from cybernetics.[28] Feedback about past performance provides information used to adjust present behavior and to plan future behavior. Feedforward on expected future performance and conditions provides information used to adjust present and future behavior. In both instances, change in organizational performance and structure are the outcomes of using research results. As we suggested in Figure 1–5 (Chapter 1), the highest use of feedback takes the form of organizational adaptation to its changing environment—consistent with Grunig's two-way symmetrical model of public relations.

STANDARDS OF ETHICS AND SOCIAL RESPONSIBILITY

Any time you intervene in the lives of others, you cannot simply operate by the test proposed by Saul Alinsky in *Rules for Radicals*: "Does this *particular* end justify this *particular* means?" Nor can you practice by his rule: "...Do what you can with what you have and clothe it with moral garments."[29] No, there are some higher-order values and guidelines for the conduct of research. An outline of some major ethical and socially responsible conditions properly ends this book. The purpose of these guidelines is to protect participants in research projects by assuring: a) no harm or deception, b) freedom of choice, and c) anonymity and confidentiality.

Assuring No Harm or Deception

As a researcher, *you* are responsible for making sure that research respondents or subjects suffer no harm, deception, embarrassment, or other injury as a result of their participation. Many organizations—especially universities and

[27]Ibid.
[28]Arthur J. Kuhn, *Organizational Cybernetics and Business Policy: System Design for Performance Control* (University Park, Pa.: The Pennsylvania State University Press, 1986), pp. 100–106.
[29]Saul D. Alinsky, *Rules for Radicals* (New York: Random House, 1971), pp. 24 and 36.

hospitals—require approval by committees charged with the protection of both human and animal research participants. Before you initiate a project, check for such a committee in your organization and comply with all requirements for getting approval of your study design and methods.

In some organizational settings, participants must be protected from having their answers used against them as individuals or groups. Likewise, participants sometimes must be protected from potentially harmful questions or questions designed to give messages rather than solicit answers. As simple as these ideas may sound, it is not always easy to assure that no harm or deception is involved. The best we can hope for is that you are sensitive to this issue and make every effort to avoid inflicting any harm or deception on your participants.

Assuring Freedom of Choice

Ethical research requires *informed consent* and *voluntary participation.* Informed consent means that participants receive complete information about the sponsor, purpose, use, and potential risks (if any) of the research. Forcing participation in research violates both professional ethics and federal regulations that apply to all organizations receiving government funds. Voluntary participation also means that people know the sponsor and purpose of the research, but such knowledge can affect both rate of participation and responses.

Babbie holds fast on the requirement that people know who sponsors a study—even admonishing against creating fictitious organizations to mask the true sponsor's name. He is less stringent on the issue of full disclosure of the purpose of research, because this information is likely to affect the quality of participation. Tell respondents whatever you can about the purposes of the research, but not information that will affect responses. Describe the purpose in general terms rather than going into detail. Never lie about the purpose for doing the study, however, even if it means losing a participant.[30]

Assuring Anonymity or Confidentiality

Protecting the dignity and well-being of participants involves keeping their identity unknown or secret. Assuring *anonymity* means that even the researcher has no way to identify the source of a particular response. For example, a mail questionnaire with no identifying codes makes it an anonymous response.

On the other hand, assuring *confidentiality* means that even though the researcher can identify the source of particular responses, he or she promises not to. For example, surveys using interviews or coded questionnaires often require that respondents be specifically identified to comply with sampling procedures. It is your responsibility to make sure that all such identifying information is removed from the interview notes and questionnaires. This typically involves

[30]Earl R. Babbie, *Survey Research Methods* (Belmont, Calif.: Wadsworth Publishing Company, Inc., 1973), pp. 352–53.

replacing this information with an identification number that no one else has access to. In effect—for both moral and legal reasons—you must protect the privacy of those participating in your research.

Ethical behavior and social responsibility in research boils down to an obligation to *respect basic human and civil rights*. Our intent has been to highlight in the research context some of the values associated with treating people with respect that guide other aspects of your personal and professional activities. If those values are not in place, there isn't much we can say here to make a difference. For a more complete discussion of the ethical problems and dilemmas applied researchers face, however, we recommend Allan J. Kimmel's *Ethics and Values in Applied Social Research*.[31]

The point is that research constitutes an intervention in the personal and organizational lives of people. As the one responsible for how research is conducted and used, you must make it conform to the highest standards of professional ethics and social responsibility. In that respect, using research in public relations is no different than any other aspect of your professional practice.

[31]Allan J. Kimmel, *Ethics and Values in Applied Social Research* (Newbury Park, Calif.: Sage Publications, Inc., 1988).

APPENDIX A

PROFESSIONAL ETHICS
AND PRACTICES

In this appendix, we provide you the March, 1986, Code of Professional Ethics and Practices of the American Association for Public Opinion Research (AAPOR). We see the AAPOR standards of professional conduct as supplementing the codes of ethics of the Public Relations Society of America and the International Association of Business Communicators. We believe that the conduct of research in public relations should—as with the practice of public relations itself—live up to the standard set by Arthur W. Page:

> . . . all business in a democratic country begins with public permission and exists by public approval.

AAPOR CODE OF PROFESSIONAL ETHICS
AND PRACTICES

We, the members of the American Association for Public Opinion Research, subscribe to the principles expressed in the following code. Our goals are to support sound and ethical practice in the conduct of public opinion research and in the use of such research for policy and decision making in the public and private sectors, as well as to improve public understanding of opinion research methods and the proper use of opinion research results.

We pledge ourselves to maintain high standards of scientific competence and integrity in conducting, analyzing, and reporting our work and in our relations with survey respondents, with our clients, with those who eventually use the research for decision-making purposes, and with the general public. We further pledge ourselves to reject all tasks or assignments that would require activities inconsistent with the principles of this code.

I. *Principles of Professional Practice in the Conduct of Our Work*

    A. We shall exercise due care in developing research designs and survey instruments, and in collecting, processing, and analyzing data, taking all reasonable steps to assure the reliability and validity of results.

        1. We shall recommend and employ only those tools and methods of analysis which, in our professional judgment, are well suited to the research problem at hand.

        2. We shall not select research tools and methods of analysis because of their capacity to yield misleading conclusions.

        3. We shall not knowingly make interpretations of research results, nor shall we tacitly permit interpretations that are inconsistent with the data available.

        4. We shall not knowingly imply that interpretations should be accorded greater confidence than the data actually warrant.

    B. We shall describe our methods and findings accurately and in appropriate detail in all research reports, adhering to the standards for minimal disclosure specified in Part III.

    C. If any of our work becomes the subject of a formal investigation of an alleged violation of this Code, undertaken with the approval of the AAPOR Executive Council, we shall provide additional information on the survey in such detail that a fellow survey practitioner would be able to conduct a professional evaluation of the survey.

II. *Principles of Professional Responsibility in Our Dealings With People*

    A. The Public:

        1. If we become aware of the appearance in public of serious distortions of our research, we shall publicly disclose what is required to correct these distortions, including, as appropriate, a statement to the public media, legislative body, regulatory agency, or other appropriate group, in or before which the distorted findings were presented.

    B. Clients or Sponsors:

        1. When undertaking work for a private client, we shall hold confidential all proprietary information obtained about the client and about the conduct and findings of the research undertaken for the client, except when the dissemination of information is expressly authorized by the client, or when disclosure becomes necessary under terms of Section I-C or II-A of this Code.

        2. We shall be mindful of the limitations of our techniques and capabilities and shall accept only those research assignments which we can reasonably expect to accomplish within these limitations.

C.   The Profession:
1. We recognize our responsibility to contribute to the science of public opinion research and to disseminate as freely as possible the ideas and findings which emerge from our research.
2. We shall not cite our membership in the Association as evidence of professional competence, since the association does not so certify any persons or organizations.

D.   The Respondent:
1. We shall strive to avoid the use of practices or methods that may harm, humiliate, or seriously mislead survey respondents.
2. Unless the respondent waives confidentiality for specified uses, we shall hold as privileged and confidential all information that might identify a respondent with his or her responses. We shall also not disclose or use the names of respondents for nonresearch purposes unless the respondents grant us permission to do so.

Part III, "Standards of Minimum Disclosure," appears in Chapter 13. Reprinted by permission.

APPENDIX B

<hr>

HOW TO SELECT AND MONITOR OUTSIDE RESEARCH CONSULTANTS

If you decide to hire outside research consultants, you still need to read this book! You can't adequately select and monitor consultants without a basic understanding of the services they provide. In this appendix, you learn the steps to take in hiring and monitoring research consultants.

STEP 1: Know Your Budget and Deadlines Before hiring research consultants, know your information needs and how you will use research findings. Know your budget limits and your deadlines. This information is the minimum you will need to provide consultants.

STEP 2: Decide Role You Want Consultant to Play Next, consider the role that you want the research consultant to play in your organization. Look at the three roles that follow. Select the appropriate role, based on your understanding of research. Communicate to prospective consultants the role you wish them to play. Determine if the consultant is comfortable and/or capable of playing that role.

- *Consultant as expert prescriber.* If you are wholly naive about public relations research, you may be tempted to hire the research consultant as an *expert prescriber.*[1] The consultant is the doctor; you are the patient. The consultant prescribes and

[1]Glen M. Broom, "Testing the Practitioner's Impact on Clients," *Public Relations Review,* Vol. 5, No. 3 (1979), pp. 47–59.

you blindly obey. While this relationship may be comforting, it leads to research that gathers dust on shelves. You and the management team play a passive role as the consultant identifies information needs and initiates research activities. Since you and the management team are not directly involved in planning and implementing the research, you don't feel you "own" the findings.

- *Consultant as problem-solving process facilitator.* Reading this book positions you to hire research consultants as *problem-solving process facilitators.* The consultant provides understanding of the research process and technical research expertise. You and the management team provide your best understanding of the public relations problems that generate research information needs. You and the management team use research results to make decisions, to implement programs, and to change the organization, its policies, and its programs. The consultant helps *you* solve *your* public relations problems by helping *you* collect and organize needed information. You "own" the research project and its findings. You have greater control over the research services you receive.

- *Consultant as service provider.* Integrating research methods into your ongoing practice of public relations allows you to hire research consultants as *service providers.* Service providers are consultants who provide specific research services such as moderating focus groups, providing focus group facilities, conducting interviews, or coding and "crunching" research data for you. You design the research and specify precisely the technical services the consultant will provide and the form that results will be presented to you and the management team. You have maximum control over research services you receive.

Avoid hiring consultants as expert prescribers. They perform the research management function for you. This relationship thwarts your professional growth and retards your research sophistication. One expensive, misdirected research endeavor by the expert prescriber will spoil you and the rest of management on the usefulness of public relations research altogether. Managing the public relations function regarding research is *your* job. Never lull yourself into believing that somebody else can do it for you.

Hire research consultants as process facilitators with great care. Such consultants, often from a full-service research company, are providing management assistance, not technical services. Talk to the consultant's past clients. Investigate the consultant's reputation within your professional network.

STEP 3: Know Your Consultant's Special Capabilities   Chapter 7 details distinctions between qualitative and quantitative research. A consultant may be good at moderating focus groups but poor at managing a large sample survey. Which consultant you call depends on whether the research is qualitative or quantitative. Carefully consider which mode of observation best satisfies your information needs before seeking research services. Review Chapter 7.

STEP 4: Research Your Research Consultants   When hiring research consultants, be careful about whom you hire and be specific about what services you need. Wimmer and Dominick describe this issue succinctly when they note that anyone.[2]

---

[2]Roger W. Wimmer and Joseph R. Dominick, *Mass Media Research: An Introduction,* 2nd ed. (Belmont, Calif.: Wadsworth Publishing, 1987), p. 33.

> *... of any age, with any qualifications, can form a research sup-*
> *ply company. There are no formal requirements, no tests to take,*
> *and no state or federal licenses to acquire. Any company can hang*
> *a "research" shingle on the door.*

Several associations represent the interest of researchers, as well as set voluntary standards of ethical practices. Among them are the American Association for Public Opinion Research (AAPOR) and the Marketing Research Association (MRA). Membership in AAPOR and/or MRA does *not* certify the research compe-tence of the member. These voluntary associations have no real power to enforce standards of professional conduct.

When you hire photographers, printers, and freelance writers, you use your professional network and your past experiences. Use the same approach for hiring research service. Here are questions research service providers should answer for you:

What Research Training Has the Consultant Completed?   Technical aspects of collecting data, data entry, and setting up focus groups do not require formal training. Research design and quantitative research analysis does. If you are deal-ing with a large firm, determine the qualifications of the person supervising *your* account. The expertise of other company members not directly involved with your research project is not as relevant as the qualifications of people working directly on your project.

For Whom Has the Consultant Provided Similar Kinds of Research Services? A competent research firm should be able to provide names and contact persons of satisfied clients. Be sure that the research services you want are the same kind of services to which former clients can attest.

What Kinds of Research Services Can the Consultant Provide?   There are a wide variety of research services available. No one company is going to be the "best buy" for every single research need. Determine the areas where your consul-tant is qualified and experienced and areas where the consultant is not qualified.

STEP 5: Tell Consultant How You Will Use Qualitative Research   Specify what you already know about the problem and what you feel you don't know. Make clear to the consultant that you intend to use these qualitative research findings to provide an initial understanding of the problem and information needs to guide further research. Sometimes decisions are made on information gleaned from qualitative research alone. We recommend against this practice. (See the limitations of qualitative research in Chapter 7.) Competent, responsible consultants will recommend against such practices as well. However, budgets and deadlines may make more extensive, quantitative research impossible. We agree, however, that some qualitative research in such situations is better than none at all—following the best-available-evidence approach to decision making. When you contract for quantitative research alone, you should do your own qualitative research and fact-finding up front. This provides an informed basis for specifying the quantitative research that follows. Sometimes, after you field a large quantitative survey, you may return to focus groups or depth interviews to unravel the meaning of puzzling quantitative findings.[3] (See Chapter 7 for a more detailed review of the modes of observation.) Following we provide a check-list for one popular qualitative technique—focus group studies.

GUIDELINES FOR FOCUS GROUP SERVICES

The details of conducting focus group studies are provided in Appendix C. In this section, we consider only issues relevant to hiring focus group services.

STEP 1: Hire a Good Moderator   The moderator is the key player in focus group studies. Good moderating is a gift, and good moderators are worth extra pay. When hiring a moderator, consult your professional network. If possible, ask to observe the moderator at work. When videotapes are made of focus group sessions, they can be reviewed to determine the moderator's skills. Work closely with the moderator to develop the moderator's guide. Make sure the moderator clearly understands your information needs.

STEP 2: Use Professional Facilities   If you have any choice in the matter, hire a field service to provide focus group facilities and to recruit participants. We see no advantage (other than cost) to practitioners recruiting and setting up temporary focus group facilities.

STEP 3: Specify the Sampling Procedures   Nonprobability samples (see Chapter 6) are generally used in focus group studies. However, make sure the sample is purposive or dimensional rather than simply convenient. Field services use any convenient list—especially including past focus group participants—to acquire "warm bodies" for focus group studies. You need to specify the exact characteristics of participants and build those requirements into the screening or recruitment questionnaire. You also need to specify the lists from which such participants will be recruited.

STEP 4: Screen for Veteran Participants   Eliminate or set a limit on the number of veteran focus group participants you will accept in the group. Recruiting "professional" focus group participants—those who have participated in several groups over the past year—is a common abuse by research firms eager to put together groups with minimum effort. Ask for the completed screening questionnaires.

---

[3]We thank Harold F. Leiendecker of Exxon Corporation for mentioning this application of qualitative research.

STEP 5: Provide for Recording Equipment   Make sure the research firm provides clear audio tapes of the session(s). The better firms will make two recordings of each session to prevent loss of data from faulty equipment.

STEP 6: Inspect Facilities   Inspect the facilities in person. Ask to see the focus group room, the observation room, the recording equipment, the kind and quality of refreshments provided, and the lists used to recruit participants. Pay attention to the neatness of the facility, the availability of parking, and transportation access to the facility.

GUIDELINES FOR LARGE SAMPLE SURVEYS

The construction of questionnaires is discussed in Appendix D. In this section, important issues in hiring and supervising survey research firms are considered.

STEP 1: Explore Piggyback Options   Several research firms offer "caravan" or "piggyback" surveys wherein multiple sponsors of the survey spread the cost of the survey among themselves. This can be advantageous when the survey costs are high and the population to be studied is common to all parties. Demographic and psychographic variables on respondents are shared with all sponsors. Other items are proprietary to individual sponsors. Such "piggyback" surveys can be conducted with other departments within a single organization or with other organizations entirely. Disadvantages of such surveys include shared (reduced) control over key design and questionnaire construction issues, a time-consuming and involved decision-making process, and the difficulty of organizing joint sponsorship in the first place.

STEP 2: Seek Competitive Bids from Competent Firms   As with all research, specify your information needs and the uses to which the research will be placed before contacting consultants. Put the requirements and uses in writing, then seek competitive bids from suppliers. Solicit bids only from suppliers you have already "checked out" through your professional network. Harold Leiendecker, now retired from Exxon Corporation's Public Affairs Department, recommends bids from three providers. More bidders than that is abusive of the bidders; fewer than three bids may mean missing out on a genuine low bid. Specify exactly what "products" will be delivered to you under the terms of the bid. If you aren't specific about what you want, you may be unhappy later.

STEP 3: Determine Involvement in Questionnaire Construction   Get involved in designing the questionnaire. Sometimes, you provide the research firm with your written information needs, and the consultant designs the instrument. Other times, you work actively with the consultant to develop the questionnaire. (See Appendix D.)

STEP 4: Set Up Sensible Instrument Review Procedure Insist on prior approval of the instrument before it is used. However, avoid using committees to approve final instruments. Virtually everyone thinks he or she can develop questionnaire items. This is not true. All key members of the management team should be actively involved in specifying information needs. One or two people with expertise in questionnaire design, however, should have authority to sign off on the instrument.

STEP 5: Specify Sample Frames Specify the sample frame for the survey. (See Chapter 6.) The findings of the survey, no matter how valid the probability sampling involved, can only be generalized to the population of the sample frame. Make sure that the sample frame includes the publics relevant to your information needs. Use qualifier questions at the beginning of the questionnaire to insure that the sample includes only those respondents specifically desired for your purposes. When random digit dialing is used, make sure you understand how the sample was generated. (See Appendix F.)

STEP 6: Pilot Test the Questionnaire Build a pilot test into questionnaire design. Some research firms—even reputable ones—may question the need for such pilot testing. Don't listen to them! We have designed dozens of questionnaires and we are *always* sorry when we inadequately pilot test a questionnaire. Help debrief the interviewers who conducted the pilot test. You will learn about problems with instrumentation—and insure that those problems are fixed in the final questionnaire. Look for items with frequent "don't know" responses or questions requiring explanation from the interviewer. The pilot debriefing may also alert you to latent issues or concerns which may involve writing new questionnaire items.

The pilot test may use as few as five respondents or as many as fifty. Larger pilots help you develop categories for precoding responses to open-ended questions. (See Appendix D.) Always pilot test questionnaires on the target public, not a convenience sample of individuals already familiar with the subject under study.

STEP 7: Observe Interviewers in Action For phone surveys, observe the first few hours of interviewing. Get to know the interviewer supervisor and see how "glitches" are handled as they come up. As Harold Leiendecker explains, "this helps you get the best of their team." Even reputable research firms do their best work when closely observed.

STEP 8: Require Response, Refusal, and Noncontact Rates Require the survey research firm to provide a complete breakdown of the outcome of every attempted interview. For intercept interviews, this information can be coded into the questionnaire itself. Build into the questionnaire and edge code a tally of refusals. Use this information to compute refusal and response rates. For telephone interviews, require a response rate log (see Appendix H). You should also require the survey firm to provide the response, completion, refusal, and noncontact rates for the survey.

STEP 9: Retain Completed Questionnaires   After the research firm enters the questionnaire data into the computer, ask for the completed questionnaires. Do spot checks of the correctness of data entered. The questionnaire may also contain open-ended responses (not machine coded) that you may wish to refer to later.

STEP 10: Obtain Copies of Data Files   Make sure that you get the data in machine-readable form, even if the research firm keeps a copy for follow-up analysis. It's never a good idea to have only one copy of data files. Establish at the outset that the data and the analysis belong to you, not the research company. Include a provision for the surrender of all data and analysis to you from the research firm, an option you may exercise at your discretion.

OTHER RESEARCH TECHNIQUES

These principles for focus groups and surveys apply to contracting for other research services as well. The more specific your instructions to the research provider, the better the job that the firm will do for you. High on the list of specifications is the form in which "deliverables" will be provided. When contracting for data collection only, specify exactly the form in which the data (audio tape, video tape, transcript, edge-coded questionnaires, ASCII-coded machine-readable medium, frequency printouts, etc.) will be delivered.

When analysis and report writing are involved, specify the types of analysis to be conducted and the topics to be covered in the report. Examine the minimal disclosure standards in the AAPOR Code of Ethics (Appendix A) and require research reports of quantitative data to include sampling error or confidence interval information. (See Chapters 6 and 10.) Share the AAPOR minimal disclosure standards with the research firm and insist that those standards be adhered to in any research reports. Regarding computer analysis, provide yourself an "elastic" clause for a reasonable amount of additional analysis of data after you have reviewed the first pass at data analysis.

RESEARCH FIRM DIRECTORIES

Your professional network is a good source of names of competent research firms. Other resources, available in any large library, include several research directories. University-based research groups can be located through the *Research Center Directory*, which lists over 9,200 university-based research centers.[4] Look under index

---

[4]M. M. Wadkins, ed., *Research Centers Directory*, 11th ed. (Detroit: Gale Research Center, 1987).

headings for marketing, public relations, public opinion, and survey research. Commercial research firms are listed in the *Research Service Directory,* a publication of the 2,200-member Marketing Research Association.[5] Commercial firms are also listed in the *Directory of U.S. & Canadian Marketing Surveys & Services.*[6] This directory lists 4,500 marketing reports and 300 consulting firms.

[5]Marketing Research Association, *Research Service Directory* (Chicago: Marketing Research Association, Inc., 1987).
[6]Rauch Associates, *Directory of U.S. & Canadian Marketing Surveys & Services* (Bridgewater, N.J.: Rauch Associates, 1987).

APPENDIX C

HOW TO CONDUCT
A FOCUS GROUP STUDY

Chapter 7 discusses focus group studies as a mode of observation and places it in context with other techniques of observation. In this appendix, you learn how to actually conduct a focus group study.

   STEP 1: Is A Focus Group Study Really Appropriate?   Before conducting a focus group study, make sure that this technique can help satisfy your information needs. (See Chapter 7 for a discussion of the strengths and weaknesses of this approach, as well as other modes of observation.)

   STEP 2: Spell Out Your Information Needs   Specify the information needs that drive the focus group sessions. Generally, these information needs involve knowledge, predispositions, and behavior of target publics in response to stimuli. Stimuli include names of organizations, public issues, message points, and media strategies in either the early or final stages of production. Focus groups provide detailed, qualitative responses to stimuli. Focus groups are useful tools in the early stages of research, followed with more rigorous quantitative research.

   STEP 3: Decide Who Will Moderate   Great moderators are exceptional people perhaps born with a special gift—and are paid accordingly. Good moderators, on the other hand, are made from ordinary people who have had experience moderating groups. *You* may be a good focus group moderator. We suggest you observe a few good professional moderators before attempting your first. Watch—and learn—what they do.

Moderating is a combination of controlling group dynamics and active listening. You control group dynamics through the moderator guide, probing for the information you need from the participants. The moderator runs the discussion—informally indicating who may speak and when. In direct tension with this control function is active listening. The moderator leans slightly forward, listens intently to each participant, and uses nods and other nonverbal cues to encourage and reward things said by participants. The moderator is free to depart from the guide and follow up on ideas, comments, or suggestions that seem fruitful, even if they were unanticipated.

STEP 4: Schedule Groups With Care Both the date and time of focus group studies require careful consideration. Avoid scheduling focus groups on days of the week when participants are likely to be busy. Avoid focus group studies on holidays or other special days that make recruitment of participants difficult. Set time of day to avoid conflict with other demands on participants' time. For example, mothers with young children or other primary care providers may be available during the day when children are in school. People working outside the home will be generally more available in the evenings. Think through the days and times that are most convenient for participants.

STEP 5: Select A Sampling Strategy As indicated in Chapter 7 and Appendix B, focus groups usually use one of the nonprobability sampling techniques described in Chapter 6. Perhaps most common is dimensional sampling, wherein participants are selected according to key attributes from one or more convenient sampling frames. For example, a ten-participant group may be made up of five males and five females, as well as four Democrats, four Republicans, and two independents. Participants may be limited by other characteristics, such as a minimum income level, a particular role in the household, or some functional linkage to the organization (see Chapter 2). You should also control or eliminate participants who have participated in other focus groups within the last year.

STEP 6: Design A Screening Questionnaire Qualifying and specifying the right participants with the right characteristics requires a screening questionnaire and a single-page checklist indicating key attributes of participants recruited for the groups. The screening questionnaire should also specify the financial (or other) payment for participation, called the *co-op* or *incentive*. Co-ops range from about $25 to over $100 per participant for groups from specialized populations (medical doctors, for example).

STEP 7: Recruit Groups of Like Minds Make sure each focus group is homogeneous. If, for example, a publicly debated issue is discussed, make sure you do separate groups for "pro" and "anti" participants. Because of the social dynamics of focus groups, people with common viewpoints reinforce and encourage each other to speak out. A sharply divided group will degenerate into a debate between two assertive individuals from either side, with others nodding but contributing little.

STEP 8: Construct A Waiting Room Questionnaire   You may choose to supplement the screening questionnaire with a second, more detailed questionnaire filled out by participants when they arrive at the facility and wait for the group discussion to start. This second questionnaire serves several functions.

- Provides more background information on those participating.
- Completing the questionnaire gives punctual participants something useful and distracting to do while waiting for laggards to arrive. (Focus groups always start late.)
- Completed questionnaire commits respondents to a particular viewpoint prior to interaction with other group members.

The moderator can use this information during the discussion to draw out viewpoints that may be buried under a dominant viewpoint expressed by a few vocal group members. Questions on this questionnaire should be open-ended, requiring short, written answers from participants. This information is very useful when writing the report of focus group findings.

STEP 9: Develop the Moderator Guide and Stimuli   The moderator guide is a series of open-ended probes and topic labels that provides a rough map to the group moderator. Tied to the moderator guide is specification of stimuli given to participants and their order of presentation. Perhaps you show participants a rough of a corporate advertisement or a series of message points about an issue important to your organization. Perhaps you use a segment of videotaped information. Whatever the stimuli, you need a medium to present them to participants. This may require paper handouts, transparencies and an overhead projector, or a videocassette recorder and monitors clearly visible to all participants and the moderator. Carefully plan and rehearse the use of stimuli to insure that they serve their appropriate focusing function.

STEP 10: Select Focus Group Observers Strategically   Commercial focus group facilities routinely provide a darkened observation room behind a two-way mirror. This permits a small number of people from your organization to observe the study. The consciousness-raising function of observation cannot be overrated. The focus group gives you an opportunity to educate the other members of the management team about issues, problems, and opportunities among target publics. Select observers strategically.

Some public relations staffers should observe because they will implement programs, write messages, and make media choices based on this research. Also include a competent note-taker as backup for the recording system. (See Step 16.)

Include managers from other organizational units because:

- You want key players in management to "own" the research, its findings, and the programs that are developed from the research.
- You want to "educate" them as well as yourself about what publics know, feel, and how they act toward the organization, its communication, and its actions, as well as issues important to the organization.
- You want them to support programs that you develop from your research findings. The vividness of focus group discussions sensitizes other managers to important issues and problems in a unique and tangible way. Focus groups help you build the understanding and support your programs require among key members of management.

STEP 11: Brief Observers Beforehand   All observers need to be briefed as to the purpose of the focus group, as well as the strengths and weaknesses of such studies. Always position the findings of focus groups as preliminary or exploratory. Make sure observers understand that they may only whisper (any loud noise can be heard by participants) and that they may not smoke (lighting cigarettes is visible to participants, distracting them and frustrating your moderator).

STEP 12: Do Your Own Thorough Facility Check   Make sure that the audio and/or video recorders used to capture focus group discussions are working on the day or evening of the study. The field service should understand that payment for services is contingent on the delivery to you of a clear, audible recording of all discussions. You may also desire to have a notetaker among the observers. (Former journalists are excellent at this task!) These notes help condense information as it occurs, reducing literally hours of listening to tapes or transcribing them. Tapes serve as backups for precise quotes or more detailed review. (See Step 16.)

STEP 13: Check Catering Arrangements   Make sure that catering is in place to provide refreshments or snacks to participants. Because focus groups are often conducted during evening meal time, a snack is a good investment in quality participant cooperation. Make sure that there are pencils and adequate copies of the preliminary questionnaire if you use one. Assume that if anything can go wrong, it will go wrong. Check everything.

STEP 14: Recruit More Participants than Needed   Always recruit more participants than needed. A group of ten may require recruitment of thirteen people, due to no-shows. Be prepared to turn some people away if everybody shows, but pay them their co-op! Turn people away based on key characteristics overrepresented among those who show. If a field service recruits participants and provides facilities, make sure you have both agreed to specific procedures for recruitment, reminder calls on the day of the study, and a strategy for dealing with low turnouts, late arrivers, and no-shows.

STEP 15: Moderate the Group   The focus group discussion begins with a brief explanation of a focus group and the purpose of the discussion.

- Explain that a recording is being made of the discussion, "because what you say is important to us." The tape recording is erased once the study is complete, and everything said in the discussion is completely confidential.
- Explain the two-way mirror by telling participants that "a few of my associates" are behind the mirror, because "they are especially interested in what you have to say."
- Explain that the discussion is informal and that there are no right answers, only points of view and perspectives. Explain that everybody's viewpoint is important, "so I want to be sure I hear from everybody."
- Go around the table; have everyone introduce themselves and answer an easy "warm-up" question related to the focal topic.
- Watch out for "dominators." Regarding control, moderators have problems with dominators, people who attempt to monopolize the discussion and suppress viewpoints different from their own. Use such techniques as "let's hear from somebody different on this question" to squelch dominators. Go around the discussion table, making sure that everyone speaks before moving on to another question or issue. Under extreme circumstances, the moderator can stop the group and leave the room. The moderator can tell support staff to wait for the discussion to resume, then call a particularly problematic dominator to the phone. The dominator is then told outside the focus group room that he or she "is too well-versed on this subject" and therefore doesn't "meet our need for only naive participants." The dominator is paid the co-op and sent home.
- Be sensitive to adversives and draw them out. You will have less trouble with adversives, people who feel shy and uncomfortable speaking their mind. The questionnaires completed while waiting for the group to start permit the moderator to draw out such participants. The "rule" that "everybody's viewpoint is important"—introduced at the beginning of the session—is reinforced on the first question or two by insuring that everyone participates. The skillful moderator controls the tempo and the direction of the discussion, using the moderator guide as a map but feeling free to take detours and explore interesting paths not shown on the map.

STEP 16: Report Focus Group Findings   Because qualitative research generates such large quantities of data, the greatest problem is organizing and reducing data to more useful forms. Video recordings of focus groups permit the use of *video bites* or brief exemplary statements by participants to illustrate key findings. These can then be used to dramatically highlight major points in later presentations.

- Use notes. Regarding written reports, good note-taking can speed report writing. Tapes are used as back-up and as the source of explicit direct quotes where the exact language is important. An example of the need for exact language is the use of opinion statements in constructing questionnaire items with "natural language." Transcripts offer the most complete record of focus group discussions, but they may prove cumbersome unless extensively excerpted and condensed. The process of writing a verbatim transcript and then editing it down to a manageable form is very costly and time-consuming.

- Make implications explicit. Spell out the implications of the findings explicitly. Implications are generally calls for further, more rigorous research, since focus groups use small, nonprobability samples and generate qualitative data. Focus group findings should always be reported along with an explicit statement of limitations of the study. (See Chapters 13 and 14 for more details on presenting research findings.)

APPENDIX D

HOW TO CONSTRUCT QUESTIONNAIRES

In this appendix, you learn the mechanics of questionnaire construction in step-by-step fashion. In order to use this appendix, you may need to read or reread other sections of this book.

   STEP 1: Develop a Research Plan   *Do not skip this step.* The research plan specifies the information needs, intended uses, and research objectives of your study. (Research plans are discussed in more detail in Chapter 9.) Questionnaire items expand rapidly during questionnaire construction, especially when several individuals or departments are involved. The research plan helps you keep the questionnaire focused on specific information needs. If other members of the management team endorse the research objectives, then such endorsement can be used to eliminate items irrelevant to research objectives. A questionnaire is a tool for gathering information. This tool must be embedded in a larger research design. Common survey designs are cross-sectional and longitudinal studies. Cross-sectional surveys collect data at one point in time. They are useful in gathering information to plan public relations programs. (See Chapter 2.) Longitudinal surveys involve collection of information from respondents at several points in time. (See Chapter 5.)

   STEP 2: Decide How to Administer the Questionnaire   Common approaches are the mailed survey, the self-administered survey, the face-to-face survey, and the telephone survey. Which approach you should follow depends on the nature of your sample frame, the content of the questionnaire, and budget. The advantages and disadvantages of the different methods of questionnaire administration are spelled out in Chapter 7, pages 154–160. You should read those pages before making a decision about how to administer your questionnaire.

Key Points about Interviews

Face-to-face and telephone questionnaires are written for the ear. As you write a face-to-face or phone questionnaire item, say the item out loud.

- **"Bench test" different versions of an item on a colleague to determine clarity and listenability.** Generally, you are restricted to three or four specified response categories in closed-ended items. Respondents are unlikely to retain more categories when they are spoken. These questionnaires must be pleasing to the ear.
- **Use complex branching instructions.** While any one item must be simple to follow and easy to understand through the ear, this disadvantage can be offset by branching and follow-up probes.
- **Supplement face-to-face interviews with visual aids provided to respondents at appropriate points in the interview.**

Key Points about Self-Administered Questionnaires

Mailed and self-administered questionnaires are written for the respondent's eyes. They must be visually pleasing, with graphics illustrating instructions and assisting the respondent through the questionnaire.

- **Take full advantage of greater response categories.** Because response categories are displayed visually, more responses can be built into a questionnaire item.
- **Keep the branching simple.** The respondent completes the questionnaire unaided by an interviewer. The questionnaire must be easy to complete.
- **General instructions must be clear.**
- **Keep it short.** These must be shorter than face-to-face questionnaires, since you can't count on respondent-interviewer relations to keep respondents on task.

STEP 3: Do Qualitative Preliminary Research Qualitative techniques such as focus groups, depth interviews, and field studies help identify unrecognized problems and dimensions relevant to the research purpose. These techniques help sensitize you to the target population's frame of reference. This proves invaluable when constructing the questionnaire. These qualitative techniques of observation are described in Chapter 7, pages 145–154.

STEP 4: Construct the Questionnaire The foregoing first four steps are often skipped by the naive researcher—often with disastrous results. Problems with "seat-of-the-pants" questionnaires become apparent when you try to report your findings or make decisions on inadequate, inappropriate, and poorly conceptualized information. So don't start here.

Developing Indices

Your research objectives guide you to constructs you need to operationalize. Some constructs, such as respondent gender or length of employment with the company, are relatively easy to operationalize. Other constructs, such as communication and job satisfaction, are more difficult, requiring multiple measures in your questionnaire. Before you attempt to operationalize complex constructs, read Chapter 8, pages 163–183. When possible, use existing item sets of known reliability and established validity from prior research. See, for example, Delbert Miller's *Handbook of Research Design and Social Measurement* for such established measures of common constructs.[1]

Insure Item Quality

When constructing a questionnaire item, avoid these common defects: ambiguous items, double-barreled questions, irrelevant items, obscure or inappropriate vocabulary, abstract questions, leading or biased items, sensitive or personal questions, and normative response items. Use the following checklist to fine-tune each questionnaire item.

- **Is item ambiguous?** Does the item mean one thing to you but several things to your respondents? Each respondent will either answer the question he or she understands to have been asked (one problem!) or will not answer at all (another problem!). For these reasons, avoid slang or jargon that may have different meanings or multiple meanings for respondents.
- **Is item double-barreled?** Does it include two implicit questions but allow only one answer? One employee might consider the employee newsletter objective (statement of facts attributed to sources) but not balanced (too few stories about clerical employees). If the question asks if the newsletter is objective and balanced, it's double-barreled. No response reflects the respondent's split feelings about the objective and balanced character of the newsletter.
- **Is item irrelevant?** Some items are irrelevant to the purposes of the study, especially when committees design questionnaires. Involve other members of the management team in the development of research objectives, but keep actual questionnaire construction limited to a few experts. Some items are irrelevant to respondents. For example, you may ask respondents how frequently they read the company magazine. Choices are often, sometimes, almost never, and never. You then ask respondents how frequently they read the promotions column, the new employee feature, and the personal announcement section. If the respondent has already indicated that he or she does not read the publication, then these follow-up questions are irrelevant. Use filter and contingency questions to avoid irrelevant questions. A *filter* question is an item with response categories that guide respondents to different sections of the questionnaire. A *contingency* question is an item that is only asked of some respondents, based on their answer to a prior filter question. For example:

[1]Delbert C. Miller, *Handbook of Research Design and Social Measurement*, 4th ed. (New York: David McKay, 1983).

1. Do you *favor* or *oppose* mandatory retirement of employees over the age of sixty-five years?
   (1) OPPOSE (SKIP TO #3)
   (2) FAVOR . . .

2. Do you think exceptions should be made for employees with special skills that can't be easily replaced?
   (1) NO
   (2) YES

Question 2 is skipped if Question 1 is "oppose." Complex designs can be developed by "nesting" filter and contingency questions within other filter questions. For example, respondents answering yes to Question 2 could be asked an additional contingency question: "For how many years past sixty-five should such employees be allowed to work?"

- **Is vocabulary too difficult?** Respondents won't tell you they don't know the meaning of words. They simply select any answer, rather than appear ignorant. Keep vocabulary simple, avoiding jargon and other specialized language unfamiliar to your respondents. Use pilot tests to detect vocabulary problems.

- **Is item abstract?** If yes, you slow completion of the questionnaire and get unreliable responses. Make questions as specific and as concrete as possible. For example, you could ask respondents how satisfied they are with their jobs. That's abstract. Ask them whether or not they feel their supervisors listen to them, whether they are given an opportunity to do the things they do best. These are more concrete. In combination, they provide multiple indicators of the "satisfaction" construct.

- **Is item leading or biased?** Management may like the kind of answers you get, but they don't meet information needs. Here's one leading item: "Most community leaders feel that XYZ Corp. has done its fair share to clean up the environment. Do you agree?" A more subtle version simply asks: "Do you agree that XYZ Corp. has done its fair share to clean up the environment?" This version takes advantage of "yea-sayers." *Yea-saying* is the tendency of some respondents to give positive responses to questionnaire items, regardless of their actual opinion.[2] A better item: "Do you agree or disagree that XYZ Corp. has done its fair share to clean up the environment?"

- **Is item sensitive or personal?** Age and income questions are frequently asked, yet some respondents regard such information as "none of your business." In telephone or face-to-face interviews, pose these questions at the end. You've established some rapport, increasing cooperation. A refusal at the end does not damage rapport for subsequent questions. Assuring anonymity at the beginning improves chances of cooperation. However, avoid using response categories for age and income questions, unless you know it improves response rates. Categories ($10K–$25K, $26K–$35K, etc.) convert ratio-level indicators to ordinal categories, reducing the statistical procedures that can be used. You violate the highest-level imperative explained in Chapter 8.

- **Is item response normative?** Some items elicit socially acceptable rather than honest responses. For example, driving after drinking alcohol is increasingly socially unacceptable. A questionnaire item asking respondents how frequently they drive after drinking will likely elicit socially acceptable rather than truthful responses. Some responses are not only socially unacceptable, they are illegal.

[2]Jerald G. Bachman and Patrick M. O'Malley, "Yea-Saying, Nay-Saying, and Going to Extremes: Black-White Differences in Response Styles," *Public Opinion Quarterly*, Vol. 48, No. 2 (Summer 1984), p. 491.

Asking employees about their use of recreational drugs such as marijuana or cocaine in a survey is not likely to elicit candid responses. Go to great lengths to assure anonymity. In one panel study of college seniors which involved questions of illegal drug use and detailed probes of sexual behavior, the interviewer (in the presence of the respondent) mailed the completed questionnaire to a colleague in Canada, where a new identification number was assigned. The respondent was assured that the questionnaire data could not be subpoenaed in the United States and his or her identity revealed. Reduce the stigma associated with certain responses. For example, introduce a question about alcohol and driving as follows: "Most people who drink find that they sometimes must drive afterwards, even though they would rather not. How often has this happened to you?"

STEP 5: Develop an Introduction   For mailed surveys, a cover letter is used to explain the purpose of the study to respondents, assure confidentiality, stress importance of respondent participation in the study, and set a deadline for returning the questionnaire. With self-administered questionnaires, this introductory function can be performed by the individual distributing the questionnaire, be such distribution to individuals or to groups. In a face-to-face or telephone questionnaire, the introduction is provided in the questionnaire itself. In each instance, the introduction is persuasive in nature; the purpose is to gain cooperation of respondents.

STEP 6: Carefully Craft Instructions   Instructions should be complete and clear. In mailed and self-administered questionnaires, each block of items generally requires specific instructions. Specify how the selected answer is to be marked (circle the number, check the box, fill in the blank, etc.). While instructions should be simple to understand, they also must be complete. For these types of questionnaires, respondents have no means of seeking clarification of ambiguous or confusing instructions.

In a telephone or face-to-face questionnaire, instructions to the interviewer must be clearly set aside from material provided directly to the respondent. This can be accomplished by putting all instructions in capital letters and setting them off in boxed areas. Such instructional material to the interviewer should also include explicit instructions for how to handle special cases where additional explanation of an item is required.

For example, most respondents in a telephone survey of employees may know about the company's profit-sharing plan. However, a minority do not. You decide that you want interviewers to provide a single-sentence description of the plan if the respondent is not familiar with the plan. This one-sentence description would be included as instructions in the questionnaire.

STEP 7: Develop Smooth Item Flow   Organize the order of questions in a logical and coherent manner. Here are some general guidelines.

- **The questionnaire should start with easy-to-answer questions.** Generally, you should follow a strategy called the *funnel technique*.[3] Start with general questions,

[3]Bernard S. Phillips, *Social Research: Strategy and Tactics,* 2nd. ed. (New York: MacMillan, 1971).

moving to more specific and detailed items as the questionnaire progresses. Open-ended questions, if used at all, occur prior to the more specific, closed-ended questions. The general questions at the beginning can be used as filter questions for more specific contingency questions that follow.

- **Group questions with similar response categories together, even if the items measure different constructs.** For example, the following items measure different constructs (job satisfaction and readership), but are grouped together because they share a common response scale.

	ALWAYS	*SOMETIMES*	*NEVER*
Do you like the sort of work you are doing?	3	2	1
Do you do the things you feel you do best?	3	2	1
Do you read the weekly employee newsletter?	3	2	1
Do you read the monthly employee magazine?	3	2	1

- **Avoid response set.** Response set is the tendency to give the same response to several questions, regardless of content. In the preceding example, respondents may be tempted to go down the left column, marking "always" to all items. Use item content to break up response sets before they start. For example, the following opinion items tend to elicit opposite responses about the quality of the employee newsletter.

	DISAGREE	*NEUTRAL*	*AGREE*
I feel the employee newsletter . . .			
. . . has too many photos & graphics	1	2	3
. . . is too "gray," too much type	1	2	3

This forces the respondent to move from the agree to disagree ends of the scale in order to be consistent. Further, an item can be stated in its negative form to check for reliability. For example, an item that states the employee newsletter "has too few photos and graphics" provides a reliability check on its opposite counterpart.

STEP 8: Clear Instrument with Key Stakeholders You want to do this prior to the pilot test, because changes in the instrument after the pilot should be based on operational issues (clarity of instructions, question order, wording of specific items), not content issues. Committees write ineffective questionnaires and have little to contribute after the pilot test. At the same time, clients and key stakeholders need to "buy in" to the study and the instrumentation. If you have done a good job of specifying information needs, anticipated uses of the information, and research objectives, then the instrument should already serve the purposes for which it was designed. This "buy-in" phase is more political than operational.

STEP 9: Pilot Test the Questionnaire A *pilot test* is the administration of the instrument to a subsample of the target population to identify problems in the questionnaire. Data from the pilot questionnaire are not used in the final analysis, since the questionnaire invariably changes as a result of the pilot test. Here are the issues you should consider during pilot testing:

- **How long does it take respondents to complete the questionnaire?** This information can be used in the cover letter or the introductory statement to inform respondents of the time required to complete the questionnaire. A start-time and stop-time block should be included on the pilot version of the questionnaire.
- **Is the introductory statement effective in eliciting the cooperation of respondents?** How might this statement be improved?
- **Is each item clearly understood by respondents?** Did the respondents frequently require clarification or explanation for certain items? If so, rewrite these items.
- **Did respondents use the full range of response categories?** If an item results in all or most respondents selecting a single response category, you are not capturing adequate variance through your item scale. Redesign the item scale so that you capture more diversity of responses.
- **Is the "unsure" or "don't know" category being frequently checked for some items?** If so, those items may be confusing or ambiguous for many respondents. A rewrite may be in order.
- **Did the questionnaire flow comfortably?** Were some transitions awkward? If so, reorder the presentation of items or write transitional statements that assist the flow from one section to the next.

The pilot test should be similar in administration to the strategy actually employed for the final survey. Mailed and self-administered questionnaires should be filled out by the respondent, unaided by the interviewer. The pilot test respondents should be encouraged to write comments or reactions to items in the questionnaire. Triple-spacing the questionnaire or leaving white space around items will encourage such feedback. You can interview pilot test respondents after they have filled out the questionnaire to insure that you fully understand their feedback. Face-to-face or telephone interviews should be administered by an interviewer, with the interviewer stopping whenever necessary to elicit feedback from the pilot test respondent.

How many pilot tests should you conduct? Major problems with vocabulary, clarity, and ambiguity in instructions can often be detected through five or ten pilot test questionnaires. The variance in response categories can be evaluated with twenty to thirty pilot questionnaires. There is no magic number. However, it is imperative that you pilot test and revise every questionnaire, even if only a few pilot tests are possible. For the novice questionnaire writer, a two-step pilot test is in order. First construct the instrument, then conduct a small pilot test to detect major problems. Revise the questionnaire, then conduct a more extensive second test to fine-tune the instrument.

STEP 10: Edge Code the Questionnaire   Once the pilot testing is complete, develop an edge coding strategy for your instrument. This process is explained in greater detail in Chapter 9. This is the final step in the design and construction of the questionnaire. Don't develop an edge coding strategy until you are "locked in" on the order and number of items in the questionnaire. Inserting, deleting, or moving an item after the edge coding is completed means redoing the edge coding. See Chapter 9 for a full explanation of edge coding.

STEP 11: Field the Study You are now ready to duplicate the questionnaire and administer your survey. Keep good field notes, indicating the day that the first questionnaires were mailed or the first interviews were conducted. Assign identification numbers to mailed questionnaires before they are mailed. These numbers can be used to track responses and permit the mailing of follow-up questionnaires to only nonresponding sample members. When face-to-face or telephone interviews are conducted from a physical sample frame, assign identification numbers to specific sample members. This can be accomplished through a form that includes the identification number, sample member information (address, phone number, etc.), and a space for recording the outcome of the contact attempts for that sample member. Note if the sample member was never contacted. Also note those sample members who were determined to not be members of the target population. Also note those who refused the interview, as well as those who completed the interview. This information is used later to compute response rates, refusal rates, and noncontact rates. See Appendix H.

APPENDIX E

HOW TO SET PROGRAM OBJECTIVES AND SELECT SAMPLE SIZE FOR STATISTICAL POWER

In this appendix, we show you how to set objectives for programs and then figure out how large a sample is required to determine if those objectives are met. To do so, you will need to do some arithmetic. We suggest you read this chapter with a pad of paper and a calculator at hand. Work through each example on your pad, using your calculator. Figuring out the appropriate sample size can be confusing, so follow carefully the step-by-step method we use here.

If you get confused, don't quit. Simply back up and work through the confusing step again. Once you've mastered the step-by-step method for the examples we provide, write your own objectives. Then use the step-by-step method you learned from the examples and the work sheet in Exhibit E–1 to figure out the appropriate sample size for measuring your objectives. But first you must understand some concepts basic to the process of sample size selection.

Statistical power is the ability of a particular statistical test and sample to detect a relationship of a given strength or size in the population *if*, indeed, such a relationship actually exists in the population.[1] Statistical power is expressed as a probability. If a test has statistical power of 0.80, that means there is an 80 percent chance of detecting the hypothesized relationship in the sample (statistically significant), given that it really exists in the population.

---

[1]The authors gratefully acknowledge the contribution of Dr. Myron Lustig, professor of speech communication at San Diego State University, who has broadened our understanding of statistical power and for the need of this appendix. We also thank Professor Lustig for his review of an earlier draft of this appendix and his suggestions for improvements. Any errors in this appendix, however, are those of the authors.

EXHIBIT E-1
Work Sheet for Computing
Sample Sizes
for Program Objectives

The following program objective is to be evaluated using a posttest-only control group design. (See Chapter 5). The Chi-Square test will be used to test whether the program achieved its desired effect.

MODEL OBJECTIVE: *To increase (awareness/positive opinion/desired behavior) of target public from _____ percent to _____ percent by end of program.*

Two groups of equal size are randomly selected. (Existing groups such as two communities or employees at two different work sites are often substituted for random groups. An equal number of people from each existing group can be randomly sampled. See Chapter 5.) The first group receives the public relations program. The second group does not receive the public relations program. At program's end, the two groups are surveyed and the impact variable (awareness, opinion, or behavior) is measured.

The *research hypothesis* is that the program worked—that the group receiving the program changed their awareness, opinions, or behavior in the desired direction and by the desired amount. That is, the group receiving the program shows the percentage from the second blank in the model objective on line d. in the Step 1 tables that follow. Line b. is computed by subtracting line d. from 100. The group not receiving the program is regarded as unchanged from the time the program was first implemented, so the percentage from the first blank in the model objective appears on line c. Line a. is computed by subtracting line c. from 100.

The *null hypothesis* is that the program had no effect at all. Both the group receiving the program and the group not receiving the program are unchanged (or changed the same amount because of other factors) from the time the program was first implemented. Lines g. and h. in the null hypothesis table contain the percentage from the first blank in the model objective.

Step 1 Tables

		RESEARCH HYPOTHESIS			NULL HYPOTHESIS	
		No Program	*Receives Program*		*No Program*	*Receives Program*
O P I N I O N	Negative	a. ____%	b. ____%	Negative	e. ____%	f. ____%
	Positive	c. ____%	d. ____%	Positive	g. ____%	h. ____%
		100%	100%		100%	100%

The proportion of the total sample (both groups) falling in each cell is computed for both the research hypothesis and the null hypothesis. This is accomplished by converting each percentage into a proportion (move the decimal point two places to the left) and multiplying by 0.5. Use the following table to make this conversion.

Step 2 Tables

OPINION		RESEARCH HYPOTHESIS	
		No Program	Receives Program
	Negative	a. ._____ × 0.5 = a. _____	b. ._____ × 0.5 = b. _____
	Positive	c. _____ × 0.5 = c. _____	d. ._____ × 0.5 = d. _____

OPINION		NULL HYPOTHESIS	
		No Program	Receives Program
	Negative	e. ._____ × 0.5 = e. _____	f. ._____ × 0.5 = f. _____
	Positive	g. ._____ × 0.5 = g. _____	h. _____ × 0.5 = h. _____

Now use these new computed proportions in the Step 3 table. In the Step 3 table, the values for each cell from the research hypothesis table and the null hypothesis table at Step 2 are computed using the following formula:

For Each Cell: $(\text{Research Value} - \text{Null Value})^2 / \text{Null Value}$

Use a calculator.

Step 3 Table

SUM THIS COLUMN
1. SUBTRACT: (a. ___ − e. ___) = ___
. . . SQUARE YOUR ANSWER: ___
. . . DIVIDE YOUR ANSWER: (___/e. ___) = ___
2. SUBTRACT: (b. ___ − f. ___) = ___
. . . SQUARE YOUR ANSWER: ___
. . . DIVIDE YOUR ANSWER: (___/f. ___) = ___
3. SUBTRACT: (c. ___ − g. ___) = ___
. . . SQUARE YOUR ANSWER: ___
. . . DIVIDE YOUR ANSWER: (___/g. ___) = ___
4. SUBTRACT: (d. ___ − h. ___) = ___
. . . SQUARE YOUR ANSWER: ___
. . . DIVIDE YOUR ANSWER: (___/h. ___) = ___
5. . . . ADD UP COLUMN: ___
6. . . . SQUARE ROOT OF ANSWER (w): ___

Congratulations. You've just computed the desired effect size (*w*) for your public relations program. Now you are ready to look up the minimum sample size needed to detect such an effect on your target public for a given level of confidence. To do so, you need to specify the decision rule (alpha = 0.05 is the industry standard) and the statistical power (power = 0.80 is the industry standard) of your evaluation study. Remember to double the alpha level (to 0.10 if you use the industry standard) because your objective specifies the direction of change (an increase in awareness, positive opinion, or desired behavior). Such an objective requires a one-tailed test. See Table E–11 for the minimum sample size.

To determine statistical power, you need to know the effect size you wish to detect in the population. *Effect size* is the strength of the relationship between the independent and dependent variable *in the population*. The stronger the relationship—the more powerful the influence of the independent variable on the dependent variable—the larger the effect size. For example, what is the relationship between informational messages about the benefits of genetic engineering and the public's willingness to permit field tests of biotechnology products in their communities? The stronger the relationship between such messages and public opinion, the greater the effect size. When the effect size is large in the population, even a small sample and/or a weak statistical procedure (in terms of power) will detect that relationship with a high degree of confidence. When effect size is small, a very large sample and/or powerful statistical procedures are required to detect it.

PEARSON CORRELATION COEFFICIENTS

When two variables are metrics, the Pearson correlation coefficient is a useful measure of the relationship between them. (See Chapter 11.) The statistical power of the Pearson correlation coefficient is perhaps easiest to understand, because Pearson correlation coefficients are directly related to effect size. The larger the coefficient in the population, the greater the effect size of the relationship.

An example helps illustrate effect size for a relationship you seek to test using the Pearson correlation coefficient. You issue a magazine called *Community Action* to people living in zip code zones around a major manufacturing plant operated by your company, MegaTech. The purpose of the magazine is to improve community perceptions of MegaTech. You wish to conduct a survey of the target community. Exposure to MegaTech's magazine is measured by asking respondents how many times they read *Community Action* over the last twelve issues. Answers range from zero (no exposure) to twelve (exposure to all issues). Opinion toward MegaTech is measured using a − 10 (very negative) to + 10 (very positive) index. The index is a combination of several opinion statements about MegaTech.

The program objective is stated in terms of a posttest-only design, in which readers are measured once after the first year of publication. (See Chapter 5 for a detailed explanation of research design. The design suggested here is vulnerable to several validity threats.)

> OBJECTIVE 1: To demonstrate a correlation of 0.40 between exposure to **Community Action** and positive opinion toward MegaTech by December 31.

The research hypothesis embedded in this objective suggests that exposure to the magazine correlates with positive opinion toward MegaTech.

How large an effect size is $r = 0.40$? The Pearson r, unlike the Chi-Square statistic, is a stand-alone indicator of the effect size. When $r = 0.10$, effect size is small. When $r = 0.30$, effect size is medium. When $r = 0.50$, effect size is large. By squaring r, you learn how much variance in the dependent variable (positive opinion of MegaTech, in this case) is explained or accounted for by the independent variable (magazine exposure). Squaring 0.10 yields 0.01 or 1 percent, when converted to percentage form. That means that if magazine exposure is correlated with positive opinion at $r = 0.10$, then only 1 percent of the variance in opinion toward MegaTech can be explained or accounted for by exposure to the magazine. A medium effect size ($r = 0.30$) explains about 10 percent of the variance in the dependent variable. A large effect size ($r = 0.50$) explains about a quarter of the variance in the dependent variable.

In this example, the effect size in Objective 1 is between medium to large. If effective, the program (magazine exposure) will account for 16 percent (0.40 squared and converted to percentage) of the variance in opinion toward Mega-Tech among its readers.

How large a sample is needed to detect an effect size of $r = 0.40$ in the population? Recall from Chapter 11 that the smaller the effect size, the larger the sample must be to detect the relationship. A small effect size implies the need for a large sample. A large effect size, on the other hand, can be detected with a small sample.

To use power tables for Pearson correlation coefficients, you specify a decision rule and a power coefficient. For this example, a 95-percent decision rule and the 90-percent power coefficient (0.90) are specified. Knowing the decision rule and the power coefficient, we turn to the power tables at the end of this appendix to determine the proper minimum sample size.

Statistical power is affected by whether the test is one-tailed or two-tailed. A two-tailed test is one where the direction of the relationship is not specified. For example, an objective could state that exposure to *Community Action* changes opinion toward the company, without specifying the direction of such change. In Objective 1, however, the direction of the relationship is specified. Exposure to

Community Action is correlated with a positive change in opinion. A one-tailed test is used.

Table E–22 at the end of this appendix is the appropriate table for selecting the proper sample size. (Note that this objective calls for a one-tailed test.) You've specified a decision rule of 95 percent (alpha=0.05) and a statistical power coefficient of 0.90. This means you are 95 percent sure you won't commit Type I error and 90 percent sure you won't commit Type II error. (See Chapter 11 for a complete explanation of error types.)

Now turn to Table E–22. Different effect sizes, ranging from small ($r=0.10$) to medium ($r=0.30$) to large ($r=0.50$) and up, appear in columns of the table. Different power coefficients are arranged down the left-hand side. The numbers in the table are minimum sample sizes needed to detect particular effect sizes in the population. Look to the column where $r=0.40$ and the row where the power coefficient equals 0.90. The intersect of this row and column is 50. This means that only 50 respondents are needed to detect an effect size of 0.40 in the population. You are 90 percent sure your Pearson correlation test will be statistically significant, given an effect size of $r=0.40$ *in the population.* This does not mean that a sample of 50 respondents will show $r=0.40$. Rather, you are 90 percent sure that—if the correlation is $r = 0.40$ *in the population*—the correlation *in the sample* will be positive and will be significantly greater than zero, using the 95-percent decision rule.

If we had specified a medium effect size of $r=0.30$ in Objective 1, Table E–22 indicates that a sample size of 93 would be required to detect the relationship at a 95-percent level of confidence and a 90-percent level of statistical power. Similarly, if Objective 1 had called for a small effect size of $r=0.10$ between magazine exposure and favorable opinion, a sample of 864 would be required. Use Table E–22 to check these sample sizes for yourself.

CHI-SQUARE STATISTICAL POWER

For the Chi-Square statistic, effect size is not directly indicated by the Chi-Square value itself, as is the case for the Pearson correlation coefficient. That's because the Chi-Square value increases as the number of cells in the contingency table increases, regardless of the effect size. To compensate for this, a different statistic is used to estimate the statistical power of the Chi Square. That "effect size" statistic is the w statistic—a number that ranges from zero to one. The higher the w statistic, the larger the effect size and the stronger the relationship between independent and dependent variables. For example, $w=0.10$ indicates a small effect size. Effect size is medium when $w=0.30$, whereas $w=0.50$ indicates a large effect size.

An example helps illustrate effect size for the Chi-Square statistic. After a year of circulating the *Community Action* magazine to a random sample of 10,000 residents, you want to see if exposure to the magazine increases reader perceptions of MegaTech as "contributing significantly to the community." A benchmark survey of the community—conducted prior to publishing *Community Action*—indicates that only 35 percent of residents agree that your company contributes significantly to the community.

Small Effect Size

You may decide that a reasonable objective is to increase agreement with the opinion statement from 35 percent to 42 percent. Stated as an objective:

> *OBJECTIVE 2: To increase the percentage of* **Community Action** *readers who agree that MegaTech contributes significantly to the community from 35 percent to 42 perent by December 31.*

Implicit in this objective is a research hypothesis stating that magazine exposure has an *effect size* of seven percentage points in positive opinion change over the time span of the program. When the program is completed, opinions of two types of residents are surveyed. Half received *Community Action;* the other half did not. (This is a posttest-only control group design. See Chapter 5.)

As shown following, this seven percentage-point shift is a small effect size. Since the Chi-Square statistic is used, effect size is measured with the w statistic. How many residents must be surveyed in order to detect an effect size this small? To determine sample size, the w statistic is computed for this research hypothesis.

The research hypothesis and the null hypothesis for this objective are stated following in the form of contingency tables, the statistical approach used in this example to measure program impact. On the left are the percentages expected *in the population* if the research hypothesis is true, if the objective is achieved. Residents not exposed to the magazine are hypothesized to remain unchanged in their opinion of MegaTech's contribution to the community. Residents exposed to the magazine increase their level of agreement with the opinion statement by seven percentage points, if the research hypothesis is true. On the right are percentages expected if the magazine had no effect at all on opinion, if the null hypothesis is true. Both magazine readers and nonreaders are unchanged in their opinion of MegaTech's contribution to the community.

O P I N I O N		*RESEARCH HYPOTHESIS*			*NULL HYPOTHESIS*	
		No Magazine	*Magazine*		*No Magazine*	*Magazine*
	Negative	65%	58%	*Negative*	65%	65%
	Positive	35%	42%	*Positive*	35%	35%
		100%	100%		100%	100%

The next step in computing the w statistic is to calculate what *proportion* of the *total* sample falls in each cell of each table. First, convert percentages to proportions by moving the decimal two places to the left:

O P I N I O N		RESEARCH HYPOTHESIS			NULL HYPOTHESIS	
		No Magazine	Magazine		No Magazine	Magazine
	Negative	0.65	0.58	*Negative*	0.65	0.65
	Positive	0.35	0.42	*Positive*	0.35	0.35

Since half the sample is drawn from magazine readers and the other half from nonreaders, multiply each (column) proportion in the table by 0.5 to find out the proportion of the *total* sample that falls in each cell. This is equivalent—in proportion rather than percent form—to the percent of total that appears as the bottom number in each cell of a contingency table. (See Chapter 11 and Appendix K.)

O P I N I O N		RESEARCH HYPOTHESIS			NULL HYPOTHESIS	
		No Magazine	Magazine		No Magazine	Magazine
	Negative	0.325	0.290	*Negative*	0.325	0.325
	Positive	0.175	0.210	*Positive*	0.175	0.175

The last two tables show the proportion of total respondents that would appear in each cell of the table for the research hypothesis (left) and for the null hypothesis (right). The next step requires some arithmetic.

For each cell, (a) *subtract* the value in the null table from the value in the research table, (b) *square* the result, then (c) *divide* by the null table value. The results appear in the cells of the table following. All the values in the cells of the table are in the column at right. Now (d) *sum* the column on the right:

		$\dfrac{(\text{RESEARCH CELL VALUE} - \text{NULL CELL VALUE})^2}{\text{NULL CELL VALUE}}$			CELL VALUES
O P I N I O N		No Magazine	Magazine		0.0000
					0.0000
					0.0038
	Negative	0.0000	0.0038		0.0070
	Positive	0.0000	0.0070	SUM OF CELLS =	0.0108

The *w statistic* is the square root of the sum of cells. In this case, *w* equals 0.104, the square root of 0.0108. The effect size, a seven percentage-point increase in favorable opinion toward MegaTech, is small.

To use the effect size to determine the appropriate sample size to use, first compute the degrees of freedom in the table. As shown in Appendix I, degrees of freedom are computed by the formula:

$$d.f. = (\text{rows} - 1) \times (\text{columns} - 1)$$

In this case, with two rows and two columns, $d.f. = 1$. That is, $(2-1) \times (2-1) = 1$.

Statistical power is affected by the decision rule used. In this example, the 95-percent decision rule (alpha=0.05) is used. Objective 1 specifies that change is toward more *favorable* opinion of MegaTech. The objective specifies the *direction of* change, so a one-tailed test is used. To do so, *double* the alpha level before using the power table, knowing that alpha=0.05 for a one-tailed test is the same as alpha=0.10 for a two-tailed test. Tables E–1 through E–20 at the end of this appendix assume a two-tailed test, so *double* the alpha level before using these tables when objectives imply a one-tailed test.

What level of power do you want your evaluation study to incorporate? You want a sample size with a 0.90 power coefficient, meaning you will be 90 percent sure of obtaining a statistically significant relationship *in your sample* if objective 1 is achieved *in the population*.

Now turn to Table E–11 at the end of this appendix. This table is used when alpha = 0.05 and a one-tailed Chi-Square test is specified by a directional relationship in the objective. (This same table is used when alpha = 0.10 and a two-tailed test is specified.) This table is specifically for Chi-Square tests for one degree of freedom (as in a two-by-two table).

Different power coefficients appear in the left column. Different effect sizes (*w*) appear across the top of the columns. In this case, look where the power coefficient—0.90—intersects with effect size—*w*=0.10. The table indicates that a sample size of 856 is required to detect a seven percentage-point shift in the population, a small program effect size (*w*=0.10).

What if you can't afford a sample size of 856? You could use a different measurement strategy and use a more powerful inferential statistic like the *F*-test (analysis of variance). An example of such a strategy is provided later in this appendix. This would permit you to use a smaller sample size.

You could use a more lenient decision rule, such as the 90-percent decision rule. You could use a smaller power coefficient, such as the 80-percent power coefficient. Both of these strategies permit you to use a smaller sample size. However, reducing the decision rule increases the probability of rejecting the null hypothesis (no program effect) when it's true. Reducing the power coefficient increases the probability of accepting the null hypothesis when it's false. (See Chapter 11.)

Another strategy, considered in the following sections, is to increase the effect size you intend to achieve through your program. With a larger effect size—greater program impact—a smaller sample will provide statistically significant indications of program effect if the objective is, in fact, achieved. If none of these is viable, don't evaluate the program. David Clavier, PhD, APR, Husk Jennings Overman Public Relations, cautions that "you need to be careful that you don't spend more asking the question than the answer's worth." Small program effect sizes go hand in hand with small programs, limited objectives, and tiny budgets. While *every* program should have measurable goals and objectives, not every program can be measured in a cost-effective manner.

Medium Effect Size

Suppose you set a more ambitious objective, such as:

*OBJECTIVE 3: To increase the percentage of **Community Action** readers who agree that MegaTech contributes significantly to the community from 35 percent to 55 percent by December 31.*

A twenty percentage-point increase in positive opinion among readers hypothesizes that the magazine will have a medium effect size. The null hypothesis is that the magazine will have no effect on opinion. Contingency tables for the research hypothesis implicit in the objective and the null hypothesis are shown following. (Percentages have been converted to proportions by moving the decimal point two places to the left.)

OPINION		*RESEARCH HYPOTHESIS*			*NULL HYPOTHESIS*	
		No Magazine	*Magazine*		*No Magazine*	*Magazine*
	Negative	0.65	0.45	*Negative*	0.65	0.65
	Positive	0.35	0.55	*Positive*	0.35	0.35

To determine the proportion of the overall population that falls in each cell, multiply each cell by 0.5 as in the example for small effect size.

OPINION		*RESEARCH HYPOTHESIS*			*NULL HYPOTHESIS*	
		No Magazine	*Magazine*		*No Magazine*	*Magazine*
	Negative	0.325	0.225	*Negative*	0.325	0.325
	Positive	0.175	0.275	*Positive*	0.175	0.175

Both tables show the proportion of the total population that would appear in each cell of the table for the research hypothesis (left) and for the null hypothesis (right). For each cell, subtract the value in the null table from the value in the research table, square the result, then divide by the value in the null table. Then sum all the values in the table (as the right column in the following table shows).

		(RESEARCH CELL VALUE - NULL CELL VALUE)^2			
		NULL CELL VALUE			
O					CELL VALUES
P.					
I		*No*			0.0000
N		*Magazine*	*Magazine*		0.0000
I					0.0308
O	*Negative*	0.0000	0.0308		0.0571
N	*Positive*	0.0000	0.0571	SUM OF CELLS =	0.0494

The square root of the sum of cells yields a value of effect size or w of 0.296.

Using the same assumptions as in the example for small effect size, again refer to Table E–11. The table shows that a sample size of 95 is large enough to detect a medium effect size ($w=0.30$) at a 90-percent level of confidence, using a one-tailed Chi-Square test and the 95-percent decision rule.

The drop in sample size is dramatic, from 856 to 95. The new sample size of 95 is too small to detect a small effect size ($w=0.10$) with any degree of confidence. By contrast, a medium effect size ($w=0.30$) is so pronounced in the population that even a small-sized sample ($N=95$) can detect it at a 90-percent level of confidence.

Large Effect Size

A large effect size is suggested by the following objective.

> OBJECTIVE 4: *To increase agreement among* **Community Action** *readers that MegaTech contributes significantly to the community from 35 percent to 70 percent by December 31.*

This objective presumes powerful impact of magazine exposure on reader opinion toward MegaTech. Exposure to the magazine is hypothesized in this objective to *double* the number who have favorable opinions of MegaTech.

How large a sample is required to detect such a large effect size? To find out, state both the research and null hypotheses in contingency tables.

		RESEARCH HYPOTHESIS			NULL HYPOTHESIS	
O						
P		*No*			*No*	
I		*Magazine*	*Magazine*		*Magazine*	*Magazine*
N						
I	*Negative*	65%	30%	*Negative*	65%	65%
O	*Positive*	35%	70%	*Positive*	35%	35%
N		100%	100%		100%	100%

Plug this information into table cells, as in the preceding examples. The computed effect size ($w=0.519$) is large. Using the same assumptions as in the preceding examples, Table E–11 shows that for a large effect size ($w=0.50$), the minimum sample size needed is only 34! That means that you can be 90 percent sure of detecting a large effect size in the population from a sample of only thirty-four respondents in the sample. However, this small sample size will not detect a medium or small effect size with any degree of confidence.

When designing a research project, you must decide *before* collecting data how large an effect size you are interested in detecting. In the preceding examples, only 34 respondents (seventeen readers and seventeen nonreaders) are needed to detect a large effect size ($w=0.50$). To detect a medium ($w=0.30$) or large ($w=0.50$) effect size, a sample of 95 is sufficient. To detect small ($w=0.10$), medium ($w=0.30$), or large ($w=0.50$) effect sizes at a 90-percent level of confidence, 856 respondents are needed. A sample of 214 would detect program impact falling between the small and medium effect size ($w=0.20$). (See Table E–11).

This is essential information for planning a research project. To use power tables effectively, specify the statistical procedure, the decision rule, the level of power, and the minimum effect size you are interested in detecting. With this information, you can use Tables E–1 through E–20 (for Chi-Square tests) to determine the required sample size.

Analysis of Variance

Because the Chi-Square test is not a powerful inferential statistic, it provides a conservative basis for determining sample size. Generally, samples required for the Chi-Square procedure are larger than samples needed for more powerful statistical procedures. Instead of a simple agree/disagree statement to measure reader opinion of MegaTech, several opinion measures are combined in an index, ranging—say—from -10 (strong negative opinion) to $+10$ (strong positive opinion). This index is potentially more reliable and valid than a single measure of opinion. (See Chapter 8.)

A benchmark survey determines current levels of opinion toward Mega-Tech. Opinion among community members averages slightly less than neutral (-1.0 on a -10 to $+10$ index). Program objectives could be restated in terms of improved reader scores on the opinion index.

> OBJECTIVE 5: *To increase positive opinion among* **Community Action** *readers from* -1.0 *on the MegaTech opinion index to 6.0 by December 31.*

As with Chi Square, the effect size of the research hypothesis implicit in the objective must be computed. To do so, refer to Jacob Cohen's *Statistical Power Analysis for the Behavioral Sciences.*[2] Methods for determining sample size for analysis of variance designs are also provided in Helena Kraemer and Sue Thiemann's *How Many Subjects?*[3] However, the explanation in the latter book is more appropriate for statisticians than public relations researchers.

Table E-1 Sample Size (N) for Chi-Square Test to Detect Effect Size (w) Using Alpha = .05 and Degrees of Freedom = 1

	EFFECT SIZE (w)								
Power	.10	.20	.30	.40	.50	.60	.70	.80	.90
.25	165	41	18	10	7	5	3	3	2
.50	384	96	43	24	15	11	8	6	5
.60	490	122	54	31	20	14	10	8	6
2/3	571	142	63	36	23	16	12	9	7
.70	617	154	69	39	25	17	13	10	8
.75	694	175	77	43	28	19	14	11	9
.80	785	196	87	49	31	22	16	12	10
.85	898	224	100	56	36	25	18	14	11
.90	1051	263	117	66	42	29	21	16	13
.95	1300	325	144	81	52	36	27	20	16
.99	1837	459	204	115	73	51	37	29	23

Table E-2 Sample Size (N) for Chi-Square Test to Detect Effect Size (w) Using Alpha = .05 and Degrees of Freedom = 2

	EFFECT SIZE (w)								
Power	.10	.20	.30	.40	.50	.60	.70	.80	.90
.25	226	56	25	14	9	6	5	4	3
.50	496	124	55	31	20	14	10	8	6
.60	621	155	69	39	25	17	13	10	8
2/3	717	179	80	45	29	20	15	11	9
.70	770	193	86	48	31	21	16	12	10
.75	859	215	95	54	34	24	18	13	11
.80	964	241	107	60	39	27	20	15	12
.85	1092	273	121	68	44	30	22	17	13
.90	1265	316	141	79	51	35	26	20	16
.95	1544	386	172	97	62	43	32	24	19
.99	2140	535	238	134	86	59	44	33	26

[2]Jacob Cohen, *Statistical Power Analysis for the Behavioral Sciences,* 2nd. ed. (Hillsdale, N.J.: Lawrence Erlbaum Associates, 1988).
[3]Helena Kraemer and Sue Thiemann, *How Many Subjects?* (Beverly Hills: Sage, 1987).

Table E-3 Sample Size (N) for Chi-Square Test to Detect Effect Size (w) Using Alpha = .05 and Degrees of Freedom = 3

	EFFECT SIZE (w)								
Power	.10	.20	.30	.40	.50	.60	.70	.80	.90
.25	258	65	29	16	10	7	5	4	3
.50	576	144	64	36	23	16	12	9	7
.60	715	179	79	45	29	20	15	11	9
2/3	820	205	91	51	33	23	17	13	10
.70	879	220	98	55	35	24	18	14	11
.75	976	244	108	61	39	27	20	15	12
.80	1090	273	121	68	44	30	22	17	13
.85	1230	308	137	77	49	34	25	19	15
.90	1417	354	157	89	57	39	29	22	17
.95	1717	429	191	107	69	48	35	27	21
.99	2352	588	261	147	94	65	48	37	29

Table E-4 Sample Size (N) for Chi-Square Test to Detect Effect Size (w) Using Alpha = .05 and Degrees of Freedom = 4

	EFFECT SIZE (w)								
Power	.10	.20	.30	.40	.50	.60	.70	.80	.90
.25	308	77	34	19	12	9	6	5	4
.50	642	160	71	40	26	18	13	10	8
.60	792	198	88	50	32	22	16	12	10
2/3	911	228	101	57	36	25	19	14	11
.70	968	242	108	61	39	27	20	15	12
.75	1072	268	119	67	43	30	22	17	13
.80	1194	298	133	75	48	33	24	19	15
.85	1342	336	149	84	54	37	27	21	17
.90	1540	385	171	96	62	43	31	24	19
.95	1857	464	206	116	74	52	38	29	23
.99	2524	631	280	158	101	70	52	39	31

Table E–5 Sample Size (N) for Chi-Square Test to Detect Effect Size (w) Using Alpha = .05 and Degrees of Freedom = 5

	EFFECT SIZE (w)								
Power	.10	.20	.30	.40	.50	.60	.70	.80	.90
.25	341	85	38	21	14	9	7	5	4
.50	699	175	78	44	28	19	14	11	9
.60	859	215	95	54	34	24	18	13	11
2/3	979	245	109	61	39	27	20	15	12
.70	1045	261	116	65	42	29	21	16	13
.75	1155	289	128	72	46	32	24	18	14
.80	1283	321	143	80	51	36	26	20	16
.85	1439	360	160	90	58	40	29	22	18
.90	1647	412	183	103	66	46	34	26	20
.95	1978	494	220	124	79	55	40	31	24
.99	2673	668	297	167	107	74	55	42	33

Table E–6 Sample Size (N) for Chi-Square Test to Detect Effect Size (w) Using Alpha = .05 and Degrees of Freedom = 6

	EFFECT SIZE (w)								
Power	.10	.20	.30	.40	.50	.60	.70	.80	.90
.25	370	92	41	23	15	10	8	6	5
.50	750	188	83	47	30	21	15	12	9
.60	919	230	102	57	37	25	19	14	11
2/3	1044	261	116	65	42	29	21	16	13
.70	1114	279	124	70	45	31	23	17	14
.75	1229	307	137	77	49	34	25	19	15
.80	1362	341	151	85	54	38	28	21	17
.85	1526	381	170	95	61	42	31	24	19
.90	1742	435	194	109	70	48	36	27	22
.95	2086	521	232	130	83	58	43	33	26
.99	2805	701	312	175	112	78	57	44	35

Table E–7 Sample Size (N) for Chi-Square Test to Detect Effect Size (w) Using Alpha = .05 and Degrees of Freedom = 7

Power	EFFECT SIZE (w)								
	.10	.20	.30	.40	.50	.60	.70	.80	.90
.25	397	99	44	25	16	11	8	6	5
.50	797	199	89	50	32	22	16	12	10
.60	973	243	108	61	39	27	20	15	12
2/3	1104	276	123	69	44	31	23	17	14
.70	1177	294	131	74	47	33	24	18	15
.75	1296	324	144	81	52	36	26	20	16
.80	1435	359	159	90	57	40	29	22	18
.85	1604	401	178	100	64	45	33	25	20
.90	1828	457	203	114	73	51	37	29	23
.95	2184	546	243	136	87	61	45	34	27
.99	2925	731	325	183	117	81	60	46	36

Table E–8 Sample Size (N) for Chi-Square Test to Detect Effect Size (w) Using Alpha = .05 and Degrees of Freedom = 8

Power	EFFECT SIZE (w)								
	.10	.20	.30	.40	.50	.60	.70	.80	.90
.25	422	105	47	26	17	12	9	7	5
.50	840	210	93	53	34	23	17	13	10
.60	1024	256	114	64	41	28	21	16	13
2/3	1160	290	129	72	46	32	24	18	14
.70	1235	309	137	77	49	34	25	19	15
.75	1359	340	151	85	54	38	28	21	17
.80	1502	376	167	94	60	42	31	23	19
.85	1677	419	186	105	67	47	34	26	21
.90	1908	477	212	119	76	53	39	30	24
.95	2274	569	253	142	91	63	46	36	28
.99	3036	759	337	189	121	84	62	47	37

Table E–9 Sample Size (N) for Chi-Square Test to Detect Effect Size (w) Using Alpha = .05 and Degrees of Freedom = 9

Power	EFFECT SIZE (w)								
	.10	.20	.30	.40	.50	.60	.70	.80	.90
.25	445	111	49	28	18	12	9	7	5
.50	881	220	98	55	35	24	13	14	11
.60	1071	268	119	67	43	30	22	17	13
2/3	1212	303	135	76	48	34	25	19	15
.70	1289	322	143	81	52	36	26	20	16
.75	1417	354	157	89	57	39	29	22	17
.80	1565	391	174	98	63	43	32	24	19
.85	1745	436	194	109	70	48	36	27	22
.90	1983	496	220	124	79	55	40	31	24
.95	2359	590	262	147	94	66	48	37	29
.99	3139	785	349	196	126	87	64	49	39

Table E–10 Sample Size (N) for Chi-Square Test to Detect Effect Size (w) Using Alpha = .05 and Degrees of Freedom = 10

Power	EFFECT SIZE (w)								
	.10	.20	.30	.40	.50	.60	.70	.80	.90
.25	467	117	52	29	19	13	10	7	6
.50	919	230	102	57	37	26	19	14	11
.60	1115	279	124	60	45	31	23	17	14
2/3	1260	315	140	79	50	35	26	20	16
.70	1340	335	149	84	54	37	27	21	17
.75	1472	368	164	92	59	41	30	23	18
.80	1624	406	180	102	65	45	33	25	20
.85	1809	452	201	113	72	50	37	28	22
.90	2053	513	228	128	82	57	42	32	25
.95	2438	610	271	152	98	68	50	38	30
.99	3236	809	360	202	129	90	66	51	40

Table E–11 Sample Size (N) for Chi-Square Test to Detect Effect Size (w) Using Alpha = .10 and Degrees of Freedom = 1

				EFFECT SIZE (w)					
Power	.10	.20	.30	.40	.50	.60	.70	.80	.90
.25	91	23	10	6	4	3	2	1	1
.50	270	68	30	17	11	8	6	4	3
.60	360	90	40	23	14	10	7	6	4
2/3	430	108	48	27	17	12	9	7	5
.70	470	118	52	29	19	13	10	7	6
.75	538	134	60	34	22	15	11	8	7
.80	618	155	69	39	25	17	13	10	8
.85	719	180	80	45	29	20	15	11	9
.90	856	214	95	53	34	24	17	13	11
.95	1082	271	120	68	43	30	22	17	13
.99	1577	394	175	99	63	44	32	25	19

Table E–12 Sample Size (N) for Chi-Square Test to Detect Effect Size (w) Using Alpha = .10 and Degrees of Freedom = 2

				EFFECT SIZE (w)					
Power	.10	.20	.30	.40	.50	.60	.70	.80	.90
.25	127	32	14	8	5	4	3	2	2
.50	356	89	40	22	14	10	7	6	4
.60	465	116	52	29	19	13	9	7	6
2/3	550	137	61	34	22	15	11	9	7
.70	597	149	66	37	24	17	12	9	7
.75	677	169	75	42	27	19	14	11	8
.80	771	193	86	48	31	21	16	12	10
.85	888	222	99	55	36	25	18	14	11
.90	1046	261	116	65	42	29	21	16	13
.95	1302	326	145	81	52	36	27	20	16
.99	1856	464	206	116	74	52	38	29	23

Table E–13   Sample Size (N) for Chi-Square Test to Detect Effect Size (w) Using Alpha = .10 and Degrees of Freedom = 3

				EFFECT SIZE (w)					
Power	.10	.20	.30	.40	.50	.60	.70	.80	.90
.25	155	39	17	10	6	4	3	2	2
.50	418	104	46	26	17	12	9	7	5
.60	541	135	60	34	22	15	11	8	7
2/3	636	159	71	40	25	18	13	10	8
.70	688	172	76	43	28	19	14	11	8
.75	776	194	86	49	31	22	16	12	10
.80	880	220	98	55	35	24	18	14	11
.85	1008	252	112	63	40	28	21	16	12
.90	1180	295	131	74	47	33	24	18	15
.95	1457	364	162	91	58	40	30	23	18
.99	2051	513	228	128	82	57	42	32	25

Table E–14   Sample Size (N) for Chi-Square Test to Detect Effect Size (w) Using Alpha = .10 and Degrees of Freedom = 4

				EFFECT SIZE (w)					
Power	.10	.20	.30	.40	.50	.60	.70	.80	.90
.25	178	44	20	11	7	5	4	3	2
.50	469	117	52	29	19	13	10	7	6
.60	604	151	67	38	24	17	12	9	7
2/3	706	176	78	44	28	20	14	11	9
.70	763	191	85	48	31	21	16	12	9
.75	857	214	95	54	34	24	17	13	11
.80	968	242	108	61	39	27	20	15	12
.85	1105	276	123	69	44	31	23	17	14
.90	1288	322	143	81	52	36	26	20	16
.95	1583	396	176	99	63	44	32	25	20
.99	2209	552	245	138	88	61	45	35	27

Table E–15 Sample Size (N) for Chi-Square Test to Detect Effect Size (w) Using Alpha $= .10$ and Degrees of Freedom $= 5$

				EFFECT SIZE (w)					
Power	.10	.20	.30	.40	.50	.60	.70	.80	.90
.25	198	50	22	12	8	6	4	3	2
.50	514	128	57	32	21	14	10	8	6
.60	658	164	73	41	26	18	13	10	8
2/3	766	192	85	48	31	21	16	12	9
.70	827	207	92	52	33	23	17	13	10
.75	927	232	103	58	37	26	19	14	11
.80	1045	261	116	65	42	29	21	16	13
.85	1189	297	132	74	48	33	24	19	15
.90	1382	345	154	86	55	38	28	22	17
.95	1691	423	188	106	68	47	35	26	21
.99	2344	586	260	147	94	65	48	37	29

Table E–16 Sample Size (N) for Chi-Square Test to Detect Effect Size (w) Using Alpha $= .10$ and Degrees of Freedom $= 6$

				EFFECT SIZE (w)					
Power	.10	.20	.30	.40	.50	.60	.70	.80	.90
.25	216	54	24	14	9	6	4	3	3
.50	553	138	61	35	22	15	11	9	7
.60	706	176	78	44	28	20	14	11	9
2/3	820	205	91	51	33	23	17	13	10
.70	884	221	98	55	35	25	18	14	11
.75	990	247	110	62	40	27	20	15	12
.80	1113	278	124	70	45	31	23	17	14
.85	1264	316	140	79	51	35	26	20	16
.90	1465	366	163	92	59	41	30	23	18
.95	1787	447	199	112	71	50	36	28	22
.99	2465	616	274	154	99	68	50	39	30

Table E-17 Sample Size (N) for Chi-Square Test to Detect Effect Size (w) Using Alpha = .10 and Degrees of Freedom = 7

	EFFECT SIZE (w)								
Power	.10	.20	.30	.40	.50	.60	.70	.80	.90
.25	233	58	26	15	9	6	5	4	3
.50	590	147	66	37	24	16	12	9	7
.60	750	187	83	47	30	21	15	12	9
2/3	870	217	97	54	35	24	18	14	11
.70	936	234	104	59	37	26	19	15	12
.75	1047	262	116	65	42	29	21	16	13
.80	1175	294	131	73	47	33	24	18	15
.85	1332	333	148	83	53	37	27	21	16
.90	1541	385	171	96	62	43	31	24	19
.95	1875	469	208	117	75	52	38	29	23
.99	2574	644	286	161	103	72	53	40	32

Table E-18 Sample Size (N) for Chi-Square Test to Detect Effect Size (w) Using Alpha = .10 and Degrees of Freedom = 8

	EFFECT SIZE (w)								
Power	.10	.20	.30	.40	.50	.60	.70	.80	.90
.25	249	62	28	16	10	7	5	4	3
.50	624	156	69	39	25	17	13	10	8
.60	791	198	88	49	32	22	16	12	10
2/3	916	229	102	57	37	25	19	14	11
.70	.985	246	109	62	39	27	20	15	12
.75	1099	275	122	69	44	31	22	17	14
.80	1232	308	137	77	49	34	25	19	15
.85	1395	349	155	87	56	39	28	22	17
.90	1611	403	179	101	64	45	33	25	20
.95	1955	489	217	122	78	54	40	31	24
.99	2676	669	297	167	107	74	55	42	33

Table E–19 Sample Size (N) for Chi-Square Test to Detect Effect Size (w) Using Alpha = .10 and Degrees of Freedom = 9

Power	EFFECT SIZE (w)								
	.10	.20	.30	.40	.50	.60	.70	.80	.90
.25	263	66	29	16	11	7	5	4	3
.50	655	164	73	41	26	18	13	10	8
.60	829	207	92	52	33	23	17	13	10
2/3	958	240	106	60	38	27	20	15	12
.70	1030	258	114	64	41	29	21	16	13
.75	1148	287	128	72	46	32	23	18	14
.80	1286	322	143	90	51	36	26	20	16
.85	1454	364	162	91	58	40	30	23	18
.90	1677	419	186	105	67	47	34	26	21
.95	2031	508	226	127	81	56	41	32	25
.99	2770	692	308	173	111	77	57	43	34

Table E–20 Sample Size (N) for Chi-Square Test to Detect Effect Size (w) Using Alpha = .10 and Degrees of Freedom = 10

Power	EFFECT SIZE (w)								
	.10	.20	.30	.40	.50	.60	.70	.80	.90
.25	277	69	31	17	11	8	6	4	3
.50	685	171	76	43	27	19	14	11	8
.60	865	216	96	54	35	24	18	14	11
2/3	999	250	111	62	40	28	20	16	12
.70	1073	268	119	67	43	30	22	17	13
.75	1195	299	133	75	48	33	24	19	15
.80	1337	334	149	84	53	37	27	21	17
.85	1510	377	168	94	60	42	31	24	19
.90	1739	435	193	109	70	48	35	27	21
.95	2102	525	234	131	84	58	43	33	26
.99	2858	715	318	179	114	79	58	45	35

Table E–21 Sample Size (N) to Detect Effect Size (r) Using One-Tailed Alpha = .01 (Two-Tailed Alpha = .02)

Power	EFFECT SIZE (r)								
	.10	.20	.30	.40	.50	.60	.70	.80	.90
.25	273	68	31	18	12	9	7	5	4
.50	540	134	59	31	20	14	10	7	5
.60	663	164	72	39	24	16	11	8	6
2/3	757	187	81	44	28	18	13	9	6
.70	809	200	87	48	29	19	13	9	6
.75	897	221	96	53	32	21	14	10	7
.80	998	246	107	58	36	23	16	11	7
.85	1126	277	120	65	40	26	17	12	8
.90	1296	319	138	75	45	29	20	13	8
.95	1585	389	168	91	55	35	23	16	10
.99	2154	529	228	123	74	47	31	20	13

Table E–22 Sample Size (N) to Detect Effect Size (r) Using One-Tailed Alpha = .05 (Two-Tailed Alpha = .10)

Power	EFFECT SIZE (r)								
	.10	.20	.30	.40	.50	.60	.70	.80	.90
.25	99	24	12	8	6	4	4	3	3
.50	277	69	30	17	11	8	6	5	4
.60	368	92	40	22	14	10	7	5	4
2/3	430	107	47	26	16	11	8	6	4
.70	470	117	51	28	18	12	8	6	4
.75	537	133	58	32	20	13	9	7	5
.80	618	153	68	37	22	15	10	7	5
.85	727	180	78	43	26	17	12	8	6
.90	864	213	93	50	31	20	13	9	6
.95	1105	272	118	64	39	25	16	11	7
.99	1585	389	168	91	55	35	23	15	10

Table E-23 Sample Size (N) to Detect Effect Size (r) Using One-Tailed Alpha = .10 (Two-Tailed Alpha = .20)

	EFFECT SIZE (r)								
Power	.10	.20	.30	.40	.50	.60	.70	.80	.90
.25	39	11	6	4	3	3	3	3	3
.50	165	42	19	11	7	5	4	3	3
.60	236	59	27	15	10	7	5	4	3
2/3	293	73	33	18	12	8	6	4	4
.70	326	81	36	20	13	9	6	5	4
.75	383	95	42	23	14	10	7	5	4
.80	450	112	49	27	17	11	8	6	4
.85	536	133	58	32	19	13	9	6	4
.90	655	162	71	39	24	16	11	7	5
.95	864	213	93	50	31	20	13	9	6
.99	1296	319	138	75	45	29	19	13	8

APPENDIX F

HOW TO CONSTRUCT SAMPLES FOR RANDOM DIGIT DIALING

Random digit dialing (RDD) is a method of sampling residential households with telephones such that every household has an equal chance of being included in the sample. The most simplified form of random digit dialing randomly samples prefixes or central office codes (COC) from a listing of such numbers assigned to the geographic area of study. The *prefix* is the three-digit number to the left of the hyphen in a seven-digit telephone number. The listing of prefixes is obtained from the telephone company or from the most recent edition of the telephone directory. The phone number *suffix*, the four-digit number to the right of the hyphen in a seven-digit phone number, is randomly assigned from a list of random numbers. (See Appendix G.)

Why RDD?

Random digit dialing is perhaps the most inexpensive way to randomly sample residences with telephones in a specified geographic a. a. Its primary advantage over face-to-face interviews for a geographically defined area is speed and cost. A random sample of several hundred households can be conducted in less than a week using random digit dialing. A similar sample of face-to-face interviews in the same geographic area would take several weeks or months to complete. Random digit dialing is inexpensive, when compared to face-to-face interviews. Actual direct interviewer costs of conducting a telephone interview range from $5 to $10 an interview. However, field services which conduct surveys for you will charge you more than these direct interviewer costs. Face-to-face interviews may cost as much as ten times that of RDD interviews.

Random digit dialing samples include only households with telephones. About 95 percent of all American households have telephones, so the exclusion of houses without telephones is not a serious limitation in most studies.[1] However, somewhere between 15 and 40 percent of households with phones do not have those numbers listed in telephone directories.[2] This is a more serious limitation. Some of these numbers are new connects added since the directory was published. Others are numbers intentionally not listed in public directories.

Are the people with unlisted numbers the same as those who appear in telephone directories? No! Households with unlisted numbers include disproportionately high numbers of people who have recently moved, who have lower income levels, who rent their homes, who are young, who are members of ethnic minorities, who live in urban areas, and who do not affiliate with voluntary organizations.[3] Telephone directories are *biased* sample frames for most research purposes. Because the sample frame is biased, meticulous random sampling from public directories nonetheless generates a biased sample.

The bias in public telephone directories is corrected through the assignment of randomly generated four-digit suffixes to specific sets of prefixes serving the geographic area of study. Because the suffix is random, unlisted numbers have an equal chance with listed numbers to be included in the sample. The sample is random.

The prefix or COC is assigned by telephone companies to designated geographic areas. The most recent telephone directory will provide a listing of prefixes and the geographic areas to which these prefixes are assigned. Take all the prefixes assigned to the geographic area you wish to study and randomly sample prefixes from the list.[4] Then sample four-digit suffixes from the list of random numbers in Appendix G. For example, here is a list of prefixes assigned to the La Jolla, California, area, a coastal community in San Diego:

[1]The 5 percent of households without telephones tend to be in isolated rural areas or in nonwhite inner-city households. These isolated individuals are underrepresented in all phone surveys. However, as indicated, they make up only 5 percent of the population. See David A. Leuthold and Raymond T. Scheele, "Patterns of Bias in Samples Based on Telephone Directories," *Public Opinion Quarterly,* Vol. 35, pp. 249–57.

[2]James H. Frey, *Survey Research By Telephone* (Beverly Hills, Calif.: Sage Publications, 1983).

[3]For more details of systematic biases in listed telephone numbers and public telephone directories, see Clyle L. Rich, "Is Random Digit Dialing Really Necessary?" *Journal of Marketing Research,* Vol. 14, pp. 300–305.

[4]A more efficient method is simply to assign random suffixes to blocks of prefixes. For example, to generate a sample of 1,000 La Jolla numbers from the twenty prefixes listed, fifty random suffixes are assigned to the 270 prefix, to the 272 prefix, and so forth. However, your sample frame is now nonrandom. If interviewers start at the top of the list and quit interviews upon 200 completions, you systematically overrepresent prefixes at the top of the list and underrepresent prefixes at the bottom of the list. This problem can be reduced by setting limits on the number of interviews completed per prefix. This problem does not occur when prefixes are selected at random.

1. 270   4. 272   7. 273   10. 274   13. 450   15. 452   18. 453
2. 454   5. 455   8. 456   11. 457   14. 458   17. 459   20. 483
3. 488   6. 534   9. 539   12. 546   15. 581   18. 587

Each prefix is numbered so that a table of random numbers (Appendix G) can be used to randomly select prefixes from this sample frame. The four-digit suffix is taken directly from the random numbers table in Appendix G. The prefix and suffix are then combined to create the sample element, the phone number actually called:

LA JOLLA PREFIXES	RANDOM SUFFIXES	SAMPLE ELEMENT
270	8578	270-8578
450	3821	450-3821
587	2180	587-2180
272	4372	272-4372
450	7327	450-7327

You continue this technique until you have constructed your full sample. Keep in mind that this sample includes disconnected numbers, business and government numbers, numbers with no answers despite repeated attempts, numbers of ineligible households (not part of your target public), and numbers where potential respondents refused to be interviewed. Therefore, you need to construct a sample much larger than your final sample of completed interviews. You should make your initial sample about *five times larger* than your desired final sample size. For example, if you wanted 200 completed interviews in the La Jolla area, you should construct an initial sample of 1,000 telephone numbers.

Note that the 450 prefix appears twice in the left column. That's because the prefixes are taken at random (with replacement) from a list of twenty prefixes assigned to the La Jolla area by Pacific Telephone. The same prefixes will appear over and over again in the left column. However, it's less likely that a four-digit suffix will appear twice.

Increasing Efficiency

The preceding example is designed for simplicity. You can construct a random digit dialing sample like the preceding one with a most recent telephone directory for the area you want to survey and Appendix G. However, there are two issues to consider. One issue is selection of prefixes. The other issue is the assignment of blocks of suffixes to business and government organizations and the assignment of other blocks of suffixes to nobody at all.

Some prefixes are connected to more homes than are other prefixes. This is because some prefixes are assigned to densely populated or rapidly growing areas, while other prefixes are assigned to sparsely populated areas or areas with declining populations. Some prefixes serve areas with many business and government phones. For this reason, some prefixes will result in a higher rate of successful residential interviews than will others. For this reason, Frey recommends you complete the same number of interviews within each prefix.[5] To do so, set a limit on the number of completed interviews per prefix. Once that limit is reached, delete all remaining numbers in your sample that have that prefix.

Telephone companies assign telephone numbers to subscribers in blocks of 100 or 1,000 numbers. Further, businesses and government agencies are often assigned entire 100 or 1,000 number blocks. These regularities allow you to develop more efficient RDD samples by eliminating blocks of numbers that are assigned to business or government. You can also eliminate blocks of numbers that are not connected to any phones at all.

To find out where these blocks of ineligible numbers occur, you need to use one of over a dozen available commercial criss-cross or cross-reference directories.[6] These directories are reorganizations of publicly listed phone numbers, so they have the same biases as the regular telephone directory. However, despite these biases, criss-cross directories usually provide a listing of phone numbers sequentially. Within each prefix, you can examine this listing to identify blocks of numbers assigned to business and government as well as unused blocks of numbers. These blocks can be listed on a sheet so that—when an RDD sample element falls within that range—you can eliminate it from the sample.

The result of these efforts is to make your sample more efficient. Interviewers won't waste time calling a number in a range or block of numbers that has no residential connections. At the same time, this technique can introduce biases. Criss-cross directories include many inaccuracies and become dated quickly. Always try to obtain the most recent edition of criss-cross directories. Banks of numbers not assigned at the time of publication may be assigned to new residences at the time of your survey. If you use simple RDD sampling, this problem is eliminated. Since the entire suffix is random, these new listings have an equal chance of being included in the sample. A more efficient list may systematically eliminate these new numbers if they fall within a bank of numbers that were not assigned when the criss-cross directory was published.

Screening or Qualifying Questions

Telephone companies assign prefixes to rough geographic areas, but the geographic areas selected by the phone company do not necessarily correspond to the geographic area you want to study. Use a criss-cross directory and a de-

---

[5]Frey, *Survey Research By Telephone*, p. 69.

[6]These directories are available at university and public libraries. The publishers and titles vary according to city and state. Some sparsely populated areas do not have such directories. A microfiche listing of telephone directories and criss-cross directories available in the United States is distributed by Bell and Howell, Inc. *Phonofiche: Current Telephone Directories on Microfiche* (Wooster, Ohio: Micro Photo Division).

tailed street map to more precisely locate the geographic areas where prefixes are assigned.

Because geographic assignment of phone prefixes is rough at best, your instrument should include screening or qualifying questions at the beginning of the questionnaire to insure that the potential respondent lives in the appropriate geographic area and meets other requirements of your target public. The Postal Service ZIP code is an efficient screening questions for geographic area.

Other Approaches

There are a number of other techniques for generating quasi-random samples from phone directories. These are discussed in a clear, detailed manner in James H. Frey's *Survey Research By Telephone*.[7] These techniques involve systematic or random samples from phone directories, then changing one, two or three of the last digits.

Add-a-Digit

For example, the add-a-digit technique involves randomly or systematically sampling a phone number from a directory, then adding a number between 0 and 9 (selected at random) to the sampled phone number. Suppose you draw a systematic sample of 200 phone numbers from the directory serving the geographic area you wish to survey. The first number is 265–3262. The digit you randomly selected to add to all your numbers is 4. So, 265–3262 + 4 = 265–3266. This new number is your sampling element. Repeat this process for every number in your systematic sample.

These are both advantages and disadvantages to techniques that involve samples from telephone directories. The advantage is that such techniques are more efficient. More of your attempted calls will result in completed interviews. That's because numbers you sample from the directory are from banks of numbers that are connected to phones. Since your sample element (directory number plus a digit) is next to a listed number, it is more likely to be connected to a phone. The disadvantage is that these techniques introduce systematic biases of unknown proportions. If new banks of numbers have been assigned since the directory was published, this sampling technique eliminates or underrepresents these numbers. A rule of thumb is: The closer your sampling element is to a directory-listed number, the more biased your sample becomes.

Changing Multiple Digits

You could reduce this source of bias by changing the last two or last three digits in the directory-listed phone number. For example, you decide to add four

[7]This book provides a detailed analysis of all types of telephone surveys and compares phone surveys to other methods of collecting data.

to the last (seventh) digit. If the sum is greater than nine, simply count 10 as 0, 11 as 1, and so forth. You decide to add seven to the sixth digit and one to the fifth digit. For example, take the number 265–7442. Add the preceding numbers to the appropriate digits.

original:	2	6	5	–	7	4	4	2
plus:						+1	+7	+4
equals:	2	6	5	–	7	5	1	6

The resulting number, 265–7516, is not very close to the number in the directory. Therefore, the sampling element reflects less bias than does a sampling element where only one digit is changed. However, the new number is less efficient because it runs a greater risk of falling into a bank of numbers not assigned to residences.

For these reasons, the simple RDD sample—where all four digits of the suffix are randomly assigned to a prefix selected at random from the available prefixes—introduces the least bias. Simple RDD samples require only convenient resources: a current telephone directory and a table of random numbers. However, the simple RDD sample is not very efficient. Many of the numbers in the sample are business and government phones. Many others are in banks of numbers that have not been assigned to phones.

APPENDIX G

━━━━━━━━━━━━━━━━━━━━━━━━━━━━━━━━

HOW TO USE A TABLE
OF RANDOM NUMBERS

Table G–1 is a table of random numbers, meaning that there is no pattern or system to the numbers or any combination of them. These numbers are useful in generating random samples from sample frames or lists.

To use Table G–1, first determine the number of elements in your sample frame. Suppose your sample frame is a list of employees at a major corporation. You wish to sample 200 employees for an internal communication survey. Your sample frame contains 8,500 names or *elements*. You use Table G–1 to generate random numbers between 1 and 8,500. Each number corresponds to a numbered name on the list. (However, the elements need not be numbered. You simply count down the list to the appropriate name.)

Enter Table G–1 at any point. Think of a number between 1 and __*. That's the *row* where you will start. Think of a number between 1 and __**. That's the *column* where you will start. If you thought of row 27 and column 5, the corresponding number in the table is: 0958. This number selects your first sampling element. That's name 958 on your list of 8,500 employees.

You proceed up or down the column, taking each four-digit random number. It does not matter which way you go, as long as you are consistent and don't change directions in the middle of sample selection.

You decide to go *up* the column. When you reach the top, you decide you will go *down* the next column on the *right*. Again, your choices are arbitrary. But you stick to your choices, once you decide.

Returning to row 27, column 5, the number above it is: 2614. This is your second sampling element. You go up the column, taking each random number, as follows: 2087, 475, 2270, 6276, 5503.

Table G–1 Random Numbers

4692	9566	7064	0180	3876	2984	1649	0598	3469	8451
6486	2286	9410	5657	0016	7431	2637	9288	5673	3221
9085	9033	1898	1843	9694	9578	2126	0485	0402	0613
4795	1333	2144	6822	3344	1576	0858	7895	6209	3401
7482	8519	6828	3995	7955	0381	3638	5546	3213	2170
0078	5242	9192	9570	4583	5270	6833	5272	0593	2818
2072	8962	6543	0073	5844	5328	5873	4222	4090	4058
7019	7453	7746	9837	3420	6954	2750	2356	3511	4912
0039	6300	0732	8513	5550	1358	3519	9948	0223	2216
5309	6402	9991	8562	4541	0064	5796	5084	4653	8118
3573	1470	4080	2756	4260	2406	6261	1163	3795	7580
9634	5527	7636	3036	8157	4395	8704	5876	9860	0410
6276	1237	4161	9411	8789	1304	1997	6090	9681	3265
9305	0133	7390	9308	7023	6224	5353	6622	1090	4055
2008	7392	2442	8311	0791	8806	7015	8681	0140	3054
5749	9852	3493	7320	4581	1512	9287	3794	4448	8346
0962	9661	1288	0045	6951	7111	6037	1293	0696	3331
4635	1780	0631	0508	8017	6193	0195	5828	2123	4219
7825	1482	7888	0546	6959	4654	1251	4861	6035	7533
3149	1852	8490	7308	9519	1207	2762	6164	1302	7611
2287	1290	4430	0755	5503	4873	9843	5324	5849	4100
3480	1006	1761	1160	6276	2489	6676	3238	4171	9460
9033	2524	8100	6608	2270	6204	4003	3618	4822	6467
2815	5179	0129	0499	0475	0980	6626	7919	5704	7753
3621	1088	9043	1947	2087	0916	5682	2644	3072	3341
5310	8281	8764	9301	2614	2299	6351	4735	7280	3133
8019	0579	3998	4220	0958	2770	2454	4000	7353	2246
7335	5907	4393	4945	8330	8381	4265	1804	0126	4860
4156	8760	2410	3780	6254	6752	9869	8578	7747	1718
2193	7693	0823	4592	4066	4562	2667	1315	5178	7622
5468	2822	0217	0312	6414	5052	8867	1068	7692	8942
5819	3327	6490	0431	0760	5528	4995	0454	8375	1108
0394	4950	8354	8503	4875	4856	5385	1154	5626	6109
9152	7495	4833	9648	4347	0966	9685	1410	0655	0003
2370	2332	2763	8043	0075	8350	0360	3526	4985	0406
8131	9886	4290	4432	5767	5564	0178	1370	7953	3996
9834	7154	4378	3619	5449	2725	9727	7870	4207	3692
5188	8297	1970	0956	9010	4908	2521	1209	7773	6225
6606	9136	4916	9436	0165	4429	8874	6730	4133	1772
3088	5294	4449	0853	5991	7314	2051	6359	1025	9978
2875	7978	6624	5475	7858	0400	6227	0992	2941	3308
8271	8715	9057	1393	6195	5833	2147	4341	8435	4533
3147	6839	8429	2003	7994	8576	4615	0430	7626	4240
0429	7000	7982	3516	4310	3903	9997	1093	9693	8325
9610	6658	5020	2456	7758	4899	3725	3480	0380	5503

4246	3586	8410	3158	0022	9961	7789	7551	9487	4794
9452	3371	6083	5272	9339	0303	8245	3581	8386	3036
4101	6910	2531	1258	8018	7445	2710	9654	7504	2377
4862	7915	6306	3889	9923	0727	7863	9170	3834	7776
0611	0410	7529	3751	7987	4793	6947	8339	8430	4509
3025	6229	5378	6744	1701	7107	7266	3686	5660	7533
2523	5594	1578	4617	5441	7687	9544	1955	9629	6129
9250	7275	1856	5382	6142	5565	0805	7627	4866	6686
3913	0673	7594	7827	7120	4207	2764	1177	1363	2917
3813	3919	2577	6489	9177	8244	1702	9613	2297	1339
4674	1976	1607	5390	2432	8263	0547	7586	0912	8164
7551	0115	1053	6366	6061	0162	8790	2557	4512	9916
5063	1423	6342	6565	5809	2652	9988	2297	1965	8888
4298	9468	5950	1480	4755	9257	2394	1201	0858	7269
9951	6487	4792	4441	3310	0779	3746	6710	2156	2510
9906	5014	1179	5121	0463	5291	0064	7048	7599	8478
3500	1731	8506	0514	1175	7603	5371	2334	7774	8104
9876	2989	1673	4079	1503	8579	0880	3006	6758	1147
1216	2184	0151	5609	1024	8725	0360	4152	1243	0822
3966	7808	7649	9975	7235	1660	4406	1259	1151	8733
7275	7897	9967	0947	8961	4664	1300	5105	7256	3637
3667	4440	1430	2005	3007	8637	9919	1955	0257	2387
6164	0675	1354	5374	8599	0352	7236	2287	0664	8172
3841	2813	0794	6325	2107	1640	2429	1998	7969	8454
4004	7377	2368	7945	8959	9651	1239	9799	5730	1008
5520	8704	7755	8633	1149	4348	3472	4716	9062	1418
6317	6443	5199	9599	4729	6003	0496	3583	2146	0582
0890	3055	7002	2368	7319	2702	2739	8548	5721	2212
7791	1311	7033	6273	5597	7842	7193	4573	4595	0332
7138	1799	8221	5965	2806	7636	4915	6930	5134	6776
8112	0416	0060	8903	6250	8607	8520	8707	2768	8694
6453	5874	6101	2864	4797	5092	9688	8301	9488	6047
1969	7196	1465	3429	6376	6736	6663	1351	9108	6023
1220	0329	1500	5479	6003	1749	6098	5971	5963	9046
0092	0787	0663	5666	8810	5160	0032	0011	8033	8772
5591	5312	2041	6310	0781	8758	6771	7461	4036	2536
3162	6913	8795	3834	7149	3497	4838	9672	4469	1577
2738	6668	6948	1473	9718	9074	6478	6622	2970	2828
2747	5464	4677	8866	0441	1435	2030	3129	9248	2972
7214	6550	3856	7417	5069	3953	1495	4829	9623	4225
0356	6634	6151	4361	8533	5021	5588	9046	9464	7178
3873	7971	1588	5292	1944	8339	6551	5736	2286	8157
3142	6189	2050	4479	2252	9239	4802	5742	6069	5825
5231	5385	1781	1884	3023	1844	1575	8351	2865	8556
2638	1168	4446	3960	7157	1270	2453	1494	2323	4593

6572	9592	0320	2078	1493	1696	8335	9659	6902	6240
8559	8276	7486	6664	3866	2935	1405	9376	7365	7933
3898	9346	4713	2171	2584	0274	6845	0334	0898	9343
9700	2110	7278	8747	4216	2187	5163	5670	6329	0252
2989	2300	6977	0993	4194	5823	2099	4097	7214	8429
4252	5490	7305	4508	1146	7456	4638	8671	9464	6552
7615	1059	1214	8424	2605	4880	4254	9248	4851	5987
7289	1929	5748	7972	4720	6580	6509	9275	8732	4143
1821	3332	6514	0553	1370	8579	0254	6748	9844	8456
7137	8665	6933	1400	9352	7243	7323	0847	4088	8419

The next number, 9519, is larger than the 8,500 names in the sample frame. In such cases, simply skip that number and take the next number in your sequence. In this case, skip 9519 and take 6959. Continue until you have selected 200 random numbers from the table. Each random number you selected identifies a sampling element in your sample frame of 8,500 names.

AN EXAMPLE

Appendix F involves selection of four digit suffixes for constructing a random digit dialing sample. These random suffixes are assigned to prefixes that serve the geographic area you wish to survey. Suppose you have three prefixes that serve your geographic area: 235, 237, and 488. You wish to assign ten random suffixes to each prefix.

You think of one number between 1 and __* and another number between 1 and __**. You think of 17 and 3 respectively. This identifies your start-point in Table G–1 as row 17, column 3. You decide you will go *down* the column and then *up* the next column to the *right*, zig-zagging down and up the page. But you are consistent in your pattern.

Enter the table at row 17, column 3. Go down the column, assigning the four digits or each random number to the three prefixes above. These are the numbers you get:

235–1288	237–3998	488–4378
235–0631	237–4393	488–1970
235–7888	237–2410	488–4916
235–8490	237–0823	488–4449
235–4430	237–0217	488–6624
235–1761	237–6490	488–9057
235–8100	237–8354	488–8429
235–0129	237–4833	488–7982
235–9043	237–2763	488–5020
235–8764	237–4290	488–8410

Try it! You now have generated an RDD sample of thirty, with equal numbers of random phone numbers within each prefix.

APPENDIX H

HOW TO COMPUTE RESPONSE, COMPLETION, REFUSAL, AND NONCONTACT RATES

All probability sampling and all inferential statistics assume that 100 percent of respondents in a sample complete the questionnaire. Nearly all survey research in public relations—and other areas as well—involves data collected from less than 100 percent of samples. For these reasons, you need to account for all sample members who do not complete a questionnaire.

Nonparticipants in your sample represent a source of bias. Under worst circumstances, a large number of nonparticipants makes a convenience sample out of an otherwise rigorous probability sample. You should provide information on nonparticipants as standard practice whenever you discuss or report research findings.

In this appendix, you learn how to account for sample members who do not participate in surveys. You learn how to compute and interpret rates or indicators of the representativeness of your final sample. These rates are the response rate, the completion rate, the refusal rate, and the noncontact rate.

TYPES OF NONPARTICIPATION

There are many sources of nonparticipation of sample members in research. Some people don't want to participate in your study. Others can't be reached. Still others didn't belong in your sample in the first place. Some types of nonparticipation are more significant as sources of sample bias than others. For example, members of your original sample may not qualify as members of the community in a community relations survey. You introduce no bias when you elect to drop them from your sample. On the other hand, if individuals hostile to your organization are refusing to participate more often than those friendly to your organization, systematic bias is introduced in your final sample. Since the nature of nonparticipation is important for analyzing bias in the final sample, you need to tally the reason for nonparticipation for each member of your original sample.

Samples within Samples

To make sense of different measures of participation, a distinction is drawn between three samples involved in every survey. The *original* sample is the sample as it is originally drawn from the sample frame. Sample frames are rarely perfect reflections of the universe you want to study. The sample frame may *exclude* some members of the population you are studying. This is a limitation you should report with your findings. The sample frame may also *include* elements that are not members of the study population. This latter category of sample elements is eliminated. The *valid* sample (also called the *eligible* sample) is the original sample, less all ineligible sample members. The valid sample is a subset of the original sample. Not all valid sample members will participate. Some will refuse while others cannot be reached. The *final* sample is the valid sample, less all respondents who refuse to participate or cannot be reached. The final sample is a subset of the valid sample. These different conceptualizations of the sample are illustrated in Figure H–1. These different forms of the sample are used to compute the response rate, the completion rate, the refusal rate, and the noncontact rate.

Modes of Observation

The technique used to collect data also affects the form that nonparticipation takes. In mailed surveys, for example, some questionnaires are returned because the sample member has moved and left no forwarding address. In phone surveys, some telephone numbers are disconnected without referral to a new number. In self-administered group surveys, some questionnaires are too illegible or incomplete to be analyzed. The tracking system you develop to monitor participation in a mailed survey differs from a similar system used in a telephone survey. Different tracking systems are shown below for different data collection techniques.

COMPLETION RATE

The completion rate is easy to compute, but is of limited use. Here is the formula for computing the completion rate in percentage form:

$$\text{Completion Rate} = \frac{\text{Completed Questionnaires}}{\text{Original Sample Size}} \times 100$$

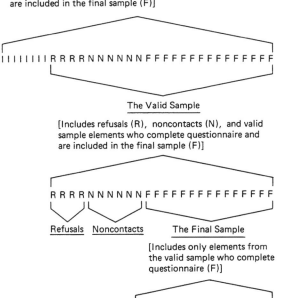

The Original Sample

[Includes ineligible elements (I), elegible elements that refuse to participate (R), eligible elements that cannot be contacted (N), and eligible elements who complete a questionnaire and are included in the final sample (F)]

I I I I I I I R R R R N N N N N N F F F F F F F F F F F F F F F

The Valid Sample

[Includes refusals (R), noncontacts (N), and valid sample elements who complete questionnaire and are included in the final sample (F)]

R R R R N N N N N N F F F F F F F F F F F F F F F

Refusals Noncontacts   The Final Sample

[Includes only elements from the valid sample who complete questionnaire (F)]

F F F F F F F F F F F F F F F

Figure H-1 An illustration of the original, valid, and final sample.

This rate is a useful planning tool, because the completion rate tells you how large your original sample has to be in order to have a designated number of completed questionnaires at the end of data collection. To determine the original sample size, divide the number of completed questionnaires you need by the completion rate (in its proportional or decimal form):

$$\text{Original Sample Size} = \frac{\text{Completed Questionnaires Needed}}{\text{Completion Rate (in decimal form)}}$$

Typically, random digit dialing samples post completion rates of about 20 percent, depending on qualifier questions.

For example, you use Appendix E to determine the proper sample size to detect a given effect of a public relations program on a target public. You determine you need a sample of 400 respondents. However, this is the *final* sample size, the number of interviews you have when data collection is complete. If you know from past studies—using the same data collection technique—that a 20 percent completion rate is likely, then you draw an original sample of 2,000 (400/0.20 = 2000) to get 400 completed questionnaires.

Because the completion rate includes both eligible and ineligible respondents in the formula, this rate does not indicate the representativeness of the final sample size. To assess the representativeness of the final sample, the valid sample is used as a base for computing the response, refusal, and noncontact rate.

THE RESPONSE RATE

The response rate is the percentage of valid or eligible sample elements that complete the questionnaire. The response rate is expressed as a percentage in the formula:

$$\text{Response Rate} = \frac{\text{Completed Questionnaires}}{\text{Valid Sample Size}} \times 100$$

As indicated, the valid sample is the original sample less ineligible elements. Some elements in the original sample are clearly ineligible. Typically, random digit dialing samples include business and government phones, as well as disconnected numbers. These sample elements are ineligible. Other sample elements include phones that ring but nobody answers after repeated attempts on different days. Are these sample elements ineligible? Perhaps. A member of your target public may live at that number, but is out of town for a few days. On the other hand, the person or persons at that number may not be members of the target public. You simply don't know. You may decide to call a single number at different times of the day for three days before classifying the number as invalid. A more conservative strategy is to increase the number of attempts before treating an unanswered number as invalid. Still more conservative is to treat these numbers as noncontacts, a valid sample elements that you were unable to reach.

Typical Response Rates

The response rates of surveys vary by the technique of data collection. Mailed surveys generally post lower response rates than phone and face-to-face surveys. Babbie describes 50 percent response rates for mailed surveys as adequate, 60 percent response rates as good, and 70 percent response rates as very good. Babbie states that properly designed and executed face-to-face surveys should post response rates of 80 to 85 percent.[1]

In a study of ninety-three published surveys in social science journals, Yu and Cooper found that the average response rate for face-to-face interviews was 82 percent while phone surveys posted a 72 percent average response rate. Mail surveys posted a 47 percent response rate average.[2] Other researchers analyzing

[1]Earl Babbie, *The Practice of Social Research*, 5th ed. (Belmont, Calif.: Wadsworth Publishing, 1989), p. 242.
[2]J. Yu and H. Cooper, "A Quantitative Review of Research Design Effects on Response Rates to Questionnaires," *Journal of Marketing Research*, Vol. 20, No. 1 (1983), pp. 36–44.

multiple surveys have generally found a similar pattern. Face-to-face interviews post the highest response rates, followed by phone surveys and mailed surveys.[3]

Improving Response Rates

Response rates can be improved by vigorous pursuit of nonrespondents. While some field services even attempt to reinterview respondents who initially refuse to participate, most efforts focus on *noncontacts,* sample elements that neither refuse nor complete the survey. Yu and Cooper found that financial and nonfinancial rewards for participation boosted response rates.[4] Precontact or prearrangements with potential respondents through the mail or by phone also improve response rates. Another tactic is to switch the mode of data collection for nonparticipants. If an initial mailed questionnaire is ignored, a telephone follow-up may be more successful. The prestige (in the respondents' eyes) of the sponsoring organization and the nature or content of the survey also affect response rates. However, these factors are not easily changed by the researcher. The length of the survey, measured either by the minute (interviews) or the page (self-administered), negatively affects response rates.[5]

REFUSAL RATE

The *refusal rate* is the percentage of the valid sample elements who refuse to participate in the survey. Refusals are either immediate or delayed. An *immediate* refusal occurs at the beginning of the phone or face-to-face interview. With mailed surveys, immediate refusals occur when the potential respondent opens the envelope, looks at the questionnaire, and *decides* not to fill it out. A *delayed* refusal occurs shortly after the interview begins, when the telephone respondent hangs up or the face-to-face respondent terminates the interview. In mailed or group self-administered surveys, the delayed refusal is indicated by an incomplete questionnaire. You must decide how much of a partially completed questionnaire is useful. You can code the unanswered items as missing values if the questions answered are important to your analysis. Otherwise, simply discard partially completed questionnaires and treat the respondent as a refusal.

The refusal rate is computed as follows:

$$\text{Refusal Rate} = \frac{\text{Refusals} + \text{Incomplete Questionnaires}}{\text{Valid Sample Size}} \times 100$$

[3]James H. Frey, *Survey Research by Telephone* (Beverly Hills, Calif.: Sage Publications, 1983), p. 39.
[4]Yu and Cooper, op. cit.
[5]The factors affecting response rates for different modes of data collection are discussed in detail in Kenneth D. Bailey, *Methods of Social Research,* 3rd ed. (New York: Free Press, 1987).

Refusal rates for mailed surveys are difficult to determine, because you often cannot separate refusals (where the potential respondent decides not to participate) from noncontacts (where the potential respondent does not receive the questionnaire or tosses it as junk mail without any knowledge of its content). Only a minority of those not completing the questionnaire will notify you that they refuse to participate. (However, with elite or specialized samples, many will write back that the questionnaire is not relevant to them.) For face-to-face and phone interviews, the refusal rate ranges from 20 to 30 percent.[6]

Refusals are different from noncontacts in their implications for sample representativeness. Refusals are conscious decisions by sample elements *not* to participate. While some people may consistently refuse to participate in *any* survey, most refusals are conditional, based on the sponsoring organization, the purpose of the study, the content of the questionnaire, or in reaction to the interviewer. Because the decision is based on *interaction* between respondents and one or more elements of the study itself, respondents are selecting themselves out of your final sample. A systematic *bias* is generated.

NONCONTACT RATE

The *noncontact rate* is the percentage of the valid sample that is not reached by the researcher. The noncontact rate, in percentage form, is computed by the formula:

$$\text{Noncontact Rate} = \frac{\text{Noncontacts}}{\text{Valid Sample Size}} \times 100$$

Noncontacts are valid sample elements left over after participating respondents and refusals are removed. Noncontacts are computed using the following formula:

$$\text{Noncontacts} = \text{Valid Sample Size} - (\text{Completes} + \text{Refusers})$$

Because noncontacts are sample elements that provide no feedback or reasons for not participating, they remain a puzzle. Noncontacts take many forms, depending on the mode of data collection. You mail a questionnaire and it is not returned. You call a number and nobody answers. You send an interviewer to a respondent's residence but nobody's home. You hand out questionnaires to 100 employees for them to fill out in a work setting. When you count them, only 96 questionnaires are returned. Follow-up efforts to make contact with these noncontacts are not successful.

Eligible Respondents

The first problem with noncontacts is whether to treat them as eligible or ineligible respondents. In phone surveys, for example, a noncontact may or

[6]Frey, op. cit., pp. 40–41.

may not be eligible. The same applies to face-to-face interviews where repeated visits to the respondent's home fail to yield contact.

In mailed surveys, a refusal involves a conscious decision *not* to complete the questionnaire, knowing something about its content. This is a serious threat to the representativeness of your sample. On the other hand, a questionnaire may be tossed because some respondents can tell by the content of the questionnaire that it was not meant for them. The former may be a valid sample element, whereas the latter is not.

The decision to treat some categories of noncontacts as ineligible sample elements should be based on a clearly stated rationale. For example, you may decide to treat three calls to the same number on three different days as an ineligible sample element because repeated calls (a dozen or more) to a subsample of those numbers did not result in contact. You conclude that there is nobody residing at a number if the phone is not answered after repeated attempts. The point is that you should explicitly state how you decided to treat some categories of noncontacts as ineligible sample elements.

Other categories of noncontacts are assumed to be eligible or valid sample elements. These valid noncontacts represent a source of bias, but generally not as serious a threat as a refusal. Generally, noncontacts are individuals who are less available than those completing a questionnaire. But noncontacts are not necessarily conscious decisions to refuse to participate, based on one or more elements of the study itself. Nonparticipation is not explicitly based on *interaction* with the questionnaire, the interviewer, or the organization sponsoring the study. The bias of noncontacts is significant only if an individual's availability is linked theoretically to differential responses to items in the questionnaire.

Increasing Contacts

Decreasing noncontact rates and increasing response rates are intertwined. Repeated follow-ups are key to lowering noncontact rates. Switching modes of data collection on follow-up attempts is likely to increase contacts. Just as some respondents are hard to reach by phone, others are unlikely to fill out a mailed questionnaire. Switching mode from mail to phone, phone to mail, or some other combination increases opportunities for contact. Further, nonrespondents may be impressed by the variety of ways you've devised to solicit their participation. This may exert a positive influence on participation and response rates.

Typical Noncontact Rates

The noncontact rate is the most frequently ignored measure of the representativeness of a sample. Commercial research firms will sometimes replace noncontacts with a new sample element, thus boosting the response rate by eliminating noncontacts altogether. This practice distorts the representativeness of the sample and prevents those examining research reports from assessing representativeness of the sample for themselves. You should not substitute new sample elements for noncontacts. Rather, compute noncontact rates as a percentage of the valid sample and report it with your findings.

Because noncontact rates are underreported or eliminated through substitution procedures, industry standards for noncontact rates are hard to determine. In a study of 182 telephone surveys, Wiseman and McDonald found an average noncontact rate of 39 percent. This figure would have been lowered to 25 percent or less with more callbacks.[7] The noncontact rate for face-to-face interviews is generally lower than for telephone surveys.[8] As indicated, it's difficult to separate refusal from noncontacts in mailed surveys.

TRACKING SYSTEMS

In order to compute response, completion, refusal, and noncontact rates, you need a system to track the outcome for every element in your original sample. Tracking systems vary somewhat with the mode of data collection. However, some characteristics of tracking systems are generic across telephone, mail, and face-to-face surveys. One document or form is used to keep track of the repeated attempts to contact each sample element. An example is provided in Table H-1 for a telephone survey. Table H-2 provides a similar form for a mailed survey.

Tracking Forms

In Table H-1, random digit dialing telephone numbers have been entered in the left column. The next three columns indicate the date and time (using the twenty-four-hour clock and tracking to the nearest hour) of attempts to reach respondents at each number. The comments column allows the interviewer to note any special circumstances. The right column indicates the outcome for each telephone number in the sample, using a series of short codes listed above the table.

In Table H-2, a tracking form for a mail survey is provided. An identification number is assigned to each name-address unit in the sample, corresponding to each potential respondent in the sample. That identification number appears in the left column of the tracking form. The next three columns indicate the date of each mailing of a questionnaire, reminder letter, or reminder card to each sampling element. The two columns on the right indicate the outcome for each sampling element and date that the outcome (completed questionnaire returned, no forwarding address return, etc.) occurred.

[7]Fredrick Wiseman and Phillip McDonald, "Noncontact and Refusal Rates in Consumer Telephone Surveys," *Journal of Marketing Research,* Vol. 16 (1979), pp. 478–84.
[8]Frey, op. cit., p. 42.

Table H-1 An Example of a Completed Interviewer Calling Record for a Phone Survey

OUTCOME CODES:	CI	= COMPLETED INTERVIEW
	DISC	= DISCONNECTED NUMBER
	ENGL	= NON-ENGLISH SPEAKING HOUSEHOLD
	NA	= NO ANSWER
	REF	= REFUSAL
	HANG	= HANG UP ON FIRST PAGE; NOT CODED
	INEL	= NO ELIGIBLE RESP IN HOUSEHOLD

[Give date and time for each attempt. Use twenty-four-hour clock]

PHONE NUMBER	FIRST ATTEMPT	SECOND ATTEMPT	THIRD ATTEMPT	COMMENTS	OUTCOME
265-3211	1-3, 19	1-4, 15	1-6, 21	ANS MACHINE	NA
272-5723	1-3, 19				DISC
223-7751	1-3, 19				DISC
488-3441	1-3, 19				CI
225-1118	1-3, 19	1-4, 15			CI
234-1142	1-3, 19	1-4, 15			INEL
222-9763	1-3, 19				ENGL
563-7379	1-3, 19				CI
262-3008	1-3, 19	1-4, 15	1-6, 21		NA
533-7779	1-3, 19				HANG
233-1179	1-3, 19				REF
223-7987	1-3, 19				CI
433-0739	1-3, 19				CI
232-7221	1-3, 19				CI

Response Rate Logs

The information that appears for each sampling element in Tables H-1 and H-2 must now be summarized. Table H-3 summarizes the outcomes for a mailed survey. (Figure 9-3 on page 194 provides a similar response rate log for a random digit dialing survey.) The original sample size is posted at the top of the response rate log. Each type of outcome for the original sample, based on the category codes in Table H-2, is posted in the right column of the log. Some elements (moved/no forwarding address and disqualified respondents) are considered ineligible and excluded from the valid sample. Other outcomes (no return, refusals, incomplete questionnaires, completed questionnaires) are treated as part of the valid sample.

The *original* sample is computed by adding together all the possible outcomes in the log. The *valid* sample is computed by summing all outcomes that are viewed as eligible respondents. The completion, response, refusal, and noncontact rates are computed from the figures in the log, according to the formulas

Table H–2 An Example of a Completed Mail Survey Return Monitoring Form

OUTCOME CODES: COMP = COMPLETED QUESTIONNAIRE RETURNED
ILEG = RETURNED QUESTIONNAIRE ILLEGIBLE, INCOMPLETE
NFA = RETURNED; NO FORWARDING ADDRESS
REF = RETURNED; REFUSED TO PARTICIPATE
DISQ = RESPONDENT DISQUALIFIED SELF
NOT = QUESTIONNAIRE NOT RETURNED IN 3 MAILINGS

ID NUMBER	FIRST MAILING	SECOND MAILING	THIRD MAILING	OUTCOME	DATE
001	1-3	3-16	5-4	NOT	
002	1-3	3-16		COMP	4-16
003	1-3	3-16		COMP	3-13
004	1-3	3-16	5-4	NOT	
005	1-3			NFA	1-12
006	1-3	3-16		COMP	3-22
007	1-3			REF	1-22
008	1-3	3-16		COMP	3-19
009	1-3			COMP	1-21
010	1-3			COMP	2-2
011	1-3			COMP	1-8
012	1-3			NFA	1-12
013	1-3			DISQ	1-14
014	1-3			COMP	1-24
015	1-5			COMP	2-21
016	1-5			COMP	2-11
017	1-5			COMP	2-13
018	1-5	3-16	5-4	NOT	
019	1-5	3-16	5-4	COMP	7-12
020	1-5	3-16	5-4	NOT	
021	1-5	3-16	5-4	NOT	
022	1-5	3-16		COMP	4-14
023	1-5	3-16	5-4	NOT	
024	1-5	3-16	5-4	NOT	
025	1-5	3-16		COMP	3-22
026	1-5	3-16	5-4	NOT	
027	1-5			COMP	1-11
028	1-5			COMP	2-13
021	1-5			NFA	1-23
022	1-5	3-16	5-4	COMP	5-20

at the bottom of Table H–3. To convert these rates (in decimal form) to percentages, multiply the results of these calculations by 100.

You should develop a tracking form and a response rate log for every survey prior to fielding the questionnaire. When contracting for survey research services from a vendor, insist that the tracking forms and a response rate log be provided you as a deliverable. Make sure that the vendor understands that you

Table H–3   A Response Rate Log for a Mailed Survey

Number in Original Sample: _____

			VALID?
Number of Moved/No Forwarding Address:	A.	____	NO
Number of Self-Disqualified Respondents:	B.	____	NO
Number Not Returned After Three Mailings:	C.	____	YES
Number of Refusing Respondents:	D.	____	YES
Number Incomplete/Illegible Questionnaires:	E.	____	YES
Number of Completed Questionnaires:	F.	____	YES
TOTAL (should equal original sample size):	G.	____	
VALID SAMPLE SIZE ($C+D+E+F$):	H.	____	

NOTE: The completion rate is equal to the number of completed questionnaires divided by original sample size (F/G). The valid sample size is equal to the original sample, less respondents who have moved with no forwarding address and ineligible respondents ($G - [A + B]$). The response rate is the number of completed interviews divided by the valid sample size (F/H). The refusal rate is the number of incomplete or refused questionnaires divided by the valid sample ($[D + E]/H$). The noncontact rate is the number of nonresponses after three mailings divided by the valid sample size (C/H). Multiply each rate (now in decimal form) by 100 to express rates in percentage form.

want every outcome accounted for—for every element in the original sample. Do not permit the vendor to substitute new sample elements for noncontacts. When reporting research findings (see Chapter 13), provide the completion, response, refusal, and noncontact rates in the report. Depending on the audiences for the report, you may elect to report these rates in the methods section or in a footnote or separate appendix. Use the industry standards in this appendix—as well as your understanding of special characteristics of your study—to assess the representativeness of your survey.

APPENDIX I

HOW TO COMPUTE THE CHI-SQUARE STATISTIC

Following are two crosstabulations. One crosstabulation is based on actual survey results of 501 readers of *SDSU Report,* a quarterly magazine circulated to 75,000 alumni and friends of San Diego State University. The other is based on what we would expect in this same sample of 501 respondents if the null hypothesis were true, if there were no relationship between reading the magazine and agreeing that the university is high-quality. Only the *number* of respondents in each cell is reported, since these are the numbers that you would use to compute the Chi-Square statistic.

OBSERVED VALUES

QUALITY	READ REPORT . . . INFREQ.	FREQ.	MAR-GINS
DIS.	12	6	18
NEUTRAL	35	21	56
AGREE	194	233	427
	241	260	501

EXPECTED VALUES UNDER NULL HYPOTHESIS

QUALITY	READ REPORT . . . INFREQ.	FREQ.	MAR-GINS
DIS.	8.7	9.3	18
NEUTRAL	26.9	29.1	56
AGREE	205.4	221.6	427
	241	260	501

The values expected under the condition of the null hypothesis are computed by using the *marginals* from the observed table. The expected value (under the null hypothesis) is computed by the formula:

Row Marginal × Column Marginal/Total = Expected Value

For the upper left cell, the row marginal is 18 (top row), the column marginal is 241 (left column), and the total is 501. Plugging these numbers into the formula:

$(18 \times 241)/501 = 4338/501 = 8.7$

This same computation is made for each cell of the "expected" value table.

To compute the Chi-Square statistic, compute a *cell value* for each cell in the table. First, subtract the expected value from the observed value. Second, square the resulting value. Third, divide that value by the expected value. This gives a *cell value* for one cell of the table. Repeat the three steps for each cell in the table. Finally, sum all the cell values in the table to compute the Chi-Square statistic. Using conventional mathematical symbols, the formula for the Chi-Square statistic:

$$\text{Chi-Square} = \sum \frac{(0 - E)^2}{E}$$

We can use the preceding table to help us do to the arithmetic. In the upper left cell, we subtract the expected value (8.7) from the observed value (12), square the results ($12 - 8.7 = 3.3$, then $3.3 \times 3.3 = 10.89$), then divide by the expected value ($10.89 / 8.7 = 1.25$). The following table on the left shows the results of this one calculation for the upper left cell. The following table on the right displays the results of this same calculation for *every* cell in the table.

CALCULATED RESULTS FOR UPPER LEFT CELL . . .

QUALITY	READ REPORT . . . INFREQ.	FREQ.
DISAGREE	1.25	
NEUTRAL		
AGREE		

CALCULATED RESULTS FOR ALL CELLS . . .

	READ REPORT . . . INFREQ.	FREQ.
DISAGREE	1.25	1.17
NEUTRAL	2.45	2.26
AGREE	0.63	0.59

To compute the actual value of the Chi Square statistic, we add together all the computed values in the table on the right:

Chi Square = $1.25 + 1.17 + 2.45 + 2.26 + .63 + .59 = 8.35$

To interpret the Chi-Square statistic, we need to compute the degrees of freedom:

$$d.f. = (\text{No. of Rows} - 1) \times (\text{No. of Columns} - 1)$$
$$= (3-1) \times (2-1) = 2 \times 1 = 2$$

The Chi Square is 8.35 with $d.f. = 2$. With this information, we refer to a table like the one following, which is exerpted from "Table of the Percentage Points of the Chi Square Distribution," *Biometrika,* Vol. 32 (1941), p. 188–89:

Critical Chi-Square Values

d.f.	p = .100	p = .050	p = .025	p = .010
1	2.7055	3.8416	5.0238	6.6349
2	4.6052	5.9915	7.3778	9.2103
3	6.2514	7.8147	9.3484	11.3349

The p over each column is the probability that the null hypothesis is true for certain critical values of the Chi-Square statistic. It's a shorter way of saying significance. Our Chi-Square value, 8.35, does not appear in the table; it falls between the two underlined values in the table, meaning that the probability of the null hypothesis being true is somewhere between 0.025 and 0.010. Converted to percentages, there's somewhere between a 1.0 percent chance and a 2.5 percent chance of the null hypothesis being true. We know from computer analysis (see Crosstabulation A in Table 11–4) that the precise probability is 1.53 percent chance of the null hypothesis being true. If you like to play computer, use the percentages in Crosstabulation B in Table 11–4 (the total sample size is 501) to compute the actual number of cases in each cell and the marginals. Then use the preceding steps to figure out the Chi-Square statistic. When you are done, be aware that our computer did the same calculations in less than a second!

APPENDIX J

HOW TO USE A TABLE OF CRITICAL CHI-SQUARE VALUES

Appendix I shows you how to compute the Chi-Square statistic. When you compute the Chi-Square statistic—or when you see a Chi-Square statistic in a report or presentation—you want to know if the relationship is statistically significant or not.

Table J–1, which provides critical values of the Chi-Square statistic, indicates the *statistical significance* of a relationship. Review Chapter 11 if the meaning of statistical significance is not clear to you.

To use Table J–1, you need to know three pieces of information: the Chi-Square value, the alpha level (or decision rule), and the degrees of freedom.

Both the Chi-Square value and the degrees of freedom are either calculated by you (see Appendix I) or provided to you in a report or computer output. Degrees of freedom appear in the left column in Table J–1. The values at the top of the other columns are alpha levels. Alpha levels correspond to the probability that no relationship exists between two variables in the population, despite some relationship in the sample. Degrees of freedom correspond to the size (number of cells) of the contingency table from which the Chi-Square statistic was computed.

AN EXAMPLE

Refer to the example in Appendix I. In that example, frequent readers of *SDSU Report* are more likely than infrequent readers to regard the university as high quality. A six-celled contingency table (*d.f.* = 2) generated a Chi-Square statistic

Table J–1 Critical Values of the Chi-Square Statistic for Different Alpha Levels and Different Degrees of Freedom

ALPHA LEVELS

d.f.	0.250	0.100	0.050	0.025	0.010	0.005	0.001
1	1.32330	2.70554	3.84146	5.02389	6.63490	7.87944	10.828
2	2.77259	4.60517	5.99147	7.37776	9.21034	11.5966	13.816
3	4.10835	6.25139	7.81473	9.34840	11.3449	12.8381	16.266
4	5.38527	7.77944	9.48773	11.1433	13.2767	14.8602	18.467
5	6.62568	9.23635	11.0705	12.8325	15.0863	16.7496	20.515
6	7.84080	10.6446	12.5916	14.4494	16.8119	18.5476	22.458
7	9.03715	12.0170	14.0671	16.0128	18.4753	20.2777	24.322
8	10.2188	13.3616	15.5073	17.5346	20.0902	21.9550	26.125
9	11.3887	14.6837	16.9190	19.0228	21.6660	23.5893	27.877
10	12.5489	15.9871	18.3070	20.4831	23.2093	25.1882	29.588
11	13.7007	17.2750	19.6751	21.9200	24.7250	26.7569	31.264
12	14.8454	18.5494	21.0261	23.3367	26.2170	28.2995	32.909
13	15.9839	19.8119	22.3621	24.7356	27.6883	29.8194	34.528
14	17.1170	21.0642	23.6848	26.1190	29.1413	31.3193	36.123
15	18.2451	22.3072	24.9958	27.4884	30.5779	32.8013	37.697
16	19.3688	23.5418	26.2962	28.8454	31.9999	34.2672	39.252
17	20.4887	24.7690	27.5871	30.1910	33.4087	35.7185	40.790
18	21.6049	25.9894	28.8693	31.5264	34.8053	37.1564	42.312
19	22.7178	27.2036	30.1435	32.8523	36.1908	38.5822	43.820
20	23.8277	28.4120	31.4104	34.1696	37.5662	39.9968	45.315
21	24.9348	29.6151	32.6705	35.4789	38.9321	41.4010	46.797
22	26.0393	30.8133	33.9244	36.7807	40.2894	42.7956	48.268
23	27.1413	32.0069	35.1725	38.0757	41.6384	44.1813	49.728
24	28.2412	33.1963	36.4151	39.3641	42.9798	45.5585	51.179
25	29.3389	34.3816	37.6525	40.6465	44.3141	46.9278	52.620
26	30.4345	35.5631	38.8852	41.9232	45.6417	48.2899	54.052
27	31.5284	36.7412	40.1133	43.1944	46.9630	49.6449	55.476
28	32.6205	37.9159	41.3372	44.4607	48.2782	50.9933	56.892
29	33.7109	39.0875	42.5569	45.7222	49.5879	52.3356	58.302
30	34.7998	40.2560	43.7729	46.9792	50.8922	53.6720	59.703
40	45.6160	51.8050	55.7585	59.3417	63.6907	66.7659	73.402
50	56.3336	63.1671	67.5048	71.4202	76.1539	79.4900	86.661
60	66.9814	74.3970	79.0819	83.2976	88.3794	91.9517	99.607
70	77.5766	85.5271	90.5312	95.0231	100.425	104.215	112.317
80	88.1303	96.5782	101.879	106.629	112.329	116.321	124.839
90	98.6499	107.565	113.145	118.136	124.116	128.299	137.208
100	109.141	118.498	124.342	129.561	135.807	140.169	149.449

Abridged from Table 8 of *Biometrica Tables for Statisticians*, Vol. I, Third Edition (1966), E. S. Pearson and H. O. Hastley (Eds.). Used with permission.

of 8.35. Refer to the second row of Table J–1. The critical values for contingency tables of this size ($d.f. = 2$) are provided for different alpha levels. The calculated value of the Chi-Square statistic (8.35) falls between alpha = 0.025 and alpha = 0.010. Converted to percentages, the probability of no relationship in the population (the null hypothesis) falls somewhere between 1.0 percent and 2.5 percent. This means that there is between a 97.5 percent chance and a 99 percent chance that the relationship in the sample can be generalized to the population from which the sample was drawn.

APPENDIX K

HOW TO INTERPRET CONTINGENCY TABLES

The contingency table on the facing page displays a crosstabulation for two variables. One variable (named READ in the SPSS-X computer program file) is frequency of reading the *SDSU Report,* which respondents reported reading frequently or infrequently. *SDSU Report* is a magazine distributed quarterly to 75,000 alumni and friends of San Diego State University. The other variable (named QUALITY in the program) is agreement, disagreement, or neutrality toward the statement: "San Diego is a high-quality, comprehensive university."

The table is a copy of the computer output of an SPSS-X program used to analyze the data from the *SDSU Report* readership survey. Our working theory is that increased exposure to the content of *SDSU Report* leads to a more favorable opinion of the university as a high-quality, comprehensive institution. According to our theory, the 241 infrequent readers in the *left* column should agree with the opinion statement less often than do the 260 frequent readers in the *right* column. We want to compare the percent of respondents who agree with the opinion statement among the infrequent and among the frequent readers of *SDSU Report.* If our theory is supported, there should be a higher percentage of frequent readers who agree with the opinion statement, when compared to infrequent readers of *SDSU Report.* Here's the first rule of thumb for interpreting crosstabulation tables:

> *RULE #1: When comparing **columns,** use **column** percentages;*
> *when comparing **rows,** use **row** percentages.*

Read How Frequently Do You Read Report?

COUNT ROW PCT COL PCT TOT PCT		INFREQ. 1	FREQ. 2	ROW TOTAL
QUALITY				
DISAGREE	1	12 66.7 5.0 2.4	6 33.3 2.3 1.2	18 3.6
NEUTRAL	2	35 62.5 14.5 7.0	21 37.5 8.1 4.2	56 11.2
AGREE	3	194 45.4 80.5 38.7	233 54.6 89.6 46.5	427 85.2
COLUMN TOTAL		241 48.1	260 51.9	501 100.0

CHI-SQUARE	D.F.	SIGNIFICANCE
8.35352	2	.0153

To report the results of this test of our working theory, we would start with the statement:

> *Among frequent readers, . . .*

We recommend that you always *stop* at the comma and figure out which numbers in the table are relevant to the rest of this statement. If you are examining frequent readers, as in this example, you are interested in the numbers in the *right column* of the .table. Since we are comparing *columns*, we are interested in *column* percentages *only.* Which numbers are the column percentages? In the upper left corner of the table, a *legend* like those found on road maps is provided. The legend indicates that the *third* number in each cell of the table is the *column* percentage. Of the twenty-four numbers that appear in the cells of this table, only *three* are relevant for reporting results among frequent readers. Those numbers are the *right column* percentages: 2.3, 8.1, and 89.6. Examine the table to see where these numbers came from and why. Use the legend in the upper left corner of the table. Now let's complete the foregoing sentence:

> *Among frequent readers, 89.6 percent agree San Diego State is*
> *a high-quality, comprehensive university.*

We pick the 89.6 percent figure because that's the *column* percentage that appears in the *bottom* row of the table, the row that contains the 427 respondents who *agree* with the opinion statement.

To analyze the relationship in the sample, we compare *frequent* to *infrequent* readers. A second statement about the relationship begins:

> Among **infrequent** readers, . . .

Stopping at the comma, we examine the table to determine which figures in the table are relevant to the analysis. Only three numbers are relevant if we are examining infrequent readers, the *left column* percentages: 5.0, 14.5, and 80.5. Examine the table and locate these numbers. Now we can complete the statement:

> Among **infrequent** readers, 80.5 percent agree that San Diego
> State is a high-quality, comprehensive university.

We pick the 80.5 percentage figure because that's the column percentage of infrequent readers who happen to *agree* with the opinion statement—the *bottom* row of the table.

We conclude from this analysis that frequent readers are more likely than infrequent readers to agree that San Diego State is a high-quality, comprehensive university (89.6 percent versus 80.5 percent).

Let's look at this same table from a different theoretical perspective. Suppose we theorize that people who *already have* a positive opinion of San Diego State as a high-quality, comprehensive university seek out information about this highly regarded institution. That is, opinion about the university (independent variable) causes increased frequency of reading *SDSU Report* (dependent variable). In other words, our new theory reverses the direction of causality and flips the independent and dependent variables.

Based on our new theory, we want to compare those who *agree* with the opinion statement with those who *disagree* and feel *neutral*. The *rows* in the table now display the independent variable. To analyze the table, we begin:

> Among those who **agree** that San Diego State is a high-quality,
> comprehensive university, . . .

Stop at the comma. The statement indicates that we are only interested in the *row* percentages for the *bottom* row in the table: 45.4 and 54.6. Look at the legend and the table to see where these numbers came from and why. Now we complete the statement:

> Among those who **agree** that San Diego State is a high-quality,
> comprehensive university, 54.6 percent are frequent readers of
> **SDSU Report.**

We pick the 54.6 percentage figure because that's the *row* percentage that appears in the *right* column of the table, the column containing the 260 frequent readers of the report.

We want to compare those who agree with the statement with those who disagree with the statement. We start the statement:

> *Among those who* **disagree** *that San Diego State is a high-quality, comprehensive university,* . . .

Stopping at the comma, we examine the table. The only numbers relevant to the rest of the statement are the *top row* percentages: 66.7 and 33.3. We complete the statement:

> *Among those who* **disagree** *that San Diego State is a high-quality, comprehensive university, 33.3 percent are frequent readers of* **SDSU Report.**

We examine the row percentages in the *middle* (neutral) *row* to complete the last statement that summarizes the relationship:

> *Among those who are* **neutral** *about San Diego State as a high-quality, comprehensive university, 37.5 percent are frequent readers of* **SDSU Report.**

We conclude from this analysis that, within our sample, a positive opinion of San Diego State leads respondents to be more frequent readers of *SDSU Report.*

As should be obvious by now, the data in the table confirm *both* theories, even though they differ entirely in terms of the direction of causality. Which one is right? This analysis, by itself, supports both theories. (In Chapter 12, you learned how to unravel the direction of causality.)

Sometimes you want to know the percentage of respondents who fall into a particular category from among *all* respondents. When the percentage is based on all respondents, the *total* percentage, the bottom number in each cell, is relevant. Use the legend and the table to see why the following statement is accurate:

> *Among* **all** *respondents, 46.5 percent are frequent readers of* **SDSU Report** *who agree that San Diego State is a high-quality, comprehensive university.*

The 233 respondents in the bottom right cell of the table both read *SDSU Report* frequently and agree with the opinion statement. They make up 46.5 percent of the 501 respondents.

The *marginal percentages* are also useful. Looking at the percentages in the right-hand margin, we see that 3.6 percent of all respondents disagree with the opinion statement, 11.2 percent are neutral, and 85.2 percent agree with the opinion statement. If the two variables were not related to each other at all in this sample of 501 respondents, we would expect 3.6 percent of frequent readers and 3.6 percent of infrequent readers to *disagree* with the opinion statement. At the same time, we would expect 85.2 percent of the frequent readers and 85.2 percent of the infrequent readers to *agree* with the opinion statement. Such results are what we would expect if the null hypothesis (two variables are unrelated) is true.

The same applies to row percentages. If the null hypothesis were true, we would expect 51.9 percent of those who agree with the opinion statement, 51.9 percent of those who disagree with the opinion statement, and 51.9 percent of those who feel neutral about the opinion statement to be *frequent* readers of *SDSU Report*. The marginal percentages are what we would expect under conditions of the null hypothesis. Practice your understanding of the interpretation of contingency tables by completing the preceding incomplete statements.

APPENDIX L

GLOSSARY OF RESEARCH TERMS

Analysis of Variance. Data analysis technique in which differences in means of a metric variable are compared for different subsamples defined by a categorical variable. The *F*-statistic tests the inference that differences in subsample means can be generalized to the population.

Anonymity. If the researcher has no way to identify respondents or subjects with the measures taken, then they are assured of anonymity when they participate in the research. (See also *confidentiality*.)

Antecedent Variable. Variable that precedes the independent variable in a causal relationship with the dependent variable.

Average. Generic label for measures of central tendency such as the mean, mode, and median.

Bivariate Analysis. Examination of the relationship between two variables, usually to determine if a relationship detected in the sample can be generalized to the population.

Cases. Individual units of analysis as they appear in the data file. Cases include data from questionnaire respondents, groups, and organizations, as well as sentences, paragraphs, stories, or entire publications in content analysis.

Case Study. Method of data collection and analysis using only one or a small number of cases examined in great detail—often over a period of time. The community case study is one type of such research.

Categorical Variable. Characteristic of an object of study that varies across cases but assumes a limited number of discrete qualities or states. Gender is a categorical variable that assumes only the qualities of male and female.

Census. Collection of data from every person, object, or other unit of analysis in a population.

Central Limit Theorem. Theory of probability that the means of repeated samples of the same size form a bell-shaped (normal) distribution around the true population mean. The mean of means converges on the true population mean.

Central Tendency. Any statistic that describes the typical or average case in the distribution of a variable.

Chi Square. Inferential statistic that tests whether a relationship indicated in a contingency table can be generalized to the population from which the sample was drawn.

Closed-ended Questions. Questionnaire or interview schedule items that limit responses to the set of options provided in the item itself.

Cluster Sampling. Probability sampling technique used when a comprehensive sample frame is not available for every sampling element, but a comprehensive frame does exist for some aggregate of sampling elements. Aggregates are first sampled from the cluster sample frame, then a probability sample is drawn from each aggregate (cluster) sampled.

Codebook. Document that links each questionnaire or content analysis item and its response categories to numeric values and the location of those values in a computerized data file.

Concept. Mental image or abstraction formed as a generalization from particulars.

Conceptualization. Thinking process whereby abstractions of real-world phenomena are clarified and defined in the abstract.

Confidence Interval. Range of numbers above and below the statistic generated from a sample that includes the true population value (parameter) at a known level of confidence. Sometimes called the margin of error. The 95-percent confidence interval is that range which we are 95 percent sure includes the parameter.

Confidence Level. Degree of certainty in an inference or knowledge claim made about a population from sample data. Generally, it is the probability that a relationship detected in a sample can be generalized to the population.

Confidentiality. If the researcher can identify respondents or subjects with measures taken but promises not to do so, then they are assured of confidentiality when they participate in the research. (See also *anonymity*.)

Construct. Mental image or abstraction created by the researcher to link a more abstract concept to a specific operationalization (variable) in the real world. A narrowly defined concept invented for a specific research purpose.

Content Analysis. Method of measuring the manifest and latent content of newspapers, news programs, or other forms of communication in a systematic, objective, and reliable manner.

Contingency Question. Question asked only of some respondents, based on their answer(s) to prior filter question(s).

Contingency Table. Table that displays the relationship between two categorical variables by indicating the number (and percent) of cases for each cell created by the intersection of values for the row and column variables.

Control Group. Comparison group of subjects in an experiment who are administered a placebo (or nothing at all), rather than the experimental treatment. Strictly defined, subjects are randomly assigned to treatment or control groups.

Control Variable. Variable that is held constant when analyzing the relationship between two other variables, so that the relationships among the three variables can be more fully understood. (Also called *test variable*.)

Convenience Sample. Nonprobability sampling technique whereby any convenient sampling element is used. (Also called *accidental sample*.)

Cronbach's Alpha Coefficient. Measure of the reliability (measurement stability) of a scale or index made up of three or more measures.

Crosstabulation or "Crosstab" Table. (See *contingency table*.)

Cross-sectional Survey. Study in which data are collected from a census or sample at one point in time.

Data File. Set of variables in machine-readable form, systematically organized for a number of cases. Generally, a data file consists of a matrix of numbers in which rows represent cases and columns represent variables. (Also called *data base*.)

Data Reduction. Process of assigning specific numeric codes to responses from questionnaire items or categories of content variables for purposes of computerized data entry.

Data Transmittal Form. Sheet of paper with columns corresponding to variable columns and rows corresponding to cases in a data file. The purpose of such forms is to reduce data from a questionnaire or other instrument and format data for computer entry. This data reduction step is eliminated through edge coding.

Decision Rule. Basis for determining the statistical significance of a relationship in a sample, based on the probability that the relationship actually exists in the population at a predetermined level of confidence. The 95-percent decision rule requires that a relation detected in a sample must be generalizable to the population at a 95-percent level of confidence before it is considered statistically significant.

Deduction. Process of logically specifying operational hypothesis within a specific research setting from a more abstract set of theoretical propositions.

Degrees of Freedom. Measure of sample size, number of cells in a contingency table, or the number of groups and sample elements within groups in an analysis of variance table. This number is needed to detemine the statistical significance of a Chi-Square value in a contingency table or an F-value in an analysis of variance table.

Dependent Variable. Variable in a bivariate relationship that is caused by or depends on the independent variable.

Depth Interview. Exploratory mode of data collection wherein the respondent is guided in an unstructured, open-ended way to a particular topic of interest to the researcher. Through active listening techniques and positive reinforcement, the respondent discusses the topic in any form or manner he or she chooses.

Descriptive Statistics. Numeric indicators of the central tendency and scatter of variables in samples, or indicators of the nature and strength of bivariate relationships within samples. Descriptive statistics summarize sample observations, whereas inferential statistics provide probabilistic statements about populations from which samples are drawn.

Dimensional Sampling. Nonprobability sampling technique used by interviewers to select sampling elements according to several variables or quotas. Within each set of characteristics, any convenient sampling element is selected.

Dispersion. Variability or scatter of a variable about its measures of central tendency.

Discrete Variable. (See *categorical variable*.)

Distorter Variable. In the elaboration model, a distorter variable changes the true relationship between the independent and dependent variables in such a way that the researcher can be misled about the causal chain.

Double-barreled Question. Questionnaire item containing two or more questions but permitting only one response.

Edge Coding. Technique for data reduction and entry in which numeric responses to questionnaire items are assigned a column location in the data file during questionnaire construction. The edge coding scheme appears as numbered blanks in the questionnaire margin with numbers corresponding to data columns in the data file.

Effect Size. Strength of a relationship between two variables as it actually exists in the population.

Elaboration Model or Process. Data analytic process in which different control (or test) variables are introduced to determine their effects on relationships between independent and dependent variables.

Empirical. Relating to the observed or observable. Phenomena that can be seen, touched, heard, smelled, or otherwise measured.

Empirical Generalization. Observed relationship in a number of real-world settings that suggests the existence of an abstract or theoretical relationship. An inductive summary based on phenomena directly observed.

Evaluation Research. Research in which information is gathered to determine the relative success or failure of programs to reach specified goals and objectives within specified deadlines.

Experiment. Research project wherein a treatment (independent variable) is administered to one group of subjects but not to control group to determine if it affects some dependent (impact) variable.

Experimental Designs. Use of various control groups and pretest-posttest measurement strategies to isolate the causal impact of the independent variable (treatment) on the dependent variable (impact measure).

Experimental Group. Collection of subjects in an experiment exposed to the treatment condition and then compared to a control group in terms of a dependent variable. Membership in a true experimental (or control) group is randomly determined.

Experimental Mortality. Any loss of subjects from an experiment or panel study, affecting the internal validity of the study.

External Validity. Generalizability of research findings. Degree to which the findings of an experiment or other study can be generalized to other settings and populations. The degree to which a measure is valid for other settings and populations.

Face Validity. Degree to which a variable is a reasonable indicator "on the face of it" of the concept it purports to measure. The quality of the logical linkage between observed phenomena and the abstractions they indicate.

Factor Analysis. Statistical analytic procedure that groups questionnaire items or other variables together based on the way items covary together. Constructs underlying the items measured can be inferred from the content of items loaded on that factor.

Field Experiments. Administration of a treatment and measurement of a dependent variable in a natural setting with reduced control over treatment administration or assignment of subjects to experimental and control groups.

Field Studies. Method of data collection wherein subjects are intensively studied in their natural context, usually over a long period of time.

Filter Question. Item in a questionnaire that directs interviewers or respondents to go to or skip a subset of subsequent items, based on answers to the filter question.

Focus Groups. Exploratory mode of observation in which six to twelve subjects selected from the population meet around a table to discuss a particular topic of focus, moderated by a group leader following a written moderator guide.

Frequency Distribution. Tabular display of the values of a single variable, giving the number and percent of cases for each value and various descriptive statistics of central tendency and dispersion.

Generalizability. Degree to which the findings from one study in one research setting can be applied to other settings and contexts.

Grounded Theory. Process of abstracting theory inductively from relationships discovered through direct, intensive observation of phenomena.

Guttman Scales. Composite measure in which items of different strength are organized hierarchically according to distribution patterns in the target population.

History. Events occurring between the pretest and posttest measures in an experiment or panel study that may affect the dependent variable and reduce the internal validity of the study.

Hypothesis. Tentative and testable statement predicting a relationship between two variables, generally deduced from theory.

Hypothesis Testing. Process of empirically determining whether the relationship specified in the hypothesis is confirmed or disconfirmed in a sample. The process of determining whether a relationship confirmed in a sample can be generalized to the population at a specified confidence level.

Independent Variable. Variable in a bivariate relationship that theoretically causes or influences the values of the other (dependent) variable.

Index. A composite measure consisting of several items designed to represent a single dimension. The accumulated scores that make up the index are said to be *unidimensional*.

Induction. Process of developing abstract generalizations from a number of specific observations.

Inferential Statistics. Data analytic procedures which permit probabilistic knowledge claims about populations from data obtained from samples.

Information Needs. Research questions that the researcher seeks to answer through research activities. A section of the research report that describes information sought that motivates the research.

Instrument Decay. Degree to which the measurement instrument in an experiment provides invalid or unreliable measures of the dependent variable, reducing the internal validity of the study.

Interaction. The intertwined effect of two or more independent variables on a dependent variable.

Interaction of Testing and Treatment. Degree to which a pretest measure in an experiment sensitizes subjects or otherwise affects the impact of the experimental treatment, such that the impact on the dependent variable would not be as great from the treatment alone. This is a threat to the internal validity of the study.

Intercoder Reliability. Degree to which two or more content analysts provide the same classification of the same media content.

Internal Validity. Degree to which an experimental design isolates the causal influence of the independent variable (treatment) on the dependent variable (impact measure) from other possible causes.

Interval-level Variables. Higher order measures of concepts that are mutually exclusive, exhaustive, ordered, and have intervals of equal size between points on the measure.

Intervening Variable. Control variable that

mediates or occurs between the independent and dependent variable in a causal chain.

Interview Schedule. Type of questionnaire used in face-to-face interviews in which questions may be open- or closed-ended.

Kendall's Tau. Nonparametric inferential statistic that tests for association between two ordinal or higher variables in a sample, then permits inferences (knowledge claims) about the population from which the sample was drawn.

Knowledge Claims. Inferential statement about the total population based on information collected from a sample drawn from the population.

Level of Significance. Probability that a relationship detected in a sample is due to sampling error, rather than due to a true relationship in the population. The probability of Type I error.

Likert items. Questionnaire items using opinion statements that respondents agree or disagree with, typically using three, five, or seven response categories developed according to procedures developed by Rensis Likert. Most composite measures that use Likert items are summative indices.

Linear Relationship. Relationship between two variables in which an increase in the value of one variable is associated with a corresponding increase or decrease in the other variable. A plot of the relationship in graph form is best described as a straight-line or linear. (See *nonlinear relationship.*)

Longitudinal Study. Generic label for research designs in which data are collected at several points in time, including trend and panel studies.

Maturation. Biological or social development of subjects in an experiment between pretest and posttest measures that may affect the dependent variable and reduce the internal validity of the study.

Margin of Error. (See *confidence interval.*)

Mean. Measure of central tendency computed as the arithmetic average (sum of all nonmissing values divided by the number of nonmissing cases).

Median. Measure of central tendency computed as the value in the middle of a distribution, such that half the cases have values greater than the median and half have values less than the median.

Metric Data. Variables with many response categories that are ordered and have equal intervals between points on the scale. Interval- and ratio-level variables produce metric data. Ordinal data are also often treated as if they are metric in order to use powerful statistical analysis procedures.

Mode. Measure of central tendency defined as the value of a variable occurring most frequently in a distribution.

Necessary Cause or Condition. Factor that must be present in order to complete a causal chain or produce an effect, even though its presence does not assure the causal relationship or effect. (See also *sufficient cause.*)

Negative Relationship. Relationship between two variables in which high values for one variable are associated with low values for the other variable.

Nominal-level Variables. Lowest level measure of a concept in which arbitrary values or symbols (mutually exclusive and exhaustive) are assigned to characteristics of people, objects, or other units of analysis. Relations between nominal variables are tested with nonparametric statistics only.

Nonparametric Statistics. Inferential statistics that do not require that variables tested be normally distributed. Nonparametric statistics possess less statistical power than parametric statistics.

Nonprobability Sampling. Generic label for sampling strategies in which the probability of selecting any given case is unknown. Such samples preclude the use of inferential statistics.

Nonlinear Relationships. Complex relationship between two variables that cannot be represented by a straight line. For example, employees with few years and employees with many years with the company frequently read the employee magazine, but employees with moderate tenure with the company are infrequent readers. When graphed, this relationship is like a U-shaped curve. (This U-shaped curve, however, is only one type of nonlinear relationship.)

Normal Distribution. Symmetrical, bell-shaped distribution of values for a variable. The normal distribution is assumed when parametric statistics are used.

Normative Response Question. Questionnaire item in which social mores and customs favor one response over another, regardless of the truth of the response. Asking respondents whether they like or dislike their mothers will generally elicit favorable responses, regardless of how they actually feel about mom.

Null Hypothesis. Statement that says two variables are not related to each other in the population. The null hypothesis suggests that any relationship observed in the sample is a product of sampling error. (See also *research hypothesis.*)

Observation. Systematic and standardized procedures for collecting research information.

Open-ended Question. Questionnaire item for which respondents can give any answer. In other words, their answers do not have to fit some predetermined set of options developed by the researcher.

Operationalization. Process of translating an abstract concept into observable phenomena in the real world.

Ordinal Level Variables. Measure in which categories are mutually exclusive, exhaustive, and ordered or ranked. Many researchers use parametric statistics with such variables, even though such measures fail to meet the equal interval assumption of parametric statistics.

Panel Studies. Type of longitudinal study in which the same respondents are studied at several points in time.

Partial Correlation. Measure of association between two variables that controls for the effect(s) of other variables on the relationship. (See also *zero-order correlation.*)

Participant Observation. Mode of observation wherein the researcher actively participates in the group or social system he or she is studying.

Pearson Product-Moment Correlation Coefficient. Parametric statistic that tests for linear relations between two variables and expresses the strength of the relationship with a number, ranging from -1 (perfect negative) to zero (no relationship) to $+1$ (perfect positive).

Pilot Test. Preliminary administration of a survey instrument to a subsample of respondents for the purpose of identifying and correcting flaws in the instrument and in its administration.

Placebo. Treatment unrelated to the true independent variable that is administered to the control group so that those subjects will feel that they were exposed to a treatment.

Population. Total set of people, organizations, or media messages that the researcher has precisely defined for purposes of study. Frequently, the researcher makes probability inferences about populations, based on data collected from samples drawn from that population. (See *universe.*)

Positive Relationship. Relationship between two variables wherein high values for one variable are associated with high values for the other variable. Low values for one variable are associated with low values for the other variable.

Posttest Measure. Measure of the dependent or impact variable taken sometime after administration of the treatment (independent variable) in the experimental group(s).

Pretest Measure. Measure of the dependent or impact variable taken sometime before administration of the treatment (independent variable) in the experimental group(s).

Purposive Sample. Nonprobability sample in which the researcher selects respondents according to his or her judgment as to their *perceived* representativeness or usefulness to the research process. (Sometimes called a *judgmental sample.*)

Q-sorting. Mode of observation in which subjects sort 60 to 100 self-referent statements or other stimuli along an eleven-point or thirteen-point scale, ranging from "most like me" to "most unlike me." The resulting Q-sort is a model of the subject's belief system about the topic of study.

Qualitative Observation. Mode of collecting information in which observations are not assigned numeric codes. Qualitative observations generally are intensive, use few cases, and attempt to discover rather than test.

Quantitative Observation. Mode of collecting information in which observations are assigned numeric codes. Quantitative observations generally are extensive, use many cases, and attempt to test rather than discover.

Quasi-experimental Design. A modification of true experimental designs in which nonequivalent comparison groups are used in place of randomly assigned control and treatment groups.

Quota Sample. Nonprobability sampling strategy wherein the interviewer selects any convenient respondent who satisfies a quota requirement defined by a single variable (for example, 50 percent males, 50 percent females).

Random Digit Dialing or RDD. Telephone sampling technique using random numbers as suffixes to telephone number prefixes assigned by the phone company in specific geographic areas. This technique permits sampling of both listed and unlisted telephone numbers.

Random Sampling. Sampling technique in which every member of the population has an equal chance of being included in the sample. In experiments, random assignment insures that each subject had an equal chance of being assigned to a treatment or control group. (NOTE: The term "random" is often used incorrectly to mean "accidental." In fact, it represents a scientific, probability method of selection.)

Range. Measure of scatter or dispersion computed as the highest value of the variable minus the lowest value of the variable.

Ratio-level Variables. Highest level of measure wherein the variable possesses the following characteristics: mutually exclusive, exhaustive, ordered, equal intervals, and true zero value associated with absolute absence of the attribute.

Record. Line of data, a single row, in a data file. A record corresponds to a computer data card, a relic of data storage prior to innovations in magnetic data storage on disk or tape.

Relationship. Degree to which two or more variables are associated with each other or co-vary. The degree to which knowing the value of one variable helps explain or predict the value of the other variable for any particular case.

Reliability. Quality of a measurement activity to yield the same results whenever the same (unchanged) object is measured. The degree to which multiple measures yield the same results—measurement stability.

Reliability Coefficients. Numeric indicator of the reliability of a scale or index, the degree to which all items in the composite co-vary, presumably because they measure the same concept.

Research Design. The overall plan and organization of research activities to answer research questions.

Research Hypothesis. Operational statement that says that two variables are related to each other in the population, often in a specified direction, based on a theoretical understanding of the concepts the two variables measure. Frequently, the research hypothesis is tested indirectly using a sample to disconfirm the null hypothesis.

Response Set. Tendency for respondents to provide similar answers to questionnaire items that share common response categories, regardless of the true or appropriate answer.

Sample. Subset of units from a population or universe that the researcher has selected for observation.

Sample Element. Individual, group, or media message selected for observation through a sampling strategy.

Sample Frame. Listing from which sample elements are selected. Generally, the sample frame operationally defines the population of study.

Sampling Interval. In systematic sampling, the number of population elements in the sample frame that are skipped over to select the next sampling unit.

Scale. Composite variable taken to be unidimensional, made up of nonequivalent measures weighted according to their ability to measure that dimension. In questionnaire construction, a scale is any strategy for labeling and ordering response categories for items in a questionnaire.

Secondary Analysis. Analysis of data collected for other purposes to answer a new research question.

Semantic Differential. A measurement technique for evaluating an object by marking a point on a scale between adjectives of opposite meaning at each end of the scale.

Skewness. Measure of how lopsided a distribution is, compared to a normal distribution. A distribution with many cases to the lower end (left side) of the distribution is positively skewed. A distribution with many cases to the upper end (right side) of the distribution is negatively skewed.

Snowball Sampling. Nonprobability sampling strategy in which respondents to one wave of data collection identify additional people for subsequent waves of data collection.

Spurious Relationship. In the elaboration model, a relationship between the independent and dependent variable is considered spurious if controlling for a third variable (which is theoretically antecendent to both) causes the initial relationship to disappear.

Standard Deviation. Measure of dispersion or scatter, computed as the square root of variance.

Standard Error. Measure of sampling error, or the standard deviation of sample means drawn from the same population. The larger the sample sizes, the smaller the standard error. The mean of means converges on the true population mean. (See *central limit theorem.*)

Statistical Power. Ability of any inferential statistical test to detect a statistically significant relationship, given that such a relationship of a given effect size actually exists in the population.

Statistical Significance. Relationship detected in a sample of sufficient strength to be generalized to the population with a specified level of confidence. The statistical significance of a relationship is indicated by a predetermined decision rule.

Stratified Random Sample. Probability sampling strategy wherein sampling elements are drawn at random from separate sample frames for different strata (values) of some key variable.

Strength of Relationship. Degree to which a change in the value of the independent variable affects, influences, or changes the value of the dependent variable.

Sufficient Cause or Condition. Factor that, when present, *always* completes the causal sequence or produces an effect. (See also *necessary cause.*)

Suppressor Variable. In the elaboration model, a suppressor variable causes a relationship between the independent and dependent variable to disappear until the influence of the suppressor variable is controlled. Once the suppressor is controlled, the relationship between the independent and dependent variables appears.

Systematic Sampling. Probability sampling strategy wherein every *n*th element (where *n* is a constant) of the sampling frame is sampled. The selection usually begins with a random start point in the sampling frame or within the selection interval.

Testing Effect. Influence that a pretest measure of the dependent variable exerts on the posttest measure of the same variable, inde-

pendent of treatment. This influence affects the internal validity of the experimental design.

Test Variable. (See *control variable.*)

Theory. Set of propositions that describe relations between concepts and seeks to explain and predict real-world phenomena.

Trend Study. Longitudinal study in which survey data are collected from the same population at several points in time, but new sample members are selected for each wave of data collection.

t-test. Inferential statistic that examines the difference between two means measured on the same scale. The procedure tests whether sample mean differences can be generalized to the population.

Type I Error. Concluding that a relationship in a sample is statistically significant when no such relationship exists in the population.

Type II Error. Concluding that a relationship in a sample is not statistically significant when such a relationship does exist in the population.

Unit of Analysis. Level of aggregation of people or mediated messages for purposes of data analysis. The unit of analysis may be the individual, the work unit, the organization or the word, the paragraph, or the news story.

Unit of Observation. Level of aggregation of people or mediated messages at which data are collected, which may or may not be the same as the unit of analysis.

Univariate Analysis. Study of research data one variable at a time, without regard to relationships between variables.

Universe. Abstract description of the entire set of people, organizations, or media messages that are the objects of study and from which samples may be drawn. (See also *population.*)

Variable. Operational indicator of a concept that takes on different values for different sampling elements or for the same sampling element at different points in time.

Variance. Measure of dispersion or scatter computed by substracting the mean from the value of every case in a distribution, squaring the difference, and computing the average for all such squared differences.

Weighted Sample. Cluster or stratified sample wherein some sampling elements are systematically oversampled or undersampled in order to insure adequate number of cases for certain subpopulations, then given greater or lesser compensatory weight in the computation of statistics.

Working Theory. Generally situation-specific set of informal propositions made up of rela-

tively concrete concepts and relationships. Such theories are developed and used by practitioners to devise program strategies.

Zero-order Correlation. Measure of association between two variables with no controls for the influence of third variables on the relationship. (See also *partial correlation.*)

INDEX